The Psychology Behind Trademark Infringement and Counterfeiting

The Psychology Behind Trademark Infringement and Counterfeiting

J. L. Zaichkowsky
Simon Fraser University

LAWRENCE ERLBAUM ASSOCIATES, PUBLISHERS

2006   Mahwah, New Jersey   London

Lawrence Erlbaum Associates, Inc., Publishers
10 Industrial Avenue
Mahwah, New Jersey 07430
www.erlbaum.com

Cover design by Kathryn Houghtaling

Library of Congress Cataloging-in-Publication Data

Zaichkowsky, Judith Lynne, 1951-
The psychology behind trademark infringement and counterfeiting /
    Judith L. Zaichkowsky.

        p. cm.
    Includes bibliographical references and index.
ISBN 0-8058-4792-8 (cloth : alk. paper)
ISBN 0-8058-4793-6 (pbk. : alk. paper)
1. Brand name products—Marketing—Management   2. Consumer be-
    havior.   3. Trademarks.   4. Industrial property.   5. Marketing—Law
    and legislation.   6. Imitation—Case studies.   I. Title.
HF5415.13.Z353 2006
658.8'27—dc22   2005055200
                                                                            CIP

Books published by Lawrence Erlbaum Associates are printed on
acid-free paper, and their bindings are chosen for strength and durability.

Printed in the United States of America
10   9   8   7   6   5   4   3   2   1

*To my wonderful parents John and Mary Zaichkowsky
And my mentor and good friend Hal Kassarjian*

Contents

Preface

The proliferation of imitation or knock-off and counterfeit goods on the marketplace has skyrocketed in the past decade. The reality is that when there is money to be made, people will flock to this profit strategy regardless of the moral, ethical, or legal underpinnings to society. My conclusion after 15 years of work in the area is that one will never stop the manufacture and selling of imitation goods when there is a customer willing to purchase them. To solve the infringement activity one must know and understand the consumer motivations to purchase the fake goods and then create and adopt a strategy to demotivate and change consumer behavior.

This book is really an extension and update of a previous book I wrote entitled *Defending Your Brand Against Imitation: Consumer Behavior, Marketing Strategies and Legal Issues* (1995, Quorum Books). That book is out of print, but can be bought used on Amazon for many times the original list price. This book extends the chapters, adding two more dimensions, one about China and the other about the Internet. I think it is superior to the first book, but first and foremost it still deals with the psychology behind stealing intellectual property in the marketplace.

The intent is to provide a background, from the consumer's point of view, to imitating brands and even counterfeiting practices. The concept of brands is not limited to products, services, or companies. This book looks at brands in the broadest sense of the word, as people, objects, and ideas, are subject to the act of others imitating or copying them. Preventing and stopping competitors and others from imitating successful brands is a difficult task. Although this book may not provide all the answers, it certainly will inform the reader concerning complexities of the issues of brand imitation.

It is quite likely that you have been prompted to buy this book after experiencing the unpleasant situation of someone infringing on your trademark. The first thing you should do, of course, is seek legal advice. This book is in no way meant to act as a self-guide for redress. My goal is to spark ideas of how to understand and prevent someone or some company from infringing on your trademark or intellectual property. You may already have excellent legal counsel that has turned you to this book for some background information on brand imitation.

The important factor is to take some action against unethical competitors who copy the identity of your business. Do not ignore them. To ignore brand imitation or counterfeiting is to condone it. Condoning current brand imitation is likely to breed future brand imitation. The ideal strategy is to prevent brand imitation or counterfeiting in the first place. The possibility of brand imitation or counterfeiting should be contemplated in the designing new products or brand packaging, just as it is in the printing of currency. Efforts to stop brand imitation once it appears in the marketplace are difficult and costly. It is the intent of this book to provide those involved in commerce with some understanding, some ideas, and perhaps some strategy for building differentiated brands that are easy to protect.

AUDIENCE

Brand managers, intellectual property attorneys, market researchers, consumers, and academics all have very different needs and interests, yet there is an area of interest in this book for each segment. For example, lawyers may find chapters 2 and 3 on consumer behavior the most useful and interesting. Marketing researchers may find chapter 6, on testing for brand imitation, a good source of ideas. Brand managers may find chapter 5, on being distinctive, beneficial for designing packaging and marketing strategy. Academics may find chapter 4, which attempts to categorize trademark infringement cases by cues, a good source of ideas for future research. Chapter 7 on cyberspace may be of interest to all groups as it covers a new way to do business. Chapter 8, passing-off in Asia, may be relevant for businesses who have chosen to move their manufacturing base to that country.

Graduate students in marketing, communication, and psychology will find a wealth of inspiration for Phd dissertations. The book may be used for supplemental reading to courses dealing with intellectual property in law schools. Marketing may find it useful for new product development, product design and consumer law courses.

OVERVIEW OF THE CONTENTS

This book attempts to cover aspects of trademark infringement as it relates to the consumer. Chapter 1 serves as an introduction to the topic and outlines the different types of imitation and passing-off in the marketplace.

The essence of branding and its role in society is discussed as well as how imitation erodes the equity of brands and the marketplace for consumers. Various legal terms are described to inform the reader of the different areas of trademark infringement.

Chapter 2 focuses on consumer behaviors in the marketplace. The concept of involvement, decision-making heuristics, and consumer intelligence levels are discussed. These concepts vary greatly among consumers and the relevance to trademark issues is outlined.

Chapter 3 is mainstream psychology. The different psychological theories show how consumers perceive goods, services and ideas in the marketplace. Consumer behavior is psychology, and biases in perception of goods and services can be predicted. Chapter 4 reviews the history of passing-off in the marketplace. Different types of trademark infringement and cases are classified into competing products, related products, and unrelated goods. Cases are also discussed according to the different cues which lead to consumer confusion, that is, color, symbols, shapes, or implied association.

Chapter 5 is perhaps the most relevant chapter for brand managers. It outlines strategies to keep one's brand distinctive and unique in the marketplace. Chapter 6 is an overview of different research methods that might be used to test for perceived similarity among brands in the marketplace. Different legal cases are used as examples for discussion.

Chapter 7 moves into the online arena. Because online commerce is the present and future, it is important to look at the unique setting of this consumer exchange. Here people do not have the benefit of examining the goods closely, instead they must rely more on brand names and the trust behind the name. Preventing trademark infringement is more difficult in cyberspace. From there the book goes to China in chapter 8. China is where most of the world's goods are manufactured. A deep understanding of the Chinese culture is useful to put the global problem of trademark infringement and counterfeiting into perspective.

The last chapter 9 is a reflection of the trademark infringement problem. It offers no ideas how to stop manufacturers from producing knock-off goods. But it does provide insight on how to prevent consumers from knowingly purchasing those goods that do not come from the true owner of a trademarked brand.

ACKNOWLEDGMENTS

Getting a book to the publisher is a major feat. I really have to thank Harry Briggs for helping me to make the second book on brand imitation a reality. The project was put on hold between 1998 and 2002 while I was MBA Director, a relentless position. Harry helped me find Erlbaum and Anne

Duffy, and no doubt put in a good word about the possibilities of the book. I want to thank Curt Haugtvedt of Ohio State University for reviewing the initial draft and ideas. The book was put on hold again between 2002 and 2003 due to my coauthorship of a consumer behavior textbook. Working on two books at once was impossible for me, and I thank Anne Duffy for her patience. My teaching, committees, conferences, and other university duties always meant that the book had to be put aside, so patience really is a virtue in writing and publishing.

Having said that, the work that went into this book covers a 10-year period and involved a lot of input from my wonderful MBA students at Simon Fraser University. Felix Tang, now a PhD student at the Chinese University of Hong Kong, prepared much of the material in chapter 8 "Trademark Infringement in China." Felix is one of the most energetic and resourceful people I have ever met. I wish him a great future in academics and for his dissertation, which also investigates the area of knock-off and counterfeit goods.

Laurie Allen, another MBA grad, was kind enough to do her final project, on "Passing-off in Cyberspace," under my supervision. Chapter 7 represents much of Laurie's data collection. Other MBA students who completed projects on the issue under me are Neil Simpson, Angela Wong, Argy Nia, Kay Lai, and Roberta Hupman. Much of their work is published in *Marketing Letters, Journal of Product and Brand Management, Asia Pacific Marketing Review,* and *Conference Proceedings of the Association for Consumer Research*. Bits of these studies are reported in this book. My colleague Colleen Collins Dodd also worked with me on the topic of retail brand imitators, and that work, too, is reported here.

I thank my colleagues at the Copenhagen Business School for their interest in my work and their eagerness to work together and coauthor papers: Ricky Wilke, who worked on the *Business Horizons* piece on the broader societal view of brand imitators, and Tore Kristensen, who got me interested in plagiarized design issues. I continue to value their insight and friendship as I learn more about design and enjoy the wonderful city of Copenhagen.

I especially thank all my colleagues at Hautes Etudes Commerciales Paris, where I spent my sabbatical year and worked on this volume. Gilles Laurent, Jean-Noel Kapferer, Frederic Dalsace, Yanghyuk Lee, Yves Evard, Marc Vanhule, and Anne Michaut all made my sabbatical time in France a warm and enriching time. Jean-Noel Kapferer, whose office was across the hall, was a great inspiration to me. He freely gave me his time and ideas, and even contributed to the title. I am not sure I captured all his input, and I am indebted to his clear thinking about brands and the intellectual generosity of his ideas. I also must thank my secretary Pascale Ardoin at H.E.C. for helping me through my many stays in France. She really made my life a lot easier. Brian Wansink, who also was on sabbatical in France at that time, was a great friend and help. I dragged him and his wife to the Counterfeit Museum, and he created a photo journal of counterfeit products for me.

I also thank the chef at the H.E.C. staff cafeteria, who supplied me with nutrients at lunchtime. These lunches are unknown to North American universities: fois gras, asparagus, smoked salmon, canard à la pêche, and of course his speciality, crème brˆullée. These lunches made working on campus an absolute must.

I give a special thanks to Rosemary Polegato, my long-time colleague and textbook coauthor. Rosemary carefully read and edited each chapter. Sometimes this was in trains, sometimes in planes and at airports, sometimes in hotel rooms, and sometimes even during the odd time in her office. She was my constant source of assurance and provided excellent critical comments on where to explain, expand, or clarify. She is a priceless friend.

I thank George Zinkhan, University of Georgia; Julie Ruth, Rutgers University; Itamar Simonson, Stanford University; Hal Kassarjian, Emeritus U.C.L.A.; and Friso Halbertsma, Elevator Design, who read chapters and simultaneously provided constructive criticism and generous reassurance when I had doubts about chapters or issues. They assured me, although not necessarily agreeing with everything I had to say, that the content was not too bad and sometimes even a very interesting read. Their time is precious, and I thank them for sharing it with me.

However, as Charles Hoffacker once relayed to me, "A manuscript is never finished; someone just comes and takes it away from you." So the final deadline has come and gone several times, and you are left to read what is started. You will realize the importance of this statement when you finish reading the volume and realize about all the questions arising from the work. There is much to be learned and researched with respect to brand imitation and counterfeiting.

Finally, I thank Betty Chung, Jean Last, and Adeel Butt, who prepared the tables, figures, and exhibits while I was constantly changing them. In conclusion, I thank you all for your time, patience, knowledge, and support.

About the Author

Judy Zaichkowsky is a Professor of Marketing at the Faculty of Business Administration and member of the Board of Governors, Simon Fraser University. She received her PhD from the University of California, Los Angeles in 1984, in Marketing, with minors in Psychology and Statistics. She holds a master's in Consumer Studies from the University of Guelph and received a Centenary Alumni award from the University of Guelph in 2003 for outstanding contributions to research. Dr. Zaichkowsky has been actively researching consumers since the early 1970s and has published works on many facets of consumer behavior. Her knowledge and expertise on the role of involvement in consumer research has had a major impact on the field of marketing. Her 1985 *Journal of Consumer Research* paper on the involvement construct is one of the top 10 cited articles in consumer behavior and one of the most influential articles in the field of advertising. Professor Zaichkowsky sits on the review boards for the *Journal of Advertising, Journal of the Academy Marketing Science, Asia Pacific Journal of Marketing, Journal of Promotion Management,* and *Psychology and Marketing.*

The decision to write this book stemmed from her personal experience as an expert witness to a passing-off case. She continues to consult on branding issues and to act as an expert witness in cases of trademark infringement.

1

Sorting Out the Issues

Each year at the world's largest consumer goods trade fair show, called the Frankfurt Ambiente fair, black gnomes with gold-tinted noses are awarded to companies judged as making "the most flagrant and unimaginative" design imitations. The reason for the gnome prize is the history of sales lost to German producers of ceramic garden gnomes because of copycat Polish knockoffs. This loss is estimated at hundreds of millions of dollars over the past 10 years. The black gnome with the gold nose symbolizes profit through plagiarism and was created by Action Plagiarus, a group that campaigns to raise awareness of copyright protection. As of 2003, Hong Kong- and Chinese-based companies have received the award 27 times (Reppert-Bismark & Fowler, 2003).

This act of intentionally taking the name, shape, symbol, color, or look associated with a successful brand and integrating it with another brand on the marketplace shifts sales away from the original brand to the new brand. This shift occurs because consumers can be led by similar cues into believing the two brands might be interchangeable. The psychology behind the perception of similarity and substitutability is important to understanding the processes and motivation of stealing brand equity or brand identity in the marketplace. In addition to the possible monetary loss to original manufacturers, there is a potential reduction in the perception of the original brand's quality or image due to the cheaper price or inferior quality of the infringing brand.

The equity of successful brands is routinely stolen because it is a cheap effective way to make short-term economic gains. This is the cost of creating a successful branded good in the marketplace that is highly visible, highly desirable, and/or highly expensive. These are the attributes that motivate manufacturers, sellers, and buyers to engage in and support the practice of brand identity theft. This theft may be in the form of a counterfeit or 100% direct copy, or it may be in the more subtle form of a brand imitator or knockoff, in which all elements are not copied, only the most salient (i.e., most market-driven) features.

These practices fall under trademark or trade dress infringement issues in the legal domain. A trademark usually is a name and/or logo, whereas the trade dress refers to the visual appearance.[1] Dollar figures for infringement activities of brand identity are routinely estimated. Interpol and the International Chamber of Commerce have estimated that on a worldwide scale, companies lose 5% to 7% of their trade because of brand and trademark abuse. These online and face-to-face trade loss figures are estimated to have been $512 billion in 2004 (Fakes, 2005).

WHY THIS BOOK

Most work on trademark infringement is from the legal perspective. Not much is written from the viewpoint espoused by the management of brands, which involves consumer behavior. The objective of this book is to provide an understanding of the issue of trademark and trade dress infringement from the standpoint of consumers and their relationship with brands in the marketplace. Determining exactly what makes a brand similar and desirable to copy is not always obvious and varies greatly among brands and products. Because litigation is costly, managers should be aware of the various cues consumers use to identify brands and how these cues transfer to the meaning consumers derive from brands.

Furthermore, the issues of marketing and consumer behavior are "soft" sciences. Often, courts allow totally unqualified individuals to offer opinions on marketing and advertising issues (McConnell & Dubas, 2004). This is likely because marketing and advertising are rather "sexy" areas of common ground and everyone can have an opinion. However, amateurs who have no formal degrees, let alone advanced degrees in consumer behavior and marketing, who have never published in a peer-reviewed journal and have no citation record often give their opinions without the basic understanding of marketing and consumer behavior in court rooms. Lawyers and judges need to know that consumer behavior theories exist, and that they are honed by those with advanced degrees in the areas.

This book focuses on the similarity of trademarks and trade dress with the intent of providing background information on consumer choice behavior, the psychological forces behind the issue of imitation, a review of selected court cases in which different cues are the basis for brand identification, an investigation of the World Wide Web as a catalyst to the business of knockoffs, and finally, a special look at China because most manufactur-

---

[1]See the glossary for detailed definitions of "trademarks" and "trade dress."

ing has moved to Asia (even Levi's are no longer manufactured in the United States), which represents the greatest growth market for branded goods.

It is the similarity of trademarks that is germane to the cueing of consumer expectations. The understanding of what creates perceived similarity, how to label it, how to avoid it, and how to test for its existence is important to the decision to take a possible infringer to court and perhaps prevent any future infringing competitors.

TYPES OF COPIES

Generally, there are two types of purchasing behavior by the consumer: knowledgeable and confused. In the case of knowledgeable behavior, the consumer is not only willing, but also eager to buy a good that copies or resembles an original brand. In such cases, the brand copy usually is sold at about 10% to 20% of the original brand cost. Consumers may think that only they will know the difference in price paid. Others who see them with the brand copy are expected to think they paid the price of the original. If the word "knockoffs" is typed into an Internet search engine, one will see hundreds of companies that make their living by selling knockoff golf clubs, purses, watches, shoes, sunglasses, and whatever else may be a publicly consumed branded good, luxury or not. It seems that the Internet has given some legitimacy to this business.

With the second type of copying, consumers do not realize they are buying a good that is not an "original" or they are "confused." This lack of knowledge may be attributable to inexperienced and uninformed customers, or customers who are just duped. It may be arrogant to assume that consumers know a good is not the original because of its low price. They may assume it is stolen merchandise. They may think that the seller has obtained the goods through parallel import arrangements, because it is not unusual for goods to sell at a lower price in a foreign country than they do in a domestic market. Consumers also may not have the knowledge about what a reasonable selling price might be for the good. Therefore, although the original manufacturer and some consumers know that the good is pirated, this may not be sufficient evidence to show that the majority of consumers know the good to be a "counterfeit."

Another global factor is that as the world's marketplace becomes borderless, well-known brands have leapt from country to country. Unfortunately, the distribution and price of these brands have not met the needs of the various worldwide markets. This situation has left a large segment open to acquiring imitation and fake brands, which are not easily recognized because of language translations. For example, the recent explosion of China as a consumer nation makes it a fertile ground for fakes and imitations. Recently, fake Harry Potter books appeared in various Chinese cities. In fact, books 5, 6, and 7 of Harry's adventures were only in Chinese because the imitators took it upon themselves to create the future adventures, making them available, along with those published by the original author, J. K. Rowling, under her name.

The problem of knockoffs and fakes is so pervasive in China that the fakes are being copied, with the copiers believing they are copying the original. Thus, the pirates themselves are being pirated. The reason this problem is so widespread in China is not because consumers want knockoff products, but more because of the country's history of intellectual property, values, transfer of brands across cultures, and laws, as well as the lack of information on original brands.

Counterfeits

Counterfeiting refers to a "direct" copy. An imitation need not be a direct copy. Imitators only need to have borrowed or copied some aspects or attributes of the original. Manufacturers tend not to differentiate between imitators and counterfeiters. Both can create similar problems for original brands because both infringe on the original brand's image and profits. The law takes the position that counterfeiting may harm society at large, especially when the counterfeit is not a direct copy in quality, but only packaged or manufactured to look like the original. When the counterfeit is sold at nearly the price of the original, the consumer cannot judge the quality (as with credence goods) and therefore is misguided by the brand name, trademark, or trade dress. As a result, the consumer may think the counterfeit good is the original.

If the quality of the ingredients or manufacturing process is inferior, then that inferiority may directly harm individual consumers or even whole nations. For example, Kenya is reported to have lost a substantial portion of its coffee crop after farmers unknowingly used ineffective counterfeit fertilizers. Some airplane crashes have been attributed to counterfeit parts, which rarely meet federal safety standards. Counterfeit auto parts are said to last only 5% to 25% as long as genuine parts (Bloch, Bush, & Campbell, 1993).

The explosion of counterfeit drugs sold around the world poses an extreme health risk. Pfizer found that its cholesterol-reducing drug Lipitor was counterfeited and sold in the United States. Novartis says that counterfeiters used yellow highway paint to get the color match for its fake painkillers (Business Week, 2005). These examples of counterfeiting, which may have an impact on the safety of society, are treated much differently by the legal system and by consumers than cases that involve goods we call publicly consumed luxury goods. However both fake luxury and

consumer goods are now at the heart of organized crime, allegedly chan-
neling hundreds of millions of dollars to subversive activities around the
globe.

Counterfeits as Pirated Goods

When a counterfeited brand is sold at a fraction of the usual selling price, it
is said to be a signal to the consumer that the good is counterfeit. This usually is referred to as piracy because the manufacturer's intention is not to
deceive the consumer about the true origin of the good. The consumer may
consciously seek out and purchase these fake products through purchase
location, low pricing or obvious differences in design details, quality, or
other features observed by the consumer. Examples are pirated CD's,
video games, and computer software sold at low prices, often with poor
packaging. Usually, the courts side with the manufacturer and see no difference between pirated and counterfeit goods. They do not take into account the many eager and satisfied consumers of fake CD's, software, or
luxury goods. Some counterfeiters use the following argument to justify
their actions:

> I tell my customers it's a copy. People can't afford the real stuff. Take
> Chanel. Their quality is great, but the bags aren't worth the price people
> pay. They have $2,800 bags I'll sell you for $150. We're doing a service by
> allowing people to have a dream. (Stipp, 1996, p. 140)

The World Wide Web exacerbates the legitimacy of this practice as a
business, both by businesses and by consumers. Some businesses advertise their wares as replicas and state boldly that they do not sell authentic
products. Because they do not manufacture them, they are but a middle-
man in the process. However, it is clear from the following customer comment (taken from a now defunct Web site) that they are selling to a public
that uses the good as an authentic product.

> I was always afraid that if I bought a replica bag people would know it
> was fake. After receiving your bag I wore it into the Louis Vuitton store
> and everyone wanted to know how I got the bag. I am no longer skeptical
> about your products! I will be ordering my Christmas presents soon.

These types of comments also help the seller portray the quality of the
pirated goods. This is a sticky point because both the buyer and seller
know the good is a knockoff or counterfeit, but the motivation to purchase
is based on the fact that the general public believes the good is "real" when
it is worn or used by the buyer. Here the lines between pirated, counterfeit,
and imitation goods are blurred by the perceptions of the marketplace.

Imitations or Knockoffs

Imitators are far more difficult to deal with because their goods are not identical, only similar in substance, name, shape, and color to an acknowledged and widely known product or service in the marketplace. Many private label brands rely on the imitation strategy. The astonishing success of private label knockoffs is not attributable to price alone. In supermarkets, private labels often have higher unit sales than national brands (Quelch & Harding, 1996). In the drug industry, the company Perrigo, which rocketed to the top of the private label nonprescription drug industry in the United States, supplies almost 1,000 look-alikes of major brands to chains such as WAL-MART and Rite Aid Corporation. The stores sell the products under their own brand names at 30% to 40% less than national brand competitors. Perrigo is constantly in court fighting trademark infringement cases. Some they win, and some they lose (Stern, 1993).

This strategy by private label brands will not go away because it "works." It works because the private label brand has cues similar to those of national brands, but at a lower price. The low price alone is not sufficient, as evidenced by the demise of the generic grocery brand. Generic brands of packaged goods were sold in plain packages and quickly acquired the reputation of low quality and ordinary substitutes. Now, by closely resembling the looks and to some extent the ingredients, private label look-alike brands are widely accepted by consumers. Perrigo admits to making packages for store labels that closely resemble those of national brands. But they insist they do not get "too close" or copy exactly (Ellison, 2002).

The problem in the court is that to say two things are similar by a specified property in common is nothing more to say they have that property in common. Comparative judgments of similarity often requires customers to weight the relative importance of a product's attributes. The variation in perceived relevance and importance of the different product attributes might be enormous. What makes two product attributes alike depends not only on which properties they share, but also on who makes that comparison and when. To compensate for the difficulties in articulating similarities, most comparisons focus on the differences. Therefore, the opinions on the acceptance of imitations are much more diverse than for pirated goods. For example, a Louis Vuitton–labeled bag that was never produced in that style by Louis Vuitton, is a knockoff, but perhaps not a counterfeit because it was never manufactured by Louis Vuitton in that style in the first place.

These examples show that the issues of trademarks, trade dress, patents, and intellectual property are sometimes hard to separate. It is a matter of interpretation. By this I mean that management should note that trademark registration does not necessarily guarantee trade dress protection because of possible differences in interpretations by the office registering the trademark and then the courts when a case is brought before them. It is suggested that only functional features are patented, whereas ornamental, incidental, and arbitrary features should be registered for trade dress protection and proven to be nonfunctional. This is why the issue is really about protecting one's equity of the brand. To understand the equity of the brand, some discussion about the language of brands is needed and provided.

THE LANGUAGE OF BRANDS

Brands today are a type of universal language. Brand names go beyond products and represent information about a variety of attributes linked to a product, service, organization, event, or even a person, such as its features, meaning, and quality, which words cannot replace easily. Instead of saying, "You should try the cold, black, sweet, fizzy water with caffeine that does not taste like coffee," you can say "You should try Coca-Cola." Thus, we use brand names not only to be specific about what we are referencing, but also to differentiate the items from what we are not referencing.

Brands Ensure Quality

The ability to identify correctly what we buy and consume has a long history dating back centuries. It started not only with pride in production and ownership, but also with the ability to identify who produced the item in case flaws were present. Economic planners in the Soviet Union found that requiring consumer goods manufacturers to imprint their individual "production marks" on their products helped guard against deteriorating standards of quality. By getting workers to identify the products for which they were responsible, the level of the quality of production was enhanced. If standards were not met, then it was likely the worker would lose his or her job. By the same token, if the standards of the brand are not met, then the brand loses customers and market share. Therefore, historically, clear branding made workers and manufacturers personally accountable for their goods and more likely to produce a standard quality product. The importance of control over one's brand, therefore, stems from both the manufacturer's fear of substandard products carrying his or her mark and the possibility of different quality goods being offered to consumers under the same trademark. Both scenarios can bring damage to the manufacturer and inconsistent products to the consumer.

In today's marketplace, ensuring quality is of the utmost importance to brands originating on the other side of the globe. When fake Harry Potter books were sold in China, they were said to make "Harry Potter look cheap." Words were misspelled, and there were grammatical errors. One loyal reader said, "I feel sick about it" (Pomfret, 2002).

Brands Reduce Risk

Consumers understand that brands make their life easier by reducing the risk of inferior or poor quality goods. Depending on the situation, the purchase may be irreversible, in that consumers cannot get their money back or undo their feelings of disappointment if the purchase does not meet their expectations. Even when consumers spend time and effort in the decision process, they may regret a "bad" purchase with hidden features that reduce quality. In the hotel industry, the brands of the "Four Seasons" and "Ibis" serve different markets, but each market is assured of exactly the same experience no matter which individual hotel in the chain they choose. The search is short and risk is reduced through common standards in each chain, regardless of the country in which you need a hotel room. Careful search for a hotel cannot guarantee this same experience. The guarantee that expectations will be met is developed through prior experience or a brand that promises to shortcut search and reduce risk through established standards.

Besides actual physical differences in product or service attributes, brands are differentiated in terms of the subjective image they impress on the consumer's mind. Brand image is created through labeling, advertising, package design, and retail distribution. The stronger the brand's image, the more the original brand can charge above its competitors because consumers are willing to put value on that image. Because of this fact, some might say that brands also could make people believe things that are not true. For example, bleach is a solution containing 5.25% sodium hypochlorite. The fact that two brands have the same chemical formula does not make them of equal quality perceptually (Landes & Posner, 1987). The major brand name in this product category charges significantly more than other competitors because it has created a superior image in the minds of the consumer.

Therefore, consumers are interested not only in the chemical formula, but also in the manufactured product, and are therefore willing to pay a premium for the assurance of the manufacturing process. Another very good example is the product category of acetylsalicylic acid (ASA or "aspirin"). It is the perception that drives the purchase, not the technical contents. The consumer will knowingly pay a premium for image and trusted quality. In many cases, this purchase of risk insurance is perceived by the consumer to be minor. I routinely pay two to three times the amount of the store brand to buy Bayer aspirin. The difference in the two dollars to my pocketbook over the year it will take me to consume the bottle is insignifi-

cant to me. Therefore, I will knowingly pay a premium for the trusted production quality of the name brand. This two-dollar insurance policy (the
brand name) is perceived to be minor in cost, but well worth it, especially
because I cannot myself objectively and accurately judge the quality of the
pill I swallow (credence good). Again, for many consumers, it is the
perception that drives the purchase, not the technical contents.

This insurance policy provided by the brand name makes the life of the
consumer easier by reducing the risk of inferior or poor quality experiences. Depending on the situation, the purchase may be irreversible. Consumers may not be able to get their money back or undo their feelings of
disappointment if the purchase does not meet their expectations. Therefore, consumers are interested not only in the ingredients, but also in the
manufactured end product. Therefore, they are willing to pay a premium
for the assurance of the manufacturing process.

Brands Create Trust

Blind and branded consumer evaluation tests show that consumers believe a known branded product to be of better quality, while judging the
same product without its brand name or packaging to be inferior. Although these tests measure the perceptions of the consumer, Consumer
Reports and other independent testing laboratories routinely carry out
tests of actual quality levels. The results of relatively objective tests routinely show major brands within product categories to be inferior to
lesser-known brand names. This fact is either unimportant or not believed
by many consumers.

The power of a known brand is exemplified in the history of the product
category of laundry detergent. In 1966, the British Monopolies Commission recommended a 40% cut in advertising by Unilever and Procter and
Gamble, accompanied by a 20% reduction in household detergent prices.
The major companies were not keen to comply with this ruling and negotiated instead to introduce new brands priced 20% less, without the heavy
advertising. The effort is said to have accomplished little, although largely
because the companies refused to admit that the quality of the new
unadvertised brand was equivalent to the quality of their main brands.
Consumers did not switch to the new lower-priced brands of the same objective quality because no trust in the new brand was created through
advertising.

Brands Communicate Image and Social Status

Viewing products simply as physical objects is too restrictive for the consumer. They have beliefs about different product brands that are not solely

a function of their physical characteristics. Different prices, different designs, and even different distribution channels all contribute to the image and become an integral part of the "soft" aspect of the brand. Therefore, brands are routinely differentiated in terms of the subjective image they impress on the consumer's mind.

In the 1950s, Gardner and Levy (1955) proposed the idea that brands have the added value of personalities, which drive preference and purchase. This is evident in some product categories. There may be minor physical product differences between brands, yet consumers see great differences among the brands. When the same experience is had without the interference of the brand image, these preferences disappear. Early work by Allison and Uhl (1964) clearly demonstrated this effect in blind and branded taste tests of bottled beer.

Jennifer Aaker (1997) has revived this complex area of brands, consumer preference, and personality. For example, Mercedes, BMW, and Jaguar all belong to the luxury car market. However a Mercedes driver has a different image than a Jaguar driver, and a different image again than a BMW driver. Therefore, brands are symbolic devices that allow the consumer to project a specific self-image, even within a certain social class. These brand images are created over time through labeling, design, distribution, and advertising. The development of the image with advertising is costly, but worth it. The advertising dollars are recouped over time because the better, clearer, and more distinct the image, the more the original can charge above its competitors.

Consumers place value on brand image because it communicates something about themselves to other people. Prestigious brands are associated with higher prices, and the higher the price, the more one can signal they are special (rich). Buying a Rolex watch over a Timex signals a different social status because the first brand costs more and may have a better standard of quality. The better standard of quality is then reflected on the individual who has the good taste and sense to "own" the brand. What parent does not know the hazards of purchasing the wrong brand of clothing for a teenage son or daughter in a world filled with wanting to belong?

HOW BRAND IMITATION ERODES BRAND EQUITY

The understanding of brand image explains the strong relationship found between brand and perceived quality. The brand perceived quality link explains the strategy of brand equity, as well as the extensions of current product lines and brands to other related and unrelated products, or just the association to the brand name itself. Most new packaged goods are brand extensions, which rely on established brand equity because of the great financial risk involved in entering new markets. The launch of a new brand can cost upwards of $100 million. The demise of a brand's equity because of others imitating the brand can be traced back to the weakening of the perceived uniqueness of the brand and possibly unfavorable associations. Poor-quality imitators or pirated goods may lead to an association effect weighted by negative information. It is like judging your worth by the company you keep.

How Counterfeiting and Imitation Destroy the Language of Brands

Consumers who do not know the true origin of goods and are not able to link the brand with the actual manufacturer will not be able to use the language of brands for communication successfully. The loss of brand language exists for both counterfeit and imitated goods. Over time the growth of imitators, which confuse consumers, may eventually destroy the language of brands as the trust, risk reduction, and communication properties of the brand become invalid. The brand name becomes invalid because it no longer identifies only the one source of the good. The same brand name or brand bundle is bought, but it is manufactured by different companies with different standards and made with different materials.

Therefore, the destruction of the language of brands is a broad event that impacts not only the copied brand, but also all other brands on the marketplace because the consumer can no longer automatically link the brand name with a company. What brand names stand for in a social welfare and global marketplace is eroded.

Destruction of Brand Equity

The destruction of brand equity is somewhat different from the destruction of the language of brands. Brand equity is something owned by an individual brand (Aaker, 1991; Keller, 1993). Brand equity captures the consumers' response to the marketing efforts of that particular brand. The components of brand equity build on the consumer's knowledge of the brand derived from their brand awareness and image of the brand. Whereas brand awareness can be defined and measured in terms of simple recognition and recall, brand image is a more complex construct derived from different types, favorability, strength, and uniqueness of brand associations. The types of brand associations are attitudes toward the brand, both functional and experiential; benefits derived from use of the brand; and perceived product attributes, which are product and nonproduct related.

A firm that imitates a competing brand's look is using the competitor's brand equity for its own benefit. For the imitating brand, this imitation strategy drastically reduces or eliminates the costs involved in launching a brand and creating a demand for it. If the imitation brands are of lower quality, as they usually are (Carratu, 1987; Fenby, 1983), purchasers may devalue the original brand, especially if they are not aware that the good is not the original nor made by the original manufacturer. Lego finds itself in this position with respect to customers who, unaware they have purchased imitation Lego building blocks, write letters of complaint to Lego about their unsatisfactory experience.

Satisfaction With Imitators.   On the other hand, if the consumer is aware of purchasing the imitation and satisfied with the brand, then the consumer also may devalue the original brand (Zaichkowsky & Simpson, 1996). This devaluation occurs because a cheaper adequate substitute has been found. Therefore, brand imitation may have very harmful effects on the equity of the original brand because it devalues the unique image, and hence the quality perception of the original brand name. This erosion of brand equity is especially acute in the case of luxury brands. The low price of the copy allows brand accessibility to a great many people, and exclusivity no longer contributes to the equity.

Moreover, a luxury brand can be broadly defined. Even commodities such as coffee and rice can be segmented into luxury brands. In a case that shocked Japan, 50 tons of tainted white rice was sold as 100% pure local rice. Over a 10-year period, the rice had been mixed with a lower-quality American rice, which retailed at half the price. When this scandal became public, consumers started to wonder whether the pure rice was worth the extra cost. Loyal buyers of the top-grade rice held in-home taste tests and could not tell the difference between the two brands (Fackler, 2003).

Misidentified Extensions.   When original brand names are applied to related or unrelated product categories by manufacturers other than the original producer, products of poor quality or poor taste may be associated with the original brand. Therefore, brand imitation extended to other product categories may have very harmful effects on the equity of the brand in its original product category. From a marketing strategy point of view, this means that certain brand extensions may be a necessary defense, although not necessarily desirable. Brand extensions may be used to block the use of the brand name by a third party in another product category. For example, Cartier, the elegant French jeweler, extended its name to textiles and tableware. This was a defensive strategy to prevent an Italian firm from registering the Cartier brand in these categories at an international level (Kapferer, 1992). Christian Dior, a French fashion house, registered its name in the product category of cigarettes in 1955 (Fletcher, 1989). Whether that was truly a defensive strategy at the time is hard to assess, but it does exemplify the protective strategy of taking one's brand name to unrelated product categories.

Diluting brand equity through unauthorized association and sponsorship is another major problem, not only of brands, but also of organizations and individuals. The concern here may be the unwelcome association, as well as the threat of confusion. Undermining a positive image or equity can lead to a diminishing of distinctiveness, uniqueness, effectiveness, or prestigious connotations. For example, the court held that the use of Tiffany's by a Boston nightclub harmed the New York jeweler's mark (*Tiffany & Co. v. Boston Club, Inc.*, 1964). The National Hockey League found itself in court objecting to its unauthorized portrayal in advertising by Pepsi-Cola (*National Hockey League v. Pepsi-Cola Canada Ltd.*, 1992). Protecting one's image is important business because images take years to build, but can be destroyed in months.

Destruction of the Product Category

There also is potential for the whole product category to be destroyed with misguided imitation product experiences. This is especially the case when the original defines the product category and there are many product substitutes. For example, when consumers buy a Lego product, they expect a certain level of quality. When a consumer unknowingly purchases an imitator of Lego (e.g., Ligo) and tries to join one of the new pieces with the original and does not get a perfect fit, then not only is the language of the Lego brand damaged, but perhaps also the whole product category of building blocks. A poor image of the brand, which defines the product category, could then mean a poor image of the whole product category. In Lego's case, building blocks give way to other play toys. Children may no longer be given building blocks as gifts, but now plasticine or game sets instead.

Another example is Coca-Cola, the definer of the product category of cola beverages. If the perceived image quality of this brand leader declines through misguided purchases, perhaps consumers will substitute other cold beverages for cola. For example, iced tea, water, and citrus-flavored drinks may be used as a substitute for colas because there is no longer a perceived consistency in the purchase of Coca-Cola. Coca-Cola's return to their distinctively shaped bottle was an important factor in preventing misguided purchases because competitors could not copy their differentiated, unique, and trademarked package.

BLURRED BORDERS: WHY PATENTS AND COPYRIGHTS ARE NOT ENOUGH

A very fine line exists between an illegal trademark or trade dress infringement and a "copycat" brand. Not only is the line a fine one. It also is sometimes dotted and curved, with major brands occasionally turning a blind eye to such activity. In some respects, it depends on how one defines copy-cat and imitation. For example, the Suave brand produced by Unilever is called a "fast follower" and known for its copycat marketing and low prices. When a hot new product comes out, Suave systematically creates a brand similar in ingredients and packaging. Procter and Gamble's Pantene Pro-V shampoo and conditioner comes in pale pearlescent bottles. So does Suave's Performance shampoo and conditioner. Both brands have smoothing versions and provitamin ingredients. However, Pantene costs two and half times as much as Suave, and Suave sells more than twice as much as Pantene in volume. Procter and Gamble chooses to use marketing tactics rather than legal ones to deal with Unilever. Smaller firms are not so lucky.

One would think the producers of successful established brands should be motivated to protect the distinct identity of their products and their brand equity by prosecuting possible infringers under trademark laws. A survey among European companies manufacturing branded products showed that more than 80% of the respondents had seen some of their products imitated at least once within the preceding 5 years. However, only about half of them had taken legal steps against the imitators, citing cumbersome procedures, high costs, and uncertainty of outcomes because of widely varying practices as the main reasons for not defending their brand against imitators (Lego Group, 1993).

Another study by Collins-Dodd and Zaichkowsky (1999) found that manufacturers who had been copied were less likely to take retail store–brand infringers to court than other manufacturers not related to re-tail store brands. Original manufacturers feared retaliation by the re-tailer's distribution system through reduction in shelf space and positioning on the store shelf.

From a social welfare perspective, the difference between counterfeit-ing and imitation may be moot. Consumers may suffer the same conse-quences from the purchase of imitators as from the purchase of counterfeits. This is because consumers sometimes are not aware of the original manufacturer and sometimes are, just as with counterfeit goods. The original manufacturer believes that imitation usually harms the broader social welfare of the marketplace by inhibiting the introduction of innovative new brands, generating unfair competition, and destroying the language of brands.

Fake luxury goods, such as copies of Hermès and Louis Vuitton allow the elevated feeling of consumption by the consumer who cannot or is un-willing to pay for the original. They allow lower income people to have a little brush with prestige, to look like a more affluent person from a dis-tance, and perhaps to feel better about themselves. However, these counterfeits also may damage the image and equity of the original brand. Very little public money is spent investigating luxury counterfeits, and the fight is left to private detectives hired by companies and trade groups. Once the case is before the courts, however, there is pressure to treat pirated goods and counterfeit goods equally under the law.

A 100% direct copy is relatively easy to identify and label as counterfeit. However, imitation is not necessarily a direct copy and, therefore, more difficult to define, identify, label as illegal, and hence prevent. Brand imitation deals with similarities, not differences. What is similar sometimes is a matter of individual perception rather than reality. What may be perceived and defined as an illegal offering in the marketplace by some may not be perceived and defined as such by others.

It Is Not About Patents or Copyright

This book is not about patents and does not cover all intellectual property rights, such as copyright. The difference is that information protected by patents and copyrights help to define technical aspects of products. Trademarks, on the other hand, affix good will and identify the source of the products placed on the market. Trademarks also retain a difference in purpose from both copyrights and patents. The name or label of a trademark communicates verifiable features to distinguish and differentiate different brands within the product category. By contrast, patents and copyrights protect unique characteristics, but do not supply the communicative element as to who produced the good or service. Consumers, therefore, do not rely on a patent or copyright to identify a product or service in the same way that they rely on a trademark. Trademarks are types of intellectual property consisting of a term, symbol, design, or combination of these cues to protect the identification of a business or product. Trademarks enable customers to correlate unique associations and meanings with a specific product or service, differentiating it from others. This "goodwill" is used by the company (owner of the trademark) to build a competitive advantage and future revenue. Trademarks also function as a signal of quality and as an instrument for advertising and promotion (Simonson, 1994).

Trademarks may be derived from various sources. The mark may come from a coined word, such as "Exxon" or "Kodak." It may be an ordinary word that has no apparent meaning in connection with the product to which it is attached, for example, "Arrow" used as a name for dress shirts. It may be a descriptive word that suggests the performance of the product, for example, "Mr Clean." It could be a foreign name, "Lux"; a founder's name, "Ford"; the name of a historically famous person, "Lincoln"; numerals, "No. 5" perfume; a picture, such as Elsie the Cow for Borden's; or a shape such as the Coca-Cola bottle (Levy & Rook, 1981). Therefore, trademarks can be as diverse as the imagination of the manufacturer. The mechanisms underlying the development of trademarks are articulated by Cohen (1986, 1991) in a discussion of trademark planning and product decisions.

The Law Understands Trademarks

Trademark policies are in place to protect trademark owners from unfair competition, in which goods are disguised as those actually desired by consumers (Burgunder, 1997). Without such protection, consumers would not be able to make product choice decisions based on their previous associations for a product. They would need to reeducate themselves with every purchase (Allen, 1991).

Trademark protection is enforced in the United States by the courts' interpretation of the Lanham Act (1946) and recent amendments, such as the Trademark Law Revision Act (1988), the Anticounterfeiting Consumer Protection Act (1996), and the Federal Trademark Dilution Act (1995). These legislative acts have clearly defined trademarks and the need for the owner to use the law to protect the trademark from counterfeiting or misappropriation ("the deliberate use of a fraudulent mark that is identical to or substantially indistinguishable from an existing mark"), infringement (the trademark's "use by another is likely to cause confusion, or cause mistake, or to deceive"), and dilution ("which occurs when the value of the mark to the owner is reduced," sometimes despite the actions of the competition) (Kopp & Suter, 2000, p. 120). Therefore, trademark infringement occurs when a registered trademark is used "by a person not entitled to its use ... who sells, distributes or advertises wares or services in association with a confusing trade-mark or trade-name"[2]

The courts have long recognized that consumers use a company's trademarks or trade dress distinctive features or cues to shortcut cognitive processing of the goods they buy and thus make their shopping more efficient. This is evident in the following statement from Mr. Justice Frankfurter in *Mishawaka Rubber and Woolen Mfg. Co. v. S.S. Kresge Co.* (1942):

> The protection of trademarks is the law's recognition of the psychological function of symbols. If it is true that we live by symbols, it is no less true that we purchase goods by them. A trademark is a merchandising shortcut which induces a purchaser to select what he wants, or what he has been led to believe he wants. The owner of a mark exploits this human propensity by making every effort to impregnate the atmosphere of the market with the drawing power of a congenial symbol. Whatever the means employed, the aim is the same—to convey through the mark, in the

---

[2]Taken from the Canadian Web site CIPO http://laws.justice.gc.ca/en/T-13/101518.html)

minds of the potential customers, the desirability of the commodity upon which it appears. Once this is attained, the trademark owner has something of value. If another poaches upon the commercial magnetism of the symbol he has created, the owner can obtain legal redress. The creation of a mark through an established symbol implies that people float on a psychological current engendered by the various advertising devices, which give a trademark its potency (Bowen, 1961, pp. 6–7)

The guidelines for the registration of trademarks and the specific laws that protect trademarks can be found in legal doctrines of each country. The World Intellectual Property Organization (WIPO) is trying to get all countries to abide by the same rules. Some of these laws are outlined in Appendix 2. Because the specific laws may vary from country to country and may change from time to time, and because all laws are open to interpretation and judgment, it is difficult to be specific about what is legal and illegal. Counterfeiting is definitely illegal, but brand imitation is not necessarily counterfeiting because it does not actually imply a direct copy.

The general purpose of trademark legislation is to prevent others from using distinctive marks that confuse people into thinking they are dealing with the owner of the trademark when they are not. When a party uses a trademark belonging to another, it is up to the original owner of the mark to convince the court of two points: first, that they actually own the trademark, and second, that the public likely has been or will be confused by the wrongful use of the trademark. It is the intent of this book to provide information with respect to the second point.

CONFUSION AND PASSING-OFF

In the eyes of the law, "consumer confusion results when two marks stimulate substantially identical psychological reactions in the minds of the purchasers when they see the marks on the goods, and a mental association is created as between the involved products or their producers" (Leeds, 1956, p. 5). This means that the consumer can be well aware that the two objects in question are not identical. The consumer only has to draw similar inferences from each based on the distinctive features common to both items. When noncompeting products or services are involved, "the court must look beyond the trademark to the nature of the products or services, and to the context in which they are marketed and sold." The closer the relationship between the products or services, and the more similar their sales contexts, the greater is the likelihood that confusion will occur.

Different criteria are applied to cases depending on whether the same, similar, or different product categories are involved. The U.S. 9th Circuit Courts use an eight-factor test for analyzing the likelihood of confusion: (a) the strength of the plaintiff's mark, (b) the degree of similarity between the two marks, (c) the proximity of the party's products, (d) the likelihood that the plaintiff will bridge the gap; (e) actual consumer confusion, (f) the defendant's good faith in adopting his or her mark, (g) the marketing channels used by both parties, and (h) the sophistication of the consumers in question (Kitts & Caditz, 2002).

Similarly, the Canadian Trade-mark Act deems a trademark to be confusing if "the use of both trade-marks in the same area would be likely to lead to the inference that the wares or services associated with those trade-marks are manufactured, sold, leased, hired or performed by the same person, whether or not the wares or services are of the same general class" (CIPO, http://laws.justice.gc.ca/en/T-13/101518.html). The Act stipulates the following criteria for the courts to use in determining whether a trademark is confusing or not: (a) the inherent distinctiveness of the trademarks or trade names and the extent to which they have become known, (b) the length of time the trademarks or trade names have been in use, (c) the nature of the wares, services, or business, (d) the nature of the trade, and (e) the degree of resemblance between the trademarks or trade names in appearance or sound or in the ideas suggested by them.

Likelihood of Confusion

The courts state that one does not have to show actual confusion, only "likelihood" of confusion. The court is supposed to weigh each factor separately, but not necessarily equally. If a consumer is confused between two trademarks, it suggests that they may not purchase the brand they intended to purchase. Confusion has been a difficult item to measure despite the large number of studies conducted to investigate it, perhaps because it is something that consumers are very reluctant to admit, perceiving it to be linked to stupidity (Simonson, 1994). Another problem is that confusion can be both conscious and unconscious. Mitchell and Papavassiliou (1999) argued that it is "more than subconscious mistakes, it is a state of mind which affects information processing and decision making" (p. 327).

Many studies have investigated consumer confusion as a result of traditional trademark infringement (Burgunder, 1997; Foxman, Muehling, & Berger, 1990; Howard, Kerin, & Gengler, 2000; Loken, Ross, & Hinkle, 1986; Simonson, 1994). These studies have found that there is a confusion rate of 17% to 25%. Mitchell and Papavassiliou (1999) looked at the implications of consumer confusion. They suggested that, "confusion can result in potential misuse of a product, which can lead to consumer dissatisfaction, lower repeat sales, more returned products, reduced customer loyalty and poorer brand image" (p. 320).

Although it is imperative for companies to understand not only what causes confusion, but also how they can help consumers minimize this confusion, Mitchell and Papavassiliou (1999) suggested prior research has focused on "very specific confusion sources" such as packaging similarity, leaving the vital concept of confusion reduction "underdeveloped and underresearched" (p. 320). Furthermore, all previous research has measured confusion in an offline environment, so little is known as to the severity of online consumer confusion.

The courts also have had a difficult time with confusion. Although they seem to have agreed on the types of confusion, there has been little agreement on who needs to be confused for the confusion to implicate trademark infringement (Allen, 1991). Is it only the purchaser, or is it also the potential purchaser? Some courts have even gone as far as to say it is the general public. And when does this confusion need to take place: before, after, or during the purchase decision? It may be that this continued lack of consensus is what drives the incentive to infringe.

Initial Interest Confusion

A variation of the confusion term called "initial interest confusion" is found in many recent court cases. The court states that the objective is "to capture initial consumer attention, even though no actual sale is finally completed as a result of the confusion" (*Dr Seuss Enters v. Penguin Books*, 1997). A further explanation is that initial interest confusion is much like posting a sign with another's trademark in front of one's store. Consumers are not confused in a narrow sense because they know where they are making the purchase. However, crucial credibility is gained in the initial phases of the consumer search process (*Interstellar Starship Services v. Epix*, 2002). Indeed, this concept greatly widens the areas of possibility for trademark infringement.

Passing-Off

The legal term used to describe the situation in which people confuse one business or product with another is passing-off action. The common law of passing-off prevents a person from misleading the public into thinking they are dealing with some other business or person when they are not. The person being harmed can request the court to order compensation or that the offending conduct be stopped. To succeed in a passing-off action, it is necessary to establish that the public was misled. However, it is not necessary to show that the copy brand was intended to mislead or confuse the public.

For example, a case involving cat litter (*A & M Pet Products v. Pieces, Inc. and Royal K-9*, 1989) found that customers purchased the imitator brand thinking it was the original. The imitator brand container had the same shape, and customers testified they just assumed it was the same product from the same manufacturer when in fact it was not. There was no actual evidence that the manufacturer intended to mislead the consumer. Most Web sites selling imitation products state in bold letters that their products are not authentic and call them replicas or representations of original brands.

Consumer Mistake

It also is possible that the consumer could make a mistake between the two objects in question because of their similarity. A consumer mistake results "when two marks sound so much alike or look so much alike that one product is purchased when the other is intended" (Leeds, 1956, p. 5). In this case, the consumer is not aware, at least at first, that a wrong purchase is made. These cases usually are confined to competing brands within a product category. For example, in *Levi Strauss v. Blue Bell* (1980), a survey among purchasers of casual clothing showed that many consumers used a small tab to identify clothing as being manufactured by Levi. Because the competition also used this small tab, it was deemed likely that consumers might mistakenly purchase the competitor's product and only later realize it was not Levi's. Lego, a Danish company that manufacturers children's building blocks and other toys, constantly receives letters of complaint about their building blocks from customers who have bought imitators' building blocks. The consumers think they are complaining about the Lego building blocks, a clear indication of a consumer mistake.

Consumer Deception

According to Leeds (1956, p. 5), "consumer deception results when two marks engender the same psychological impression, or look so much alike, or sound so much alike that unscrupulous dealers are led to believe that they can sell the second user's good for those of the first without fear of detection, or if detected, with an excuse believed sufficient to excuse the action." A case that might exemplify deception is that of *Hartford House Ltd. v. Hallmark Cards Inc.* (1986). In this case, the imitator deceived even the manufacturer of the original brand. Court documents showed that Hallmark deliberately set out to eliminate Hartford House as a competitor with their imitator product.

A consumer can be confused, make a mistake, or suffer from a deceptive practice with respect to products or services involving manufacturers, the source of the goods, or sponsorship or association (Boal, 1973). Whereas confusion and mistake are discovered from the standpoint of the consumer, deception is rooted in the intent of the seller of the good. It is the seller or manufacturer of brand imitators who causes consumer confusion through the use of similar cues in selling their products. Marketers, not wanting to confuse brands, but wanting to sell in the same product category, go to great lengths to provide consumer cues distinctive from those of their competitors.

The factors that the courts considers in deciding consumer confusion vary from court to court and from case to case. Anthony Fletcher (1989), in reviewing the different legal courts in the United States, came to the conclusion that there is very little agreement among the court circuits on which factors to consider for the determination of confusion. Given that the court may deal with confusion, mistake, and deception differently, it is not too surprising that there is such disagreement.

Secondary Meaning

Secondary meaning is an important term from the legal language used in discussing brand confusion. It is the notion that a trademark or trade dress need not identify the source of a product by name, but rather that the look of the product provides the consumer with similar expectations. There appear to be three levels of secondary meaning (Palladino, 1983): (a) liberal (the trademark or dress identifies one product), (b) accepted (the trademark or dress identifies the product of one, perhaps anonymous, company), (c) conservative (the trademark or dress identifies one specific company).

Secondary meaning, in the liberal sense, has been applied to drugs. For example, a company that produces a drug and packages it in a certain color has no ownership of the particular color of the particular drug. All drugs may be of that color despite the origin of manufacturer (*Inwood Laboratories, Inc. v. Ives Laboratories, Inc.*, 1982). An example of color in the conservative interpretation can be seen in the case of *Eastman Kodak v. Fotomat Corp.* (1971). In this case, Fotomat was prevented from using the same colors on their buildings that Kodak used on their film. The court ruled that the color combination could mean only Kodak to the customer.

In the case of design or trade dress features, are these features functional/utilitarian, aesthetic, or both? Is the trademark "strength" fanciful/coined, arbitrary, suggestive, or merely descriptive? The determination of secondary meaning may be through long extensive use of a product or service, size or prominence of a business, successes of promotional efforts by manufacturers, or direct evidence such as consumer research (Fletcher, 1989). For a comprehensive legal discussion and review of trademarks and secondary meaning, the reader is referred to an article by Armstrong (1992).

Genericism

A name is generic if its primary significance to the consuming public is the product rather than the producer (source). That is, does the name signify a common name for a (kind) of thing, or does it signify a particular brand of that (kind of) thing? Many brand names have fallen into the generic pit. Examples include Thermos for an insulated jug, RollarBlades for in-line skates, and Xerox for photocopying. Perhaps the most common one is Aspirin. The word no longer identifies the source of the product. Instead, the public uses the word to identify the product.

More recently, Microsoft's Windows was in the courts fighting off "Lindows" for trademark infringement. The judge stated that because the term "windows" is a common term, it logically follows that the use of "windows," "window," and "windowing" also are generic when referring to the computer domain. The major problem for the originating company is that once a brand name becomes generic, it is at risk of being removed as a trademark.

Brand Dilution

Dilution is the court's version of eroding brand equity. The United States created the Federal Dilution Act of 1995 to identify trademark injury when a trademark is used on noncompeting goods or for unrelated categories. The law specifically states that dilution exists even if the owner of the famous mark and the diluting party are not in competition with one another, and even if the actions of the accused diluter does not infringe on the trademark. If the dilution is planned and intended to prey off the famous brand, the owner of the famous brand may seek monetary damages (Lans Retsky, 2003).

However, proving actual dilution of a brand is elusive. It is the opposite of measuring brand equity. In determining whether a trademark is distinctive and famous, a court may consider factors such as, but not limited, to

- the degree of inherent or acquired distinctiveness of the mark
- the duration and extent of use of the mark in connection with the goods or services with which the mark is used
- the duration and extent of advertising and publicity of the mark
- the geographic extent of the trading area in which the mark is used
- the degree of recognition of the mark in the trading areas and trade channels used by the mark's owner and the person against whom the injunction is sought
- the nature and extent of the use of the same name or similar marks by third parties.

In the case of *Moseley et al. dba Victor' Little Secret v. V. Secret Catalogue Inc. et al.* (2003), Victoria's Secret (women's lingerie and catalogs) claimed that Victor's Little Secret (men and women's lingerie, sex toys, and adult videos) diluted their brand. The Supreme Court ruled that Victoria's Secret presented no actual dilution to the courts. Yet in the case of *Hasbro Inc. v. Internet Entertainment Group Ltd.* (1996) "Candyland" was deemed a famous trademark associated with family entertainment. Because Internet Entertainment Group was running an adult entertainment site at the domain name "candyland.com" the court found Internet Entertainment was liable for the dilution and tarnishment of Hasbro's famous trademark "Candyland." There is thus difficulty in showing dilution, especially because the law states that the trademark owner need not show actual lost sales or profits to have the alleged infringer stopped.

KNOWLEDGEABLE PURCHASERS

When the consumer is knowledgeable about the source of the good, then one may argue, as the luxury counterfeiters do, that there is little harm and perhaps even some benefit to the consumer. Perhaps this is why most imitated and pirated goods seem to be tolerated or given a low priority for elimination. Consumers are not perceived to be cheated because they use their own free will to purchase these lower priced, but usually lower quality, goods. Naturally, the consumer might be disappointed in the quality, but then they would lose trust in the pirated or imitated good and probably not purchase it again.

When the pirated or imitator good is of better quality than the original, this follows Schnaar's (1994) argument of a contribution to the welfare of society, giving consumers more and better products from which to chose. However, not one example of a better quality counterfeit, pirated, or imitated good comes to mind. There are perhaps many examples of goods perceived by consumers as close enough to the quality of the original, in content, that follow an imitation strategy. These goods, it is argued, contribute to the social welfare if the goods are of better value or priced much lower than the original. One example is the public's basic acceptance of generic drugs. Society is given the option of purchasing a substitute brand at a lower price.

If the consumer perceives the poor quality imitator to be an unsuitable substitute, then the imitating brand may die quickly in the marketplace. This is the hope of many major brand managers. The problem scenario, from a broad marketing point of view, occurs when the selling price is very low. Then the price-sensitive consumer still may buy the imitator, and its poor quality may destroy the equity of the original brand merely through its presence on the market.

For example, if luxury brands are copied using inferior materials and workmanship and then knowingly purchased by the masses, the original is seen as losing its exclusivity. Some people want goods simply because they are exclusive. The proliferation of look-alikes would mean the original brand will no longer be exclusive, an inherent attribute of the brand. If exclusivity is the desired important characteristic, then the equity of the brand will be seriously eroded. Over time, no one would want either the imitator or the original, because it was the attribute of exclusivity that motivated the purchase. The brand would no longer provide the elevated feeling of prestige to those who could afford the original. The problem is that consumers who own the original no longer are privy to the image of publicly consumed luxury goods. People wearing a real Rolex watch are now asked if it is fake! This question does not enhance the experience of owning the real thing. Once the brand loses its appeal to the target segment, the imitator also loses its market because the imitator no longer represents a brand that communicates prestige based on exclusivity.

SUMMARY

This book is not written from a legal perspective, but provides a guide for how to understand the concept of brand imitation from the perspective of the physical cues and how the consumer perceives these physical cues for identification and association. The book is not meant to be a blueprint of how to copy, but a manual for understanding the consumer motivations, meanings, and perceptions of brands so owners of brands and intellectual property can protect and keep their brand image. It fosters on understanding of how to portray that owning the real is to be real.

The act of true counterfeiting, in which the buyer (or even seller) is deceived about the origin of the good, usually is seen as immoral, unethical, and subject to penalties of the law. The current problem is that on the market many goods are made to look as nearly like the original as possible, with the full knowledge of the buyer and seller that these goods are not original. They are advertised and sold as copies, fakes, or replicas, so there can be no possible deception to the buyer. Perhaps this is why the courts see no difference between counterfeit and pirated goods and do not ask if the consumer knows the true origin of the good.

The link to imitators is more obtuse. Different standards are applied to imitators because they are not direct copies. The observer determines the perception of imitation and the meaning derived from the brand. Measurements of perceptual confusion as to the manufacturer are difficult and time-consuming to perform.

The most serious problems arise when the consumer is misguided about the origin of the good, regardless of the quality. In all cases, no matter what the value or quality, there is destruction in the language of brands.

Too often, marketing competitors choose to imitate a very successful brand through their trademark or trade dress in order to appropriate some goodwill (i.e., brand equity) that already exists in the marketplace. This practice can potentially cause harm to the original seller in several ways. First, when the confusion involves competing brands, there may be some economic loss to the original producer or supplier because some consumers divert their purchases. These diversions can be conscious, in that the consumers know they are not purchasing the original.

Second, some diversions are a real mistake on the part of the consumer at the point of purchase. If the consumer never becomes aware of the mistake and the good is inferior, then the consumer may never purchase the good again because they believe the quality now to be below their accepted level. The essence of this argument is captured in Fig. 1.1, which discusses the benefits and costs to society from brand imitation.

Third, a manufacturer or a supplier also should be alarmed when a seller of an unrelated good uses its well-known trademark or trade dress to sell a good in a different product category. Although the good sold may be a noncompeting product, the brand equity of the original brand may be ex-

| | | QUALITY OF IMITATOR COMPARED TO ORIGINAL | | |
		Better	Equal	Worse
CONSUMERS' AWARENESS OF TRUE MANUFACTURER OR IMITATOR	Knowledgeable	Society better off	Depends on price ratio: better value, society better off	Has potential to destroy equity of original brand
	Confused	Destroys the language of brands	Destroys the language of brands	Destroys the language of brands and can destroy the whole product category

FIG. 1.1. Assessing the costs and benefits of imitation brands.
Source: Wilke, R. & Zaichkowsky, J. L. (1999). Brand Imitation and Its Effects on Innovation, Competition, and Brand Equity. *Business Horizons*, November-December, 9–18.

propriated or even eroded by its sale in another product or service category. This transfer also applies to unrelated goods in the form of unauthorized sponsorship or association.

REFERENCES

Aaker, D. A. (1991). *Managing brand equity.* New York: The Free Press.

Aaker, J. L. (1997). Dimensions of brand personality. *Journal of Marketing Research, 34,* 347–356.

A & M Pet Products Inc. v. Pieces Inc., and Royal K-9 (South West United States District Court, Central District of Los Angeles, case no. 89-4923, 1989).

Allen, M. J. (1991). Who must be confused and when? The scope of confusion actionable under trademark law. *Trademark Reporter, 81*(2), 209–259.

Allison, R. I., & Uhl, K. P. (1964). Influence of beer brand identification on taste perception. *Journal of Marketing Research, Vol. 1 August,* 36–39.

Armstrong, J. S. (1992). Secondary meaning "in the making" in trademark infringement actions under Section 43(a) of the Lanham Act. *George Mason University Law Review, 14*(3), 603–635.

Bloch, P. H., Bush, R. F., & Campbell, L. (1993). Consumer "accomplices" in product counterfeiting: A demand-side investigation. *Journal of Consumer Marketing, 10*(4), 27–36.

Boal, R. B. (1973). Techniques for ascertaining likelihood of confusion and the meaning of advertising communications. *The Trademark Reporter, 73,* 405–435.

Bowen, D. C. (1961) Applied psychology and trademarks. *The Trademark Reporter, 51,* 1–26.

Burgunder, L. B. (1997). Trademark protection of product characteristics: A predictive model. *Journal of Public Policy and Marketing, 16*(2), 277–288.

Carratu, V. (1987). Commercial counterfeiting. In J. M. Murphy (Ed.), *Branding: A key marketing tool* (pp. 59–72). London: Macmillian Press.

Cohen, D. (1986). Trademark strategy. *Journal of Marketing, 50,* 61–74.

Cohen, D. (1991). Trademark strategy revisited. *Journal of Marketing, 55,* 46–59.

Collins-Dodd, C., & Zaichkowsky, J. L. (1999). National brand responses to brand imitation: Retailers versus other manufacturers. *Journal of Product and Brand Management, 8*(2), 96–105.

Dr. Seuss Enters v. Penguin Books, 109 F.3d 1394, 1405 (9th Cir. 1997).

Eastman Kodak Co. v. Fotomat Corp., 317 F. Supp. 304 (N.D. Ga. 1969), appeal 441 F. 2d 1079 (5th Cir 1971).

Ellison, S. (2002, November 15–17). Shampoo maker mimics rivals, repeats. *Wall Street Journal Europe,* A6.

Fackler, M. (2003, October 30). Japan's ingrained favourite, in current short supply, spurs white-kernal crime. *Wall Street Journal,* A1.

Fakes. (2005, February 5). *Business Week.*54–64.

Fenby, J. (1983). *Privacy and the public.* London: Frederick Muller Ltd.

Fletcher, A. L. (1989). Trademark infringement and unfair competition in courts of general jurisdiction. *The Trademark Reporter, 79,* 794–882.

Foxman, E. R., Muehling D. D., & Berger, P. W. (1990). An investigation of factors contributing to consumer brand confusion. *The Journal of Consumer Affairs, 24*(1), 170–189.

Gardner, B. B., & Levy, S. J. (1955, March–April). The product and the brand. *Harvard Business Review, 33,* 33–39.

Hartford House Ltd. v. Hallmark Cards Incorporated, CA10 (Colo), 846 F2d 1268-Fed Cts 815,862; Trade Reg 43, 334, 576, 626 (1986).

Hasbro, Inc. v. Internet Entertainment Group Ltd., 40 U.S.P.Q.2d 1479 (W.D. Wash. 1996)

Howard, D. J., Kerin, R. A., & Gengler, C. (2000). The effects of brand name similarity on brand source confusion: Implications for trademark infringement. *Journal of Public Policy and Marketing, 19*(2), 250–264.

Interstellar Starship Services Ltd. v. Epix, Inc. 304 F 3d 936 (9th Cir) USPQ2d D.or (2002).

Inwood Laboratories Inc. v. Ives Laboratories Inc., 4 56 US 844 (1982).

Kapferer, J. N. (1992). *Strategic brand management.* London: Kogan Page.

Keller, K. L. (1993). Conceptualizing, measuring, and managing consumer-based brand equity. *Journal of Marketing, 57*(1), 1–22.

Kitts, K. T., & Caditz, C. L. (2002, September). Domain-name registrations and on-line trademark infringement. *Washington State Bar News.* [On-line] Available: http://www.wsba.org/barnews/2002/09/kitts-caditz.htm (Accessed March 6, 2003).

Kopp, S. W., & Suter, T. A. (2000). Trademark strategies online: Implications for intellectual property protection. *Journal of Public Policy and Marketing, 19*(1), 119–131.

Landes, W. M., & Posner, R. A. (1987). Trademark law: An economic perspective. *The Journal of Law and Economics, 30,* 265–309.

Lans Retsky, M. (2003, May 12). Dilution of trademarks hard to prove. *Marketing News,* p. 6.

Leeds, D. (1956). Confusion and consumer psychology. *The Trademark Reporter, 46,* 1–7.

Lego Group (1993). *Fair play.* Billund, Denmark: Author.

Levi Strauss v. Blue Bell Inc., 632 F.2d 817 (9th Cir. 1980).

Levy, S. J., & Rook, D. W. (1981). Brands, trademarks, and the law. In B. M. Enis & K. J. Roering (Eds.), *Review of Marketing* (pp. 185–190). Chicago, IL: American Marketing Association.

Loken, B., Ross, I., & Hinkle, R. L. (1986). Consumer "confusion" of origin and brand similarity perceptions. *Journal of Public Policy and Marketing, 5*(1), 195–211.

McConnell S. J., & Dubas, J. E. (2004). Marketing experts' misplaced expertise in the courtroom. *Journal of Consumer Marketing, 21*(6), 378–380.

Mishawaka Rubber & Woolen Mfg. Co. v. S.S. Kresge Co., 316 US 203, 205 53 USPQ 323, 324-25 (1942).

Mitchell, V. W., & Papavassiliou, V. (1999). Marketing causes and implications of consumer confusion. *Journal of Product and Brand Management, 8*(4), 319–339.

Moseley et al., dba Victors Little Secret v. V Secret Catalogue, Inc., et al. US Ct aappeals for the Sixth Circuit No. 011015 March 4, 2003.

National Hockey League v. Pepsi-Cola Canada Ltd., No. C902104 (Supreme Court of British Columbia, June 2, 1992).

Palladino, V. N. (1983). Techniques for ascertaining if there is secondary meaning. *The Trademark Reporter, 73*, 391–404.

Pomfret, J. (2002, November 2–3). It's Harry Potter versus the Pirates: Bogus books abound in China. *The International Herald Tribune*, A1.

Quelch, J. A., & Harding, D. (1996, January–February). Brands versus private labels. *Harvard Business Review*, 99–109.

Reppert-Bismark, J., & Flowler, G. A. (2003, January 31). The Frankfurt Fair: Where imitation isn't a form of flattery. *Wall Street Journal Europe*, A6.

Schnaars, S. P. (1994). *Managing imitation strategies: How later entrants seize markets from pioneers*. Don Mills, Ontario: The Free Press.

Simonson, I. (1994). Trademark infringement from the buyer perspective: Conceptual analysis and measurement implications. *Journal of Public Policy and Marketing, 13*(2), 181.

Stern, G. (1993, July 15). Perrigo's knockoffs of name-brand drugs turn into big sellers. *Wall Street Journal*, A1.

Stipp, D. (1996, May 27). Farewell my logo. *Fortune*, pp. 128–140.

Tiffany & Co. v. Boston Club, Inc., 231 F. Supp. 836 143 USPQ2 (D. Mass. 1964).

Trademarks Act, R.S.C. C T-13, (1985).

Wilke, R., & Zaichkowsky, J. L. (1999, November–December). Brand imitation and its effects on innovation, competition, and brand equity. *Business Horizons*, pp. 9–19.

Zaichkowsky, J. L., & Simpson, R. N. (1996). The effects experience with a brand imitator on the original brand. *Marketing Letters, 7*(1), 31–39.

2

Understanding the Consumer

Two main issues with respect to consumer behavior are mentioned routinely in the investigation of trademark infringement issues: the "sophistication" of the consumer and the consumer's "state of mind." Although the main purpose of this book is to provide information about how trademarks might be similarly perceived, the behavior of consumers is very important in determining what it is they see, perceive, and pay attention to. The various consumer points of shopping behavior, involvement with the purchase or situation, comparison points, intelligence levels, and memory storage are noted in court cases.

The earliest insight is from an article entitled "The Unwary Purchaser" printed in the *Michigan Law Review* (Rogers, 1910). Although the voice is masculine, the points remain the same today:

> The "unwary purchaser" is judicially known to act in certain ways; he has certain duties imposed upon him, and there are certain things which he need not do or know. He is not bound to make comparisons between labels or brands and usually has no opportunity to do so. He is likely in making his purchase to act on the moment and is not bound to study or reflect, to analyze labels or packages, or to read or examine them. He is not bound to remember more than the general features of a mark, brand, or label and is not expected to have in mind the details. He is not supposed to know that imitations exist. The courts recognize he has not the experience of an equity judge in analyzing the elements, which make up the general appearance of a package. Some courts indeed have gone so far as to hold that he has the right to be careless and that the use of the mark or label will be enjoined where deception is a probable or even a possible consequence. (pp. 614–615)

The main point of this early article is that the unwary purchaser usually is transformed in the courtroom. Objectively, the consumer is understood, but the problem is that the behavior becomes subjective when viewed through the lens of the judge and the courts. The claim, which can still happen today, is that the judge unconsciously projects his mental abilities on the consumer's situation, and through that lens, transforms the purchaser into what the court thinks he ought to be, and more frequently into what the court itself is. This happens when judges closely view the evidence themselves and give opinions. For example in *National Hockey League v. Pepsi Cola* (1992), the judge disregarded the reactions of 300 consumers to Pepsi advertisements and stated that after closely watching the ads, in his opinion, there was no way consumers could be confused about who was sponsoring the ads.

Rogers (1910) went on to say that the unwary purchaser would probably not recognize himself if he was suddenly confronted with the person he is thought to be. "His judicially injected intelligence and perception would doubtless astonish him" (p. 617). Therefore, this chapter is about the average individual with certain faculties and certain failings, acting in the current marketplace.

CONSUMER SHOPPING BEHAVIOR

The relative importance of consumer decisions, as opposed to concurrently happening decisions regarding relationships with spouse or significant others, children, career or job, one's health, and everyday hassles of traveling crowded freeways, subways, and other transportation venues, is so minor that the selection of brands within product categories may not even be rated in comparison. It is this perspective that must be kept in mind when the importance and effort put into purchase decisions are examined. Kassarjian (1978) put it best when he said that the average consumer who blithely purchases, consumes, and discards the product most likely could not care less about these purchases. Unconcernedly, he or she makes the purchase, switches brands, ignores commercials, and worries about the important decisions in his or her life and not the purchase of toilet paper.

This behavior is confounded with the tens of thousands of products on the shelves of supermarkets, with the consumer's desire to speed through the aisles, and with the great impatience of consumers when they have to wait at the checkout counter. Most shopping studies show consumers zipping through the aisles, mainly looking at one brand (Dickson & Sawyer, 1990; Hoyer, 1984). A study by Burke (1995) found that consumers purchased an average of 48 different items in just 39 minutes.

All the aforementioned stand in contrast to what happens when a brand comes before the courts in an issue of trademark infringement and all those party to the case become very involved. Lawyers, judges, manufacturers, marketers, and advertisers are aware of every detail that identifies the brand. They are keenly aware of any differences that exist between the two opposing brands in court. It is this close scrutiny that highlights the behavior of being involved. Judges must remember that most consumers almost never achieve this level of scrutiny of the products and services they buy.

A review of the law literature around the concept of the "average" consumer is supplied by Davis (2005). Most of the cases reviewed are from European law, but all the arguments are universal in nature. This concept of the average consumer is germane to main arguments of trademark infringement.

Level of Involvement

In the past 30 years, there have been numerous conceptualizations and investigations of both low- and high-involved behavior. In academic terms, the concept of involvement means that the person is motivated or aroused to think about the object in question. Involvement can be defined as "a person's perceived relevance of the object based on inherent needs, values, and interests."[1] The word "object" is used in the generic sense and refers to a product (or brand), an advertisement, or a purchase situation. Consumers can find "involvement" in all these objects. Besides the internal factors, involvement can be caused by factors relating to the object in question, such as degree of differentiation for the attributes of the object and also factors relating to the usage or purchase situation of the object. Because involvement is a motivational construct, one or more of these antecedent factors can trigger it. These relationships are depicted in Fig. 2.1.

The right side of Fig. 2.1 shows some consequences of being involved with the various objects, products, advertisements, or purchase decisions. When consumers are highly involved, more importance is attached to the object and more evaluation takes place. Because when consumers are intent on doing what they can to satisfy a need, they will be more motivated to pay attention to and process any information relevant to reaching their goals. Also they see more differences among brands, whether the differences are real or imagined.

Although definitions may vary, it is clear that the recognition of individual differences from product category to product category or from person to person has a tremendous impact on how consumers in the shopping environment are viewed. The pervasive effect of involvement with the product category on consumers' motivation to distinguish details and differences, especially with respect to confusion, was first documented in a

---

[1]See Zaichkowsky (1985a, 1986) for detailed information on this topic.

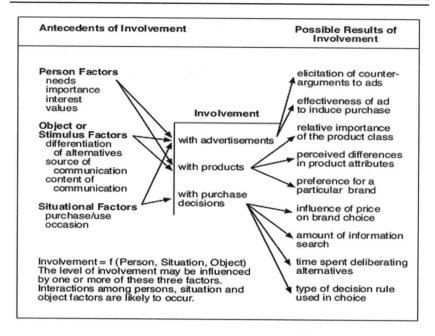

FIG. 2.1. Conceptualizing involvement. From Zaichkowsky (1986).

study by Foxman, Meuhling, and Berger (1990). Involvement with the product, along with memory and certainty of judgment, significantly separated those consumers confused with similar-looking brands from those who correctly identified brands of soups and decongestant products.

When one has low involvement, little or no arousal exists to motivate the consumer to evaluate the object in question. Alternatives seem very similar, and price becomes a primary differentiating factor. That is why customers with low involvement are much more price sensitive than consumers who are highly involved in what they are buying. Therefore, consumer behavior theorists speak of low-involved consumers, low-involvement products, low-involving advertisements, and low-involving purchase decisions. These are usual and frequent conditions of consumers in the marketplace. The implication is that decision making is minimal, and the most common form of purchase decision is just pure and simple recognition of the product. The legal system does recognize the concept of the low-involved purchaser. It is this difference between the low- and high-involved purchaser that leads to the differences in views of the object. That is why one gets such varied views on the perception of similarities or differences among the objects in question. Consumers highly involved with the object under investigation may not be confused at any time, whereas those with low involvement may be easily confused at any time.

Emotionally High Involved.   To delineate further the concept of involvement, marketing researchers and practitioners view a second dimension of motivation types: thinking to feeling. This second dimension explains why consumers may be highly motivated toward products, yet secure so little hard information about them. It departs from the original model, which implies that high-involvement products require a thinking or cognitive orientation first, whereas low-involvement products are more suited to an affective or noninformational appeal. The expansion of involvement along an orthogonal continuum from thinking to feeling allows a more complex approach, which takes into account the excitement that accompanies certain purchases.

The original classification scheme for products was proposed by Vaughn (1980) for the advertising firm Foote, Cone, and Belding in Los Angeles. It implies that different marketing strategies, different decision-making styles, and different advertising copy are needed for different types of products. The scheme is depicted in Fig. 2.2. It proposes that for a great deal of products, the decision process is based on emotion rather than thought or facts. This model heavily influenced consumer behavior research in the 1980s.

In a case involving brand imitation of handguns (*Sturm, Ruger, & Co. Inc. v. Arcadia Machine & Tool Inc.*, 1988), this theory of emotional involvement was used to explain the likely consumer decision-making process with respect to the product category of handguns:

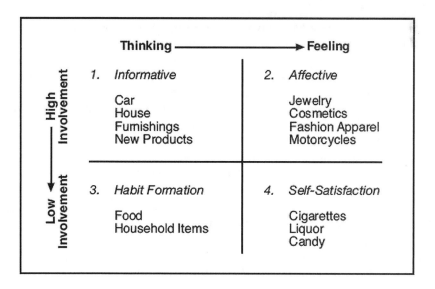

FIG. 2.2. The Foote, Cone, and Belding grid for product classification.

Gun purchasers are more interested or involved than they would be if they were buying a bar of soap, but heightened interest does not necessarily mean that more care is exercised. That only happens when more actual intelligence is brought to bear. It does not happen if the purchaser's heightened interest is more emotional than intellectual. Gun purchasers tend to be emotional. Guns often have psychological attraction for people who buy them. When various complex subliminal factors have convinced a customer to buy a particular gun, he buys it without spending much time finding and reading the objective technical literature. The average customer probably does not exercise a high degree of care in purchasing a gun. (Fletcher 1989, p. 823)

This testimony also brings to light the notion that involvement and knowledge are not the same thing. They may be correlated, but they predict different avenues to decision making. Someone highly involved with a product is not necessarily an expert on that product. Having knowledge is definitely different from being involved and leads to different types of information seeking and processing.[2]

The emotion consumers get from the ownership of luxury goods is the key driver of their purchase, not the functional benefits. The fake goods that copy luxury goods are much sought after by consumers because the consumer can "pass themselves off" as being associated with the luxury goods and get an elevated emotional feeling without the luxury price tag. Only by severing the positive feeling with fake luxury can the informed purchase of counterfeiting or copying of luxury goods be arrested.

Strategies to Increase or Decrease Involvement. Although consumers have very low involvement with purchases for many everyday routinely purchased goods, marketers can increase their level of involvement so that they do pay more attention to the purchase. Close examination of Fig. 2.1 to discover what causes involvement will result in some understanding concerning the creation of involvement. Examples of ways to increase involvement include appealing to the consumer's hedonic needs by using sensory appeals, creating actual differences in the elements of the object, and building a bond to the consumer whereby he or she becomes brand loyal. To decrease involvement, just the opposite strategies are needed: similarity of goods, reduced association with values and interests, and private consumption experiences.

Brand Loyalty Overrides Experience

In a research study investigating the effects of consumption experience with a positive or negative brand imitator on the original brand, brand loy-

---

[2]See Zaichkowsky 1985a for more detail.

alty was found to be an interesting explanatory variable (Zaichkowsky & Simpson, 1996). The study was conducted in the product category of colas. Coca-Cola was used as the original brand, and a fictitious imitation brand, Lora Cola, was created. There were two treatments of the imitation cola, Lora Cola: a positive experience and a negative experience. The original comparison product was Coca-Cola for both treatments.

To create the positive test cola, the new Lora Cola labels were pasted on a two-liter bottle of Coca Cola. To create the negative test cola, the new Lora Cola labels were put on identical bottles of Fountain Fresh, a cola judged in blind taste tests to have a poor taste.

Regular cola drinkers were asked about their involvement with colas, their frequency of consumption, their brand awareness, and the highest and lowest prices they would pay for a large bottle of cola. They were then asked to evaluate the brand Coca-Cola and state their preference for Coke over other brands (measures of brand loyalty). Subjects were then poured samples of each cola for tasting and asked to evaluate the new Lora Cola. Next, they were asked to reevaluate Coca-Cola and their likelihood of purchasing the new Lora Cola and different price structures. When the poor-tasting cola was put in the Coca-Cola bottle, those who were most brand loyal to Coca-Cola continued to rate that taste experience higher than the good tasting (the real Coke) from the fake Lora Cola bottle. Such is the power of brand equity and loyalty that the perception that comes with the well-known trademark and trade dress overrides the actual experience of what is inside the package.

DECISION-MAKING CUES AND HEURISTICS

Over time, consumer behavior theorists have kept up-to-date in studying how decisions are made in the marketplace. It appears that consumers are very adaptive decision makers, changing their behavior to meet the demands of the environment. This adaptation is largely a result of the change in lifestyles and the change in the marketplace. It is important to survey some history of consumer behavior and constructs relevant to decision making. It also is important to review the diversity that exists in the consumer base. Too often, it is forgotten that not all consumers make decisions as we would or do, or think we do, ourselves.

The Economist's View

Early models of consumer behavior were rooted in economic theory. In this paradigm, purchasing decisions were thought to be the result of largely "rational" and conscious economic calculations. Several problems became apparent in applying this assumption to actual consumer consumption.

First, consumers do not have perfect information in the marketplace, nor do they have the same information about the existing alternatives or the attributes of known alternatives. Instead, each consumer has fragmented knowledge of his or her own set of known alternatives and, as a result, consumers cannot always rank order a set of alternatives available to them. In addition, preferences often violate utility theory. Different people prefer different styles, have different tastes, and hence make choices built on preferences of style or images rather than objective information, such as price.

Recognition of the biases in individual decision making is evidenced by the awarding of the Noble Prize in Economics to Daniel Kahneman and Amos Tversky, two psychologists without extensive training in economic models. Their research on systematic biases in choice behavior shows that consumers rarely make rational choices and seem inherently unable to transfer objective information equally to choices (Tversky & Kahneman, 1974).

The Cognitive Consumer

In the 1960s, Kennedy put forth The Consumer Bill of Rights (1963) as a social contract between business and society. As a result of the Kennedy mandate, the government poured millions of dollars into departments whose goal was to make sure the consumer had access to information. Labels were put on products listing all ingredients. Advertising was regulated, and if it was misleading, then corrective advertising was necessary. Information to the consumer was in great supply.

However, according to consumer researchers, although consumers are given information, they often fail to use that information to make decisions. In one choice and evaluation experiment (Scammon, 1977), consumers were given objective product information about several brands available in the marketplace. The study showed that recall of product attributes decreased with increasing information, and that those consumers with more information felt better about their brand selections, but actually made poorer choices. Consumers were limited by the extent of their knowledge about the marketplace and their capacity to store information about the marketplace in short-term memory. The general relationship between the amount of information available and the consumer's use of that information is shown in Fig. 2.3. Generally, people use and search only for the amount of information they can actively process.

This finding is commensurate with other research about the individual's ability to use information. Jacoby, Speller, and Kohn (1974) showed how package information in a supermarket environment could be ignored just because of the volume of information available to the consumer. Generally, it is known that humans can store only a limited amount of informa-

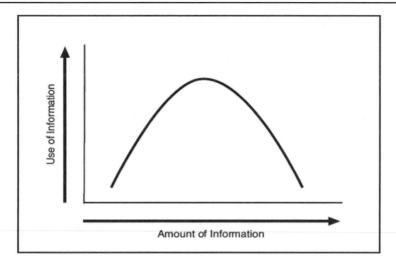

FIG. 2.3. Relationship between information search and ability to process information.

tion in their short-term memory, which in turn imposes limitations on the amount of information the individual is able to process and remember in the long run. Miller's (1956) analyses of the individual's cognitive capacity for seven, plus or minus two, pieces of information as the optimum ability for decision making held for consumer contexts.

Developing Heuristics

Although consumers' skills are limited, the number of choices available to the consumer increases every day. As a coping mechanism for this overwhelming choice environment, consumers have become "cognitive misers" in the marketplace, meaning that they are unable or unwilling to engage in extensive decision-making activities and will settle for "satisfactory" decisions. An in-store study showed that consumers go through almost no brand price comparison behavior (Hoyer, 1984). Decision heuristics such as "buy the cheapest," "buy name brands," or "buy what my friend bought" give the consumer a satisfactory choice in the marketplace that supplants an optimal choice. Consumers must use these simple rules because too many goods clutter too many store shelves.

Wal-Mart, the leading retailer, epitomizes the type of store that carries tens of thousands of items. Currently, major superstores carry more than 50,000 items. There are said to be 400 different brands of beer available to the American beer drinker. A new car purchaser might have 300 different types of cars and light trucks, domestic and imported, from which to choose. The market actually provides overchoice to today's consumer, and the decision-making effort must be simplified.

Alongside this change, working mothers still are mainly in charge of regular family shopping, and now shopping usually is squeezed into minutes between returning home after work and meal preparation. Most consumers simply do not take the time to look carefully at the items they buy because they simply do not have the time or the inclination to do so. It is no wonder that the consumer develops rules of thumb or heuristics to simplify purchase behavior.

The Major Heuristics: Brand Name and Price

The use of brand name and price as major signals for consumer decision making are well documented. Hoyer and Brown (1990) found that these cues could even override objective quality ratings given to consumers. These effects were replicated, by MacDonald and Sharp (2000), 10 years later in a different country with different product categories. When the brand name is known, consumers make choices faster and consider fewer alternatives. They give more weight to the brand cue than the price cue, although the weight given to either can vary across individuals and some situations.

In another study by Dawar and Parker (1994) using electronic goods rather than frequently consumed package goods, the same ordering of the choice heuristics (brand name and price) was found to be universal across cultures. Using several definitions of culture and three different criteria for universality, these authors evaluated the use of brand name, price, retailer reputation, and physical product appearance as signals of quality. Using a sample of 640 adults from 38 nationalities, they found that brand name rated highest—well above the price cue, which was rated as second. Physical appearance rated third, and retailer reputation rated last in consumer importance for decision making.

Interestingly, the correlation between the ratings for price and brand was .37. Although this correlation was significant, it nevertheless shows that the two signals are *not* interchangeable. Price signals different things than brand name. People who are more brand-prone are more price-inelastic, reflecting the value of the brand signal.

INDIVIDUAL DIFFERENCES

Ability Levels

When one is directly involved in passing-off cases, with lawyers, brand managers, and judges, it is sometimes difficult to remember that they probably are more intelligent, more educated, and more involved than most of the consuming public. What appears to be obvious and a matter of common sense under scrutiny may not be such for the consumer of average or below-average intelligence, education, and involvement (or even highly intelligent people under real market and live conditions). Courts have used the following with respect to the average person:

> It is the probability of the average person endowed with average intelligence acting with ordinary caution being deceived that is the criterion. To measure that probability of confusion, the Register of Trademarks or the Judge must assess the normal attitudes and reactions of such persons. (*Canadian Schenley Distilleries Ltd. v. Canada's Manitoba Distillery Ltd.,* 1975, p. 5)

The problem is that we soon forget what is average. Simple decision heuristics are so widely used because a vast number of people are just not able to make more complex informed decisions because of ability, time pressures, or a focus on other aspects of their lives.

Illiteracy

Figures on the extent of functional illiteracy vary. In the United States, approximately 10% of the population older than 16 years of age cannot read or write, and hence are basically unfit for literate employment. Approximately 22% of the population lack the basic skills of reading and arithmetic for retail shopping, and approximately 50% lack the more complex skills for credit card application and sales agreements. This state of affairs certainly is not limited to the United States, and the numbers are even higher for developing countries (*UN Chronicles*, 1990; UNESCO, 2000). These alarming statistics need explanation for a full understanding of the relevance of illiteracy to brand imitation in the marketplace and the consumer's use of simple heuristics and cues to make decisions and choices.

What Does Illiteracy Mean? Literacy measurement has always been controversial because there is no one accepted definition for literacy. In 1948, a United Nations commission proposed "the ability to read and write a single message" as a working definition. More recently, literacy was defined as "the information-processing skills necessary to use the printed material commonly encountered at work, at home, and in the community" (Statistics Canada, 1992). In 1991, Congress defined literacy as

> an individual's ability to read, write, and speak English, and compute and solve problems at levels of proficiency necessary to function on the job and in society, to achieve one's goals, and develop one's knowledge potential. (National Adult Literacy Survey, 1992, p. 2)

In a survey of Canadians, a respondent scoring less than seven on the following ten questions was classified as illiterate:

1. Read and understand the right dosage from an ordinary bottle of cough syrup (10% cannot)
2. From six road signs, pick out which one warns of a traffic light ahead (13% cannot)
3. Figure out the change from $3 if you ordered a soup and sandwich (33% cannot)
4. Sign your name in the correct spot on a social insurance card (11% cannot)
5. Circle the expiry date on a driver's licence (6% cannot)
6. Answer four questions about a meeting arrangement, including the date, time, and people involved (15 to 17% cannot)
7. Circle the long-distance charges on a telephone bill (29% cannot). (Calamai, 1987).

Many of the functionally illiterate are older (age 65 years or older), and illiteracy is higher among men than women. A more extensive study was undertaken in the United States by the Department of Education: the National Adult Literacy Survey (1992). This survey found a total 40 to 44 million American adults functional at the lowest literacy level. The following are examples of questions in these tests:

1. Locate an intersection on a street map.
2. Locate two pieces of information in a sports article.
3. Calculate costs of purchase from an order form.

Because of these low literacy levels, great numbers of people are not able to read labels accurately. The coping and shopping skills of the functionally illiterate were investigated by Viswanathen, Rosa, and Harris (2005). These authors found that the functionally illiterate have different cognitive predilections, decision rules, trade-offs, and coping behavior than consumers who are functionally literate.

The functionally illiterate usually rely on one dimension for decision making or use concrete reasoning. For example, they focus on price or size, but cannot combine different values of each to determine a best buy. They have difficulty transferring knowledge from one product category to another. Price is the usual cue for decision making.

A related predilection is for pictographic thinking, or the attachment of literal and concrete information to the pictures on packages, their color and even font. In this case, a consumer relies on familiar logos and images seen in advertisements when making decisions. This reality must not be ignored.

It was an interesting lesson to retailers who developed generic products to target at low-income and very price-sensitive consumers. These generic goods had only the contents written on the package as the label. There were no logos, mixed colors, or pictures on the package to indicate quality. Consequently, much of the low-income target market did not readily identify what was in the package. The main buyers of generics were the more affluent, but they did not make up a sufficiently large segment on their own to warrant the continued selling of plain-labeled generic products. Most of these generics are now off the shelves of the retailers, making space for more store brands with identifiable cues on the packages.

The functionally illiterate usually rely on a single heuristic for decision making. The most common one is price, but other single cues may be used. To cope with embarrassment , they refuse to ask for help from strangers and shop routinely at corner stores, where anxiety can be kept to a minimum.

Language Abilities

The inclusion of the English language as a criterion for literacy has a great deal of relevance for North America because of the high immigrant population. The foreign-born population in the United States in 2002 was 32.5 million people (Schmidley, 2003). Very few of these people were born in English-speaking countries. Whereas some consumers may rely on visual cues for choice because of illiteracy, other consumers may use the same cues because of language difficulties.

The number of legal non–native-speaking residents in our large cities can be observed casually during the selection of juries for the court system. On any given day, one can count the number, as a percentage, of people who ask to be excused from jury duty because they do not speak the language well enough to understand the court proceedings. Some of those asking to be excused have lived in the country more than 20 years. Our large cities are set up so that immigrants can gather together and continue with their own language, culture, and religion, all recognized in public domains, such as hospitals, where the importance of correct communication may be the difference between life and death. A general hospital in Vancouver posts patient instructions in six languages: English, French, Cantonese, Punjabi, Farsi, and Italian.

In many instances, immigrants are not able to learn their new host culture language. That is left for the children to do at school, with the parents then relying on the children as interpreters. People who do not speak the local language purchase goods every day in our stores and supermarkets. It is likely that many of these immigrants are not literate in English. Hence, their shopping world is guided by nonverbal cues such as pictures on the package.

Relevance of the Literacy Issue

Educated and intelligent people involved in commerce tend to have a very specific social world and thus are not fully aware of the "below average" abilities of many consumers. People of one social class rarely interact on a regular basis with members of another social class. Therefore, they often "forget" that other people may view things differently. A substantive question is what intelligence level of the consumer should be used as the standard in evaluating the level of confusion in the marketplace? This question becomes relevant because determinations of trademark infringement relies on consumer surveys for evidence.

A whole history of consumer research shows that people who choose to participate in surveys are of higher intelligence and education than those who do not participate. Because the majority of consumer research uses convenience samples, subjects are inherently self-selected, with the result that the findings usually are more biased toward higher education than if a truly random sample were chosen.

The particular product under question has a great deal to do with the sample used in determining confusion. However, most products subject to consumer confusion, whether they are frequently purchased branded goods, such as cat litter and soft drinks, or specialty products, such as faucets or guns, are bought by consumers of various intelligence and educational levels. Therefore, it must be kept in mind that surveys may be biased toward the conservative end of confusion detection because, on the average, those who respond are likely to be more literate, educated, and intelligent than those who do not respond. In the final analysis, actual confusion and potential confusion are likely to play a greater role in consumer choice than previously determined because of the many consumers who cannot correctly read and interpret package labels.

Microview of Confused Shopping

Levy and Rook (1981) first interviewed consumers about their encounters with confusion in the marketplace. Generally, they found that consumers had three different views with respect to this issue. First, some consumers blamed themselves for the mistake. Those that blamed themselves admitted to being embarrassed and said that perhaps they were not careful enough in the purchasing environment. Second, some consumers expected brands to be similar from time to time, and therefore thought consumers should be sufficiently aware to make adequate discrimination. Third, some consumers saw the need for legislation to protect companies, and perhaps themselves, from imitators.

Able But Low Involvement Dominates.   The majority of the literate population still may make mistakes in the marketplace because other cues, such as symbols, color, and shape, supersede any careful decision making. The mistakes made are viewed often by the consumer as not being serious enough for any action to be taken. It must be remembered that purchasing is viewed by consumers in the context of all the things they must think about during the day.

Colleagues have relayed the following situations during discussions about brand confusion. Shopping in a drug store, Professor Wilson decided to buy some vitamins. These vitamins were a major brand heavily advertised on television. He walked to the vitamin shelf, looked, and picked up what he thought were Centrum vitamins. He had bought Centrum before and was well aware of their appearance. When he looked more closely at the package, he noticed it was not the Centrum, but the store brand, which had a design and package color very similar to Centrum. Instead of returning the store brand to the shelf and picking up the real Centrum vitamins, he put the store brand in the basket and proceeded to purchase it.

He did not go back and buy what he intended for two reasons. First, he thought it was only vitamins and questioned how different they could be. Second, he did not want to give the impression that he had made a mistake. He thought other people might think he was not very bright for making such a mistake at the point of purchase. (This consumer was a full professor who taught advertising and consumer behavior. Even the experts are consumers from time to time!)

Another business colleague told a story of shopping for Head-and-Shoulders dandruff shampoo, also in a drug store. Upon examining the brand on the shelf, Professor Smith noticed a similar-looking bottle next to it, picked it up, and examined it. He decided he wanted to buy the real thing and picked out a bottle to take to the cash register. When the professor arrived home and unpacked his purchases, he discovered he actually had purchased the similar-looking bottle rather than the bottle of Head-and-Shoulders he really wanted. He did not take the imitator brand back to the store for an exchange. Professor Smith did not think it was worth his time, and he said he felt a little stupid about making such a mistake, especially because he had consciously decided not to purchase the imitation.

Why Mistakes Matter to the Individual.   These types of purchase situations exist every day for most of us. The relative cost of such mistakes is mostly inconsequential for the consumer. The damage is not done to the consumer, but to the equity of the original brand. What consumers do not think about when they purchase a look-a-like brand, knowingly or not, is the potential harm to the original manufacturer. Just as brands reduce search costs and risk for consumers in the buying process, so new brands are simultaneously created to give consumers more and different attributes from which to choose. That may be in the interests of consumers. Gillette, for example, has a goal that 40% of Gillette sales every 5 years come from entirely new products, not just line extensions (Morris, 1996). The Sensor razor, which reportedly required 10 years to perfect, exemplifies the time, money, and effort required for innovation. It is doubtful that Gillette would be so committed to this strategy if the company felt its efforts would not be protected under its world famous brand name. Therefore, protection from imitation actually may provide more products from which the consumer can choose.

An older, and perhaps more established, company is Procter and Gamble. This company deals with brand imitation over a wide number of brands, especially its historic brands such as Tide and Head and Shoulders shampoo. Procter and Gamble has made 70 separate improvements to Tide laundry detergent since its launch in 1956. Tide's core promise is that it gets clothes cleaner than any other laundry detergent on the market. Procter and Gamble's consistent investment in product improvements enhances Tide's perceived and real superiority and provides the basis for information to differentiate brands (Quelch & Harding, 1996). Procter and Gamble devotes $1.2 billion annually to research and development. The company holds more than 2,500 active patents and employs 1,250 Ph.D. scientists (Henkoff, 1996). It is clearly committed to innovation through research.

Because of this commitment to introduce new products, it is in the interest of consumers, and hence, society, that firms cannot easily imitate each other. Therefore, a restrictive trademark law can be seen as being in the interest of consumers because the development of new brands gives them the possibility to choose among brands with different attributes, to have a broad category of brands at their disposal, and to live in a society that values new process technologies.

Companies that copy some identifying aspect of a competitor's brand usually do not advertise their brand at all. They rely solely on the in-store identification and decision making of the consumer. This means that the consumer may have some idea of the brand they are seeking before entering the store, on the basis of previous experience or advertising. The imitator is able to find its way to the consumer's basket because the consumer does not have the exact picture of the product stored in memory, only a reasonable image. The concept of imperfect recollection is a real phenomenon.

SUMMARY

The points of shopping behavior, decision heuristics, literacy rates, and memory storage usually are clouded in dealings with brand imitation. It is the goal of the lawyer to do the best job possible for his or her client and "win" the case. Lawyers are very good at clouding the issues and emphasizing the points in favor of their client. That is what they are paid to do. Therefore, these points sometimes get lost in courtrooms. An article on defending trademark infringement cases cites tactics such as presenting incorrect legal rulings and getting the plaintiff to focus on irrelevant issues (Robin, 1992). Thus, the consumer gets lost in the shuffle.

When investigating any case of brand confusion in the marketplace, it is important to keep in mind the following aspects of consumer decision making:

1. Consumers have limited short-term memory and are not able or willing to process all available product information at the time of purchase. They are likely to use simple decision heuristics that allow for a time-efficient choice. The most used heuristics are brand name and price, in that order.
2. Currently, consumers suffer from overchoice. There are simply too many alternatives in the marketplace for the consumer to consider rationally. To cope with this environment, consumers make what they believe to be satisfactory choices, not necessarily optimal ones.
3. Consumers spend less time shopping because they feel rushed and tired from their workdays. The combination of mental fatigue and increased time pressure is likely to lead to less concentration or awareness of specific brand attributes when consumers are purchasing.
4. Not all consumer purchase decisions are based on rational thinking. Some are based on emotion and also can be independent of the cost of the good.
5. Not all consumers have the ability to function fully in a literate world. Due to the illiteracy of our population, we might expect one in five consumers to rely heavily on symbols for identification. These people may be more likely than the literate consumer to use cues such as color, shape, and design to select brands. Illiterate consumers are less likely to use written information to make their choices.
6. Immigrants often cannot read the package information given in English. They are perhaps more likely to rely on package cues such as pictures and color for their choice.
7. Highly intelligent articulate people also rely on external cues when they are "low involved" and hence are not motivated to evaluate carefully the product purchase in question.
8. Consumers who do make mistakes in the marketplace usually do not feel it is worth their time and energy to correct them. They also may not want to admit that they purchased something they did not intend to purchase.

These points should be emphasized in efforts to understand how the consumer reacts to imitators in the marketplace. Too often judges, lawyers, and other well-educated persons involved in these cases forget that they are not necessarily "average" consumers. Often they project their own decision-making patterns onto the court cases in question. In addition, well-educated people may not want to admit that they, too, are capable of making mistakes in the marketplace.

REFERENCES

Burke, R. R. (1995). *Marsh Supermarkets, Inc. (A): The Marsh Supermarket Study.* Boston: Harvard Business School Publishing, Case number 042.

Calamai, P. (1987, September). Broken words, why five million Canadians are illiterate. A Special Southam Survey, Southam: Canada.

Canadian Schenley Distilleries Ltd. v. Canada's Manitoba Distillery Ltd., 25 C.P.R. (2d) 1 (F.C. T.D.), (1975).

Davis, J. (2005). Locating the average consumer: His judicial origins, intellectual influences and current role in European trademark law. *Intellectual Property Quarterly, 2,* 183–192.

Dawar, N., & Parker, P. (1994). Marketing universals: Consumers' use of brand name, price, physical appearance, and retailer reputation as signals of product quality. *Journal of Marketing, 58,* 81–95.

Dickson, P. R., & Sawyer, A. G. (1990). The price knowledge and search of supermarket shoppers. *Journal of Marketing, 54,* 42–54.

Fletcher, A. L. (1989). Trademark infringement and unfair competition in courts of general jurisdiction. *The Trademark Reporter, 79,* 794–882.

Foxman, E. R., Meuhling, D. D., & Berger, P. W. (1990). An investigation of factors contributing to consumer brand confusion. *Journal of Consumer Affairs, 24*(1), 170–189.

Henkoff, R. (1996, October 14). P&G new and improved. *Fortune,* 151–161.

Hoyer, W. D. (1984). An examination of consumer decision making for a common repeat purchase product. *Journal of Consumer Research, 11*(3), 822–829.

Hoyer, W. D., & Brown, S. P. (1990). Effects of brand awareness on choice for a common, repeat-purchase product. *Journal of Consumer Research, 17,* 141–148.

Jacoby, J., Speller, D. E., & Kohn, C. A. (1974). Brand choice behavior as a function of information load. *Journal of Marketing Research, 8,* 47–55.

Kassarjian, H. H. (1978). Presidential address, 1977: Anthropomorphism and parsimony. In K. Hunt (Ed.), *Advances in consumer research* (Vol. 5, pp. xiii–xiv). Ann Arbor, MI: Association for Consumer Research.

Levy, S. J., & Rook, D. W. (1981). Brands, trademarks, and the law. In B. M. Enis & K. J. Roering (Eds.), *Review of marketing* (pp. 742–775). Chicago, IL: American Marketing Association.

MacDonald, E. K., & Sharp, B. M. (2000). Brand awareness effects on consumer decision making for a common, repeat purchase product: A replication. *Journal of Business Research, 48,* 5–15.

Miller, G. A. (1956). The magical number seven, plus or minus two: Some limits on our capacity for processing information. *Psychological Review, 63*, 81–97.

Morris, B. (1996). The brand's the thing. *Fortune*, 72–80.

National Adult Literacy Survey (1992). National Center for the Study of Adult Learning and Literacy. Available: http://gseweb.harvard.edu/ncsall/ (Accessed November 2, 2003).

National Hockey League v. Pepsi-Cola Canada LTD., No. C902104 (Supreme Court Of British Columbia, 1992, June 2).

Quelch, J. A., & Harding, D. (1996). Brands versus private labels: Fighting to win. *Harvard Business Review, 74*(1), 99–109.

Robin, A. (1992). The defense of a trademark infringement case. *IDEA—The Journal of Law and Technology, 32*(4), 383–390.

Rogers, E. S. (1910). The unwary purchaser. *Michigan Law Review, VIII*(8), 613–622.

Scammon, D. L. (1977). Information load and consumers. *Journal of Consumer Research, 4*(3), 148–155.

Schmidley, D. (2003). The foreign-born population in the United States: March 2002. *Current Population Reports*, P20-539. Washington, DC: U.S. Census Bureau.

Statistics Canada. (1992). *Adult literacy in Canada*. Ottawa, Ontario: Author.

Sturm, Ruger & Co. Inc. v. Arcadia Machine & Tool Inc., 10 USPQ2d 1522 1527 (CD Calif., 1988).

The Consumer Bill of Rights. (1963) In Consumer Advisory Council, first report. Washington, DC: U.S. Government Printing Office.

Tvesky, A., & Kahneman, D. (1974). Judgement under uncertainty: Heuristics and biases. *Science, 185*, 1124–1131.

UN Chronicles (1990, March). Illiteracy knows no borders, p. 59.

UNESCO (2000). Regional adult literacy rate and population by gender. UNESCO Institute for Statistics. Available: http://www.uis.unesco.org/en/stats/statistics/literacy2000.htm (Accessed May 1, 2003).

Vaughn, R. (1980). How advertising works: A planning model. *Journal of Advertising Research, 20*(5), 27–33.

Viswanathan, M., Rosa, J. A., & Harris, J. E. (2005). Decision making and coping of functionally illiterate consumers and some implications for marketing management. *Journal of Marketing, 69*, 15–31.

Zaichkowsky, J. L. (1985a). Measuring the involvement construct. *Journal of Consumer Research, 12*, 341–352.

Zaichkowsky, J. L. (1985b). Familiarity: Product use, involvement, or expertise? In E. C. Hirshman & M. B. Holbrook (Eds.), *Advances in Consumer Research* (Vol.XII, pp. 296–299). Provo, UT: Association for Consumer Research.

Zaichkowsky, J. L. (1986). Conceptualizing involvement. *Journal of Advertising, 15*(2), 4–14, 34.

Zaichkowsky, J. L., & Simpson, N. R. (1996). The effect of experience with a brand imitator on the original brand. *Marketing Letters, 7*(1), 31–39.

3

Psychological Principles Underlying Consumer Perceptions of Imitation Brands

Because consumer behavior is just another aspect of human behavior, marketers have often turned to cognitive and social psychology for explanation and prediction of consumers' activities in the marketplace. For the concept of brand imitation, learning theory from cognitive psychology is highly relevant. A framework for understanding how consumers learn to make choices and discriminations is based on their learning from the environment. Also, from cognitive psychology, theories of perception and attention provide understanding for occasions when objects actually are perceived or noticed by the consumer.

Social psychology, specifically attitude and group influence theories, are important to the understanding of why others would want to associate with owners of successful trademarks and why consumers are knowingly motivated to buy fake products. The premise is that positive attitudes can be developed through simple association with well-liked objects, and that these positive attitudes can lead to purchase of the associated product, as well as the original product. Most of the theories relevant to brand imitation are very simple to comprehend.

STIMULUS GENERALIZATION

The reason why imitation as a strategy even exists may be partly explained by a concept termed "stimulus generalization." *Stimulus generalization* means that the individual generalizes from one incident or stimulus object to another similar incident or stimulus object. The phenomenon is rooted in the theory of classical conditioning, which states that learning depends not only on repetition, but also on the ability of individuals to generalize from one object to the next.

Classical Conditioning

Classical conditioning gets its name from the fact that it is the kind of learning originally studied in the "classical" experiments of Ivan P. Pavlov (1849–1936). Pavlov, a Russian psychologist, undertook experiments conditioning dogs to salivate at the sound of a bell. To condition the dogs, a neutral stimulus or bell acted as the conditioned stimulus. This bell was paired several times with the meat paste (unconditioned stimulus) presented to the dog. The dog would salivate, which was an unconditioned or natural response. After a while, the meat paste was taken away and only the bell was presented to the dog. As a result of the continued pairing, the dog salivated at the bell although there was no food accompanying it. This is called a conditioned response. The process is outlined in Fig. 3.1.

In Pavlov's case, the dog was conditioned to salivate at the sound of the bell when there was no meat paste present. Although the possibility of applying this type of learning to humans might seem outrageous, consider the conditioning that takes place with food. Moviegoers have been bombarded by the smell of popcorn at theaters for decades. The sight and smell of popcorn entices them to purchase popcorn to eat during the movie. It is a

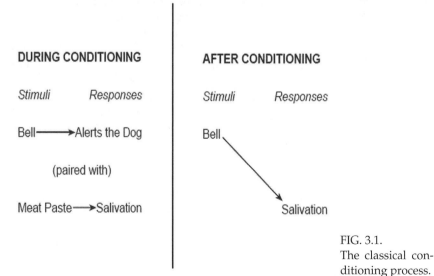

DURING CONDITIONING

Stimuli   *Responses*

Bell ⟶ Alerts the Dog

(paired with)

Meat Paste ⟶ Salivation

AFTER CONDITIONING

Stimuli   *Responses*

Bell ⟍

⟍ Salivation

FIG. 3.1.
The classical conditioning process.

learned pairing of movies and popcorn. Now, with the saturation of DVDs in the home, the renting and buying of movies is a weekly occurrence for many households. Coupled with this is the proliferation of sales of microwave popcorn and bagged popcorn. Sales of home-eaten popcorn are at an all-time high, far exceeding sales of popcorn eaten outside the home. People have been conditioned to eat popcorn when they watch a movie. The movie watching rather than the sight or smell of popcorn leads to the purchase of popcorn to be eaten when consumers view the movie in their own home.

Getting back to the relevance of brand imitation, according to classical conditioning theorists, learning depends not only on repetition, but also on the ability of individuals to generalize. Over time, Pavlov noticed that his dog salivated, not only to the sound of a bell, but also to the sound of keys jangling, a buzzer, or even a metronome. These were sounds that only resembled a bell. Thus, the animal tended to generalize the conditioned response to stimuli that differed from the original sound of the bell, but somewhat similar to a sound to which it was specifically conditioned. It is this same response to a slightly different stimuli, or stimulus generalization, that facilitates learning or is a key aspect of learning.

Marketing Studies of Stimulus Generalization

Stimulus generalization provides the theory to explain why consumers react similarly to, or desire imitators that, closely resemble original brands. It also explains why manufacturers of private brands try to make their packaging resemble those of the national brand leaders. They want the consumer to generalize national brand images to perceptions of store brands.

An academic study of brand imitation dealing with manufacturers of private brands and national brands found that the similarity in physical appearance of originals and imitators was significantly related to consumer perceptions of a common business origin between them (Loken, Ross, & Hinkle, 1986). Respondents thought the look-alike brands (national vs. private) were produced at the same manufacturing plant. In addition, the researchers speculated that the physical similarities between brands, such as color and shape, have marketing consequences independent of the product origin perceptions. External package cues, such as color, were used to evaluate product attributes and to motivate purchase behaviors.

A follow-up study by Ward, Loken, Ross, and Hasapopoulos (1986) provided support for their speculation. In this study, subjects were given various brands of shampoo to evaluate. The results confirmed that different brands with similar-looking packages were rated as similar in quality and perceived performance. The subjects appeared to generalize from the physical appearance of the package to the contents inside the package.

A field experiment, based on the concept of stimulus generalization, provided evidence in a trademark infringement case of breath mints (Miaoulis & D'Amato, 1978). The manufacturers of the original brand, Tic Tac mints, thought two new competitors (Mighty Mints and Dynamints) had infringed on their trade dress by copying the "look" of their package and mint. In this study, Mighty Mints and Dynamints were placed for sale in retail outlets in cities where Tic Tac was an established brand, but where neither Mighty Mints nor Dynamints were known. Consumers were questioned about their reasons for purchase after buying either the Mighty Mints or Dynamints, but before eating the product. The responses suggested that the consumers purchased the new competing products mainly because of the expectations raised by the physical appearance of the package and the mint. Consumers said these expectations were learned from previous experiences with Tic Tac brand mints.

Another study of national and look-alike store brands was conducted in a shopping mall (Hupman & Zaichkowsky, 1995). Regular purchasers of hair conditioner, antiperspirant, and cellophane tape were asked to rate the similarity of each pair of brands on perceived quality, benefits, and different product attributes. They then were asked whether they thought the two brands were manufactured at the same source or by different manufacturers. The consumers also were asked what it was that caused them to believe the two brands were similar. Two groups emerged: respondents who believed the product pair was made by the same manufacturer and those who believed the product pair was made by different manufacturers. For all product categories, respondents who thought the brands were manufactured at the same source perceived the brands to be more similar. These results are presented in Table 3.1.

When these consumers were asked to articulate the source of the similarity, the overwhelming response was "the package."

To further this investigation, a second study was conducted in which the level of involvement with the product category was measured. People were asked whether brand name, color, shape, or overall design was used to judge similarity. The results showed that subjects with lower involvement rated the brands as more similar than those more highly involved with the product category (Table 3.2).

When asked about the cues used to judge similarity, the stated reason still focused on overall design (Table 3.3). Although it was thought that brand name and color cues would be more important than shape and overall design, self-reports focused on the overall design answer. The respondents might have considered that overall design incorporated the other cues and therefore may have considered it more important. Also, people may not be cognitively aware of specific cues, such as brand name or color, they are using to identify brands. It is likely that this can be tested only by

TABLE 3.1
Perceptions of Origin of Manufacturer and Similarity of the Product

	Users Only (n)	Similarity[a]
Antiperspirant (national/store)		
Different origin	17	5.06 ± 1.30
Same origin	49	5.55 ± 1.00
		p < .05
Hair conditioner (national/national)		
Different origin	40	5.08 ± 0.97
Same origin	20	5.65 ± 0.81
		p < .05
Cellophane tape (national/store)		
Different origin	38	3.71 ± 1.45
Same origin	30	4.90 ± 1.40
		p < .05

[a]Measured on a 7-point scale: 7 (extremely likely the same origin) to 1 (extremely likely a different origin)

Source: Hupman and Zaichkowsky (1995).

TABLE 3.2
Involvement With Product and Perception of Same Manufacturer

	n	Perceived Similarity of Manufacturer	t Value
Antiperspirant			
Low involvement	41	6.00 ± 0.95[a]	3.20
High involvement	26	5.08 ± 1.41	p < .01
Hair conditioner			
Low involvement	36	5.19 ± 1.14	NS
High involvement	32	4.97 ± 1.23	
Cellophane tape			
Low involvement	52	5.13 ± 1.30	4.72
High involvement	19	3.37 ± 1.64	p < .001

NS, not significant

[a]Scale: 1 (most likely different manufacturer) to 7 (most likely same manufacturer).

Source: Hupman and Zaichkowsky (1995).

using nonverbal experiments measuring reactions to product packages. Support for this premise comes from feature integration theory discussed later in this chapter (Triesman & Gelade, 1980).

In conclusion, the major cues used by consumers to evaluate their expectations of product performance and brand similarity seem to be color, shape, overall design, and brand name. Experimental and survey evidence sug-

TABLE 3.3
Stated Importance of Visual Cues in Judging Similarity

	Color	Brand Name	Shape	Overall Design
Antiperspirants	3.84 ± 1.10[a]	3.12 ± 1.07	3.61 ± 0.97	4.15 ± 0.96
Hair conditioners	3.52 ± 1.03	3.38 ± 0.98	3.79 ± 0.99	4.01 ± 0.91
Cellophane tapes	2.99 ± 0.93	3.20 ± 1.17	3.42 ± 1.14	3.66 ± 1.07

[a]Measured on a 5-point scale: 1 (very unimportant) to 5 (very important).

Source: Hupman and Zaichkowsky (1995).

gests that consumers do generalize between look-alike brands and may form similar expectations about product attributes and performance on the basis of external product cues. The weight given to each cue may vary over different situations, but color is important in the initial brand identification.

THE CUE OF COLOR

Although many researchers focus on the importance of brand name, color is an integral and important aspect of the brand's logo, packaging, and identity. Color also is important because it conveys emotion, mood, (Bellizzi, Crowley, & Hasty, 1983), advertising context (Gorn, Dahl, Yi, & Chattopadhyay, 1997), or differences in the meaning of colors cross-culturally (Madden, Hewett, & Roth, 2000). These research streams are fed by a great body of literature on the psychology of color that spans more than 100 years of studies investigating color reactions as functions of personality, physiological reactions to color, color preferences, color effects on emotions, and color effects on behavior (see Valdez & Mehrabian, 1994, for a review).

Louis Cheskin's (1947, 1954) early work on color in marketing showed that consumers do not know why they react or what they react to. He said it is a false premise that what people say is equal to what they do. One basis for this sweeping statement is an experiment that investigated the reactions to butter and margarine on the basis of preconceived notions about the color of the substances:

> A large number of women at a luncheon were asked whether they could tell the difference between butter and margarine. Over 90 percent said they preferred butter because margarine tasted oily, greasy, and more like shortening than butter. Two pats were served, one yellow (margarine) and one white (butter). The ladies were asked whether they could discern any differences. The yellow pat (margarine) tasted like butter, claimed 99 percent of luncheon guests, but the white pat (butter) tasted oily like margarine. (Cheskin 1954; p. 95)

Cheskin said this test showed how people confuse sensations. In other words, the ladies attributed to the sense of taste the characteristic that belonged to the sense of sight. This interdependency of the senses is well known among sensory specialists. If you blindfold a subject before a taste test, it is unlikely that they will be able to distinguish between Coke and Seven-Up, or red wine and white wine. The sight of the color primes the senses with expectations.[1]

Color and Identification

According to the Institute of Color Research, consumers make subconscious judgments within 90 seconds of viewing an object, and 90% to 60% of the acceptance or rejection of an object is based on color. Because color impressions are both quickly made and long held, decisions regarding color can be highly important to success.

Colors are used to associate and identify in the broadest sense. For example, grass is green and the sky is blue, just as Coke is red and Pepsi is blue. Marketing companies know that over time, consumers come to associate specific colors with certain well-known brands, partly because of carefully controlled advertising and promotion strategies, which include color associated closely with brand name. For example, Player's cigarettes, Kodak film, and Coca-Cola are just a few brands that are associated quickly with a specific color on their package. These associated colors are carefully regulated and controlled by the company, and the colors in different aspects of the ad must be the same as those on the package. For example, the red in Santa Claus's suit (Coca-Cola), the blue in the sky (Player's), and the yellow/black (Kodak) in photo finishing stores all are carefully matched to the package for quick and congruent identification and association.

Identification by color also is a point of differentiation from competitors. For example, sports teams wear different colored uniforms for games at home and away to identify themselves as visitors. Brands also use color to distinguish themselves from their competitors. Consumers usually have a low level of involvement with routine purchases of packaged goods and often use color as an easy signal or as the first cue of the brand they wish to purchase. Although there are many external cues that consumers use to identify brands, color and specific color combinations are identified easily and cross language and literacy barriers. Therefore, color may be an even more important cue than brand name in unfamiliar purchase environments.

---

[1]On an unrelated matter, sensory specialists also know that the sense of taste is dependent on the sense of smell. Without the ability to smell, one loses his or her sense of taste.

Academic documentation of the role that color plays in brand identification is limited to a study by Kapferer (1996), who found color to be the attribute most likely used in initial brand identification. The U.S. court only recently ruled, in 1995, that color may serve as a trademark (Burgunder, 1997). Moreover, academic research applied to brand identification and association due to color is just emerging in marketing (e.g., Alvaro & Zaichkowsky, 2001; Garber, Burke, & Jones, 2000). This legal ruling also is important for brands with "line extensions" because manufacturers may want to stick with colors of original brands when they take their brand to other product categories to ensure that their rights are preserved.

Contributions From Psychology.   Christ (1975) conducted a meta-analyses of the experimental literature on color and its effects on visual search, and found that if the color of a "target" is unique and known in advance, then color indeed assists both the search task and the identification task. This finding was supported by Jansson, Marlow, and Bristow (2004), who studied the use of color for searching in cluttered environments. The implication for brand management is that brands with unique, well-known packages are more easily identified on the retailer's shelf.

Christ (1975) also found that color could be identified more accurately than sizes, brightness, and shapes, but with less accuracy than alphanumeric symbols. Color improved identification accuracy by at least 176% compared with size, 32% compared with brightness, and 202% compared with shape.

Boynton and Dolensky (1979) conducted a study to examine these findings in a real-life setting, with other cues competing against color for the consumer's attention. Subjects presented with a randomly selected group of 17 books spread out on a table were allowed to inspect them for 45 seconds. Some subjects were made color-blind with red filter glasses worn either in the first or second part of the experiment or during the entire experiment. After 17 decoys had been added to the original selection of books, subjects were asked to identify as many of the original books as possible within 3 minutes. The results indicated that color cues did not appear to be used to a significant extent. It could have been that subjects used the book titles as cues.

A second experiment was conducted in which the titles of the books were covered. In this experiment, the results showed that the performance of subjects was indeed enhanced by the use of color cues. Overall, this study suggests that color cues often are used in conjunction with alphanumeric cues and, as shown in the second experiment, color cues are used more extensively than size or shape.

The Stroop Effect.   Early work in psychology by Stroop (1935, 1992) showed that people have a difficult time reading the name of a color when the actual color of the print deviates from the letters being read. For example, it took people longer to read green when it was printed in red than if the color of the print was also green. This caused a 74% increase in the mean time it took to name colors, as compared with the time required when they were just presented in squares. When the effect of practice or repetition was taken into account, this delay effect was diminished, but still significant.

Extrapolating from this work, there could be interference between package colors and brand names with well-known and long-established brands. The law of associative inhibition states: "If a is already associated with b, then it is difficult to connect it with k; b gets in the way" (Stroop, 1992). Furthermore, the degree to which b gets in the way is curvilinearly dependent on association with a, with most of the interference occurring at average levels of association (Exhibit 3.1). Thus, it follows that if a brand is associated with a particular color, it is difficult to connect it with a new color, especially when the consumer is an average purchaser. The original color will get in the way of brand identification once the color has been modified, or if a new brand is brought forward into the marketplace with the same or similar color packaging as the original brand it is attempting to imitate, it may come to be confused with the original brand.

Stroop's findings may be applied to brand package identification in studies investigating the relative impact of new brands with the same color combination package as the long-established product category

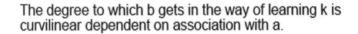

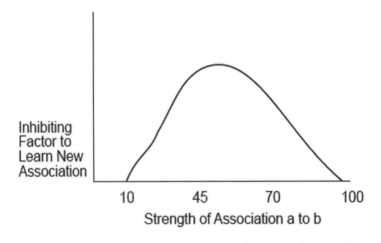

EXHIBIT 3.1   Studies of Interference in Serial Verbal Reactions (Kline, 1921).

leader. A consumer may see a brand package with a specific color combination and have an immediate response to his or her stored knowledge association of these colors. It is easier for a person to identify the word "red" when it is in red lettering than when it is in blue lettering. An example applied to marketing would be the identification of a label. If the traditional or original label was blue in color with the brand name in red, the identification would be first of the colors, a sensory cue, then second of the printed word, a semantic cue. An imitator brand using the same colors but a different brand name might easily be misidentified as the first brand because of the superior selection of sensory cues, such as color, over semantic cues, such as brand name.

ATTENTION AND PERCEPTION

Sometimes consumers initially pick out an imitator brand because they think it is the original brand. The image they have of the original brand is in their mind, and it is this image they are looking for. This preperception is 50% of the object or brand they are looking for. They make a mistake or misperceive the actual differences between the original and the imitator. This mistake may be only in the initial identification, and may be discovered once the item is in the hand of the consumer. The mistake may also go unnoticed by the consumer until the product is about to be used. In some cases, the mistake may be entirely undiscovered by the consumer. In all these cases, it is not stimulus generalization that is primary, but perception and attention to the object.

The initial step in understanding perception is to understand what kind of things can be perceived at all. For the consumer to use marketing cues in decision making, the cues must first be perceived by the individual. For the cues to be perceived, the individual must first pay attention to them. Attention has two parts, intensity and direction, that sometimes exist in a nonconscious environment. In other words, attention usually is immediate and effortless.

Intensity has to do with the time spent looking at the object. The longer an individual is exposed to a stimulus, the more likely it is to be perceived. Direction means the individual must have the stimulus in focus. For example, a disclaimer on an advertisement likely will not be perceived unless the person is led to focus on it. This focus could be aided by size, color, contrast, and position or context. These all are important factors in directing attention. The reader must keep in mind that the consumer's main response to marketing communication might be one of disinterest as compared with other aspects of the consumer's personal environment. Therefore, attention to marketing communication is likely to be fleeting and superficial, with little intensity and fluttering direction.

Attention to Visual Information

There are several physical properties that do direct attention when considered in the context of the visual field. For example, it has long been known in advertising that the size of an advertisement can account for more than 25% of the variance in readership scores (Troldahl & Jones, 1975; Twedt, 1952). There is an abundance of evidence to suggest that color increases attention to an advertisement, although many studies of color could be interpreted as supporting the effectiveness of color as a contrast tool. Thus, the impact of color depends on the surrounding information. The manner in which individuals direct their attention to areas in a visual display is sensitive to both the characteristics of each piece of information relative to competing information and the consumer's goals associated with the processing of the stimulus or information in question. In most cases of product choice, the goals are to recognize and choose rather than to examine and evaluate.

The fleeting aspect of attention is detailed by Janiszewski (1991). The first look at a stimulus (i.e., the first 200 msec) is characterized by a nonfixation, indicating a holistic analysis of the information available. During this preattentive state, decisions are made about where to look (fixate) first. A decision on where to look involves a comparison between the potential benefits associated with an additional fixation and the costs of being "temporarily blind" while engaged in movement to that area. In many cases, assessment of the potential benefits associated with the next fixation may be nothing more than an assessment of the density or uniqueness of information in that area.

The resulting patterns of looking or direction are highly dependent on the viewer's processing goals. Greater variability can occur when an individual is asked to view a picture for seven different purposes because seven unique scan patterns will emerge, few of them comparable with those used by other individuals (Janiszewski, 1993). In some ways, this notion of goals is related to the idea of selective attention. The individual's processing capacity, in the short term, is limited in some central mechanism. This mechanism is associated with consciousness and controlled processing, and it delimits divided attention (Johnson & Dark, 1986). Selective attention therefore refers to the differential processing of simultaneous information sources. Early research on selective attention shows that sensory selection is consistently more accurate and less effortful than semantic selection.

Perception and Weber's Law

Of basic interest in the detection of any stimulus is Weber's Law. It states that with any given kind of perceiving, equal relative (not absolute) differences are perceptible. Weber's Law is a description of the "just noticeable difference" (JND) or differential threshold level that can be perceived by an individual. This is the minimum difference in a stimulus or the minimum difference between stimuli that will be noticed by the individual. The quantification and expression of this ratio is shown in Exhibit 3.2.

The main point is that Weber's Law is an expression of the fact that the ratios, not the absolute difference, are important in describing the least perceptible differences in sensory discrimination. The differential threshold varies not only with the sensitivity of the receptor and the type of stimuli, but also with the absolute intensity of the stimuli being compared. The size of the least detectable change or increment in intensity is a function of the initial intensity, that is, the stronger the initial stimulus, the greater the difference that needs to be noticed.

The application of Weber's Law to the selling of goods is important (Britt, 1975). Manufacturers and marketers endeavor to determine the relevant JND for their products for two very different reasons: (a) so that reductions in product size, increases in product price, or changes in packaging are not readily discernible to the public; and (b) so that product improvements are readily discernible to the public. The need to update existing packaging without losing the consumers ready recognition of the package involves a number of small changes, each carefully designed to fall below the JND so that consumers will not perceive the difference. For example, Ivory soap, Campbell's soup, and Betty Crocker cake mixes all have gone through many package changes over the years to update their image. Brand imitators also may design their package so it is just below the noticeable level of difference from the original so that differences are not readily noticed. From the two images in Exhibit 3.3, one can see there are many similarities between the two packages. There similarities may cause a consumer to mistake one brand for another.

$$K = \frac{\Delta I}{I}$$

Where:

ΔI = the minimal change in intensity of the stimulus required to be just noticeable to the person (j.n.d.)

I = the intensity of the stimulus before the change occurs

K = the constant increase or decrease necessary for the stimulus to be noticed (this varies across the senses)

EXHIBIT 3.2 Weber' Law

EXHIBIT 3.3   Examples of Packaging which may be Below the J.N.D.

The JND in which the threshold was too low and people could not notice the name involved Royal Doulton China and Coast Hotels. Coast bought Royal Doulton China specifically to upgrade the perception of their hotel in the mind of the consumer. The problem was that when the hotel got the china from Royal Doulton, Royal had minimized the size of their name stamped on the bottom of the china and the pieces were therefore not immediately recognized as Royal Doulton China. A spokesperson for the hotel said that the smaller brand name diminished the value of the tableware, and they asked for a refund. In the court case, Royal Doulton argued that it never dreamed the size of the brand name would be of such importance to Coast Hotels (Armstrong, 2000).

Comparison Points.   It must not be forgotten that the objects of trademark infringement cases are viewed out of the real purchasing environment. As Judge Cattanch remarked:

> In considering the similarity of trademarks it has been held repeatedly that it is not the proper approach to set the marks side by side and to critically analyze them for points of similarities and differences, but rather to determine the matter in a general way as a question of impression. (*Canadian Schenley Distilleries Ltd. v. Canada's Manitoba Distillery Ltd.*, 1975, p. 5).

These general aspects of the consumer environment emphasize the consumer's natural decision and behavior patterns. Therefore, Weber's Law also can be heavily influenced by context. For example, with respect to disclaimers, contrast is particularly effective in facilitating perception. Contrasts in size, form, color, and brightness are well known to be effective in altering our JND levels. Weber's Law also is important in determining the size of warning labels or disclaimers in the context of advertisements or package sizes. The print and size of the warning or disclaimer must be proportional and relative to its context. The specifics of warning label size and print are detailed in chapter 5, which discusses avoiding confusion.

PERCEPTIONS CAN BE BIASED

The perception for the existence of brand imitation usually is not a point of agreement. Usually, the party accused of imitation denies it, whereas the accuser is certain of the intent of imitation. To understand why these differing viewpoints of the same stimulus are so rooted, further information on the interpretation of perceptions is necessary.

Perceptions Are Selective

Perceptions are best regarded as interpretations made in the light of previous experience. This interpretation occurs unconsciously, and the existence of this step is apt to be denied, because one instinctively places great reliance on the validity and directness of perceptions. However, a lifetime of previous experience must influence what one perceives. Our perceptions, then, are not always valid, and they are not the direct appreciation of the environment. They are interpretations of sensory messages, and these interpretations have important consequences. For instance, two people often give different reports when they witness the same scene, not because one is a liar, unobservant, or crazy, but simply because the past experiences of the two people are different. Hence, their interpretations, based on their prior experiences, lead to different results. In other words, they genuinely have different perceptions of the scene. One need not cease to accept that "seeing is believing," but one comes to realize that seeing is only believing, and that beliefs are based on prejudice as well as fact (Barlow & Mollon, 1982).

Therefore, perception depends a great deal on personal factors. Past experiences and social interactions may help to form certain expectations that provide categories or alternatives used by individuals to interpret stimuli: the narrower the individual's experience, the more limited the person's access to alternative interpretive possibilities.

The concept of imperfect recollection also was recognized early in the courts by Lord Justice Luxmore (application by Rysta Ltd., 1943) and quoted by Judge Cattanch. Imperfect recollection emphasizes the natural process of memory and the reconstruction of events seen in the past.

The answer to the question whether the sound of one word resembles too nearly the sound of another so as to bring the former within the limits ... of the Trade Marks Act ... must nearly always depend on first impression, for obviously a person who is familiar with both words will neither be deceived nor confused. It is the person who only knows the one word, and has perhaps an imperfect recollection of it, who is likely to be deceived or confused. Little assistance, therefore, is to be obtained from a meticulous comparison of the two words, letter-by-letter and syllable-by-syllable, pronounced with clarity expected from a teacher of elocution. (*Canadian Schenley Distilleries Ltd. v. Canada's Manitoba Distillery Ltd.*, 1975, p. 13)

Perceptions and Memory

There are a number of instances in which memory of the specific can be mistaken for memory of the general, and vice versa (Jacoby, Kelley, & Dywan, 1989). Such is the case of misattribution, memory, and brands (names, trade dress, and even advertising) in marketing. For example, if a successful brand/product is on the market, the marketer of a new brand/product can potentially benefit from the misattribution of the favorable characteristics of the older established brand to the new one. The marketer of the new brand may attempt to cause this misattribution by developing a name that is semantically similar to that of the older brand (e.g., Minute Lube v. Jiffy Lube; TeleTubbies v. Bubbly Chubbies).

An application of memory and source misattribution to the confusion of claims in advertising further demonstrates the generalizability of the effects (Law, 1995). Ads that imitate the claims of original ads were analyzed for the consumers' perception. Consumers' belief in imitator claims was influenced by their feelings of familiarity of the message and whether they could recall the original source of the advertising exposure. Memory for the source of the imitator ad was a major factor in its believability. When subjects were confused about the source, they believed it more. Only when they correctly remembered the original did they discount the imitator.

Perception and Expectations

The interpretation of the incoming stimulus guided by selective attention is the perception, perceptual organization, or perceptual interpretation of the stimulus. The typical course of perception proceeds (a) from a real world object or event, (b) through a medium, (c) to sensory surfaces and receptors, and (d) to the central nervous system (Cutting, 1987). Once the perception hits the central nervous system, inferences from the stimulus can be of two kinds. They can be deductively valid or inductively strong. Perception could be deductive if all premises came from stimulus information, but that is hardly ever the case. Experience, familiarity, and anticipation usually play a part in the passing of stimulus information on to perceptual objects (Fig. 3.2). Therefore, most perception is inductive, with some premises coming from memory and cognition.

An example showing the effect of induction on attention to and perception of a stimulus object is illustrated by the connection to our sense organs. Whenever our interest in an object is derived from or connected to other interests, our senses adjust to form a close connection in all our behavior and perception. The image in the mind is the attention, and the preperception is half the looked-for object.

This effect of induction on consumer responses can be typified by a personal story. I recall driving to work with a colleague who had just bought a new house and was in the process of preparing his lawn and garden. We drove by a sign that said BEDDING SALE, and he said he wanted to go in and buy some plants. I said I did not think they sold plants at that store. Then he noticed it was a furniture store selling mattresses. He was so preoccupied in his mind with gardening that the sign BEDDING SALE for him meant, through an inductive process, a sale of bedding plants for the garden. He did not initially process the surrounding cues that indicated a furniture store, but focused only on the sign that was relevant to him at the time. He was deductively weak and inductively strong in his perceptions.

Feature Integration Theory

Feature integration theory proposes that features are perceived before objects, and in parallel across the field of vision. Objects are differentiated afterward and require focused attention to be identified correctly. For

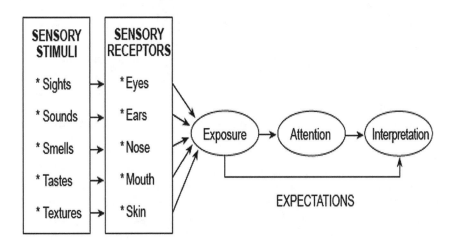

FIG. 3.2. Overview of the perceptual process.

example, the consumer may be faced with a number of different dimensions, such as color and shape, which may or may not help distinguish among brands. Think about Coca-Cola and various store brands with red cola labels in big 2-liter bottles. If a feature, "a particular value on a dimension" (Treisman & Gelade, 1980), is the same across objects, that feature cannot be used to distinguish between them. Only features that are different across objects will help to distinguish them from each other. However, differentiation requires focused attention and serial processing of the objects. Describing what is similar between objects is more difficult than describing what is different because similar features are not serially processed. Only different features are noticed.[2]

To put this theory into the context of consumer behavior, similarly packaged products located together on a shelf in a retail establishment would be perceived as the same. Focused attention is required to distinguish among brands with similar packaging, and each brand would have to be examined individually. If the consumer was pressed for time, or had other distractions, the likelihood of the consumer selecting a brand other than the one intended would be higher the more similar the two brands are.

A product may be searched by individual features or by the combination of features (termed a "conjunction"). It is assumed that there is no need for attention in the search for an individual feature (e.g., color of the package). Therefore, interference would have no effect. On the other hand, if it is necessary to search by conjunction (e.g., packaging is so similar among competing brands), focused attention is required. Otherwise, an unintended brand is purchased.

Illusory Conjunctions. Sometimes people tell us not what they saw, but what they have seen by putting together the different parts of the object. Experiments in cognitive psychology by Treisman and Schmidt (1982) suggest that individual features of objects are registered separately, and that in the absence of focused attention, they may be wrongly combined to form illusory conjunctions. This process is diagramed in Figure 3.3. That is, people may state that they perceive something they have not actually seen.

The dimensions of color and shape appear to be the most susceptible to separate coding and incorrect reconstruction by consumers. In situations wherein the consumer's attention is not focused because of distractions or time pressures, illusory conjunctions may be perceived. That is, consumers may combine features incorrectly. They may believe they are purchasing the intended brand, but in actuality have selected a brand that may be similar in features. Features may not be linked to a particular brand, and brands would not be identified through conjunctions of features, but by individual features. Therefore, imitation brands take advantage by imitating features that consumers use to identify the original brand.

---

[2]See Coca-Cola bottles on p.131

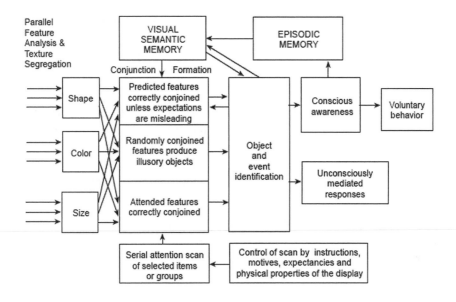

FIG. 3.3. Processing operations involved in perceiving objects.
Source: Triesman and Schmidt (1982), Illusory conjunctions in the perception of objects. *Cognitive Psychology*, 14,110. Reproduced with permission from Elsevier.

The implication of these findings in studies of illusory conjunctions suggest that if we see a blue, small triangle, only the labels "blue," "small," and "triangle" are registered. The individual then supplies his or her conscious image with the correct quantity of blue coloring to fill the specified area, regardless how much color was presented originally. Moreover, the person may use the image to color the area within the specified shape, regardless whether this matches the shape that was blue originally. Studies of illusory conjunctions place conscious seeing at a greater remove from the physical stimulus than might be assumed intuitively. In other words, individuals may cognitively rearrange what is actually seen to coincide with what they think they would most likely see logically. In so doing, individuals make mistakes in what they actually see as compared with what they think they saw.

GESTALT

The specific principles underlying perceptual organization often are referred to as Gestalt psychology. *Gestalt*, a German word that means pattern, configuration, form, or organization, was founded by Max

Wertheimer (1880–1943) and his colleagues K. Koffka and W. Kohler. Gestalt has no direct translation to the English language, but is commonly defined as "the whole is more than the sum of its parts."

The basic premise of gestalt is that people do not experience the numerous stimuli they select from the environment as separate and discrete sensations. Rather, they tend to organize them into groups and perceive them as unified wholes. Thus, the perceived characteristics of even the simplest stimuli are viewed as a function of the whole to which the stimulus appears to belong. For example, a piece of gray paper is gray only in relation to its background or to something with which it is compared. On a black background, it appears light, whereas against a white background, it appears dark.

This type of perceptual organization is called figure and ground. The figure usually is perceived clearly because to its ground it appears to be well defined, solid, and in the forefront. The ground usually is perceived as hazy and in the background. The point is that the gray will be either figure or ground depending on the context. The eye does not perceive objects in isolation, but rather with the surroundings. A very famous figure and ground example used in introductory psychology is shown in Exhibit 3.4. One either sees faces or a vase in the picture, but not both at the same time.

Another example of gestalt is grouping. That is, individuals tend to group stimuli automatically, so that they form a unified picture or impression. The point of grouping is that patterns or forms of our experience cannot be explained by compounding elements. The perception of stimuli as groups rather than as discrete bits of information facilitates their memory and recall. For example, it is easier to attend to the global features of a triangle than to broken component lines because the Gestalt property of closure makes the global figure more salient perceptually. In the case of a brand, the consumer may remember the total "look" of the package, but may be

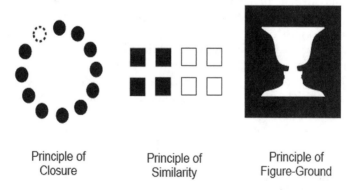

<table>
<tr><td>Principle of
Closure</td><td>Principle of
Similarity</td><td>Principle of
Figure-Ground</td></tr>
</table>

EXHIBIT 3.4   Principles of Stimulus Organization Derived From Gestalt Psychology.

unable to recall small details individually, such as type of lettering, the exact hue of color, or the specific picture on the package.

The following are types of perceptual organizations of Gestalt that mainly affect our interpretation of stimuli:

1. *Similarity.* Similar elements are seen as belonging to each other more than to other elements equally close, but less similar. What the individual perceives from the environment belongs to certain categories. For example, two packages of equally similar shape and color each seen separately likely will be categorized in the person's memory in the same space. Therefore, the consumer may make a mistake in selecting the one package over the other because they are organized together. The two packages are too similar to be categorized separately in the consumer's mind.

2. *Proximity.* Elements that are physically close are seen as belonging to each other more than to similar elements farther away. Proximity also can make things look more alike than they really are.

Gestalt psychology explains why objects can be detailed differently but still look the same to the observer. There are many cases of brand imitation in which no one feature of the object is the same; all features are similar. Examples of infringement cases involving gestalt are found in toys, handguns, and greeting cards. These are detailed in the exhibit in chapter 4 that presents cues that cause confusion.

BALANCE THEORY

Balance theory comes from social psychology and the study of attitude formation. It postulates that individuals seek information that is consistent with their needs, interests, and attitudes, and avoid information that is not. This theory provides the rationale for cases involving unauthorized use or association of a successful trademark as in *Bette Midler v. Ford Motor Company* (1988), in which a Bette Midler sound-alike was used in the Ford commercial. The underlying idea behind the use of balance theory to explain why authorized association to a successful brand would take place is that, overall, marketers want customers to have a very positive attitude toward the goods and services they are selling. When consumers have a positive attitude, it is likely that positive behavior in the form of purchases will follow. It is as simple as that.

Getting customers to have a positive attitude toward their product or service is a major task for marketers. While there are several complex, time-consuming, and expensive ways to build positive attitudes based on the creation of good products and images, a very simple way is just to associate your good to an object toward which consumers already have a very positive attitude. This implies the use of balance theory.

Balance theory was developed by Heider in 1946 to explain how individuals cope with their environment. The basic premise is that people seek to balance their cognitive and affective states. In other words, people want their attitudes and feelings to be consistent with their objective thoughts and beliefs. The meaning of this can be understood by examining Figure 3.4. The link between the person (P) and the attitude object (O) is the attitude in question. The attitude is represented solely by its valence, which is either positive (+) or negative (–).

The link between O and X (some other person or object) represents an association (+) or disassociation (–) between the attitude object and some related object, broadly construed to include people, attributes, or consequences. According to Heider, the valence of the attitude between the person and the first object (P–O) can be predicted on the basis of the valences attached to the person and the second object (P–X) and the links between the two objects (O–X links). Because the individual is motivated to achieve a balanced state, the P–O valence will be determined by the algebraic multiplication of the two valences (see Lutz, 1991, for more detail). For example, if Kate Hudson, the movie personality, is liked by a majority of consumers, they will hold a positive attitude toward her (+). If she endorses Revlon, this leads to a positive connection between Kate Hudson and Revlon products (+). The prediction then is that the consumer will like Revlon Products (+) and hence be motivated to purchase that line of cosmetics. In doing so, the consumer maintains a balanced state.

Balance theory also explains why successful companies bring lawsuits against other companies who use their property unlawfully or in bad taste. Unauthorized use of a trademark to associate it with a lesser object or a negatively perceived object can bring harm to the original trademark. The mere association can cause a decrease in the consumer's attitude toward the original because the negative perception of the tainted or negative ob-

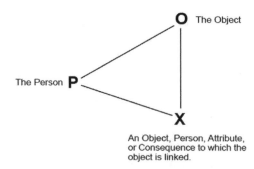

FIG. 3.4. Heider's balance theory.

ject "rubs off" on the original's image. In *Girl Scouts of the United States v. Personality Posters Mfg. Co.* (1969), the Girl Scouts of America tried to enjoin a company that was manufacturing and selling posters of visibly pregnant girls in Girl Scout uniforms with the headline "Be Prepared." The association of "pure girl scouts" (+) with unwed mothers (–) would lead to an unbalanced (–) state, and perhaps harm the reputation of Girl Scouts (Fig. 3.5). This is attributable to the pairing of Girl Scouts with unwed mothers simply by association. The individual has a constant (–) association to unwed mothers. To maintain balance, the previous positive sign for Girl Scouts changes to a negative sign. In this way, tension is reduced because the overall state returns to positive (negative × negative = positive).

Prior Attitude

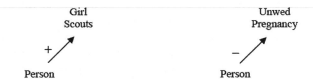

Person stores images as unrelated in their mind

Pairing

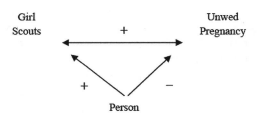

Result

Person is in an unbalanced state and strives for balance

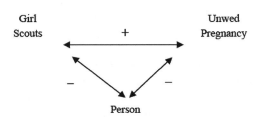

FIG. 3.5.
Changing images
and attitudes.

The Case of Balance Theory in Marketing

The unauthorized use of someone else's trademark or trade dress is done to imply an association, which should help in building a positive attitude toward the infringer's product. Every day, hundreds of authorized endorsements bring profits to companies. One of the highest paid endorsers is now Tiger Woods. Tiger Woods turned pro in 1996 and made $2.7 million in tournament winnings his first year. According to one estimate, Woods generated $650 million in new revenues for television networks, equipment manufacturers, and other businesses that first year. He now earns more than $20 million a year from Nike alone.

At least Nike is a related product category, in which Tiger's expertise comes into play. His link to Accenture is a better example of how balance theory can work. Clearly, Tiger Woods' expertise is not business consulting. Yet his picture in advertisements for the company are thought to make buyers of consulting services feel that Accenture is a leader and winner in their own field. There is no direct link that would make Accenture customers think Tiger Woods would come to their company and analyze their books. It is only the image of a winner and an expert that Accenture is buying by associating its brand name with Tiger Woods.

REFERENCE GROUPS

Besides knowing a company's motivation for copying a successful brand, there is also the question of what motivates a consumer knowingly to purchase fake or imitator products. There are two answers to this question because the answer depends on the type of product in question. For privately consumed necessity goods, which are mainly frequently purchased consumable goods, the answer usually is price. Most of these types of imitators are sold 40% to 50% cheaper than the original goods. Because the goods are consumed privately, and usually have a low-involved purchaser, the consumer feels that substitutes are fine. Moreover, they also save money. These goods would not be bought if they were priced at the same level as the original good. It is the price cue that drives the purchase.

For fakes and imitations of publicly consumed goods, such as watches, handbags, and neckties, the answer is more complex. Low price plays a role, but other factors become relevant, especially because brand names are so important. The relative influence of groups on purchase decisions is shown in Exhibit 3.5.

Three segments of consumers can be used to illustrate the influence of groups. Two of the segments are purchasers of fake goods, and the remaining segment avoids both fakes and the brands they copy. The first group of consumers knowingly purchases these fake goods, but only because they

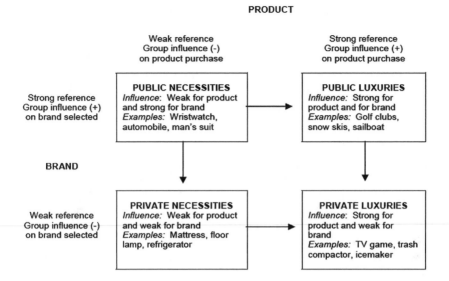

EXHIBIT 3.5 Relative Group Influence on Purchase Decisions.
Adapted from William O. Bearden and Michael J. Etzel (September 1982).
Reference group influence on product and brand purchase decisions. *Journal of Consumer Research*, 185. Reprinted with permission by the University of Chicago Press.

think others (the general public) will think they are authentic and not copies. These consumers would not purchase the goods if they thought other people would immediately recognize their purchase as fake or replica, and not the original. Thus, it is not the purchaser who is confused. Rather, the purchaser wants to confuse others.

Then there is a small segment of buyers who do own authentic goods, but buy fakes and counterfeits for the value they represent and for "fun." These buyers may even buy some fakes to use as substitutes for originals while traveling in case their goods are stolen or lost. These consumers continue to buy both types of goods, but they do not expect most observers to know the goods are fake, and they really do not care (Nia & Zaichkowsky, 2000).

There also is a segment that used to buy the authentic good, but now due to the popularity and wide distribution of imitation goods, no longer want the brand because it has lost its exclusivity. They do not want to own the same goods as the "masses." Such is the price of "success" that the brand suffers from eroded equity in the original market.

These motivations can be explained through social psychology and reference group influence. Humans are social animals. We all belong to groups, try to please others, and take cues about how to behave by observing the actions of those around us. Our desire to fit in or to identify with desirable individuals or groups is the primary motivation for many of our purchases and activities. A *reference group* can be formally defined as "an actual or imaginary individual or group conceived of having significant relevance upon an individual's evaluations, aspirations, or behavior" (Park & Lessig, 1977, p. 102). The form of influence that reference groups have with respect to these publicly consumed goods is mainly of a value-expressive nature. The many types of value-expressive influences are shown in Table 3.4.

Aspirational and Avoidance Groups

Although two or more people usually are required for the formation of any group, the term "reference group" often is used to describe any external influence that provides social cues. In the case of brand imitation, we are interested in membership groups and aspirational groups. Membership groups influence buyers of original luxury goods. To them, the good signals that they belong to a certain social class, or club-like group, which is small, cohesive, and exclusive.

Aspirational groups are groups that individuals hold in high esteem and "aspire" to be like. These groups can be work-related (e.g., accountants), or they can be social groups (e.g., patrons of the arts or movie stars). The consumer may not have any direct contact with this reference group, but the aspirational group still can have a powerful influence on what the consumer prefers and buys because the group provides guidance as to the types of products/brands used by admired people. Generally, people aspire to a

TABLE 3.4
The Value Expressive Influence of Groups[a]

The individual feels that the purchase of a particular brand will enhance the image others have of him or her.

The individual feels that those who purchase or use a particular brand possess the characteristics that he or she would like to have.

The individual sometimes feels that it would be nice to be like the type of person that advertisements show using a particular band.

The individual feels that people who purchase a particular brand are admired or respected by others.

The individual feels that the purchase of a particular brand would help show others what he or she is or would like to be (e.g., an athlete, successful business person, good parent).

[a]Adapted from C. Whan Park and V. Parker Lessig (1977, September). Students and housewives: Differences in susceptibility to reference group influence." *Journal of Consumer Research, 4*, 102. Reprinted with permission of the University of Chicago Press.

higher social class because people of a higher social class are "rich." These rich people have certain products and brands that lower classes do not have. By having the same good as the higher social class, the consumer can have the same signal that he or she is special and "rich." The consumer also can have the feeling imitated by owning the imitated product/brand.

Higher social class groups may see lower social classes as *avoidance groups*. They do not want to have things that the lower classes own. For example, plastic lawn chairs are signals of low class, whereas teak lawn chairs are signals of high class. When goods that once were exclusive to the higher social class are used by the lower classes, the higher class then will avoid these goods because the association of the good has changed hands from them to someone of a lower class. What happens is that over time, as the brand or imitation good becomes more widely held by their avoidance group, they avoid the associated product.

SUMMARY

Theories from psychology help to explain why imitation, as a marketing strategy, is a threat to the selection and perception of the original brand. Consumers generalize expectations from experiences with original brands to other similar looking goods and services in the marketplace. Because of fleeting attention and perceptual biases, individuals often make mistakes in their perception of similar, but not the same, brands in the marketplace.

In the interests of economizing attentional effort, individuals do three things. First, they narrow the selectivity of their attention more or less to those things that are somehow essential to the task at hand. For example, in purchasing goods, the consumer may focus on price, but not on the weight of the package. Hence, they may buy a lower priced good, but one of actually poorer value because the package contains less than others. Second, individuals "recode" into a simpler form the diversity of events encountered so that their limited attention and memory span can be protected. For example, instead of trying to remember the exact price of a good, consumers may remember only that it was the most expensive of the alternatives available, which may preserve the necessary information and allow the recreation of any specific information with regard to those alternatives. Finally, individuals deal with information overload relative to their limited capacities for noticing, registering, and remembering by using aids that are designed to lengthen the noticing process. A simple example would be a shopping list, or tearing an ad from the paper and bringing it to the choice environment. All these methods help, but none of them can guarantee an accurate perception of what is seen.

Often, objects are reconstructed from memory, and errors subsequently occur in what people say they saw, as opposed to what they actually saw.

This is what Lord Justice Luxmore called "imperfect recollection" back in 1943. Individuals may be guided in their visual perceptions by their cognitive expectations. This bias may be inherent and enduring. One function of perceptual judgment is to accentuate the apparent differences in magnitudes between objects that differ in value, provided the difference in magnitude is associated with the difference in value. When there is little difference in value, objects appear to be similar, and consumers tend to lump them together even more than they actually are. It is this lumping together of similar objects that causes confusion.

The psychological principles of attention and perception guide our identification of objects. Misperception usually is caused by inattention to parts of the message or product, similarity to other products, and/or associations of cues to consumers' expectations of the inherent meaning of the cues. By analyzing prior court cases of confusion with the concepts of attention and perception, the strength of the cues consumers use to identify and interpret the object become apparent.

Balance theory and reference group theories from social psychology have little to do with perception or attention per se, but are important to understanding the motive for unauthorized association, purchase, or both. The simple association with a likable object leads to two likable objects. Marketers know that simple celebrity endorsement or association with other successful products can increase sales far beyond the benefits actually inherent in their products. Preventing unauthorized association is extremely important to brand managers and consumers of originals, especially when the connection is made to an object with lesser status than that of the original.

REFERENCES

Alvaro, C., & Zaichkowsky, J. L. (2001). *The effects of color on brand identification.* Division 23, APA Conference, San Francisco.

Armstrong, J. (2000, July 20). The size does matter in dishes, court rules. *Globe and Mail*, A7.

Barlow, H. D., & Mollon, J. D. (Eds.). (1982). *The senses.* London: Cambridge University Press.

Bette Midler v. Ford Motor Company, 849 F. 2d 460 (9th Cir., 1988).

Bellizzi, J. A., Crowley, A. E., & Hasty, R.W. (1983). The effects of color in store design. *Journal of Retailing, 59*(1), 21–45.

Britt, S. H. (1975, February). How Weber's Law can be applied to marketing. *Business Horizons, 18,* 21–29.

Boynton, R. M., & Dolensky, S. (1979). On knowing books by their colors. *Perceptual and Motor Skills, 48*(2), 479–488.

Burgunder L. B. (1997). Trademark protection of product characteristics: A predictive model. *Journal of Public Policy and Marketing, 16*(2), 277–288.

Canadian Schenley Distilleries Ltd. v. Canada's Manitoba Distillery Ltd., (1975) 25 C.P.R. (2d) 1 (F.C.T.D).

Cheskin, L. (1947). *Colors: What they can do for you.* New York: Liveright Publishing Corporation.

Cheskin, L. (1954). *Color guide for the marketing medic.* New York: The MacMillan Company.

Christ, R. E. (1975). Review and analysis of color coding research for visual displays. *Human Factors, 17,* 542–570.

Cutting, J. E. (1987). Perception and information. *Annual Review of Psychology, 38,* 61–90.

Garber, L. L., Jr., Burke, R., & Jones, J. M. (2000). *The role of package color in consumer purchase consideration and choice.* Working paper report 006104, Marketing Science Institute, Boston.

Girl Scouts of the United States v. Personality Posters Mfg. Co., 304 F. Supp. 1228 (S.D.N.Y., 1969).

Gorn, G., Dahl, D., Yi, T., & Chattopadhyay, A. (1997). The effects of color as an advertising execution cue: They're in the shade. *Management Science, 43*(10), 466–476.

Hupman, R., & Zaichkowsky, J. L. (1995). Cues used in self-reports of judgment of brand similarity. In S. MacKenzie, & D. M. Stayman (Eds.), *Proceedings of the Society of Consumer Psychology* American Psychological Association, La Jolla, California (pp. 28–34).

Jacoby, L. L., Kelley, C., & Dywan, J. (1989). Memory attributions. In H. L. Roediger & F. I. M. Craik (Eds.), *Varieties of memory and consciousness: Essays in honor of Endel Tulving* (pp. 391–422). Hillsdale, NJ: Lawrence Erlbaum Associates.

Janiszewski, C. (1991). The relationship between stimulus display and nonconsciously directed attention. Research proposal, University if Florida, unpublished.

Janiszewski, C. (1993). Preattentive mere-exposure effects. *Journal of Consumer Research, 20*(3), 376–392.

Jansson, C., Marlow, N., & Bristow, M. (2004). The influence of colour on visual search times in cluttered environments. *Journal of Marketing Communications, 10*(3), 183–193.

Johnson, W. A., & Dark, V. J. (1986). Selective attention. *Annual Review of Psychology, 37,* 43–75.

Kapferer, J. N. (1996, May). Stealing brand equity: Measuring perceptual confusion between national brands and "copy-cat" own-label products. *Marketing and Research Today, 23,* 96–103.

Law, S. (1995). Belief in imitator claims: The role of source memory. *Advances in Consumer Research, 22,* 165–170.

Loken, B., Ross, I., & Hinkle, R. L. (1986). Consumer confusion of origin and brand similarity perceptions. *Journal of Public Policy and Marketing, 5,* 195–211.

Lutz, R. J. (1991). The role of attitude theory in marketing. In H. H. Kassarjian & T. S. Robertson (Eds.), *Perspectives in consumer behavior* (pp. 317–357). Englewood Cliffs, NJ: Prentice-Hall.

Madden, T. J., Hewett, K., & Roth, M. S. (2000). Managing images in different cultures: A cross-national study of color meanings and preferences. *Journal of International Marketing, 8*(4), 90–107.

Miaoulis, G., & D'Amato, N. (1978). Consumer confusion and trademark infringement. *Journal of Marketing, 42,* 48–55.

Nia, A., & Zaichkowsky, J. L. (2000). Do counterfeits devalue the ownership of luxury brands? *Journal of Product and Brand Management, 9*(7), 485–497.

Park, C. W., & Lessig, V. P. (1977). Students and housewives: Differences in susceptibility to reference group influence. *Journal of Consumer Research, 4,* 102.

Rysta Ltd.'s, Appn. 60R.P.C. 87. (1943).

Stroop, J. R. (1935). Studies of interference in serial verbal reactions. *Journal of Experimental Psychology, 18,* 643–662.

Stroop, J. R. (1992). Studies of interference in serial verbal reactions. *Journal of Experimental Psychology, 18,* 643–662.

Treisman, A., & Gelade, G. (1980). A feature-integration theory of attention. *Cognitive Psychology, 12,* 97–136.

Triesman, A. & Schmidt, H. (1982) Illusory conjunctions in the perception of objects. *Cognitive Psychology, 14,* 107–141.

Troldahl, V. C., & Jones, R. L. (1975). Predictors of newspaper advertising readership. *Journal of Advertising Research, 5,* 23–27.

Twedt, D. W. (1952). A multiple factor analysis of advertising readership. *Journal of Applied Psychology, 26,* 207–215.

Valdez P., & Mehrabian, A. (1994). Effects of color on emotions. *Journal of Experimental Psychology, 128*(4), 394–409.

Ward, J., Loken, B., Ross, I., & Hasapopoulos, T. (1986). The influence of physical similarity on generalization of affect and attribute perceptions from national brands to private label brands. In T. Shimp, S. Sharma, W. Dillan, R. T. Dyer, M. Gardner, G. John, et al. (Eds.), *American educator's proceedings* (No. 52, pp. 51–56). Chicago, Il: American Marketing Association.

4

Cases of Imitation in the Marketplace

Literally tens of thousands of trademark infringement cases can be found in legal libraries. The number of cases has grown exponentially over the past 10 years because companies, and even famous people, are increasingly aware of the concept of brand equity. The fact that brand equity is not limited to consumer goods is evidenced by the trademark claim made by yoga master Bikram Choudhury. He makes claim to a series of 26 yoga postures, exercises, breathing techniques, and dialogues done with a heater blasting (National Post, 2005).

It is beyond the scope of this book to present a sample representing all the different types of issues and legal cases. What this chapter does provide are examples of passing-off cases with regard to specific cues that may have led consumers to consider two objects as coming from the same source, mistake one object for another, think of an association between two products or objects, or devalue or defame the original brand or object. The aim was to find disputes that exemplify the importance of brand name, shape, symbols, color, and gestalt over competing brands, related products, and unrelated product categories. Although infringement of competing brands is the most obvious cause of legal action, the documentation of court cases involving related or even unrelated products pertaining to consumer confusion is of utmost interest to those wondering about the extension of their brand equity. Lists of cases, as classified in this chapter, are found in Appendix 2.

The products and brands involved in each case have their own complex issues, which are then interpreted by the law. Furthermore, the decisions are sometimes inconsistent because different people have different views and interpretations based on their own experiences. One lawyer has commented as follows on the apparent inconsistencies: "Court increasingly clueless when it comes to trademarks" (Lans Retsky, 2000).

A prime example of the complexities involved in trademark litigation is observed in the case of the "Swiss army knife" made in China. The question for the courts was: Is a red, multiblade, multifunction knife emblazoned with a shield and a cross a Swiss-made army knife, or is it a knife used by the Swiss Army, or is it a knife that could just as easily be made in China? (Cava, 1996). The answers of the court were yes, no, and maybe.[1] The issues of brand name, design, color, country of origin, manufacturer, quality, customer confusion, generics, external cues, and advertising claims all were being interpreted and evaluated by teams of lawyers and different judges, and only sometimes the consuming public and/or marketing experts.

A HISTORICAL PERSPECTIVE
OF BRAND NAME LITIGATION

It seems that confusion over brand names for the same product started the history of passing-off litigation. In *Thomson v. Winchester* (1837), Thomson sold certain medicines of his own preparation under the name "Thomsonian Medicines." Winchester then began to sell inferior medicines under the same name. In this early case, the court recognized that there is no exclusive right in the name if it has become generic and descriptive of a class of medicines, even though the customer may be harmed by the inferiority of the medicines sold under the same name. Unfortunately, for Thomson medicine, the law paid little attention to the perceptions of the consumer on this issue, or the reputation of Thomson medicines, deciding that Winchester's actions were not illegal. Consumers and original producers were not protected, and the way was clear for copy artists to benefit from name similarity.

A later case, *Faber v. Faber* (1867), involved the sale of lead pencils by two brothers. Originally A. W. Faber created and sold lead pencils with great success. His brother, realizing this success, also started to produce and sell pencils with his name, "John H. Faber," stenciled on them. There is no information on the quality level of John Faber's pencils in relation to those of his brother, but that did not seem to matter. The court ruled that John Faber was entitled to use his own name, without fraud, despite the fact that it was his brother who had created the market for Faber lead pencils.

Fortunately, outcomes of litigation changed after these early days as the consumer became more important in the evaluation of the situation. In the case of *Montgomery v. Thompson* (1891), two pubs were selling beer under the same name, "Stone Ale.". Montgomery had been selling Stone Ale at its

---

[1]For details see The Forschner Group, Inc. and Swiss Army Brands, Ltd. v. Arrow Trading Co. Inc. 833 F. Supp. 385 (S.D.N.Y. 1993).

popular roadside pub since 1780, more than 100 years longer than its recent competitor. The court ruled that the name "Stone Ale" meant the beer was from the first pub, Montgomery, and not Thompson. Hence, the idea of consumer confusion with the source or the maker of the product became increasingly important.

The idea that brand name signaled quality control as well as the manufacturer is found in *Spalding A. G. & Bros. v. A. W. Gamage Ltd.* (1915). Spalding made certain balls called "Orb." The balls that did not meet the quality standards of Spalding were sold off to a waste rubber merchant for disposal and recycling. A new and "improved" ball then was made by Spalding and sold under the name "Improved Orb." The problem was that the waste manufacturer did not destroy the Orb balls sold to them, but began reselling these substandard balls as "Improved Orb." Both balls really were made by Spalding, but only one had the quality Spalding wanted to have on the market.

Similar Names

Because brand name is the crucial identifier and clearly protected by trademarks, the most common method of trademark infringement deemed effective to gain market share by a competitor without traditional marketing effort is to adapt a brand name extremely similar in sound to the original. One of the earliest cases involving a similar name is *Slazenger and Sons v. Feltham & Co.* (1889). Slazenger and Sons branded their tennis racquets "The Demon," and their competitor, Feltham, stamped the brand "Demotic" on its racquet handle. The court ruled that Feltham had to plane out the similar brand name "Demontic," and then they would be allowed to continue selling its racquets.

Other Cues

Manufacturers learned that besides the same or similar brand names, their customers relied on other heuristics or cues to identify the brand they wanted to buy. An early example showing the importance of the gestalt of a package can be found in *Fischer v. Blank* (1893). In 1888, Benedickt Fischer began marketing its Russian Caravan tea in oblong boxes with black wrappers that had the following features: the name "Black Package Tea"; three scenes in white, one depicting a caravan crossing a desert and another two representing snow scenes; a silver label on which the Russian words for "Russian Caravan Tea" were printed; and a white, diamond-shaped label bearing the plaintiff's business name.

Some time later, Berthold Blank began to sell the same type of tea in boxes the same size and shape as Fischer's, also in black wrappers, and also called "Black Package Tea." This package also bore scenes and labels substantially identical to the distinctive designs of the original. The only difference was in the words printed on the labels. On the white label, the name Blank replaced the name Fischer; and on the silver label, the Russian printing designated different words. The court drew the following inference, stressing the limited significance of individual packaging elements when viewed in an isolated context:

> There is no single point of resemblance or imitation, which would of itself be regarded as adequate grounds for the grant of equitable relief. Form alone would not be sufficient; nor size; nor color; nor the general decoration of the panels; nor the disks of the same size and color arranged the same way; or a label of the same shape and color attached to the same part; nor the use of the same name to designate the kind of quality of the product. Each one of these distinguishing features might be separately used and no harm result. (Schultz, 1977, p. 661)

Clearly, the combination of features is considered the important factor enabling consumers to identify the brand they want to purchase.

TODAY'S GLOBAL MARKETPLACE

A hundred years of experience and some attention to consumer perceptions has changed the way the courts regard companies who appropriate brand names of established successful business entities. This is especially so because the 1990s were the era of big brand names and brand equity research. Therefore, awareness of the ability to capitalize on well-known brand names became more apparent to the layperson. Products and services, in both consumer and business markets, found their way to court to protect the value in their original brand names from being used by parasite copycat organizations. No market was to small (e.g., dietary rice supplements: Cholestin v. Cholestene) or too specialized (e.g., spices: Old Plantation v. Olde Plantation Spice) to escape brand name appropriation by another competitor.

BRAND NAMES

Brand name is the single most used cue, after price, in determining consumer choice and evaluation. This is probably why most infringing competitors focus their confusion tactics on the name they use to label their goods and services. Similar brand names can exist between competing brands, between related product categories, or even between unrelated product categories.

Competing Products

Today's courts also have come a long way to recognize an idea called "initial interest confusion." In *Grotrian, Helfferich, and Schulz v. Steinway & Sons* (1975), two competing pianos were clearly labeled "Grotrian-Steinweig" and "Steinway & Sons," respectively, but the court nevertheless found a likelihood of confusion. The court ruled that the issue was not the possibility that a purchaser would buy a Grotrian-Steinweig thinking it was actually a Steinway, or that Grotrian had some connection with Steinway and Sons. Rather, the harm, to Steinway, was the likelihood that a consumer hearing the Grotrian-Steinweig name, and thinking it had some connection with Steinway, would consider it on that basis.

The Grotrian-Steinweig name therefore would attract attention from potential customers based on the reputation built up by Steinway over many years. Potential Steinway buyers could be misled into an initial interest, perhaps thinking that the less expensive Grotrian-Steinweig is at least as good, if not better, than a Steinway. Deception and confusion were thus deemed to appropriate the Steinway's history of goodwill. It seems in this case that the judge was most perceptive concerning the psychological influences of stimulus generalization.

The name may not even be a brand name, but a name for which the consumer has developed a strong meaning and association. Napa Valley wines of California are to be made of grapes grown only in Napa Valley, California. In the case of *Bronco Wine Company and Barrel Ten Quarter Circle, Inc. v. Department of Alcohol Beverage Control, Napa Valley Vintners Association* (2003), Bronco wine company had bought Napa Ridge, a Napa Valley company, and then had started using non-Napa grapes in its production. Consumer research was submitted showing that 52% of the consumers who examined the Napa Ridge brand wine associated it with the Napa Valley brand. A full 42% of the consumers said that the wine was made with Napa grapes. Failure to protect the name Napa in the category of wine from being truly associated with Napa Valley Wines was seen as detrimental to the long-term viability of the Napa wine industry.

Partial Brand Names. The courts also deemed that partial redundancy of names was enough to establish confusion for competing brands (*Maidenform, Inc. v. Bestform Foundations, Inc.*, 1969). Maidenform originally had a whole line of dream bras: Day Dreams, Dreamliners, and Dream-Aire. Bestform subsequently launched a brand named "Teen-Dream." Both sides submitted lengthy discussions centered on the use of the word "dream." The court held that there was likely to be confusion in the consumer's mind on who manufactured the Teen-Dream Bra.

I really doubt if there is any instance too trivial to fight over. For example, an ice-cream flavor called "Moose Tracks" represented a vanilla ice cream with fudge and chocolate-covered peanut butter cups. It was produced by Denali Flavors in Michigan. The Michigan company took another ice-cream producer, based in Minnesota, to court because it claimed they copied Moose Tracks ice cream with a product called "Cow Tracks" (Ice-cream makers fight in court, 2002).

Descriptive Brand Names. The court says that when names are descriptive of the object being sold, the litigation may not be successful. For example, an action was dismissed in a case involving two magazines (*Toronto Parent* and *Today's Parent*) that competed in the same geographic area. The court ruled that *Toronto Parent* did indeed infringe on *Today's Parent*, but that the registration of *Today's Parent* was invalid because it was clearly descriptive of the audience for the product to which it was registered (*Professional Publishing Associates Ltd. v. Toronto Parent Magazine, Inc.*, 1986).

Advertising Slogans. Expropriation from a brand name to a competing brand's slogan happened in *Big O Tire Dealers v. Goodyear Tire and Rubber* (1977). In the fall of 1973, Big O decided to identify two lines of its private brand tires as "Big O Big Foot 60" and "Big O Big Foot 70." These names were placed on the sidewalls of the respective tires in raised white letters. In July 1974, Goodyear decided to use the term "Big Foot" in a nationwide advertising campaign. At the time of the trial, Big O's total net worth was approximately $200,000, as compared with Goodyear's net sales totaling more than $5.25 billion. The court ordered damages payable by Goodyear to Big O of slightly less than $5 million.

In a similar case, *Carnival Corporation v. Seascape Casino Cruises Inc.* (1999), Carnival sued for dilution of its "Fun Ship" mark. The company claimed that Seascape's slogan of "Seascape to a Ship Full of Fun" infringed on and diluted their mark of "Fun Ships." A consumer tracking study showed that 58% of the respondents interested in taking a cruise identified Carnival as using the "Fun Ships" slogan. Nonetheless, the court decided that the "Fun Ships" slogan was not sufficiently famous for protection under the law.

Related Product Categories

The perceived relation between products and their use plays a major role in the examination of the evidence and the seriousness of the alleged trademark infringement. The closer the two products/services are in use, the more likely the courts may feel that confusion exists. But again, this is not always the finding.

Same Brand Name.   Two early examples of related business activities with the same name are *The Clock Ltd. v. The Clock House Hotel Ltd.* (1936) and *Mountain Shadows Resort Ltd. v. Pemsall Enterprises Ltd.* (1973). In both cases, the first establishment offered meals and resort activities (bathing, tennis, and golf) to the public, but did not offer overnight accommodation. The other establishments opened years later and essentially were hotels offering lodging, meals, and liquor. Much evidence was presented describing people arranging to meet but ending up at different places. Both later hotels were ordered to change their name.

A classic case of confusion for related products is *Vidal Sassoon Inc. v. Beverly Sassoon and Slim Lines, Inc.* (1982). The infringing product was a skin-tightening cream to be used in conjunction with a plastic wrap endorsed by the estranged wife of Vidal Sassoon, the highly successful manufacturer of hair care products. The product, called "Slim Lines Body Contour Crème" claimed to reduce inches off the body and was marketed with the name "Beverly Sassoon" on the jar. A consumer survey of 450 target market customers in a mall found that they did not perceive the body contour cream to be a Slim Lines product even after careful scrutiny of the package and jar. Instead, the consumers believed that the source of the product was Beverly Sassoon, Sassoon, Vidal Sassoon, or Vidal Sassoon Inc. An expert witness advised that the only truly effective way to end the deception would be to remove the photograph and the name of Beverly Sassoon from the package, jar, brochures, and promotional materials.

In *Union Carbide Corp. v. Ever-Ready Inc.* (1976), the related products were batteries and light bulbs. Union Carbide produced and advertised an extensive line of electric batteries, flashlights, and miniature bulbs for automobile and marine use under the name of "Eveready." Ever-Ready commenced importing miniature lamp bulbs with the term "Ever-Ready" stamped on their base. These bulbs were sold in blister packages containing the term "Ever-Ready" in a four-sided logo, and the package indicated their use in high-density lamps. Although the products were not exactly the same, the two lines were very closely related.

The court originally ruled for Ever-Ready. However, on appeal, a higher court reversed the judgment. The higher court gave weight to a consumer survey, which showed that 55% to 60% of consumers were confused about the source of the products.

In *Sears, Roebuck & Co. v. Sears Realty Co. Inc.* (1996), Sears Roebuck objected to Sears Realty naming convenience stores and credit cards under the "Sears" name. Sears is a widely known household name in the United States, and many consumers already have a Sears card in their wallet. Therefore, the relatedness of the two businesses was in the credit card domain.

Unrelated Product Categories

The degree to which two product categories are unrelated may not be obvious, or there may be disagreement on this issue. The degree of relatedness of two product categories is perhaps a matter of judgment by the courts, how widely the products are used by the public, and the length of time the products are in use. The question of consumers' actual perceptions of relatedness of the product categories is seldom asked in surveys for court cases. Rather, the judge seems to decide this issue.

Unsuccessful Cases of Defense for the Same Brand Name. The difficulty experienced by the courts in seeing the possibility for consumer confusion with unrelated product categories, despite identical distinctive names and established confusion in the minds of the consumer, is well documented. In *Lego Australia Pty. Ltd. v. Paul's (Merchants) Pty. Ltd.* (1982), the Australian company sold irrigation equipment bearing the name "Lego" in Australia. The Danes had sold "Lego" children's building block toys in Australia since 1978, and Lego toys had been marketed in Australia since 1962. Several witnesses said they had assumed that the irrigation equipment had been made by Lego Ltd. because of the name Lego, because the hose was predominantly colorful plastic, and because companies appear to diversify.

The court concluded that companies may and sometimes do expand the range of products they produce. However, this in and of itself cannot warrant a conclusion that a particular company has done so, and although consumers made unwarranted assumptions or had misconceptions, that was the fault of the consumer, not the company. The judgment was in favor of the Australian irrigation company. The very same issue, with the same arguments, was brought to court in England (*Lego System A/S v. Lego M. Lemelstrich*, 1983). This time, the Danish company won, despite weaker consumer evidence than found in the Australian case.

It is likely that most people think of a hamburger in conjunction with the words "Big Mac." However "Big Mac" was used in advertising a 2-liter wine bottle in Australia (*McWilliams Wines Pty., Ltd. v. McDonald's System of Australia Pty. Ltd.*, 1980). The main complaint of McDonald's about the advertisement was the appearance of the words "Big Mac" in letters about 3 ½ cm in height extending substantially right across the advertisement immediately below the word "McWilliams," which was in letters about 1 ½ cm in height. Hence, the case was a classic example of "just noticeable difference" or Weber's Law.

The Australian judge ruled that the words "Big Mac" are descriptive. When used by McDonald's, they describe and refer to a particular type of large hamburger. When used by McWilliams, they describe and refer to a particular type of large container of wine. It seems the judge agreed that there was confusion, but considered the confusion not misleading in the choice of products. McWilliams was cleared of any infringement. This shows the overwhelming influence the judge, and perhaps even the culture, might have in cases of passing-off.

In *Hormel Foods Corporation v. Jim Henson Production, Inc.* (1995), the court asked Hormel foods to "lighten up." They had brought suit because a new Muppet called Spa'am had joined the cast in a movie, Muppet Treasure Island. Hormel foods claimed that the use of such a character would cause a drop in consumption of Spam luncheon meat and related marketing merchandise. The judge disagreed. Upon appeal the marketing of the merchandise was limited (*Hormel Foods Corporation v. Jim Henson Production, Inc.*, 1996).

A prestige brand may be Jaguar, the luxury car. Jaguar was involved in a 10-year court battle with a small Canadian-leather importing company called Remo, who had used the trademark of Jaguar since 1981 in Canada (Olijnyk, 1999a). Jaguar argued that Remo's licensing of the term "Jaguar" for leather products in Canada was an attempt to "deceive the public." Large companies with famous trademarks fight these smaller trademark disputes because they are seen as a defense of their rights against potentially far greater abuse. They are protecting their territory (see *Jaguar Cars Ltd. And Jaguar Cars, a Division of Ford Motor Co. v. Manufactures des Montres Jaguar S. A. Festina*, 2000).

Gideons International was a Business and Professional Men's Association that brought suit against Gideon 300, a homeless ministry (*The Gideons International, Inc. v. Gideon 300 Ministries, Inc.*, 1999). The trial court denied both parties motions for summary judgment because questions of fact existed as to whether the name was likely to cause consumer confusion and whether the two parties were in the same market.

A U.S. software company, M2 Software, sued MTV cable company for calling their channel "M2: Music Television." The court held that the cable company did not infringe on the software company, and that there could be no likelihood of confusion because the software company was not famous according to a survey conducted by the cable company. Only 1% of the 501 people interviewed by telephone associated the label M2 with CDs or music videos (*M2 Software Inc. v. Viacom International, Inc.*, 2000). Furthermore, the label M2 was associated with a variety of products.

Businesses See Brand Names Differently

Whereas the court is hard pressed to find a problem with the same or similar names for totally unrelated product categories, the business world finds otherwise due to the value of brand names. The value of a reputable brand name is routinely measured by surveys such as the one found in Business Week Online (2003), Global Brands Scorecard. At the top of the list is Coca-Cola, with a brand evaluation exceeding $70 billion. These numbers are important to assessments of what firms are willing to pay for brand names, both outright and through licensing of the brand name. For example, Sunkist received $10.3 million in royalties by licensing its name for use as Sunkist fruit gums (Ben Myerson Candy), Sunkist orange soda (Cadbury Schweppes), and Sunkist juice drinks (Lipton) (Aaker, 1991). Such practices have increased the opportunity for confusion among consumers faced with the same brand names applied to different product categories.

There is a lot more recognition in the value of a successful brand, especially if that brand has a lifestyle and prestige image to the buyer. A lifestyle brand may be "Roots," the Canadian clothing company (owned by Americans). The Roots brand has been extended to cover almost everything from sunglasses to home accessories to a luxury lodge in British Columbia. The extension of brand names to other product categories, which may be related or even unrelated, is of great interest to the marketing discipline.

These types of extensions are not limited to consumer products, and may be applied to the industrial or B2B market. In *Falconbridge Nickel Mines Ltd. v. Falconbridge Land Development Co.* (1974), the first older established company traded on the stock exchange, whereas the second company had just started business and just picked the name randomly out of the phone book.

Protecting one's brand name from use in unrelated product categories serves two purposes. First, if another manufacturer uses the brand name to label an unrelated product and that product is of inferior quality, the poor image may reflect back on the original product. Manufacturers should not want to risk their brand name being attached to inferior products, no matter how far they are removed from the original product class.

Second, protecting one's name in unrelated markets protects future options, because the manufacturer may some day want to extend the name to different product categories. Perhaps the more frequently brands extend to unrelated product categories, the more likely courts will be to grant protection of their trademark.

COLOR

Color is an extremely important cue for identification. Color connotes cognitive meanings such as quality and emotional meanings such as energy. The idea that color can be an overwhelming part of the trademark or trade dress is recognized by business, but color still is a very difficult cue to protect. Color usually is accorded trademark protection only upon a showing of secondary meaning. Factors determining whether secondary meaning has developed include long use, advertising, sales volume, and identity of a particular source or origin in the minds of the purchasing public.

Color protection has been denied unless it is an integral part of the design, its use clearly distinguishes it from the goods of others, a substantial promotional use has been made of the color, and advertising has established a secondary meaning for the color (Grubbs, 1974). The plaintiff bears the burden of establishing a secondary meaning for his product. The court must decide whether the ordinary user, using due care in the marketplace, would be likely to confuse the products based on color.

The protection of color as a trademark owes much to a business-to-business case involving dry cleaning pressing pads colored a special shade of green-gold (*Qualitex Company, Petitioner v. Jacobsen Products Company, Inc.,* 1995). Qualitex had produced and sold these green-gold pads for years, and then Jacobsen entered the market producing pressing pads and giving them the same color as his competitor. The court found that the green-gold color acted as a "symbol," which had a secondary meaning of the Qualitex manufacturer. Hence the color green-gold could be a registered trademark for Qualitex.

The inherent understanding of the role of color by the businessperson is evident in the marketing community. A Vancouver business wanted to sell tea, mainly to the East Indian community, with a package greatly similar to the leading local brand, Nabob. The name was changed from Nabob to Maharajah, but all other aspects of the package were extremely similar or the same. In fact, the brand imitator even (erroneously) copied the exact supermarket scanner bar code from the original brand.

In settling this dispute out of court, Nabob proposed that the imitator could keep all aspects of its package the same if it agreed to change the color from the copycat red to blue or green. The Maharajah tea seller initially refused. He inherently knew the value of keeping the color the same as the original. In negotiations, he did offer to lighten or darken the color of his red package slightly away from the original red. Hence, it is easy to see how squabbles over shade and hue might occur.

Competing Products

A case of color and secondary meaning is the "Yellow Pages" telephone directory (*Southwestern Bell Telephone Co. v. Nationwide Directory Service, Inc.,* 1974). The term "yellow pages" appears with the yellow pages symbol on the front cover of the telephone directory and on the yellow-colored pages in the advertising section. The court found that the yellow pages format had achieved trademark status and granted a permanent injunction against the other "Yellow Pages."

Related Product Categories

The overriding use of color for brand identification is found in *Eastman Kodak Co. v. Fotomat Corp.* (1969). Fotomat simulated the trade dress of Eastman Kodak Co. by using a yellow color for its roof and by using yellow, red, and black colors on signs. In addition, Fotomat used large "Kodak Film" signs without clear identification of Fotomat itself. The court decided the likely result was that customers assumed Fotomat was associated with Kodak. The court thus ruled for Eastman Kodak Co.

Unrelated Product Categories

The overwhelming impression created by a combination of colors is not only unique design, but also the ability to cross cultures with the same information. In *Visa International Service Association v. Visa Motel Corp.* (1985), portable modular structures were painted in the same bands of blue, white, and gold that Visa credit cards use for identification. The opinion of the court was that if both marks were in the same area, people would believe that the two businesses had the same owner.

Color was a secondary attribute contributing to confusion in *Church & Dwight Co., Inc. v. Helene Curtis Industries, Inc.* (1977). Helene Curtis brought onto the market a new brand of deodorant called "Arm and Arm" using the colors of yellow and red to identify its package. In previous years, Church and Dwight had sold Arm & Hammer baking soda with yellow and red packaging. The leap that could happen in the mind of the consumer was that the same company was now selling deodorant as well as baking soda.

The Special Case for Color in the Drug Industry

One of the major users of color for identification is the drug industry. Here, color can be thought of as a "safety" factor. Pills without their packages are very difficult to label, so color combinations often are used as surrogates for labels. This color-coding can be a life or death matter because the colors are functional to patients as well as to doctors, nurses, and hospitals. This functional aspect of color was germane to *Inwood Laboratories, Inc. v. Ives Laboratories, Inc.* (1982). In 1955 Ives received a patent on the drug cyclandelate. After Ives' patent expired, Inwood copied the appearance of the original capsules, selling cyclandelate in 200- and 400-mg capsules with colors identical to those selected by Ives. The Supreme Court ruled that specific color combinations helped to avoid confusion among chemically different drugs by those responsible for dispensing them. A similar ruling is found in Canada, where the Federal Court ruled that a generic, Novopharm, could copy the colors of Eli Lilly's lucrative antidepressant drug, Prozac, because the color was a safety factor.

A review of the legal and technical arguments with respect to color, size, and shape of prescription drugs is found in an article by Furlanetto (1996). There are issues of the drug's functionality, as well as advertising issues and packaging issues. However drugmakers who want to be distinctive to the courts seem to have no trouble altering color, shape, packaging, advertising, and whatever else it takes to be perceived differently. For example, recent patent battles around Viagra, the little blue pill with a triangular shape, involved Pfizer's competitors, Bayer and Elli Lilly, who developed their own erectile dysfunction medication. Court documents showed much discussion about the distinctive nature of the look of the competitors' pills. In Eli Lilly's case, their distinctive drug was yellow and oval-shaped, whereas Bayer's was round and white. The distinctiveness of the shape and color of the competitor's pills certainly was used by the lawyers to play up a perceptually different pill from the blue-diamond Viagra. The different look of the pills supported arguments of a different pill from a different producer in the mind of the consumer who sought relief for similar medical problems.

CONFUSION AND SIMILAR SHAPES

Sometimes consumers identify brands or products not by their brand name or color, but by their shape. The protection of shape can be found in law under the expression "distinguishing guise." It can be the shaping of the goods themselves, the shaping of their containers, their mode of wrapping, or the way the good is packaged. All these methods are used to distinguish goods or services from those of competitors. The shape itself may be desirable, or the shape may represent to the customer the quality of the product through identification of the brand. The shape of the article may be protected by a design patent on the aesthetics, but not on the function of the package (Fitzell, 1982). Nevertheless, the shape is meaningful to the consumer. Shape may be the initial cue to identification of the desired product. Identification by shape and design takes place in both the consumer and industrial marketplaces. If a product obtains commercial success, and this is seen to be related to its design, competitors are quick to copy the design of the product, but usually at a lower price.

Manufacturers are eager to seek trademark protection of product shapes or configurations because this form of product differentiation might have four significant anticompetitive effects. First, it might permit the seller to acquire a control over price that he or she could not otherwise maintain. By differentiating the appearance and protecting the distinction, the seller can influence consumers to buy the product even though the quality level is no higher than a nondifferentiated product. Second, shape aids quick identification of the brand for the consumer, further utilizing noncontent cues in the decision-making process. Third, shape adds to the cost of production and marketing by requiring expenditures for differentiation not related to the quality or actual needs of the product. Fourth, entry into an industry is made more expensive because of higher initial losses while the consumer learns to identify the product by a new shape (Minnesota Law Review, 1975).

One example of the distinctive shape issue is the Head and Shoulders shampoo brand. The cost of litigating and trying to prevent hundreds of copycat manufacturers of this shampoo likely led the strategy to change the shape to the brand's distinctive bottle. It was likely less expensive for the company to change and to promote its new look than to spend the time, money, and effort in litigating against copy artists. Pictures of the before and after bottle, is found in Exhibit 4.1.

The Product as Shape

A similar case of shape serving to identify a product but having no particular function is found with water faucets (*Price Pfister v. Mundo Corporation*, 1989). Seven consumer surveys were carried out to identify associations to product shape and to address the issue of brand confusion. In the shape recognition surveys, respondents were shown a Price Pfister product and two similar handles, then asked to identify each handle. For some consumers, the exposure to the actual brand name did not lessen their identifica-

EXHIBIT 4.1   Changing the Shape of Shampoo Bottles.

tion of that imitator as the original. It appears that the cue of shape can be so powerful that the consumer may continue to confuse a copy with the original even when the different brand name of the copy is supplied.

A very similar case is *Versa Products Company, Inc. v. Bifold Company Ltd.* (1994). Here Versa Products sold valves with contoured lines and shaping, which were allegedly copied by Bifold. The initial ruling was in favor of Versa Products, but was reversed upon appeal (*Versa Products Company, Inc. v. Bifold Company Ltd.*, 1995) because Versa did not have any research to show consumer confusion. Versa Products then tried to have the Supreme Court rule on the case, but their petition was denied.

In *Sears, Roebuck & Co. v. Stiffel Co.* (1964), the Stiffel Company secured design and mechanical patents on a pole lamp, a vertical tube with lamp fixtures along the outside. The tube was made so that it would stand upright between the floor and the ceiling of a room. Sears, Roebuck and Co. put a substantially identical lamp on the market that sold at a retail price similar to Stiffel's wholesale price. Because furniture has a style but little overt brand labeling, it is unlikely that the average consumer was aware whether the lamp was a genuine Stiffel. The courts decided in favor of Sears, which continued to sell its copycat lamps to the public at a lower price.

The Stiffel case served as a precedent for many furniture cases over the years (e.g., *Parkdale Custom Built Furniture Pty. Ltd. v. Puxu Pty. Ltd.*, 1982). Knock-off furniture is inferior in quality and lower in price than the original. Confusion surrounding the origin of the furniture may be extensive. Because no labels are visible, salespeople employed by retailers have given misleading information to buyers. Retail companies can easily substitute one picture, thinking it is another. Evidence may show the two manufacturers' furniture to be so similar that a person could easily interchange them.

In a step that might help designers of furniture, the U.S. Patent and Trademark Office granted trademark protection to the furniture company Knoll for four famous designs of the popular Barcelona collection: a chair, a stool, a couch and a table. Although Knoll has had trademark protection for the name Barcelona since 1968, the new registration extends to the actual design. It is unlikely that this registration will prevent near copies, but it will make litigation a little easier (Beck, 2004).

The product does not even have to be a durable product to have a unique and identifiable shape. An example of protection in which the customer may never know the actual brand name is found in *Chocolates à la Carte v. Presidential Confections Inc.* (Felsenthal, 1992). In this case, a Philadelphia jury ruled that the California chocolatier's copyrighted creations, nautilus-shaped seashells, was original chocolate artwork, and ruled that Presidential Confections' look-a-like chocolates infringed on the original brand.

Buildings as Shape

The identification of establishments by their distinctive shape or structure is quite common. Because the highways and streets are so crowded, an instantly recognizable symbol of standards and quality can turn travelers and commuters into customers. A uniquely designed building can function as a trademark and convey relatively complex messages in a form of graphic shorthand (Fletcher, 1979). This is exemplified in *Fotomat Corp. v. Houck* (1970), in which the court held that the overall appearance and design of the Fotomat's building represented "an exercise in inventive skill and creative talent resulting in a building that is attractive and distinctive because of shape, configuration, utilization of colors, design of the roof, and design of the trim" (Oppenheim & Weston, 1977, p. 200). This same identification of the shape as a symbol of the establishment is exemplified in McDonald's golden arches, Tower Pizza, Holiday Inn, and Howard Johnson's to name a few. Just the sight of a pair of golden arches brings pictures of hamburgers and children to mind.

The protection of famous and not so famous landmarks through copyright laws is very important in the United States. The trademarking of buildings by landlords is very much related to the "royalties" or licensing fees that may be available through registering the building or parts of it as a trademark. Use of the building for a movie set or backdrop can bring the landlord a good income. Images of a famous or unique building put on T-shirts for tourists are another form of licensing and income. Even the skyline of Manhattan, New York, seems to be trademarked, because almost every building is registered. For example, the New York Stock Exchange sued the New York–New York Hotel and Casino of Las Vegas, for building a one-third scale model of the New York Stock Exchange's façade on the gambling floor (Dunlap, 1998).

Consumer Packages as Shape

The specific shape of a package provides an easy way for the consumer to identify products, especially when the color of the packaging is coupled with the shape. One of the most important package shapes is observed with perfume bottles. The identity of each and every perfume is closely associated with a distinctively shaped bottle. One of the first cases involving the shape of perfume bottles was *Lucian Lelong Inc. v. George W. Button Corp.* (1943). Lucian Lelong successfully protected their brand of perfume by protecting the shape of their bottle. Since then, the design of distinctive perfume bottles contributes to the multimillion-dollar perfume business. Some consumers buy the perfume only for the bottle because it is seen as a collection piece.

The following case, involving the product category of cat litter, demonstrates how similar packaging, despite distinctive brand names, results in brand confusion, as seen in *A & M Pet Products v. Pieces Inc. and Royal K-9* (1989). Originally, A & M had introduced a new form of cat litter, "Ever-Clean," which consisted of a sandlike material for use in the usual cat litter box possessed by most cat owners. This sandlike material contained ingredients that made the litter absorb liquid wastes into a well-defined clump without contaminating the remaining litter in the box.

To differentiate Ever-Clean cat litter from regular cat litter sold by many other companies, A & M decided to market its sandlike clumping litter in standard plastic jug–like containers rather than the various size bags that were the industry standard form of packaging for cat litter products. Hence, A & M differentiated its brand from other brands by the shape of the package.

In 1989, a competitor, Pieces, began selling its brand, "Forever Fresh," at the same retail outlets in identically shaped and sized containers, but at a cheaper price and with a different color label. Affidavits from consumers showed that they bought Forever Fresh, mistakenly believing it was Ever-Clean. They stated that they were so dissatisfied with the product purchased under the belief that it was Ever-Clean, they decided not to buy Ever-Clean again.

The belief of the consumers that they were purchasing Ever-Clean was perhaps due to the identical shape of the Forever Fresh and Ever-Clean containers, despite different brand labels. One customer testified that she assumed the makers of Ever-Clean had simply changed the color scheme of their labels. This is a reasonable assumption because brands do go through face-lifts and updating from time to time.

Summary

The shape of the package, the shape of the brand, and even the shape of the building associated with the goods are common cues used by consumers to identify brands. Changing the shape may have no impact on the concrete benefits derived from the product, but may be crucial in brand identification. The ease with which packaging may be differentiated was summed up by the court in an early case regarding the packages of toothbrushes (*Florence Mfg. Co. v. J. C. Dowd & Co.*, 1910).

It is so easy for the honest businessman, who wishes to sell his goods upon their merits, to select from the entire material universe, which is before him, symbols, marks, and coverings which by no possibility can cause confusion between his goods and those of competitors, that the courts look with suspicion upon one who in dressing his goods for the market, approaches so near to his successful rival that the public may fail to distinguish between them. (Grubbs 1974, p.385)

CONFUSION AND SYMBOLS

A symbol may be something specifically associated with a name brand. The customer may use the symbol to identify the brand. It may be directly attached to the object, serving no direct purpose other than identification. Two of the most recognized symbols in the world are the words Olympic Games and the five entwined colored rings. These symbols have been found used without authority on everything from pizza parlors to presidential advertising campaigns (Bisetty, 2004). The Olympic committee finds they are extremely busy fighting unauthorized use, especially in cities hosting future and current games.

Tags as Symbols

Coach Leatherware Co. Inc. v. Ann Taylor, Inc. (1991) involved Coach handbags branded by leather luggage tag–like tags attached to them with small brass chains. Ann Taylor sold a line of handbags very similar in total appearance to Coach's bags. In addition, Ann Taylor also put a leather tag with a brass chain on the bag. A consumer study showed 60% of the respondents were confused as to the origin of the Ann Taylor handbag and thought it might be a Coach handbag. Hence, the leather tag acted as a symbol for Coach's products.

A similar example is found in the manufacture of clothing (*Levi Strauss & Co. v. Blue Bell, Inc.*, 1980). Since 1936 Levi Strauss has used a small marker or tab affixed to the exterior of the garment at the hip pocket to identify its jeans as Levi's. The company also has used this tab on other products it manufactures, such as shirts or jean jackets. Wrangler jeans, which had a significantly smaller share of the market, also started to put the same size tab on their casual garments. Wrangler's tabs were of different colors such as red, black, brown, white, olive, yellow, pink, orange, and green. Despite these different color tabs, a consumer survey showed that Wrangler garments with the tab were identified as Levis. To identify the brand as Levi's irrespective of the tab's color, the customer was therefore using the tab. This was key evidence in the judgment for Levi's.

Symbols in Brand Names

The symbol can also be an integral part of the brand name. In *Safeway Stores, Inc. v. Stephens* (1967), a comparison of pictures of the stores of the two parties showed that the block-type lettering used in the sign on the Save-Way store (owned by Stephens) was extremely similar to the type of lettering long used by Safeway. The court ruled that Save-Way deliberately failed to avoid confusion, mistake, or deception in this situation.

In *World Carpets, Inc. v. Dick Littrell's New World Carpets* (1971), World Carpets was the owner of two federally registered trademarks for carpeting that contained the word "world" along with globe pictures. Dick Littrell used the name New World Carpets with a globe showing latitudinal and longitudinal lines as his brand identity. Therefore, the globe was the common symbol, whether it was a literal or a representational depiction. The court ruled for World Carpets, and Dick Littrell could no longer use the globe to identify his company.

In another David and Goliath case, owners of "Cotton Basics" fought against The Gap Clothing stores, which used the Cotton Basics label on their clothing. Despite a legal battle, the Gap continued to sell merchandise with the "Cotton Basics" on its label long after the trial. The legal battle cost the little company $22,000, yet they still did not get complete satisfaction (Olijnyk, 1999b).

Symbols in Associated Words

Although Harley-Davidson was successful in trademarking the hoglike sound from the exhaust of its motorcycles, it was unsuccessful in legally taking the word "hog" to be associated exclusively with its brand. Harley-Davidson had sued a motorcycle repair shop in New York, called the "Hog Farm," for trademark infringement (McMorris, 1999). A lower court agreed with Harley-Davidson, but on appeal, a higher court sided with the little guy and stated that the word "hog" is found in the dictionary to represent "large motorcycles" and not a particular brand. Under trademark law, this is evidence that the word is descriptive and common and not protected under the law.

Symbols in Advertising

Advertising always strives to catch the viewer's attention and break through the clutter. It is important that each advertisement have a strong and unique connection to the brand it is selling. However, look-alike advertisements are sometimes created. The advertising agency of Chiat/Day/Mojo created an American Express Co. charge card commercial with images of young bathing beauties in a water ballet. The advertisement was pulled immediately after an agency representing European American Bank charged Chiat/Day/Mojo with creative pilfering. They had aired an advertisement using an adolescent synchronized swim team in the bank advertisement 2 ½ years previously. It seems that the Chiat/Day/Mojo group saw the original advertisement and unwittingly copied the spot (Goldman, 1992).

Advertising Slogans as Symbols.   Not only do people rely on visual cues for identification, but consumers also may use advertising slogans as a cue that triggers association to the brand name. In *Maidenform, Inc. v. Munsingwear, Inc.* (1977), debate centered on the rights of both parties to use the slogan "Underneath it all" in conjunction with their respective trade names in their advertising. Munsingwear adopted the name "Vassarette" to identify its woman's apparel division, whereas Maidenform made use of its corporate name for identification. For many years, Munsingwear used the words "Underneath it all" in conjunction with the name "Vassarette" as a slogan to promote its women's undergarment products. In June 1977, Munsingwear learned that Maidenform intended to use the words "Underneath it all" in conjunction with the words "I'm a Maidenform woman." Therefore, no brand name per se was contested in this case, but rather, a phrase used to associate the product in the minds of the consumers. The court determined that the slogan was entitled to protection, and Maidenform was enjoined from further diluting and infringing on the Munsingwear's trademark.

SIMILAR GROUPING OR GESTALT

People do not perceive situations or events as made up of many discrete elements, but rather as dynamic wholes. This emphasis on perceiving the environment as a whole that is more than the sum of its parts is known as "gestalt," from the German word for shape or form. A core idea in this perspective is that people tend spontaneously to group and categorize objects. When individuals need to retrieve previous images from memory, they cannot get it all back in one complete accurate picture. Any analysis of product/brand perception must start out by acknowledging our limited processing abilities. Consumers do not try to perceive or remember all possible bits of product information. They do only what is necessary to get a clear impression of what is going on. People take in information selectively, then organize it into a meaningful gestalt that makes sense out of the selective information. This is why products with the same trade dress may be confused with one another, despite very different brand names.

Competing Brands

Because gestalt refers to the overall look of the item, many distinctive features may be grouped together to give an overall impression of the object. In *Kendall-Jackson Winery, Ltd. v. E. & J. Gallo Winery* (1998), Kendall claimed a unique combination of five elements to identify their chardonnay wine: a lip, or "flange," around the bottle opening, a visible cork, a wrapper around the bottle neck, a white label, and a picture of a grape leaf. Kendall argued that Gallo copied these elements to confuse consumers with their cheaper chardonnay. No one aspect was singled out, but all were deemed to be important in making the impression of the brand. The claims from both sides depended upon whether these features were distinctive and nonfunctional, and whether Gallo's bottle created a likelihood of confusion. The court ruled that Kendall-Jackson's trade dress was not sufficiently distinctive, and that the look of their bottle was functional. The court further stated that granting Kendall-Jackson exclusive rights to the look would put competitors at a disadvantage.

Other prevailing cases of gestalt is found in children's plush toys (*American Greetings Corp. v. Dan-Dee Imports, Inc.*, 1985), in handguns (*Sturm, Ruger & Co., Inc. v. Arcadia Machine & Tool Inc.*, 1988), and in greeting cards (*Hartford House Ltd. v. Hallmark Cards Incorporated*, 1986). A detailed description of the original brands is given in Exhibit 4.2. Confusion is pervasive but elusive because there is no one or overriding aspect that is important in these cases. In the first case, plush toys were sold under the name of "Care Bears" versus "Good Time Gang." The infringing bears had various graphic symbols placed on the white background of their bellies. The original manufacturer had used the same device to develop a strong product appearance with a clear secondary meaning. The competitor knowingly copied the overall appearance of the first manufacturer's bears. The overall appearance of the two product lines was so similar that the manufacturers' survey showed that 42% of customers associated the competitor's products in some way with those of the original manufacturer.

In *Sturm, Ruger & Co., Inc. v. Arcadia Machine & Tool Inc.* (1988), the basis for confusion was between two brands of handguns. Photographs and drawings of the AMT Lightning pistols appearing in gun magazine articles and advertisements were misidentified as Ruger's in the accompanying printed explanations or advertising copy. A market research study was conducted to measure the distinctiveness of the Ruger Mark II within the product category and the extent of confusion between the AMT and Ruger pistols. A sample of 311 people who had purchased a handgun in the preceding 5 years was divided into two groups, shown pictures of five pistols, and asked to identify them. One group had the Ruger in the five pictures and the other group had the AMT in the pictures. On an unaided basis, 46% of those shown the photograph of the Ruger pistol correctly identified it as a Ruger. However, 39% of handgun buyers identified the AMT as the Ruger, whereas on 3% correctly identified the AMT. Ruger won its case.

A particularly aggressive instance of brand imitation can be found in *Hartford House v. Hallmark Cards Co.* (1986). In March 1985, Hallmark's CEO came to visit Blue Mountain to negotiate a joint venture, but Blue Moun-

Blue Mountain Greeting Card

- A two fold card containing poetry on the first and third pages.
- Unprinted surfaces on the inside three panels.
- A deckle edge on the right side of the first page.
- A rough edge stripe of color wide stripe on the outside of the deck edge of the first page.
- A high quality, uncoated, and textured art paper for the cards.
- Florescent ink for some of the colors printed on the cards.
- Length of poetry, written in free verse, typically with a personal message.
- Appearance of hand-lettered calligraphy on the first and third pages with the first letter of the words sometimes enlarged.
- The illustration on the cards "wraps around" the card and is spread over three pages including the back of the card.
- The actual style and "look" of the cards is characterized by backgrounds of soft colors done with airbrush blend or light watercolor strokes; they usually depict simple contrasting foreground scenes superimposed in the background.

Ruger Guns.

- Shape and angle of the grip to the barrel.
- Shape and slant of the bottom of the grip.
- Shape of the external portions of the magazine and the location of the magazine release.
- Slant of the back of the bolt and receiver.
- Shape of the bolt ears used for pulling the bolt back in preparation of firing.
- The shape and location of the ejection port.
- The location and style of the safety and bolt stop.
- The angle and shape of the front portion of the grip frame.
- The shape of the trigger and trigger guard.
- The amount of the barrel which is left exposed.

Care Bears

- Pastel coloration.
- An inverted triangular "jowly" shaped head.
- Heart-shaped paws.
- Pear-shaped body.
- An oval-shaped abdominal area.
- A heart-shaped nose.
- A tuft of hair atop the head.
- A white plush abdominal area.
- Tummy graphics.

EXHIBIT 4.2   Distinctive Features Giving Gestalt.

tain declined. In September 1985, Hallmark conducted market research to determine the effectiveness of its copycat product, Personal Touch, as compared with the Blue Mountain product. The report advised that the sales force could use the information to reduce or eliminate Blue Mountain art displays and insert its own Personal Touch displays. In April 1986, the owner of Blue Mountain testified that she went to straighten an in-store display of her cards, and turning over a card, to her shock and disbelief, she discovered it was an imitation bearing the Hallmark name. The copy was so convincing that it fooled even the owner of the original company. The request for damages and costs from Hallmark was $50 million. It took Blue Mountain years to develop the style and look of its cards. Hallmark tried to do it in a matter of months. The court ruled that Hallmark must select and incorporate alternative features to avoid the potential for confusion. It was told to alter and rearrange the features of its cards in such a way as to produce a card different from the Blue Mountain product.

Therefore, the roles of David and Goliath are sometimes reversed. Established companies originally created Ruger guns and Care Bears, and lesser companies tried to piggyback on the coattails of their success. However, the Blue Mountain greeting card case is an example of a "little guy" who created and built a successful business only to have an established multimillion dollar company, Hallmark, try to reduce or eliminate it (Schultz, 2004).

Gestalt of Buildings

In *Maternally Yours, Inc. v. Your Maternity Shop , Inc.* (1956), the two retail establishments had similar signs, labels, boxes, advertising slogans, and telephone listings. The total visual image was deemed more important in confusing the two establishments than any one aspect. A similar concern involving gestalt is found in *Palace Station Inc. v. Ramada Station, Inc.* (1988). Ramada was accused of using a railroad station theme, confusingly similar to Palace Station's old time railroad station motif, in connection with the advertising, promotion, development, and operation of its Laughlin, Nevada hotel–casino. The judge ruled that the exterior and interior thematic design of a hotel–casino serves no engineering or scientific purpose. It does not make the facility safer, more energy efficient, or less costly to construct or maintain, nor does it enable the patron to gamble more conveniently or more effectively. Therefore, the look or gestalt of the infringing structure as a railroad station had to be changed.

Gestalt of Advertising

Courts look at advertising copyright infringement cases by comparing the "look and feel" of the commercials instead of using single elements

(Goldman, 1992). The idea behind using the whole advertisement is that one would have had to see the original to create the infringing advertisement. Unfortunately, sometimes this "look and feel" is taken apart by focusing on the different individual small elements.

In the *National Hockey League v. Pepsi-Cola Canada Ltd.* (1992), market research showed that 68% of viewers of the advertisement in question believed the NHL to have sponsored or to be associated with Pepsi's promotion and advertising. This belief might have been largely attributable to the incorporation of several factors common to the NHL in Pepsi's advertising: the Stanley Cup Playoffs, the look-alike team uniforms, and the hockey commentators.

IMPLIED ASSOCIATION AND UNAUTHORIZED USE

Endorsement by or a simple association of a product or brand with a celebrity or well-liked image can transfer popularity to the product in the minds of consumers. Under the simple rules of Heider's balance theory (See chapter 3 for a detailed discussion of balance theory), the individual seeks to maintain a steady state among his or her relationships. Thus, if the consumer likes a certain pop star, say Britney Spears, and Britney Spears endorses Coca-Cola, then the consumer should like Coca-Cola to maintain the state of balance. It is the association in the minds of consumers that is important. Knowing how important association is to sales leads companies to use association without consent. This use without consent creates problems in the marketplace.

Merchandise Associated With Events

Merchandise associated with "events" are extremely popular. They tell of the wearer's associations, travels, and entertainment habits. They show support, liking, and in some cases, prestige travel of the wearer by the information printed on the merchandise on one's back. This can be an alma mater the wearer would like to be associated with, a sports team, a rock group, or even a destination. The production and sale of these items, such as T-shirts, hats, jackets, can bring in millions of dollars of revenue to the associated organization. The items usually are sold at a great premium over material costs due to the desirability of the affiliation. Authorized goods usually are of good quality to enhance the association and pride in wearing the garment and to justify the premium price in the mind of the consumer.

The big problem here is that events are fleeting, and a seller who gives the same name association but at a lower price than authorized dealers usually can get a big part of the market. Concerts, such as those by the Rolling Stones, have seen sellers of unauthorized merchandise, which is inferior in the quality. Also the printing on the T-shirts has not been carefully controlled. For example in *Brockum Company v. Baylock* (1990), shirts were sold stamped with "I saw the Stones at the Vet" or

> I was there!
>
> The Rolling Stones
>
> Veterans Stadium
>
> Philadelphia, PA.
>
> August 31
>
> September 1, 1989

This script was 3 to 4 inches in height, whereas in quarter-inch writing underneath was a disclaimer: "This shirt is produced by LTS merchandise Co. and is not sponsored or authorized by the Rolling Stones." Of course, the reading and the effectiveness of the disclaimer is likely nonexistent. Because of the lower quality of the merchandise, the argument was that the merchandise would create confusion among purchasers and others by conveying the impression of reduced standards by the Rolling Stones. For these types of events, it is unlikely that the consumer cares too much about the quality because the merchandise is likely a souvenir and will be worn only a few times until the next concert. For example, in one case for an INXS event, the unauthorized seller not only had disclaimers on the merchandise, but the stall from which the goods were sold bore a sign "Bootleg T-shirts" (*Hutchence and Others v. South Seas Bubble Co. Pty. Ltd.*, 1986).

Not only are music events subject to this unauthorized selling, but sports also are a universal passion. Football, hockey, and baseball are big businesses that make huge margins from licensing agreements. Knowing how important association is to sales leads manufacturers to use association without consent, sometimes after failed negotiations with the owner of the mark. In *National Football League v. Wichita Falls Sportwear* (1982), a survey found that 50% of the public believed the manufacturer would have to get permission to put the sports logo on merchandise. This use without consent is what creates problems in the marketplace because many times the logo is already sold to another for exclusive use. In *Boston Athletic Association v. Sullivan* (1989), the Boston marathon already had a sponsor who had the exclusive rights to produce T-shirts. The cost of such an arrangement is factored into the price of the official T-shirt. To have an unauthorized shirt at half the price on the market certainly would diminish the value of that mark to the event organizers the next time they look for a sponsor.

The First Amendment of the U. S. Constitution

Under the laws in the United States, there is the First Amendment Protection. It says that if there is artistic impression and/or dissemination of information, then the unique use of a mark may not be so protected by law. The question is what is art and what is information? Of course, there are times when art is really art. In *ETW Corp. v. Jireh Publishing Inc.* (2000), prints of the golfer Tiger Woods on the golf course were being sold without authorization from Tiger Woods. In this case, the artist had three different images and had made prints of the art for sale to the public. The argument was made that none of these three specific images were trademarked and therefore should be considered art.

A similar argument was made by an advertising agency that wanted to use the song "Sing, Sing, Sing," by Benny Goodman to sell golf clubs (*EMI Catalogue Partnership and EMI Robbins Catalogue Inc. v. Hill, Holiday, Connors, Cosmospulos Inc. & Spalding Sports Worldwide*, 2000). The ad agency approached the company holding the rights to the song, but found that the cost of the royalties attached to the song quite expensive, so they instead looked for a similar tune and wrote the lyrics "Swing, Swing, Swing" for the advertisement. The advertising agency said that the song in their ad was protected by the First Amendment because the ad described both the action of the players depicted in it and the musical style of the sound track.

Altering Identities

The association may be made using the gestalt of the person (*Motschenbacher v. R. J. Reynolds Tobacco Co.*, 1974) or a specific symbol (*Bette Midler v. Ford Motor Company*, 1988). In the first case, an R. J. Reynolds television commercial for Winston cigarettes, the photograph of a famous professional racing driver's car was used without his permission. Although the number on the car was changed and a wing-like device known as a spoiler was attached to the car, other features were not disguised. The car still had white pinpointing, an oval medallion, and a solid red coloring. The driver, Motschenbacher, was in the car but his features were not visible. On viewing the commercial, some people correctly inferred that the car was his, and that he was in the car and was therefore endorsing the product. The lower court ruled in favor of R. J. Reynolds. However, on appeal, a higher court overturned the judgment. The appeal court ruled it irrelevant that Motschenbacher could not be identified in the advertisement. The advertisement suggested that he was in the car by emphasizing distinctive signs or symbols associated with him.

Myriam Bedard, the famous double-gold Canadian Olympic Biathlete, found huge pictures of herself endorsing Wrigley Gum on the sides of buses. The problem was the picture had been altered to "make her look like a man." Saying she was insulted, humiliated, and traumatized by the ad, which stripped her of her femininity, she sued Wrigley Canada and the advertising firm BBDO Canada for $725,000 (Gatehouse, 2000). The case was subsequently settled out of court.

In a symbolic case, Bette Midler successfully sued Ford Motor Co. (*Bette Midler v. Ford Motor Company*, 1988) and its advertising agency, Young and Rubicam, Inc. for $400,000 over an advertisement for Ford Lincoln Mercury that used a "sound-alike" singer. Neither the name nor the picture of Bette Midler was used in the commercial. The advertising agency had originally approached Ms. Midler's manager for approval, who had flatly refused the offer. Undeterred, the advertising agency recruited one of Midler's backup singers with instructions to sound as much like Midler as possible. The district court described Ford's conduct as that "of the average thief," saying it had decided "If we can't buy it, we'll take it". The cue in this case was a very distinctive voice, expertly copied.

Who Owns What?

Sometimes who owns the rights of a celebrity is more complex. In 2001, after 5 years of legal bills and battles, Paramount Pictures settled with George Wendt and John Ratzenberger of Cheers fame. Paramount had granted an advertising company approval to use the Cheers show and character likeness, but had not sought approval from the actors. The actors were not pleased to see their likeness in advertising without their approval and sued Paramount. This case went back and forth from court to court, finally reaching the U.S. Supreme Court, which refused to hear the case (Lans Retsky, 2002). Once again, different opinions prevailed from court to court.

Implied Image Association

The association that leads to liking does not have to be a person. It can be an image falsely implied. In *Narhex Australia Pty. Ltd. v. Sunspot Products Pty. Ltd.* (1990), Narhex misleadingly or deceptively represented a connection between its Japanese-manufactured skin care products and France by the impression conveyed in the packaging or labeling of the products. This French image was created by the use of the word "Paris" and the phrase "crème des yeux pour les rides à l'elastine," which was on the front and sides of the package. Instructions were written in French and English inside the package, and reference was made to "laboratoire de Narhex Paris-France" and to the work of French scientists at the University of Paris.

In fact, Narhex elastin was manufactured in Japan for Narhex Australia Pty Limited and was not distributed in France. The court considered that the color and labeling on the package combined to convey the impression of a connection with France. A reference to a French origin for a product or an indication of its acceptance by French people, especially Parisians, serves greatly to enhance consumer expectations as to its efficacy and to increase consumer willingness to pay a higher price for it. He considered that these facts were well and truly known to all mankind.

The Wonderful World of Parody

Humor is a wonderful thing. However, humor, like beauty, is in the eye of the beholder. When one is the object of laughter, or when others are laughing at, rather than with one, this is quite likely to be considered offensive by the target of the laughter. Mastercard Inc. sued Ralph Nader to stop the political candidate from running a commercial that listed the campaign expenses of other politicians in a take-off of the credit cards "Priceless" campaign. An example of the parody was "Grilled Tenderloin for fundraiser: $1,000 a plate," finding out the Truth "Priceless." The judge ruled that there was no infringement on Mastercard's trademark by these types of parodies.

There also are different types of humor. Humor related to sexual or bodily functions usually are seen as particularly bad taste. It is this idea of bad taste that will get you in a courtroom for sure. Of all the sources of imitations, parody seems to be divided into good and bad taste, and taste is a matter of culture and preference. Anything pornographic probably is judged to be bad taste and detrimental, but what is pornography can be a matter of opinion.

For example, the Aids Committee of Toronto (ACT) put out an ad in 2001 that parodied the Marlboro cowboy ad. The ad had two cowboys on the same horse about to kiss. The headline of the ad said, "Welcome to Condom Country," and at the bottom it said "HIV Is on the Rise in Toronto; Ride Safely." Phillip Morris never challenged this campaign in court. In fact, this campaign was deemed to be the most successful and effective advertising by ACT ever (www.actoronto.org/actweb/info.ns). Although many people might find the ad offensive, it may have not displeased Phillip Morris that much because for them, it might have been seen as "good and effective," and even welcome advertising. Remember, this is a company for which most advertising is banned, so any association, even with a gay group, may be a positive for the company. Cigarette smoking is not confined to heterosexuals, and because this ad campaign was so well liked by the gay community, it may even have caused many a gay smoker to switch to Marlboro.

Even the Girl Scouts of America have found themselves in court. They were unable to prevent the use of their trademarks on a poster depicting a pregnant scout and the motto "Be Prepared" (*Girl Scouts of the United States v. Personality Posters Mfg. Co.*, 1969). It seems pregnancy and HIV prevention are good things for society because the court allowed these parodies to continue.

Sexual innuendos are less likely to be accepted. The Dallas Cowboy Cheerleaders have been successful in stopping both a pornographic movie featuring an actress occasionally clad in a Cheerleader's uniform (*Dallas Cowboys Cheerleaders, Inc. v. Pussycat Cinema, Ltd.*, 1979) and a poster depicting a group of past members wearing only a portion of their former attire (*Dallas Cowboys Cheerleaders, Inc. v. Scoreboard Posters, Inc.*, 1979). In the first case, the central character of the pornographic film is selected to become a "Texas Cowgirl," a name sometimes used for the cheerleaders. To raise money for the trip to Dallas, the heroine engages in a variety of sexual activities, sometimes attired in a uniform strikingly similar to that worn by the actual Dallas Cowboys Cheerleaders. The court stated, "It is hard to believe that anyone who had seen the sexually depraved film could ever thereafter disassociate it from the Dallas cheerleaders" (Denicola, 1982, p. 206).

The judicial concern here is the unwelcome association rather than the threat of confusion. The owner of the mark wants to prevent the appearance of their mark in an unwholesome or inappropriate environment. In this vein, General Electric was granted an injunction against the use of "Genital Electric" on T-shirts and briefs (*General Electric Co. v. Alumpa Coal Co.*, 1979). In another case, the Pillsbury trade characters Poppin Fresh and Poppie Fresh were depicted in an adult newspaper engaged in sexual activities incompatible with the wholesome image sought by their owner (*Pillsbury Co. v. Milky Way Prods. Inc.*, 1981).

Besides, sex, drugs, and violence also do not make good parodies. The court stopped the use of a well-known Enjoy Coca-Cola design on a poster featuring a facsimile of the symbol, but advocating instead, Enjoy Cocaine (*Coca-Cola Co. v. Gemini Rising, Inc.*, 1972). Fred Rogers, the soft-spoken 70-year-old host of PBS's Mister Rogers' Neighborhood sued a Texas-based novelty store for selling T-shirts displaying a picture of Rogers with his trademark sweater and smile and a silver handgun. Instead of saying "Won't you be my neighbor?" the t-shirt had "Welcome to my hood" written on it. This was called sick humor, which wrongly benefited from Mister Rogers' image.

Parodies of Products.   Transferring human products to animal domains is seen as funny by some, and terribly serious by others. When it is done in a perceived positive fashion, it seems to be accepted, but not when it is done in a negative light. This was the case when Tommy Hilfiger challenged Timmy Holedigger's dog perfume (*Tommy Hilfiger Licensing Inc. V.*

Nature Labs, 2002). Nature Labs made, marketed, and sold pet perfumes with names that parody elegant brands sold for human consumption. Here, the court ruled that the dog perfume could be continued on the market. It was decided that there was no chance the original brand would be confused with the dog perfume.

Nature Labs asserted that the use was an obvious parody, and even if confusing, trademark parodies are protected under the First Amendment. Even if not technically a parody, the use was a pun or comical expression entitled to constitutional protection. The whimsical substitution of a dog-related pun on dog perfume was said to convey clearly a joking variation on the original. It was argued that the original cologne and the pet cologne did not fall within the same class of fragrances and thus were not in competitive proximity. The intent of the lighthearted parody was not to confuse, but to amuse.

In a more negative light, a company called Gag Foods produced and sold a product called "Roadkill Helper." From a distance, the package looked identical to the "Hamburger Helper" product by General Mills (Gibson, 1993). This image suggestive of eating the inedible is not very appetizing.

Parodies of Fictional Characters.   Just because you do not really exist does not mean that you do not have an image to protect. D.C. Comics, property of Time Warner Entertainment LP, owns all intellectual property of Superman. In 1998, a local Canadian middle-aged jeweler developed a character named Cashman dressed in a costume similar to Superman. Cashman changed in a phone booth using rapid physical spinning. The jeweler found himself in court defending Cashman. The worry was that if this character was allowed, one might have Cashmen springing up in every city, and then Superman's image would be at risk.

Coca-Cola's recent icons are polar bears enjoying Coca-Cola in various scenarios. Pepsi-Cola Canada tried to parody these ads by depicting the Polar Bears participating in a blind taste test against Pepsi-Cola and finding that their cola of preference really is Pepsi. These ads were pulled, after threat of legal action by Coca-Cola (Stewart, 2000).

Even Mattel's Barbie doll has been the object of parody. A photographer developed a series of photographs titled Food Chain Barbie, which depicted Barbie dolls in a variety of absurd and sexually provocative poses, often involving household appliances. Here the court ruled that Mattel had created a cultural icon ripe for social comment, and that the artist had a right to create and sell photographs of naked Barbie (Valis, 2003).

However, take away the artistic element and the parody disappears. Selling pornographic sex with the Barbie image is judged to be damaging to the brand, especially in an online environment (Murray, 2004 for a detailed discussion).

Association and Defamation of Character

Companies sometimes make money by selling their name to other manufacturers. In these instances, the trademark does not serve as an indication of source, but rather of quality. Consumers who have come to expect a specific level of quality through their prior experience with the original product bearing the brand may then transfer that expectation to the second product. This is why cases dealing with sponsorship or even just association may provide a basis for infringement. If a second firm implies that they are associated with a successful brand, any consumer dissatisfaction with its product or service will be at the expense of the original's reputation and goodwill, even when the two parties are not in direct competition.

The reasoning behind keeping one's product away from unwanted association can be explained by the balance theory of attitudes. Just as companies want to associate with positive images to form positive attitudes and hence lead to purchase, negative associations lead to negative attitudes and images and avoidance of the product.

The courts recognized the wide-reaching nature of trademarks in 1934:

> His mark is this authentic seal; by it he vouches for the goods, which bear it; it carries his name for good or ill. If another uses it, he borrows the owner's reputation, whose quality no longer lies within his own control. This is an injury, even though the borrower does not tarnish it, or divert any sales by its use; for a reputation, like a face, is the symbol of its possessor and creator, and another can use it only as a mask. (Denicola, 1982, p. 164)

The association or connection does not have to be direct. The simple fact that the sight of a familiar trademark will call to mind the trademark owner is enough to cause infringement. A legal action in these cases is likely to be brought because the association dilutes or harms the image and reputation of the first party. The chief value of a trademark is its selling power, which depends not only on the quality of the goods or services sold under the mark, but also on the impression or image created by the mark itself.

Undermining the positive image can even be a case for diminishing distinctiveness, uniqueness, effectiveness, or prestigious connotations. This was exemplified when Catherine Zeta-Jones found her picture next to partially nude women on the Web page of The Spice House, a topless cabaret in Nevada. She contended that the site would dilute the value of her celebrity endorsement. The Spice House had downloaded the images from a German Web site that offered them for free without knowing who she was (*Marketing News*, 2004b, p. 21).

SUMMARY

The imitation of brand name, shape, symbol, color, and trade dress over competing brands, related product categories, and even unrelated product categories is an ongoing problem for ethical marketers. The decisions in cases brought to court have not always been consistent.

Some early cases of passing-off that dealt with infringement of brand name were decided for the alleged infringer, and little or no protection was given to the original manufacturer despite the sale of identical goods under the same name (e.g., *Thomson v. Winchester*, 1837, and *Faber v. Faber*, 1867). However, some years later in *Fischer v. Blank* (1893), courts recognized the importance of the total look of the object being sold. Despite different names, the total look of the package or the gestalt was so similar that the courts found the infringer guilty and ruled that he could no longer sell his look-alike tea on the market.

Taking well-established names to related or even unrelated product categories is an important strategy that allows marketers to take advantage of their brand's equity. However, when someone other than the original owner takes a brand name to the other product category, some confusion as to the source of the product may exist on the part of the consumer. It is extremely important to protect one's brand name even in noncompeting markets.

Protection of far more than brand name is needed. This is because consumers sometimes do not identify only with the name, but also use some other feature. The feature may or may not be associated with the name. For example, the Stiffel lamp was known by its shape and called by its name. The seashell-shaped chocolates are identified by their shape and probably not by their brand name or manufacturer. It is the shape that is desirable.

Symbols may be attached to or associated with products. Tags on Coach leather handbags identify their products. Color in distinctive combinations or patterns can be critical to product or brand identification. There may be a problem in copying certain colors, but when colors are coupled with other factors such as shape or name, it may be easier to protect them.

Imitating the trade dress or copying the gestalt of a product or object is extremely common. Unscrupulous competitors seem to think they can put their own brand name on a package or object that has the overall look and feel of another very successful brand on the market. Fortunately, courts have generally upheld the rights of original manufacturers despite attempts by imitators to focus on minute differences that might exist.

Companies also must protect themselves from unpaid and unauthorized associations. Associations with positive images of the original well-known brands can contribute substantially to the infringer's profits. Associations with negative images may decrease the value of the original brand identity and may lead consumers to avoid the original brand in the future. Thus, future sales can be hurt by negative company images.

REFERENCES

Aaker, D. A. (1991). *Managing brand equity.* New York: The Free Press.

A & M Pet Products v. Pieces, Inc. and Royal K-9 (South West United States District Court, Central District of Los Angeles Case No. 89-4923 1989).

American Greetings Corp. v. Dan-Dee Imports, Inc., 619 F. Supp. 1204 (D.N.J. 1985).

Beck, E. (2004, October 30). Knocking out the knockoff. *Globe and Mail,* L8.

Bette Midler v. Ford Motor Company, 849 F2d 460 (9th Cir. 1988).

Big O Tire Dealers v. Goodyear Tire and Rubber 561 F.2d 1365 (US Ct of Appeals, 10th Cir. 1977).

Bisetty, K. (2004, November 1) Trademark battles are signs of the times. *Vancouver Sun,* B1.

Boston Athletic Association v. Sullivan, 867 F. 2d 22 (U.S.C.A., 1st Cir. 1989).

Brockum Company v. Blaylock, 729 F. Supp. 438 (U.S.D.C., E.D. Penn. 1990).

Bronco Wine Company and Barrel Ten Quarter Circle, Inc. v. Department of Alcohol Beverage Control, Napa Valley Vintners Association Case No. C037254 (California Court of Appeal 2003).

Business Week Online. (2003). Global brands scoreboard. [On-line]. Available: http://bwnt.businessweek.com/brand2003/index.asp (Accessed December 1, 2003).

Carnival Corporation v. Seascape Casino Cruises Inc., 74 F. Supp. 2d 1261 (U.S. Dist. Lexis 17546; 52 1999).

Cava, A. (1996). A Swiss army knife: Should it be known by another name if it is made in China. *Journal of the Academy of Marketing Science,* 24(2), 184–185.

Church & Dwight Co., Inc. v. Helene Curtis Industries, Inc., Achter's Key Drug, Inc., and N.W. A Industries, Inc., Achter's Key Drug, Inc., and N.W. Ayer & Son, Inc., d.b.a. N.W. Ayer International, CCH. 61, 279 (D.C.N. Ill., January, 1977), BNA ATRR No. 802 (February 22, 1977), A-19.

Coach Leatherware Co. Inc. v. Ann Taylor, Inc., 933 F2d 162, 18 USPQ2d 1907 (CA 2 1991).

Coca-Cola Co. v. Gemini Rising, Inc., 346 F. Supp. 1183 (E.D.N.Y. 1972).

Dallas Cowboys Cheerleaders, Inc. v. Pussycat Cinema, Ltd., 604 F. 2d 200 (2d Cir. 1979).

Dallas Cowboys Cheerleaders, Inc. v. Scoreboard Posters, Inc., 600 F. 2d 1184 (5th Cir. 1979).

Denicola, R. C. (1982). Trademarks as speech: Constitutional implications of the emerging rationales for the protection of trade symbols. *Wisconsin Law Review,* 158–207.

Dunlap, D. W. (1998, September 12). Even the skyline is trademarked. *Globe and Mail,* C9.

Eastman Kodak Co. v. Fotomat Corp. 317 F. Supp. 304 (N.D. Ga. 1969), appeal 441 F.2d 1079 (5th Cir. 1971).

EMI Catalogue Partnership & EMI Robbins Catalogue Inc. v. Hill, Holiday, Conors Cosmopulos Inc. & Spalding Sports Worldwide (U.S. Ct of Appeals for 2nd Circuit Lexis 30461. 2000) Docket No. 99-7922.

ETW Corp., v. Jireh Publishing, Inc., Case No. 1:98 CV 1485, United States District Court for the Northern District of Ohio, Eastern Division, 99 f. Supp. 2d 829; 2000 U.S. Dist. Lexis 4816

Faber v. Faber, 49 Barb 3 Abb Pr (NS) 115 (NY Sup 1867), Cox 1892, supra note 5, cited in Pattishall, 1978, Vol. 68.

Falconbridge Nickel Mines Ltd. v. Falconbridge Land Development Co. 5 W.W.R. 385 (B.C.S.C. 1974)

Felsenthal, E. (1992, July 16). Ice sculptors view this outcome as a means to a lasting legacy. *Wall Street Journal*, B1.

Fischer v. Blank, 138 N.Y. 244 N.E. 1040, (1893).

Fitzell, P. B. (1982). *Private labels: Store brands and generic products.* Westport, CT: Avi, Publishing Company.

Fletcher, A. L. (1979). Buildings as trademarks. *The Trademark Reporter, 69,* 229–245.

Florence Mfg. Co. v. J.C. Dowd & Co., 178 F. 73, 75 (2d Cir. 1910).

Fotomat Corp. v. Houck, 166 U.S.P.Q. 271 (Fla. Cir. Ct., Pinellas County 1970).

Furlanetto, A. (1996). Prescription pharmaceuticals and the passing-off action. *Intellectual Property Journal,* December, 79–109.

Gatehouse, J. (2000, January). Doctored photograph in gum ad makes me look like a man. *Financial Post,* 2(70), A1–3.

General Electric Co. v. Alumpa Coal Co., 205 USPQ (BNA) 1036 (D. Mass. 1979).

Gibson, R. (1993, January 6). He hasn't got anything to spoof spaghetti and meat sauce—yet. *Wall Street Journal,* B1.

Girl Scouts of the United States v. Personality Posters Mfg. Co., 304 F. Supp. 1228 (S.D.N.Y. 1969).

Goldman, K. (1992, February 14). American Express's ad snafu revives spot on creative pilfering. *The Wall Street Journal,* B12.

Grotrian, Helfferich and Schulz v. Steinway & Sons, CA2 NY, 523 F2d 1331, 186 USPQ 436 (1975).

Grubbs, M. L. (1974). Trade protection for descriptive name and color. *Arkansas Law Review, 28,* 381–387.

Hartford House Ltd. v. Hallmark Cards Incorporated, CA10 (Colo), 846 F2d 1268-Fed Cts 815, 862; Trade Reg 43, 334, 576, 626, (1986).

Hormel Foods Corporation v. Jim Henson Productions, Inc. 1995 U.S. Dist. Lexis 13886; 36 U.S.P.Q.2D (BNA) 1812; 1995-2 Trade Cas. (CCH) P71,154.

Hormel Foods Corporation v. Jim Henson Productions, Inc. 73 F.3d 497; 1996 U.S. App. Lexis 338; U.S.P.Q.2D (BNA) 1516.

Hutchence and others v. South Seas Bubble Co. Pty Ltd., 64 A.L.R. 330 (Aust. Fed. Ct. 1986).

Ice-cream makers fight in court. (2002, July 9). *Financial Post,* 2.

Inwood Laboratories, Inc. v. Ives Laboratories, Inc., U.S. 102 S. ct. 2182, 72 L.Ed. 2d 606, (1982).

It's a Joke. (2004a, April 15). *Marketing News,* p. 4.

Jaguar Cars Ltd., and Jaguar Cars, a Division of Ford Motor Co. v. Manufactures des Montres Jaguar, S.A., Festina, U.S.A. 196 F.R.D. 306 (U.S. Dist. LEXIS 13027 2000).

Kendall-Jackson Winery, Ltd. v. E. & J. Gallo Winery, WL 390795 (9th Cir. Jul. 8, 1998).

Lans Retsky, M. (2000, April 10). Court increasingly clueless when it comes to trademarks. *Marketing News*, 17.

Lans Retsky, M. (2002, February 4). Image is everything, sometimes legally. *Marketing News*, 9.

Lego Australia Pty. Ltd. v. Paul's (Merchants) Pty. Ltd. (Fed. Ct. of Australia. Gen. Divn., Sydney, July, 1982).

Lego System A/S v. Lego M. Lemelstrich, F.S.R. 155 (Ch. D. 1983).

Levi Strauss & Co. v. Blue Bell, Inc., 632 F.2d 817 (9th Cir. 1980).

Lucian Lelong Inc. v. George W. Button Corp., 50 F. Supp. 708 (S.D.N.Y. 1943).

M2 Software Inc. v. Viacom International, Inc. 119 F. Supp. 2d 1061 (U.S. Dist Lexis 11753 2000).

Maidenform, Inc. v. Bestform Foundations, Inc., Patent Office Trademark Trial and Appeal Board, 161 USPQ 805, (1969).

Maidenform, Inc. v. Munsingwear, Inc., United States District Court, Southern District, N.Y., 195 U.S.P.Q. 297, (1977).

Maternally Yours, Inc. v. Your Maternity Shop, Inc., 234 F 2d 538, 546, 110 USPQ 462 (CA Z 1956).

McMorris, F. A. (1999, January 18). It seems a hog is a hog is a hog, even if it isn't a Harley-Davidson. *Wall Street Journal*, B1.

McWilliam's Wines Pty. Ltd. v. McDonald's System of Australia Pty. Ltd. (Fed. Ct. of Australia. Gen. Divn 1980).

Montgomery v. Thompson (1891) A.C. 217 (H.L.).

Motschenbacher v. R. J. Reynolds Tobacco Co., 498 F2d 821 (9th Cir. 1974).

Mountain Shadows Resort Ltd. V. Pemsall Enterprises Ltd., 9 C.P.R. (2d) 172 (B.C.S.C. 1973).

Murray, B. H. (2004). *Defending the brand: Aggressive strategies for protecting your brand in the online arena*. New York: American Management Association.

Narhex Australia Pty. Ltd. v. Sunspot Products Pty. Ltd. (Federal Court of Australia, Perth, July, 1990).

National Football League Properties Inc. v. Wichita Falls Sportswear Inc. 532 F Supp 651, 215 USPQ 174 (W.D. Wash 1982).

National Hockey League v. Pepsi-Cola Canada Ltd. No. C902104 (Supreme Court of British Columbia, June 2, 1992).

Newest spice girl—or not. (2004b, December 15). *Marketing News*, p. 21.

Olijnyk, Z. (1999a, July 2). Jaguar gets territorial in trademark dispute. *Financial Post*, p. C6.

Olijnyk, Z. (1999b, February 9). Cotton basics back in battle. *Financial Post*, p. C3.

Oppenheim, S. C., & Weston, G. E. (1977). *Unfair trade practices and consumer protection: Cases and comments*. St. Paul, MN: West Publishing Co.

Palace Station Inc. v. Ramada Station, Inc. (United States District Court, District of Nevada 1988).

Parkdale Custom Built Furniture Pty. Ltd. v. Puxu Pty. Ltd. (High Court of Australia 1981–1982).

Pillsbury Co. v. Milky Way Prods. Inc., 566 Pat. Trademark and Copyright J. (BNA) A-3 (N.D. Ga. Dec. 24, 1981).

Price Pfister v. Mundo Corporation; Renco Sales, Inc.; Laloo Manufacturing; Callahan Wholesale Hardware Company; CWH Co.; Pioneer Industries, Inc.; and Does 7 through 500, (1989), Superior Court of the State of California.

Professional Publishing Associates Ltd v. Toronto Parent Magazine Inc. (1986) C.P.R. (3d) 2 No.

Qualitex Company, Petitioner v. Jacobson Products Company, Inc No. 93-1577, S.C.U.S., 514 U.S.

Safeway Stores, Inc. v. Stephens, 281 F. Supp. 517 (U.S. District Court for the Western District of Louisiana 1967).

Schultz, A. B. (1977). Trade dress and unfair competition in publishing and packaging: When imitation is not the sincerest form of flattery. *Brooklyn Law Review, 43,* 643–679.

Schultz, S. P. (2004). *Blue Mountain: Turning dreams into reality.* Boulder, CO: Blue Mountain Publishing.

Sears, Roebuck & Co. v. Sears Realty Co. Inc. et al. 932 F Supp. 392, 1996 U.S. Dist. Lexis 10651.

Sears, Roebuck & Co. v. Stiffel Co., 376 U.S. 225, 84 S. Ct. 784, 11 L.Ed. 2d 661 (1964).

Silcoff, S. (2002, August 3). Taking chips off Lego's old blocks. *Financial Post,* 1, 6.

Slazenger & Sons v. Feltham & Co., 6 R.P.C. 531 (Ch.D. 1889).

Southwestern Bell Telephone Co. v. Nationwide Directory Service, Inc., 371 F. Supp. 900 (W.D. Ark. 1974).

Spalding (AG) & Bros. v. A.W. Gamage Ltd., 32 R.P.C. 273 (H.L. 1915).

Stewart, S. (2000, December 4). Coke foaming mad about Pepsi ads, threatens lawsuit. *Financial Post,* p. C5.

Sturm, Ruger & Co., Inc. v. Arcadia Machine & Tool Inc. 10 USPQ 2nd 1522 (United States District Court, Central District of California 1988).

The Clock Ltd. v. Clock House Hotel Ltd., 53 R.PC. 269 (C.A. 1936).

The Forschner Group, Inc. and Swiss Army Brands, Ltd. v. Arrow Trading Co, Inc. 833 F. Supp. 385 (S.D.N.Y. 1993), reversed, 30 F3d 348 (2nd Cir. 1994), on remand, 1995 U.S. Dist. LEXIS 15826 (S.D.N.Y., October 24, 1995).

The Gideons International, Inc. v. Gideon 300 Ministries, Inc. Civil Action No. 97-7251 (United States District Court for the Eastern District of Pennsylvania 1999, U.S. Dist. Lexis 6239).

Thomson v. Winchester, 36 Mass (19 Pick) 214 (Sup. Ct. 1837).

Tommy Hilfiger Licensing Inc. v. Nature Labs, LLC 99 Civ. 10713 (MBM) (.S. Dist. Lexis 14841 2002).

Trademark protection of objects and configurations: A critical analysis. (1975). *Minnesota Law Review, 59,* 541–573.

Union Carbide Corp. v. Ever-Ready, Inc., 531 F. 2d 366, 381-382, 188 USPQ 623 (CA-7 1976).

Valis, M. (2003, December 31). Mattel loses appeal in case of Barbie art. *National Post,* A9.

Versa products Company, Inc. v. Bifold Company Ltd. No. 93-2734 (AJL) U.S.D.C. for the district of New Jersey (U.S. Dist Lexis 19053 1994).

Versa Products Company, Inc. v Bifold Company Ltd. 94-1863, Supreme Court of the United States, 116 S. Ct. 54 (U.S. Lexis 5333 1995).

Vidal Sassoon, Inc. v. Beverly Sassoon and Slim Lines, Inc. (United States District Court, Central Division of California 1982).

Visa International Service Association v. Visa Motel Corp. (1985), 1 C.P.R. (3d) 109 (Proudfoot, J. aff'd by C.A.)

World Carpets Inc. v. Dick Litterll's New World Carpets, 438 F2d 482 (United States Court of Appeals, Fifth Circuit 1971).

Yoga master copyrights and trademarks particular serious of postures. (2005, May 2). *National Post*, FP7.

5

Strategies to Be Distinctive

For the consumer to identify brands with their respective manufacturers, the brands must be sold with distinctive features supplied by that particular manufacturer. This differentiation, or identity, may be achieved through a well-known brand name, color, shape, and a particular look and feel, as well as the distinctive design of the package or product. Brand identity is an important component of the brand equity model, as shown in Exhibit 5.1.

The phrase "Products are produced in the factory, but brands are produced in the minds of the consumer" is true because the costs of brand differentiation are in the initial and additional dollars spent on production

EXHIBIT 5.1 Brand Equity Model. *Source:* H. M. Meyers & M. J. Lubliner. (1998). *The Marketer's guide to successful package design.* American Marketing Association, NTC, Chicago: Business Books, p. 25.

and marketing, which may not be related to the quality or necessary benefits of the product. Take Grey Goose vodka, for example, a recent entrant to the vodka market. In this case, an unknown brand was elevated to international luxury status by linking itself to France, home of the luxury goods market. Advertisement stating that experts rated Grey Goose as the number one vodka in the world provided objective concrete information for consumer decision making. Demand and brand image skyrocketed, and the brand was recently sold to Baccardi for $2 billion. France has no history of expertise in producing vodka. This is an example showing sheer marketing genius of brand differentiation and positioning by Sidney Frank, who now has his sights set on the tequila market.[1]

UNIQUE SELLING POINTS

Some brands may be able to claim a unique selling point in their brand name, for example 2000 Flushes or Five Minute Rice. Others may rely on image and marketing efforts to be different, for example Mike's Hard Lemonade or Obsession perfume. For its unique selling point, Owens-Corning manufactures Fiberglass Pink insulation, which is dyed pink. The pink color is an added cost with no value added quality or necessary benefit to the product other than as identification. In the first 10 years of the product (1972 to 1981), Owens-Corning spent more than $42 million on advertising to build unique brand identification by associating their pink insulation with pink flamingos and the Pink Panther cartoon character. This campaign (or advertising strategy) resulted in an overwhelming consumer association of pink insulation with Owens-Corning. This identity is still going strong and dominates their communication strategy. Their phone number for customer inquiries is 1-800-GET-PINK. Their Web site is printed in pink, and the Pink Panther cartoon character remains their mascot/spokesperson (Exhibit 5.2).

The benefits of a differentiation strategy, along with an extensive advertising campaign informing of the brand differentiation, should permit companies to set a higher price for their goods than they otherwise could have achieved or maintained. For example, Di-Star Inc. started as a generic diamond manufacturer in 1978. In 1996, it changed its name to "Hearts on Fire" to match its branding program for a new diamond cut it had trademarked, which refracted light into hearts and arrows. As a result of the unique cut and sales-force training program to teach customers about the differentiation, sales and profits for the company have skyrocketed, whereas industry sales have increased only marginally (Heckman, 1999).

---

[1]For a complete and thorough understanding of creating and managing distinctive brands, the reader is directed to *The New Strategic Brand Management*, (Kapferer, 2004).

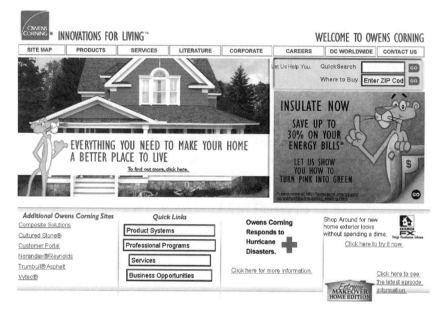

EXHIBIT 5.2   Get Pink web page.

The suggestion is that if manufacturers can differentiate their product in appearance and protect the distinction through advertising and consumer perception, purchasers will buy the product even though the quality level is no higher than that of a nondifferentiated product.

Another benefit of product differentiation is that because of the advertising, purchase decisions are partly based on the advertising rather than on any active comparison of product attributes that the consumer makes among the different brands. The advertising should drive the purchase decision emphasizing the relative quality, source of the goods, and desired image. Being distinctive is not difficult, but it may be expensive to communicate the unique identity of the brand.

TO LITIGATE OR NOT? FIGHTING RETAIL LOOK-ALIKES

Anecdotal evidence in the academic literature and business press suggests that manufacturers will take legal action against each other when they believe their trademarks or trade dress have been infringed upon, but they are reluctant to take legal action when retailers undertake the same copycat activity (Hollinger, 1997; Kapferer, 1995a, 1995b). The reason put forth is that manufacturers are fearful of being delisted or losing shelf space if they confront retailers who copy their brands (Finch, 1996).

This practice is said to be so extensive in the cereal category that no major brands remain to be imitated, thereby limiting projections for private label growth in the category (Burns, 1995). A British survey of 100 brand managers found that 51% had their brands copied by supermarkets, and that 82% of those lost sales to imitators (*Marketing*, 1994).[2] In one reported case, the size of the loss was considerable—a 25% decline in market share over 3 years—despite increases in advertising. The European Association of Industries of Branded Products surveyed their members and found that 80% of companies had their brand imitated between 1985 and 1990 (June 8, 1990). Procter & Gamble Co. alone filed 13 package design infringement suits from 1994 to 1995, all of which were settled or had judgments imposed in the company's favor (*Wall Street Journal*, May 16, 1995; May, 19, 1995). Procter & Gamble launched its first suit against a retailer in 1994 (Rosendahl & Brookman, 1994) and reached a negotiated settlement.

Are Retail Brands Treated Differently?

It is thought that manufacturers may have a more difficult task when suing a retailer rather than another manufacturer for infringement. In the case of Vaseline Intensive Care (*Conopco Inc. d/b/a Cheesebrough-Pond's USA Co. v. May Department Stores Co. and Venture Stores, Inc.*, 1994), the U.S. Courts made note of the fact that the retailer used its name on the packaging and that given the ubiquity of the name in the store, there was no possibility of confusion between the national brand and the private label product (Woo, 1994, October). Another example of a manufacturer bringing suit against a retailer is the Penguin-Puffin case in Britain. Court documents report that retailer Asda's Puffin brand package and product imitated McVitie's Penguin brand chocolate biscuit, and that the 65-year-old Penguin brand sales declined from £40 million to £30 million during a 3-year period, despite an increase in advertising spending (Stuart, 1997). The judge ruled that Puffin's packaging could lead to customer confusion. However, he did not agree that the manufacturer's trademark had been violated (Hollinger, 1997). The case then went to the high court, and the retailer was ordered to redesign its package (Rogers, 1997).

To investigate this special area of retail store–brand look-alikes, a study examining the actions and expectations of national brands in relation to both retailers and other manufacturers as imitators was conducted (Collins-Dodd & Zaichkowsky, 1999). Four types of information were collected from brand managers:

---

[2]To the authors' knowledge, similar data for North America is not available.

1. Incidence of brand imitation as well as the firms' responses to imitation by retailers and manufacturers, including legal action, package changes, product improvements, negotiated settlements, enhanced promotion, and increased trade support

2. Expectations of retailers' responses to litigation, including package redesign immediately, package redesign within 6 months, loss of shelf placement priority, loss of shelf space (and estimated amount), brand delisted, other brands delisted, and enhanced distribution by other retailers

3. Expectations of firms' likelihood of using litigation against other firms varying in size or type (a major manufacturer, a minor manufacturer, a major national retail chain, a minor regional retail chain, a small local retailer, a close channel partner, and an antagonistic channel partner)

4. Firm characteristics.

A total of 30 firms representing a variety of product categories including beverages, personal care products, processed foods, snack foods, and paper products responded to the survey. Sales ranged from $9.5 million to $1 billion, with average sales of $242 million. The respondent firms had been in business from 3 to 130 years, produced 1 to 300 different products, and represented a range of 1 to 85 different brands. Slightly more than half of the firms had in-house legal counsel. Four firms were currently involved in brand imitation litigation. Fourteen firms had been imitated by manufacturers and retailers: six by manufacturers only and five by retailers only. On the average, each firm had previously dealt with 10 different brand imitators.

Response to Imitation. Among the firms that had been imitated, 80% took legal action against the manufacturers, but only 42% initiated legal action against retailers. Firms also were more likely to make product improvements when other manufacturers were accused of an imitation strategy (Table 5.1). The most commonly reported strategy used to deal with retail imitators was negotiation (58%), followed by legal action, enhanced promotion, and trade support. Firms that took legal action against a retail brand also tended to reach negotiated settlements to a much greater degree. Whereas 89% used negotiated settlements with the threat of a lawsuit, only 14% used negotiations without also taking legal action. It is clear that legal action is an important tool for facilitating a negotiated settlement with retailers.

The shortest case reported for litigation against a retailer was 1 week, and the longest was 36 months. For legal action against other manufacturers, the shortest case was 3 months, and the longest reported case was 54 months. Eight brand managers reported that retailers had threatened to

TABLE 5.1
Manufacturers' Response to Brand Imitators:
Retailers Versus Other Manufacturers

Action Taken by Manufacturer	Source of Imitation	
	Retailers	Manufacturers
	(n = 19)	(n = 20)
Legal action	9	16
Package redesign	6	5
Product improvements	5	11
Negotiated settlement	11	10
Enhanced consumer promotion	8	10
Increased trade support	8	8
Total Number of Actions	47	60

Source: Collins-Dodd & Zaichkowsky (1999). National brand responses to brand imitation: Retailers versus other manufacturers. *Journal of Product and Brand Management, 8*(2), p. 99.

delist their brands when confronted with alleged trademark infringement by the retailer's own brand.

Differing Responses to Retailers. Given that two-thirds of the firms had been imitated by retailers, but that only half of them had initiated legal action, responses from these were compared with those of the manufacturers that had taken no prior legal action against retailers. These results are reported in Table 5.2. Generally, those firms that had previously taken legal action against retailers were more willing to take legal action against both major and regional retailers.

Virtually all the manufacturers in the total sample reported that they would be at least somewhat likely to bring legal action against another manufacturer who imitated their products, and they appeared to make no distinction between major and minor manufacturers. However, only 59% thought they would take legal action against a major national retail chain. The proportion that would take legal action fell to only 28% if the manufacturer had a close relationship with the retailer. This supports the premise found in the literature and trade press that manufacturers deal with imitations less aggressively when the imitator is a retailer rather than another manufacturer.

Expectations of Retailers' Reactions. Firms were asked how they thought retailers would respond to their threat of legal action, and these responses were again analyzed by previous litigation experience with retail-

TABLE 5.2
Manufacturers' Propensity for Legal Action

Type of Imitator	% Likely[a]	Legal Action Against Retailers[b]	
		Taken	Never Taken
	(n = 29)	(n = 9)	(n = 20)
Major manufacturer[c]	93	4.7 ± .5	4.4 ± .8
Minor manufacturer	93	4.6 ± .7	4.4 ± .8
Major retailer	59	4.0 ± .7**	3.2 ± 1.2
Regional retailer	48	3.9 ± .8*	3.2 ± 1.1
Local retailer	55	3.9 ± .8	3.4 ± 1.1
Close relationship[d]	28	3.6 ± 1.*	2.8 ± 1.2
Antagonistic relationship	55	3.9 ± .8	3.7 ± 1

[a]Percentage of responses including "likely" and "very likely."
[b]Mean on 5-point scale: 1 (very unlikely) to 5 (very likely).
[c]Major manufacturer significantly different from major retailer ($p < .01$)
[d]Close relationship with retailer significantly different from antagonistic relationship ($p < .01$)
*$p < .1$.
**$p < .05$

Source: Collins-Dodd & Zaichkowsky (1999). National brand responses to brand imitation: Retailers versus other manufacturers. *Journal of Product and Brand Management, 8*(2), p. 100.

ers. Only 20% of the total sample thought retailers would immediately redesign their package in response to legal action. Firms who had previously litigated against retailers were more likely to believe retailers would change their package. These same manufacturers were less likely to expect losing shelf placement priority. They expected less loss of shelf space, and generally were not worried about having their brands delisted by the retailer. These results are listed in Table 5.3.

There also is some speculation that major national brands are engaged in imitating their own brands for partners in retail channels. A marketing article states, "It's hard for brand owners to protest about own-label 'copy-catting' when many of them are actually producing the goods for retailers" (Murphy, 1997). This is true, but most companies that do produce private label products for retailers are not the brand leader. They are likely to be the number two or three in the market, with a need to stay on the right side of the retailer to maintain brand stock levels. Brand leaders can make it on their own. A Kellogg's advertisement declared, "We don't make Corn Flakes for anyone else."

Summary.   In summary, national brand manufacturers should not hesitate to litigate against infringers to maintain their brand equity, even if it is against the entity that actually sells their brand. One major point made by this study is that differentiation is the key to keeping imitators at bay. Constant product and package improvements can leave the imitators scrambling to catch up. It is much more difficult for imitators to deny that they are copying the look and feel of national brands when they follow product and package changes regularly brought to the market by the original brand. There is some evidence that retailers themselves realize that the days of national brand imitation are behind them. Sainsbury, a leading retailer often accused of imitation, has recently adopted a new distinctive private label strategy emphasizing improved product quality (Lee, 1997). National brands should not be complacent about their offerings. A successful look today does not make for a successful look tomorrow. Plans should be in place for constant review and updates of packaging to discourage and keep ahead of imitators.

Additionally, retailers need major brands, just as major brands need retailers (Hoch, 1996). Customers of national brands are less price sensitive and bigger spenders. Hence, retailers do not want to remove national brands from their shelves. So yet another response to prevent imitation is to build strong relationships with the retail trade (Quelch & Harding,

TABLE 5.3
A Comparison of Expected Retailer Response to Legal Action

Expected Retailer Response	*Previous Legal Action Against Retailers*	
	Taken	*Never Taken*
	(n = 9)	*(n = 20)*
Redesign package immediately	2.9 ± 1.6	2.1 ± 1.1
Redesign in 6 months	3.7 ± .8*	2.7 ± 1.4
Lose shelf placement priority	3.0 ± 1.2**	4.0 ± 1.2
Lose shelf space	3.3 ± 1.3	4.0 ± 1
How Much?	18% ± 18%***	46% ± 26%
Brand delisted	1.8 ± .9***	3.1 ± 1.4
Increased distribution by other retailers	2.0 ± .8	2.1 ± 1.1
Other products delisted	2.8 ± 1.6	3.0 ± 1.5

*$p < .05$. **$p < .1$. ***$p < .01$.

Source: Collins-Dodd & Zaichkowsky (1999). National brand responses to brand imitation: Retailers versus other manufacturers. *Journal of Product and Brand Management, 8*(2), p. 101.

1996). When a leading manufacturer is "good friends and business partners" of the retailer, there is likely to be good information exchange and targeted trade spending on promotions, which can build a partnership to reduce the incentive for a retailer imitation. The retailer can build profit margins from increased sales of national brands.

SELECTING A DISTINCT BRAND IDENTITY

Brand Names

Because consumers rely heavily on brand names to identify goods and services for purchase, it is no wonder that competitors want to select a similar-sounding brand name. Honest and ethical competitors, on the other hand, will select a name that is distinctly theirs when they want to stand behind their products in the marketplace. The kind of name selected for identifying one's goods may range from strong distinctive coined letter combinations that have no meaning whatsoever (e.g., ACCENTURE for business consulting), to less strong inherently distinctive words that have a meaning in English but have no reference or relationship to the goods or services associated with the mark (e.g., CREST for toothpaste), to relatively weak inherently distinctive words that are suggestive rather than descriptive of the character or quality of the goods or services (e.g., SUNKIST for oranges), to weak inherently distinctive words that describe but arguably do not clearly describe the character or quality of the goods or services associated with the mark (e.g., GARDENFRESH for frozen vegetables). Whatever type of brand name is desired by the company, the objective is to have the brand name linked to only the goods of the owner of the name. This distinctiveness is accomplished over time through extensive advertising with quality products, service, and image building.

Abstract Versus Figurative Logos and Brand Names

Brand names with descriptive terms are not only more difficult to trademark. They also are less distinct in the mind of the consumer, and have less protection from trademark infringement. As we saw in the 1990s, the focus was on branding, especially on building global brands, and quite a few businesses were built up around helping companies find new unique names for their products or companies. Some of these firms are worldwide, charging hundreds of thousands of dollars to develop brand names that will "work" globally.

Although brand names are central to the identity of the brand, the name itself may not be sufficiently distinctive. The company also must think about how that name is portrayed through its graphics or logo. The attention to the design or logo portraying the brand name is extremely important in the global marketplace, where the identity of the brand must transcend language and even alphabets. The company then can follow different decision trees for names and logos from abstract to figurative.[3] These decision trees by Lencastre and Beirao (2004) are shown in Figs. 5.1 and 5.2.

Apple computers[4] is a good example. The name is Apple, and the logo is a rainbow-colored apple with a bite out of it. The objective of the firm is to have high recall and recognition of their brand identity or name and logo (Fig. 5.3). The creation of a name or logo can be analyzed within this framework. Generally, names harder to pronounce are more difficult to remember. Then there is the initials mania of simple abbreviations, for example, IBM for International Business Machines. Also, there are many spelling abbreviations or acronyms, which have lexical of phonetic proximity with existing words (e.g., Palmolive joins "palm" with "olive"). New words are coined by manipulating the existing lexis such as Swatch from "Swiss

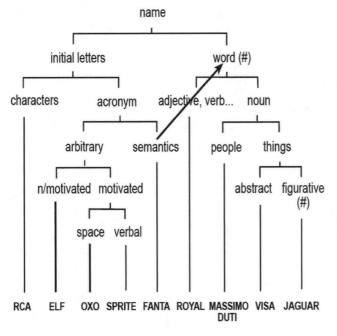

FIG. 5.1.
Decision tree for the brand name choice.
Source:
P. Lencastre & A. F. Beirae (2004). *The figurativeness of brand signs: An empirical research on names and logos memorization.* In 3rd International Conference on research in Advertising, Oslo, Norway, pp. 36–44.

---

[3]There is a body of literature on the interactive effects of pictures and words in advertising starting with Lutz and Lutz, *Journal of Applied Psychology*, August 1977. Researchers have found enhanced processing and recall when relevant images accompany brand names.

[4]Although the Apple name was trademarked by The Beatles, there was little chance for brand confusion across a different category at the time. Also the logo and colors were unique.

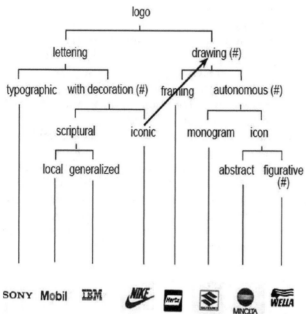

FIG. 5.2. Design tree for the brand logo choice.
Source: P. Lencastre & A. F. Beirae (2004). *The figurativeness of brand signs: An empirical research on names and logos memorization*. In 3rd International Conference on Research in Advertising, Oslo, Norway, pp. 36–44.

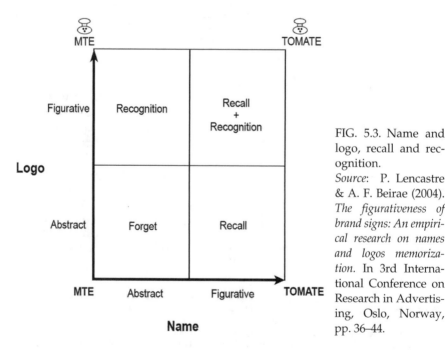

FIG. 5.3. Name and logo, recall and recognition.
Source: P. Lencastre & A. F. Beirae (2004). *The figurativeness of brand signs: An empirical research on names and logos memorization*. In 3rd International Conference on Research in Advertising, Oslo, Norway, pp. 36–44.

Watches." Finally, there are strong symbolic names such as Jaguar. On the left side of Fig. 5.1 are the abbreviations, and then there is a continuum of names from most abstract to most concrete on the far right.

The same search for motivating images inspires the logo creators and the decision tree in Fig. 5.2. On the left side are logos with a dominant lettering component, such as SONY (hence more abstract), and on the right side are more abstract logos that have a dominant drawing component, such as WELLA, and hence are more figurative. The same reasoning is found in the brands MacDonald's, Dove soap, and Turtle Wax. Theories from cognitive psychology and applications from marketing (Henderson & Cote, 1998; MacInnis & Price, 1987) predict that when both the name and the logo are abstract, more forgetting should take place. When both the brand name and corresponding logo are extremely figurative, then both visual recognition and cognitive recall occur. This is shown in Fig. 5.3.

In an empirical study examining 21 prototypes of names and logos along these continua (9 variations in name and 12 variations in logo), Lencastre and Beirao (2004) found that memorization scores increased when they moved from abstract names and logos to figurative names and logos (Fig. 5.4). Therefore, it may be that the most distinctive names and logos are those

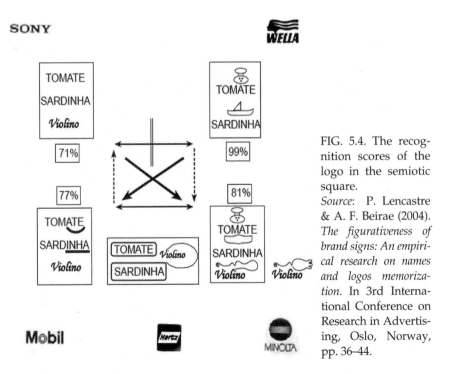

FIG. 5.4. The recognition scores of the logo in the semiotic square.
Source: P. Lencastre & A. F. Beirae (2004). *The figurativeness of brand signs: An empirical research on names and logos memorization*. In 3rd International Conference on Research in Advertising, Oslo, Norway, pp. 36–44.

that use both figurative brand names and logos. These brands also may have trademarks that are more difficult to infringe upon because of their distinctive nature. The understanding of why Apple is better than IBM, and why a stripped IBM is better than a plain IBM is demonstrated through the grid. In semiotic terms, the differences make sense to the consumer.

Unique Brand Names Are Easier to Protect

The amount of time, research, effort, and money that goes into the selection of a good brand name is demonstrated by the classic case of Standard Oil, New Jersey (Enis, 1978). Standard Oil had four other company names (Esso, Enco, Enjay, and Humble) and sought to have only one name to build its identity. Five names also were very expensive to keep up because of regional advertising, duplicate inventories of product and equipment, and continuing legal struggles to protect all the different names.

The company's objectives were to select a brand name that was easily identified on a worldwide basis, available and appropriate for use on a wide range of products, suitable to convey a desirable image for all audiences, and free from legal restrictions on usage. Consumer analysis and research suggested that the new name should have no meaning at all and be very simple.

The search for a new name began with a team of linguistic experts, a leading graphics design firm, a battery of lawyers, and a computer. The computer search generated 10,000 words of four and five letters. More consumer research and testing reduced the number of names to 234. The committee then cut that list to 16 for further testing. Six names, including two existing trademarks (Enco and Enjay), were selected for final testing.

The six names were tested worldwide in 56 languages spoken by more than 5 million people. As a result, the two existing company names were eliminated: Enco, which meant "staled car" in Japanese, and Enjay, which had translation problems in Chinese. Exxon became the clear choice for both the company and brand names. The research indicated that it conveyed the idea of a large, international enterprise, and that it portrayed the petroleum and chemical business in a way that was significantly superior to others. Exxon is easy to pronounce and remember, and it has no meaning in any language.

After developing the name and logo, Exxon spent $100 million to promote its new identity. After just 1 month of advertising that incorporated the new name, 92% of the company's customers and 88% of its competitors' customers were aware of the name change. Furthermore, one-half of those surveyed could cite why the name was changed. Although the total amount spent on this process may seem outrageous, it should be viewed in relation to sales and profits. When a company is earning billions of dollars in profit, a few million in development costs may be viewed strictly as investment dollars.

The strength and uniqueness of the Exxon trademark was subsequently tested in court (*Exxon Corp. v. Texas Motor Exchange of Houston, Inc.*, 1980). The court decision was that the Exxon trademark was infringed upon by the mark "Texxon," but not by the mark "Tex-on." That one little x made all the difference in consumer perception of identification and ownership.

It also may be that there is nothing more distinctive than one's own surname. Consider Donald Trump, for example, and his branding of buildings. However, there may be some trouble from Australia in protecting even your own name. An Englishman born Carl Anderson legally changed his name to Bill Gates and registered a company called Microhard, Down Under (Fotheringham, 2000). It seems Australians love to be independent, and they appear to have little sympathy for big multinationals. The history of successful litigation in Australia against a multinational company based in another country is weak. For example, both Lego and MacDonald's have lost cases in Australian courts, but have won similar stronger cases in other countries.

Innovative Products

If a company is first in the market, it can reap profits by having a brand so well known that all other similar products become known by the original's brand name. Manufacturers often view this as an ideal situation as consumers often end up buying the trademark product unsure whether competing products are of the same quality. The cost of this success is that consumers may use the original brand name as the name for the product category, for example, Thermos for a container to hold hot beverages, Jell-o for gelatine desserts, and Kleenex for tissues. Over time, consumers may not realize that these are brand names.

Taylor and Walsh (2002) called this "genericide," or the threat of the brand name being used as a generic term and subsequently leading to cancellation of the trademark under the Trademark Revision Act. Research by other academics, such as Simonson (1994) and Oakenfull and Gelb (1996), has shown the difficulty courts encounter in deciding to keep such trademarks. This is illustrated by *Anti-Monopoly Inc. v. General Mills Fun Group* (1979). Parker had registered Monopoly as a trademark in 1935. In 1973, Anti-Monopoly was established to produce and sell a game it called Anti-Monopoly. Several surveys were introduced as evidence, including one describing consumer motivation to purchase the product. The argument was that Monopoly had become a generic name. After several appeals, the court ruled that Monopoly had become a word pertaining to the product rather than a brand of board game.

Trademark owners can take steps to prevent genericide from happening. First, they can use the trademark as a descriptive adjective, such as RollarBlade® in-line skates (Goerne, 1992). A trademark identifies a particular brand of some product. Hence, grammatically, it is an adjective. It is not the name of the product itself, and it is not a noun.

Second, a company can make sure that the media uses the trademark properly to ensure that the consumer recognizes the trademark as a trademark. In other words, firms should use the trademark notice in advertising and labeling (e.g., RollarBlade®).

Third, companies need to display the mark with some form of special typographic treatment. Nothing contributes more strongly to the impression that a trademark is generic than its appearance in lowercase letters. Furthermore, special fonts, as seen in Exhibit 5.3, are important to the meaning associated with the brand (Doyle & Bottomly, 2004).

Fourth, if the trademark gets into the dictionary, firms need to make sure it is identified as such. Finally, the trademark name should be extended to other products, as Kimberly-Clark Corp. has done with its Kleenex trademark. This tactic tells consumers that the name represents a whole line of products (Verespej, 1980).

RIO TROPICS	PARADISE ISLAND	JAMMIN TIME!
THIRSTIES	SHORT STOP	JAVA JUICER
Juice n' Java Isle	Thirsty Isle	ROCK N' RIO
JoJo Juicer	Columbia Classics	PARADISE KEY
Daily Pit-Stop	Trango Isle	GOURMET ISLAND
Commuter Pit-Stop	RIO STOP	Paradise Pit Stop
TASTE TROPICS	JOURNEY OASIS	Beverage Time
JOURNEY STOP	Thirsty Tropics	Jolly Juicer
RIO CLASSICS	Java-Joocer	TEXAS KEYS
DAILY BLAST	Juic-n-Java	Jazzy Tropics
JAMAICA JAVA JUICED		

EXHIBIT 5.3   Fonts courtesy of NAME-IT®.

In summary, companies that launch new product brands should actively pursue any misuse of their brand name, differentiate their product on more than brand name, and extend the brand name to other related product categories. Successfully protecting one's brand name involves much more than attention to the brand name. It may involve a whole company strategy.

DIFFERENTIATION THROUGH GESTALT

It is important to have different manufacturers producing the same products to reduce prices paid by the consumer. However, the first manufacturer wants the competition to sell the goods in a different manner to differentiate them from its own. A good example of "fair" play in the marketplace based on total product presentation, or gestalt, is demonstrated in the lawsuit of the *Kellogg Co. v. National Biscuit Co.* (1938) involving shredded wheat. Up until 1912, the National Biscuit Company held the patent on producing shredded wheat in a pillow-shaped biscuit form. In that year, the patent expired, and Kellogg started to produce shredded wheat.

Kellogg put forth great effort to sell their product differently than their competitor, and to associate its own brand name with its new product. This differentiation was accomplished in several ways. First, the standard Kellogg carton contained 15 biscuits, whereas the National brand contained 12. The Kellogg cartons were distinctive in form and color. The Kellogg label was distinct, bearing in bold script the name "Kellogg Whole Wheat Biscuit" or "Kellogg Shredded Whole Wheat Biscuit." It was perhaps impossible not to register the brand as a Kellogg product due to the size and spacing of the name.

The Kellogg biscuit was significantly smaller than that of the National brand, about two-thirds as large. It also had a different appearance. Therefore, consumers could easily tell the difference between the two brands even without the package. In this case, Kellogg took every reasonable precaution to prevent consumer confusion with the original National brand. The stimulus factors of size, color, and contrast were used to establish Kellogg's own brand identity, both on the package and with the product.

UNIQUE COLOR COMBINATIONS ARE EASIER TO PROTECT

Color and brands can be regarded as the modern form of heraldry, in which distinctively colored emblems pertain to a specific individual, family, or community. The first coats of arms, which appeared on battlefields and at tournaments, needed to be seen from a distance, so bright and contrasting colors helped to identify the bearer (Pastoureau, 2001). Brands should be thought of in the same way to distinguish themselves from competitors in the cluttered retail environment. Moreover, we know that colors are remembered more than shapes.

It is very easy to use color to differentiate one's brand. The National Bureau of Standards lists 267 distinctive colors (Woo, 1993). Given this vast array of colors from which to choose, companies should have little difficulty selecting distinctive color combinations to identify themselves or their brands. The color combinations should be limited because designs with a multitude of colors have no specific identity, whereas designs with one or two colors are recalled with ease (Cheskin 1947). Of course, the color combination needs to be congruent with the target population for the product, because the perceived meaning of color does vary across cultures and nationalities (Mortimer, 2004).

Although single colors are most often used in the marketplace, their protection may not be as straightforward as that for distinctive color combinations. A company cannot lay claim to a single hue unless there is overwhelming evidence that the customer identifies only that one brand or company with that particular color. Strong evidence would be that the customers asked for the product by color and that the color is not an integral part of the product for function, but used as a cue for identification.

Although some companies are successful in building identification with one color as an integral quality cue of the product, such as Corning's pink fibreglass or Qualitex's green-gold pressing pads, the package or logo of the product is a more likely place for color identification. This is where distinctive combinations are crucial along with a particular design. If the company selects only a single hue for the package, there is greater likelihood that a similar or even the same hue will be used by subsequent competing brands brought to the marketplace.

Sometimes the defense for using the same color is that the color has somehow become generic for the product category. There is evidence that color does provide certain images when associated with certain names and certain shapes (Klink, 2003), but color as indicative of a product category is not proven. Although some product packages do seem to have the same color, this is more convention than identification.

Color, whether in packaging or product makeup, is an easy cue to use to differentiate brands. Combinations of colors are superior to a single color for identification because protection for a single color is extremely difficult.

DIFFERENTIATION BY SHAPE

Avoiding confusion by shape can be unrealistic in some markets and integral in others. Examples of shape that is standard and difficult to differentiate include cereal boxes, cracker boxes, and pasta boxes. Cardboard boxes are important packaging for some products, and the square shape makes the package very easy to display and stock. In these cases, the design and color are even more critical to a distinctive identity than the shape of the package.

On the other hand goods packaged in aluminum, plastic, or glass are easy to differentiate by shape. The packaging products manufacturer Crown Holdings Inc. creates new and distinctive shapes combined with unusual graphics to ward off counterfeiters and knockoffs. Instead of normal cylinder-shaped beverage, food, or aerosol cans, their technology can create cans in distinctive shapes that become part of the brand image, for example, a keg-shaped can for Heineken Beer (NYSE Magazine, 2005)

The distinctive Coca-Cola bottle was one of the prime factors in warding off store imitation brands. Coca-Cola had been using a 2-liter cylinder-shaped bottle just like those of the store brands. After switching to the uniquely shaped bottle they owned, Coca Cola's sales took off at the expense of their store-brand imitators (Exhibit 5.4).

Shampoo bottles, perfume bottles, and deodorant bottles are but a few product categories in which distinctively designed shapes lead to distinctive brand identity. Manufacturers of perfume put great effort into linking the distinctive shape of the perfume bottle to the brand name. This has been a relatively successful practice over the years. The success is perhaps because perfume is a relatively expensive product, which conveys a strong image and symbolic meaning to the consumer, in contrast to a product

EXHIBIT 5.4 By adopting the trademarked shape for its 2 liter bottle, Coca-Cola was able to differentiate itself from storebrand competitors and regain marketshare.

such as hair shampoo. Shampoo brands may develop distinctively shaped bottles, but competitors readily copy their bottles. They fight off imitators by constantly redoing and updating even their best-selling brands, with few packages being the same for more than a year or two.

Shape may not be enough due to the recycling of bottles. Budweiser was plagued by knockoffs in China because local brewers were refilling "real" bottles. To counteract this practice, Budweiser started using expensive imported foil and technologically advanced heat-sensitive labels, which turned red when cold. Therefore, consumers could easily distinguish the real Bud from a knockoff (*Business Week*, 2005).

USE OF DISCLAIMERS

When copy artists try to avoid passing-off litigation, they sometimes affix a statement that denies any connection to the original good. This is called a disclaimer. Disclaimers may be viewed in two ways. First, any company that thinks it needs to use a disclaimer may be freely admitting that it has infringed on a trademark. Otherwise, why would the company want to emphasize that there was no association? Just the presence of a disclaimer might be thought to imply a guilty party. The second view is that disclaimers are effective in alerting consumers who might mistakenly infer association. The legal rulings on this issue are far from conclusive and seem to vacillate between these two views of disclaimers. However, from the perspective of consumer behavior, research shows fairly conclusively that disclaimers are not a good way to provide consumers with supplemental information (Foxman, Muehling, & Moore, 1988).

Attention and Disclaimers

The effectiveness or ineffectiveness of disclaimers might be explained by the integration of attention and Weber's Law with the concept of advertising. When an advertisement contains many messages or space-consuming words, figures, and pictures, attempts to emphasize any one message are more difficult. To focus attention on the main point in print ads, the advertiser can increase the size of the particular printed message relative to the rest of the copy, supply it with a unique position or appearance, or repeat it several times.

When one wants some aspect of the message to be perceived, that aspect must be viewed relative to the complete presentation. A disclaimer may appear to attract attention when viewed in isolation. However, taken in context, this may not be so.

One case that points out the importance of gaining attention is *Coca Cola Co. v. Dorris* (1970). In this case (Erickson, Dunfee, & Gibson, 1977), customers asked for Coke and received Dorris's Cola. Coke was written on their receipt. The restaurant had signs posted that read: "We do not serve Coke or Coca-Cola. We serve Dorris House Cola." The courts ruled that the signs placed in the restaurant were insufficient to constitute notice of the substitution of another product. They said the customer must be verbally advised that the specified product is not available. In this case, the customer's attention was not directed to the sign. Given the total gestalt of the restaurant, there was no reason for the customer to perceive the sign. The verbal notification would have provided context and contrast for the perception of the disclaimer.

Even if the disclaimer is brought to the attention of the consumer, the prior image and experience of the consumer may be too strong for the disclaimer to have any weight. This was the case with *Elliot Knitwear, Inc.* (1961). Elliot sold a sweater made of "Cashmora," which consumers thought meant cashmere. The Federal Trade Commission found that consumers would have the impression that it was cashmere even though the labels contained a statement about fiber content and a disclaimer of cashmere content. The label "Cashmora" was accompanied by "No Cashmere" in smaller print below. After reading the label, 22% of the viewers surveyed thought the sweater contained cashmere. In this case, the size and position of the disclaimer were overridden by the prior image and association of the word "cashmere" with "cashmora."

The court articulated these phenomena in a case involving the name of a restaurant (*Calamari Fisheries Inc. v. Village Catch Inc.*, 1988). It concluded

> that the use of the disclaimer could ... become a subtle, indirect, and ironic means for the defendants to communicate and reinforce association with the plaintiff. Any disclaimer will appear to some customers to be little more than an attempt to impose a meaningless, hyper technical legal requirement. By coupling the plaintiff's name with the defendant's establishment through litotic presentation of the plaintiff's protected name in a disclaimer, defendants will continue to achieve indirectly what they are proscribed even from suggesting directly. (Fletcher, 1989, p. 850)

Effective Disclaimers

Previous examples have shown that disclaimers usually are ineffective because of Weber's Law relating to size and positioning of the disclaimer. There is a case of a disclaimer effective due to its size, color, and positioning, which all led to good contrast effects. In the case of *CBS Inc. v. Gusto Records, Inc.* (1974), two record companies produced recordings of Charlie Rich. These records had different content, but were virtually the same product with the same name. The Gusto label contained old monograph songs, and CBS wanted to stop the sale and distribution of Gusto in case customers confused the inferior recording with that of the CBS stereo album.

The court ordered a disclaimer be affixed directly over Charlie Rich's photograph. The position of the disclaimer was central to the directing of attention to it. The disclaimer was 3 ½ inches by 1 ½ inches in size. It was therefore large enough to meet Weber's Law of threshold effects and to be perceived in the context of the record album, which was roughly a foot square. Finally, the decal was bright orange with black ink lettering. The color of the decal grabbed the attention of the customer, especially in contrast to the album background. These perceptual factors of size, color, positioning, and contrast likely led to a successful disclaimer perceived by the customer. The customer likely would not have perceived the same disclaimer in a dark color on a smaller label placed on the back of the album.

Ineffective Disclaimers

Unfortunately, most disclaimers follow the example of *John B. Stetson Co. v. Stephen L. Stetson Co. Ltd.* (1942). In this case, the courts stipulated a disclaimer to be put on Stephen Stetson's hats and used in its advertising. The decree provided that in any advertising done by Stephen Stetson, the words "Never Connected in Any Way" should be printed in letters substantially larger and in bolder type than any printing above or below it. An exception was made for the linings and labels inside caps or hats, where the disclaimer could be printed curved upward immediately adjacent to the other part of the label and in letters of the same size and boldness as the other words.

Although the court had good intentions, Stephen Stetson was adept at rendering the disclaimer totally ineffective. Over time, the disclaimer became part of the label's background design to the label and was virtually lost in any advertising. The disclaimer appeared on the hats as the name "Stephen L. Stetson" in headline type on the entire first line, the corporate name and address in large type on the bottom lines, the disclaimer surrounded by ornamental scroll, and the words "Never Connected" printed in letters one-sixth the size of the name. In the display ads, the name "Stephen L. Stetson" appeared in huge type five times and once in the corporate name, whereas the disclaimer was tucked away obscurely in a margin or corner.

Several perceptual factors accounted for the ineffectiveness of the disclaimer: figure and ground, size, context, and primacy versus recency. The disclaimer was the background, not the figure or center of attention. In fact, it looked like a decoration. The disclaimer was so much smaller than the rest of the print that it probably was below the perceptual threshold level of the consumer. It also was buried in the middle of the text, rendering neither a primacy nor recency effect.[5]

---

[5]It is well-known in cognitive psychology that those items presented first and last in a string of items are better remembered. This is why bookend advertisements are sought after when a series of commercials are shown between programming.

An even more obvious ineffective disclaimer involves the case in which it is hidden from view. In *Ford Motor Company; Jaguar Cars, Ltd.; and Aston Martin Lagonda Ltd. v. Lloyd Design Corporation* (2001), the object of the suit was a car floor mat bearing the names of famous car brands, such as Jaguar, Mustang, and Lincoln, produced by Lloyd Design. Here, the disclaimer was on the underside of the floor mat and clearly not visible when the product was used. The famous marks were on the top of the floor mat and used as the primary selling point by Lloyd. Lloyd claimed its floor mats were of a better quality, and this argument originally stood up in court. However, the court turned back the case to the parties involved, with new instructions for appeal.

Summary. Even if disclaimers are the center of attention, the a priori association may be so complete in the mind of the consumer that very little can be done to distinguish the original brand. In *Vidal Sassoon Inc. v. Beverly Sassoon and Slim Lines, Inc.* (1982), Harold Kassarjian, the noted Fellow of Consumer Behavior, stated in his declaration:

> Based on my knowledge of information processing and consumer perception of advertising and labels, my conclusion is that a written or oral disclaimer of association with Vidal Sassoon would not be an effective solution. Many potential customers would simply be oblivious to a disclaimer, or ignore it. Others would focus on or notice the words "Vidal Sassoon" and conclude that Sassoon produced the product. Still other consumers would misperceive a disclaimer as actually an endorsement of the product by Vidal Sassoon, Inc. and Beverly Sassoon. Finally, a group of consumers might perceive a disclaimer as it is intended to be understood. Nevertheless, the risks of placing a disclaimer on the product are great. There is greater probability that the message will be ignored or misunderstood than there is that it will be perceived as intended. It is even possible that a majority of consumers would misperceive or ignore any disclaimer. (pp. 6–7)

Given the aging of the population and the increased need for reading glasses, it is likely more and more consumers will not be able to read disclaimers, even when they are brought to their attention, while shopping in the marketplace.

How to Set Up Disclaimers

Guidelines for disclaimers are put forth for industry by the Federal Trade Commission in the United States. These are not laws, but self-administered guidelines. There are many deficiencies in the disclosure program due to the information processing limitations of consumers (see Stoltman, Morgan, & Muehling, 1991, for a complete discussion), but the first step is to implement the recommended procedure for disclosures or disclaimers.

Television Disclaimers. The Federal Trade Commission (1979) has an enforcement policy statement with regard to "clear and conspicuous" disclosures in television advertising. The words "clear" and "conspicuous" refer to technical factors (e.g., size of letters, duration of disclosure) used in presenting the disclosure to a television audience, as well as the substance of the individual disclosure. The commission believes that the following standards should be met for a television disclosure to be deemed clear and conspicuous:

1. The disclosure should be presented simultaneously in both the audio and video portions of the television advertisement.
2. The video portion of the disclosure must contain letters of sufficient size so that it can be seen and read easily on all television sets, regardless of picture tube size, that are commercially available for the consuming public.
3. The video portion of the disclosure should contain letters of a color or shade that readily contrast with the background. The background should consist of only one color of shade.
4. During the audio portion of the disclosure, no other sounds, including music, should be presented.
5. The video portion of the disclosure should appear on the screen for a sufficient duration to enable it to be completely read by the viewer.
6. The audio and video portions of the disclosure should immediately follow the specific sales representation to which they relate, and should be presented each time the representation is presented during the advertisement. In cases wherein a disclosure is required, but is not linked to a specific representation, it should appear in immediate conjunction with the major sales theme of the advertisement. (Federal Trade Commission 1979, pp. 114–115)

Print Disclaimers. Getting similar messages across to consumers in print requires that the size of the message be specifically detailed in relation to the context of the package or advertisement size. This is another application of Weber's Law and the relative size of the disclaimer in relation to its context. One example among print messages is health warnings that currently are part of alcohol labeling in the United States (Code of Federal Regulations, 1992). The guidelines are as follows:

1. The warning must be stated on the brand label or separate front label or on a back or side label separate and apart from all other information.
2. The warning must be on a contrasting background.
3. The words "GOVERNMENT WARNING" must be in bold letters and capitals. The remainder of the warning must not appear in bold type.

4. The warning statement shall appear in a maximum number of characters per inch as follows:

a. Maximum of 40 characters when type size is 1 mm
b. Maximum of 25 characters when type size is 2 mm
c. Maximum of 12 characters when type size is 3 mm.

5. The size of type shall be proportional to the size of the container, as follows:

a. Containers of 8 ounces or less, a minimum of 1 mm
b. Containers between 8 ounces and 101 ounces, a minimum of 2 mm
c. Containers larger than 101 ounces, a minimum of 3 mm.

6. The labels must be firmly affixed so that neither water nor other solvents will remove them.

The Canadian Department of Consumer and Corporate Affairs (1990) also has outlined some very general rules about print disclaimers. Canadian guidelines address content, placement, format, symbols used, symbol placement, and size of the fine print. They generally take into account the effects of size and placement of the disclaimer and their effect on the consumer's perception of the information. The usual placement of disclaimers in small print at the bottom of a message usually ensures the very opposite results of the reason for using a disclaimer in the first place. If the information in the disclosure is intended to be read and absorbed, it should be included in the main part of the message in a format likely to be read and understood, and not at the bottom of the message in fine print.

One of the reasons given for the use of disclaimers is that advertisers believe they can avoid charges of misleading advertising by using them. This was the case in *National Hockey League v. Pepsi-Cola Canada Ltd.* (1992). Pepsi was accused of using the National Hockey League (N.H.L.) in its soda pop promotion without the League's authorization. Pepsi included a disclaimer in its television advertising, which was not perceived by 99% of those exposed to the advertisement during a mall-intercept marketing research study. Pepsi also included the disclaimer in fine print on the back of its contest entry form. Consumer research showed that 68% of those surveyed thought that the N.H.L. was either sponsoring or associated with the Pepsi promotion. The judge read the disclaimer (with his reading glasses) and announced that anyone carefully reading the disclaimer could not possibly be confused as to any association or sponsorship. The problem was that the vast majority of consumers never read the disclaimer or had any idea there even was a disclaimer present.

SUMMARY

Avoiding a competitor's imitation is not an easy task. To keep ahead of brand imitators, leading brands need a distinct and sometimes changing identity. Manufacturers must think seriously about the prevention of trademark infringement when developing their brands and products. Because only successful brands, such as product category leaders, usually are copied, it may be difficult to remain aware of the possibility of infringement during development. It is rare to have a crystal ball that would tell of the brand's future success. In creating distinctive brands, the following major areas need to be kept in mind:

1. Brand names in a product class should be unique in terms of sound, pronunciation, spelling, and meaning. A company should use the brand name before the name of the product category to reinforce the brand name to customers. For example, the manufacturer should refer to Breton crackers in advertising, not just Breton's.

2. Color combinations are superior to single colors for brand identification. The protection of color combinations in the courtroom is much easier than the protection of a single color.

3. The gestalt or the total look of the brand, whether it be the product consumed or just the package, is important to distinctive identity. The size, color, design or picture, brand name, and shape all combine to give the consumer's eye the "look" of the brand. Distinctly different brand names may not be sufficient to form distinctly different identities in the mind of the consumer. Consumers purchase from many product categories, not primarily by brand name, but by the "look" of the product.

4. Unique shapes of containers, packages, or products help to create a distinctive identity. These unique shapes might be best coupled, where possible, with distinctive colored labels for identification.

5. The use of disclaimers by a company to provide distinction is misguided. If a company even thinks it needs to use a disclaimer, it is likely to be infringing on another's trademark or trade dress. Brands should speak for themselves, not the fine print.

This century may bring a new age of defense against imitators. New developments in nanotechnology are making it easier and more affordable to embed identities into products. Holographic three-dimensional labels and special ink, as used in currency, are used currently to identify and distinguish genuine articles from their imitators. Pfizer will put radiofrequency ID tags on all Viagra sold in the United States so it can track the real drugs from the laboratory to the consumer (*Business Week,* 2005). Just as technology has helped the counterfeiters to copy well-known brands easily, so technology also may make it easier for consumers to identify originals.

REFERENCES

Anti-counterfeiting: Shaping a brand. (2005, March–April). *NYSE Magazine*, p. 11.

Anti-Monopoly Inc. v. General Mills Fun Group, 611 F. 2d 296, 301 (9th Cir. 1979).

Burns, G. (1995, June 26). A fruit loop by any other name. *Business Week*, 73–76.

Calamari Fisheries Inc. v. Village Catch Inc., 698 F. Supp. 994, 997, 8 USPQ2d 153, 1954 (D Mass 1988).

Canadian Department of Consumer and Corporate Affairs. (1990). *Asterisks, disclaimers, and other fine print.* Misleading Advertising Bulletin, 4. Director of Investigation and Research, Competition Act, Ottawa Canada.

CBS Inc. v. Gusto Records Inc. 403 F. Supp. 447 (U.S. District Court for the Middle District of Tennessee 1974).

Cheskin, L. (1947). *Colors: What they can do for You.* New York: Liveright Publishing Corporation.

Coca Cola Company v. Dorris. 311 F. Supp. 287 (E.D. Ark. 1970).

Collins-Dodd, C., & Zaichkowsky, J. L. (1999). National brand responses to brand imitation: Retailers versus other manufacturers. *Journal of Product and Brand Management, 8*(2), 96–105.

Conopco, Inc. d/b/a Chesebrough-Pond's USA Co. v. May Department Stores Co. and Venture Stores, Inc., 46 F3d 1556, 1565 (Fed Cir 1994), and 115 S Ct 1724 (1994). USA.

Design-infringement suit is filed against island maid. (1995, May 16). *Wall Street Journal*, B4.

Doyle, J. R., & Bottomly, P. (2004). Font appropriateness and brand choice. *Journal of Business Research, 57*(8), 873–880.

Elliot Knitwear Inc. 59 F.T.C. 893, 904 911 (1961).

Enis, B. M. (1978). Exxon marks the spot. *Journal of Advertising Research, 18*(6), 7–12.

Erickson, M. L., Dunfee, T. W., & Gibson, F. F. (1977). *Antitrust and trade regulation.* Columbus, OH: Grid Inc.

Exxon Corp. v. Texas Motor Exchange of Houston, Inc., 628 F. 2d 500 (5th Cir. 1980).

Fakes. (2005, February 7). *Business Week*, 54–64.

Federal Trade Commission. (1979, June). Consumer information remedies policy session. FTC Bureau of Consumer Protection Washington DC.

Finch, A. C. (1996). When imitation is the sincerest form of flattery: Private label products and the role of intention in determining trade dress infringement. *The University of Chicago Law Review, 63*(3), 1243–1276.

Fletcher, A. L. (1989). Trademark infringement and unfair competition in courts of general jurisdiction. *The Trademark Reporter, 79*, 794–882.

Ford Motor Company; Jaguar Cars, Ltd., and Aston Martin Lagonda Ltd. v. Lloyd Design Corporation, U.S. App. LEXIS 23668; 22 Fed. Appx. 464 (2001).

Fotheringham, A. (2000, September 23). Australia's gates still trying to nail down first billion. *Globe and Mail*, O6.

Foxman E. R., Muehling, D. D., & Moore, P. A. (1988). Disclaimer footnotes in ads: Discrepancies between purpose and performance. *Journal of Public Policy and Marketing, 7,* 127–137.

Goerne, C. (1992, March 2). Rollerblade reminds everyone that its success is not generic. *Marketing News,* p. 1.

Heckman, J. (1999, August 30). Copycat cutting. *Marketing News,* p. 13.

Henderson, P. W., & Cote, J. A. (1998, April). Guidelines for selecting or modifying logos. *Journal of Marketing, 62,* 14–30.

Hoch, S. J. (1996). How should national brands think about private labels? *Sloan Management Review, 37*(2), 89–102.

Hollinger, P. (1997, March 25). Confusion reigns over "Lookalikes." *Financial Times.*

John B. Stetson Co. v. Stephen L. Stetson Co. Ltd. 14 F. Supp. 74 (S.D.N.Y. 1936). Modified and affirmed 85 F.2d 586 (2d Cir.), cert. denied 299 U.S. 605, 57 S. Ct. 230, 81 L. Ed. 445: 128 F.2d 981 (1942).

Kapferer, J. N. (1995a). Stealing brand equity: Measuring perceptual confusion between national brands and "copycat" own-label products. *Marketing and Research Today* (May), 96–103.

Kapferer, J. N. (1995b). Brand confusion: Empirical study of a legal concept. *Psychology and Marketing, 12*(6), 551–568.

Kapferer, J. N. (2004). *The new strategic brand management.* London, Great Britain: Kogan Page.

Kellogg Co. v. National Biscuit Co., 305 U.S. 111, 83 L. Ed. 73, 59 S. Ct. 109 (1938).

Klink, R. R. (2003). Creating meaningful brands: The relationship between brand name and brand mark. *Marketing Letters, 14*(3), 143–157.

Lee, J. (1997, April 24). Sainsbury ends copycat battle. *Marketing,* p. 1.

Lencastre, P., & Beirao, A. F. (2004). *The figurativeness of brand signs: An empirical research on names and logos memorization.* In conference proceedings, 3rd International Conference on Research in Advertising, Oslo, Norway, pp. 36–44.

Lutz, K. A., & Lutz, R. J. (1977). The effects of interactive imagery and learning: Application to advertising. *Journal Of Applied Psychology, 62,* 493–498.

MacInnis, D. J., & Price, L. L. (1987, March). The role of imagery in information processing: Review and extensions. *Journal of Consumer Research, 13,* 473–491.

Marketing. (1994, March 3). Brand managers back lookalikes crackdown.

Meyers, H. M., & Lubliner, M. J. (1998). *The marketer's guide to successful package design.* Chicago: American Marketing Association, NTC Business Books.

Mortimer, M. (2004, October 6). Branding and colour: The colour of money. *Brand Strategy,* p. 24.

Murphy, C. (1997, June 5). Sleeping with the enemy. *Marketing,* p. 20.

National Hockey League v. Pepsi-Cola Canada Ltd./Pepsi-Cola Canada Ltd. No. C902104 (Supreme Court of British Columbia 1992, June 2).

Oakenfull, G., & Gelb, B. (1996, September/October). Research-based advertising to preserve brand equity but avoid genericide. *Journal of Advertising Research, 36,* 65–72.

Office of the Federal Register National Archives and Records Administration. (1992). *Code of Federal Regulations: Alcohol, Tobacco Products, and Firearms, 27,* p. 204.

Package-infringement suit won against Honolulu firm. (1995, May 19). *Wall Street Journal,* A4.

Pastoureau, M. (2001). *Heraldry: Its origins and meaning*. London: Thames and Hudson Ltd.

Quelch, J. A., & Harding, D. (1996, January–February). Brands versus private labels: Fighting to win. *Harvard Business Review, 99*–109.

Rogers, D. (1997, July 10). Puffin redesign ends copy row. *Marketing*, p. 3.

Rosendahl, I., & Brookman, F. (1994, October 24). Too close for comfort. *Drug Topics, 138*(20), p. 77.

Simonson, I. (1994, Fall). Trademark infringement from the buyer's perspective: Conceptual analysis and measurement implications. *Journal of Public Policy and Marketing, 13,* 181–194.

Stoltman, J., Morgan, F., & Muehling, D. D. (1991). Televised advertising disclosures: A review and synthesis. In R. Holman (Ed.), Proceedings of the 1991 Conference of the American Academy of Advertising (p. 16).

Stuart, L. (1997, March). Prryhic victory hits brands the hardest. *Marketing Week, 19,* 28.

Taylor, C., & Walsh, M. G. (2002). Legal strategies for protecting brands from genericide: Recent trends in evidence weighted in court cases. *Journal of Public Policy and Marketing, 21*(1), 160–167.

Verespej, M. A. (1980, April 14). When is a trademark not a trademark? *Industry Week,* pp. 69–73.

Vidal Sassoon Inc. v. Beverly Sassoon and Slim Lines, Inc., No. 82-2916 WMP (United States District Court, Central District of California 1982).

Woo, J. (1993, February 25). Trademark law protects colors, court rules. *Wall Street Journal,* B1.

Woo, J. (1994, January 5). Product's color alone can't get trademark protection. *Wall Street Journal,* B5.

Woo, J. (1994, October 7). Vaseline ruling deals blow to big brands. *Wall Street Journal,* B10.

Testing for Brand Imitation

RESEARCH IS IMPERFECT BY IMPLICIT DEFINITION

One thing to remember about any research study is that it will never be perfect. Even when the most experienced researchers work collectively without any time constraints or pressure, flaws appear only after the work is complete and the results are studied. Research is undertaken to discover, and in that process of discovery, under incomplete information, researchers learn where to take their next inquiry. Therefore, there is little chance that research done for litigation purposes, often by a sole researcher sworn to secrecy about the project, can produce perfect work under considerable time constraints. This needs to be understood by all parties involved before the research is undertaken.

Professional people will do the best job possible given their information and time limitations. Market research by highly trained professionals rarely has "fatal" flaws. However, it almost always has minor flaws that could be improved. Arguing over minor flaws is a favorite tactic of litigation lawyers, who try to divert attention from major issues and discredit the professionals who did the research. Minor flaws also might be used by judges to devalue the consumer research so they may be more comfortable making a ruling based on their own personal opinion of the evidence before them. Therefore, expert witnesses hired to carry out litigation research need to have a knowledgeable background of their discipline and how the legal system works, as well as an equal load of self-confidence (Weiss, 1990).

A survey of field research submitted in trademark cases shows that in only 14 of 67 instances was the research accorded substantial weight (Jacoby, 1985). In most of the cases, the court did not document why the consumer research did not play a major role. It seems that consumer data collected for cases of trademark infringement play a very uncertain role. Part of this uncertainty may be the result of blurring between public opinion poll research methodology and market research methodology. Fortunately, there is some evidence that courts are becoming more accepting of consumer research as they are becoming better informed about the issue of nonprobability samples (Gastwirth, 2003).

Research in trademark infringement is based in marketing. Marketing research, at the consumer level, usually relies on consumers' reactions to marketing stimuli. The aim of the research is to measure the consumers' perceptions and reactions to the product, service, or communication strategy under very controlled conditions. The techniques and methods used to measure reactions usually are experimental in nature and carried out with relatively small samples, which means that the evaluator of such research needs a solid grounding in both experimental design and survey methodology.

Public opinion polls, on the other hand, usually require random sampling of the population in some proportional representative manner so that predictions of public sentiment can be made. The criteria and methods used for public opinion polling are different from the criteria and methods used in consumer research for marketing purposes. The two different areas require different tools from the social scientist.

This point is important because the courts, legal scholars, and attorneys have erroneously labeled all field research as "surveys" or "public opinion polls." In fact, most research done in trademark infringement cases rarely consists of surveys or public opinion polls. Data from relevant consumers usually are gathered to support or provide evidence of the relevant points in each case of trademark infringement. The type of data and techniques used to generate the data will vary by the nature of the issue at hand.

HOW LARGE A SAMPLE?

The first question usually asked in designing research is "How many people do I need to sample?" This is an important question because the answer affects the cost of the research and the time taken to complete the data collection. The number of subjects needed for any survey or study depends on the desired accuracy of the results, how many subgroups need to be analyzed, the question being asked, the critical effect or the number of people who need to be confused, and how difficult it is to find those confused people. A misunderstanding of the statistical power or ability of the study to detect real differences often leads to wastes in time, money, and effort in sampling too many or too few people to make the study meaningful. A misunderstanding of critical effect may lead to undersampling if the critical effect is very small and oversampling if the critical effect is relatively large. (For a detailed explanation of these concepts, see Chumura Kraemer & Thiemann, 1987.)

Critical Effect

The critical effect relates to the central question: What percentage of consumers out of what size market need to be confused for the court to rule that confusion occurs beyond a reasonable doubt in the marketplace. A "substantial" or "appreciable" number of consumers need not be a majority of the total consumers. This distinction may be crucial where a study shows a low percentage of confused customers that can be extrapolated over a large, relevant "universe" of potential customers. For example, in the case of *Humble Oil and Refining Co. v. American Oil Co.* (1969), the court indicated that 11% of a national market comprising millions of consumers constitutes a very large number of potentially confused consumers. Another example would be the billion-dollar soft drink industry, in which 1% confusion might mean millions of dollars and people. In these cases, the critical effect may be very small, and larger samples are needed to find that important 1%.

In cases for which the critical effect is predetermined to be very large (e.g., more than 20% of consumers are perceived as necessary evidence to indicate likelihood of confusion) then smaller samples would suffice. The number or percentage of consumers who need to be confused with respect to the object of the investigation is a matter that seems to vary widely in the courts. The courts may do some of the calculation intuitively, as figures of 8.5% (*Grotrian, Helfferich, Schultz Steinweg Nach v. Steinway and Sons*, 1975), 11% (*Jockey International Inc. v. Burkard*, 1975), and 15% to 20% (*RJR Foods, Inc. v. White Rock Corp.*, 1978) all have been found to indicate confusion among the consuming public.

Another issue with respect to the required level of confusion is that there may be a double standard concerning harm to consumers and their costs, as compared with harm to corporations and their profits. In many cases involving frequently purchased branded goods, in which the consumer easily interchanges brands under low involvement, more harm attributable to consumer confusion or passing-off may be done to the company than to the consumer. That is, the original company suffers loss of sales, but the consumer is not perceived by the courts as being harmed. When the consumer suffers no threat of personal injury or incurs no apparent costs, the courts might require a higher level of confusion documented in the marketplace. However, when consumers suffer obvious harm or personal injury because of their confusion or perceptions of association, the courts may judge a smaller percentage to be the criterion. The courts may thus have a double standard with respect to protecting the consumer and protecting the large company. When it is evident that consumers are greatly harmed by inferior products, perhaps a smaller percentage will justify confusion. When the company is mainly harmed by lost sales and there seems to be little or no harm done to consumers, the courts may want a higher level of confusion to justify action.

Significance Level

The second point to make about sample sizes is with respect to significance level, or the probability that the outcome occurred by chance rather than confusion. The significance level usually is reported as a p value less than .01, .05, or .10. A p value less than .01 means that the odds are 1 in 100 that the finding occurred by chance. The usual significance level accepted in social science research is 1 in 20, or a p value less than .05. However, 1 in 10, or a p value less than .10, may be adequate depending on the problem and the sample size. Clearly, 1 in 100 or a p value less than .01 leads to greater confidence in the outcome. It exhibits very strongly that the results are highly unlikely to have happened by chance.

The Adequacy of Small Samples

An analysis of prior court cases gives some indication of the critical effect or necessary number of people who must be confused to confirm the presence of infringement. Table 6.1 provides an estimate of how many subjects are needed to achieve the criterion level using different probability levels and confidence intervals in achieving that result. The 99% power level may be interpreted as close to certainty.

The research design needs more participants when the confusion of a small percentage of consumers is an important consideration. When a large percentage of customers need to be confused, a smaller sample will suffice. Gathering data from large samples, say 500, when the criterion is 20% confusion, leads the researcher to be extremely confident that more than enough people have participated in the research to find that level of confusion.

Just what the criterion for confusion should be varies with the issue. However, Preston (1990) noted that a likely criterion is 20% to 25% or more. Given the 20% baseline, sample sizes at different power levels are listed in Table 6.2.

However, the determination of sample size is derived from many factors, and the exact criterion level for confusion may not be known before data collection.

Another important issue with respect to sample size is the number and size of subgroups involved in the data analysis. It may be important to show an overall level of confusion, and then look more closely at consum-

TABLE 6.1
Prior Passing-Off Cases: Projected Sample Sizes
Needed Over Different Power Levels

Case	Research Results % Confused in Case	Sample Size Needed to Achieve Power Level One-Tailed Test[a] at $p < .01$[b] ($p < .05$)[c]		
		99%[d] ~N[e]	90% ~N	80% ~N
Grotrian, et. al. v. Steinway & Sons (1975)	8.5	3000 (2200)	1800 (1200)	1400 (800)
Jockey International v. Burkard (1975)	11	1776 (1294)	1069 (704)	824 (508)
RJR Foods v. White Rock (1978)	15-20	949–528 (692–385)	571–318 (376–210)	441–246 (272–152)
NFL v. Delaware (1977)	19-20	587–528 (428–385)	353–318 (233–210)	273–246 (169–152)
Smith v. Sturm, Ruger (1985)	39	130 (110)	79 (63)	57 (48)
Federal Glass Co. v. Corning Glass Works (1969)	52	70 (50)	45 (35)	35 (20)
International Milling v. Robin Hood Popcorn (1956)	61.5	45 (32)	28 (18)	21 (14)
NHL v. Pepsi-Cola Canada (1992)	68	34 (25)	19 (14)	15 (11)

NFL, National Football League; NHL, National Hockey League
[a]Tests only for similarity, not differences.
[b]One in 100 this will occur by chance.
[c]One in 20 this will occur by chance.
[d]Power to find a significant result.
[e]Sample size needed to test at this level.

TABLE 6.2
Sample Sizes Required at Different Confusion Criteria and Power Levels

Confusion Criterion	Power at $p < .05$		
	95%	90%	80%
20%	265	210	152
30%	114	91	66

ers with a similar grouping characteristic. For example, if there is some question whether older people would be more susceptible to confusion than younger people, sufficient numbers of consumers in the different age groups are needed. Similarly, if comparisons between males and females are important, the researcher would want to make sure the power within each subgroup was sufficient to determine whether there were any intragroup differences.

Incomplete Questionnaires

A further practical consideration is the problem of incomplete questionnaires. It is not uncommon for a respondent to start answering the questions of a study, and then decide not to finish the interview. If there is a self-completion part, some critical questions may be deliberately omitted by the respondent because he or she judged it to be irrelevant or too personal. Sometimes incomplete questionnaires are not useful because critical questions are not answered. In these cases, the whole questionnaire might have to be removed from the tabulation. This is a common problem in research, particularly in North America. A colleague received a frantic phone call from a data analysis company in Japan telling him that 6% to 7% of the questionnaires filled out by the American sample were not complete. The nonresponse from the matched Japanese sample was only 1%. The colleague had to tell the company not to worry, that a 6% to 7% nonresponse for North America actually was very good. Sample sizes should be sufficient to allow for up to 10% percent deletion of possible incomplete questionnaires.

"Don't Know" Responses

"Don't know" responses are a peculiar problem. On one hand, "don't know" may reflect confusion. On the other hand, it may mean "don't care." "Don't know" also may reflect its literal meaning. The researcher may want to delete these responses or analyze them separately to avoid criticism and show conservatism in data analysis. By deleting persons who state they do not know, one is left with a sample of people who do have a certain perception of the problem at hand. They should represent people confident in their judgments. An alternative method might be for the researcher to tabulate the results in a manner that both includes and separates the "don't know" respondents to give a complete picture of the data analyses.

In a study by Leifeld (2003), the data showed very different results for confusion of branded goods when the respondents were allowed "don't know" as a response. Using three experiments involving actual purchase behavior of branded goods, consumers were shown pictures of products and asked for the identification of the manufacturer or owner of the trademark. He found that the number of "don't know" responses dropped when the consumers were given "strong filters," or more detailed questions concerning their thoughts about the brand, which eliminated guessing from the responses. He offers that in Western culture people are very cooperative with research, so they search their memory for images similar to the product/brand being shown to them. He speculates that these produced images may not be related to the task at hand.

WHO SHOULD BE SURVEYED?

Perhaps even more important than the number of people sampled is the type of people used in the research. Decisions in both Federal Trade Commission Act and Lanham Act cases dealing with consumer perceptions of advertising content have held that to determine conveyed meanings, there is no need for samples to be national probability samples, to include only those who use the product or have characteristics indicating the probability of such usage, or to include only those exposed to the media running the advertisement (Preston, 1990). The explanation is that the sheer perception of what a message is saying should not differ from one sort of person to another. However, the extent to which the preceding statements are generalizable to all consumer research does depend on the situation. There are cases in which the courts have not been inclined to accept consumer research that contains nonusers of the product.

Users Versus Purchasers

In most cases in which the judicial system ignored or gave little weight to the study, the criticism concerned the type of people used in the sample. In *Jenkins Bros. v. Newman Hender & Co. Ltd.* (1959), the issue was a diamond-shaped design of a valve used in industrial settings. Jenkins took a survey of plant supervisors and operation and maintenance personnel who were users, but not necessarily purchasers, of the product. The results of the survey were judged to be inconclusive and generally indicated that users of valves identified them by shape or type rather than by the design in question. This case is in contrast to the case of *Price Pfister, Inc. v. Mundo Corp.* (1989), in which the issue also was shape, but the product was faucets. In this case, purchasers of faucets were interviewed, not just users. Faucets are likely to be bought by homebuilders, whereas the users of faucets are not likely to be purchasers unless they build their own homes. Thus, purchasers are sometimes different from users, but both have perceptions relevant to the issue.

Limited Users

In *Mead Data Central Inc. v. Toyota Motor Sales, U.S.A., Inc.* (1988), the issue was the name LEXIS versus LEXUS. A survey showed that 76% of lawyers and 26% of accountants identified LEXIS as a computerized search service. Indeed, it is a service used mainly by lawyers. However, only 2% of the general public correctly identified it as such. The point is that the LEXUS car market was not limited to lawyers and accountants, but to the general public within a certain income bracket. Using a sample of lawyers and accountants to identify the name did not represent all potential car purchasers.

Unlikely Purchasers

To be more precise about potential purchasers, one may need to identify past purchasers, intended purchasers, or those who might influence purchase decisions (Reiner, 1983). Identifying these subtle differences in the sample might ward off criticism about the type of person used in the research. One of the most widely cited cases concerning inappropriate samples is *Amstar Corp. v. Domino Pizza, Inc.* (1980). Both sides presented research studies, which were judged to be lacking. The court suggested that the relevant sample for purchasers of Domino's pizzas would be single, male, college-aged persons. The court ruled that the perceptions of middle-aged females with respect to pizza would lend no relevant information on which an expert could rely when testifying about marketing choices of potential purchasers of pizza products.

Specific Users

The complexity of the issue is exemplified in *Weight Watchers International Inc. v. The Stouffer Corp.* (1990). Weight Watchers alleged that Stouffers' advertising represented an endorsement of the Stouffer product. Weight Watchers had to prove that the public believed it had approved or endorsed Stouffer products. Stouffers' advertising did not use the Weight Watchers' trademark to designate its own product, but instead used it on "compatibility advertising or advertising about the fit with a competitor's product or service." The judge found fault with the research of both sides in this case.

The research of both Stouffers and Weight Watchers focused on individuals who bought and ate frozen food and/or who had tried to lose weight. The alleged problem was that neither survey focused on people who ate diet or low-calorie frozen foods, or even people who were trying to lose weight through dieting as opposed to exercise. Given this reasoning by the court, some of the respondents may not have been in the market for diet food of any kind, so the samples of both studies were judged to be too broad.

The theoretical rationale is that respondents who are not potential customers may well be less likely than potential customers to be aware of and to make relevant distinctions when reading advertisements. The judge ruled that the research methodology was so flawed he had no alternative but to assess the advertisements personally. However, a highly informed sample of one is never better at judging perception than a naive group of "average" consumers.

Summary

The type of people who constitute the universe in a trademark litigation study is defined in terms of the following characteristics (Sorensen, 1983):

   1. *Relevance.* The beliefs, perceptions, attitudes, and behaviors of individuals are of interest to the case at hand. Generally, the subject in a consumer research study of brand imitation should be either a purchaser or a user of the good or service. There are instances in which the user may not be the purchaser or the purchaser may not be the user.
   2. *Accessibility.* The relevant individuals should be available for an interview. It is not always necessary for a random probability sample to be used in consumer research.
   3. *Identifiability.* The relevant individuals must be identified by certain characteristics, which can be used to screen qualified respondents without alerting them to the purpose of the research.
   4. *Cooperation.* The relevant individuals must permit themselves to be interviewed about the object of investigation in sufficient numbers.

DIFFERENT METHODS OF CONSUMER RESEARCH

Early Work From Psychology

Early work on testing for trademark infringement is found in Paynter's (1920) work, A Psychological Study of Trademark Infringement; and Rogers' (1919) work, An Account of Some Psychological Experiments on the Subject of Trademark Infringement. These studies relied on recall and recognition measures based in psychology and psychometric methods to test for confusion among trademarks, mainly by brand names and the sounds of the names when provided. One piece of research by Rogers (1919) sought to build an index of confusion based on sounds, and to relate the index back to actual decisions in infringement cases (Table 6.3).

The first column of Table 6.3 shows whether the court found infringement or not. The second column is the original mark, and the third col-

TABLE 6.3
The Grades and Probable Errors of the Word "Chero-Cola":
Each of the Five Infringements and Four Noninfringements

| Decision | Trademark | | Average | Probable Error |
	Original	Imitative		
Infringement	Cascarets	Castorets	1.2	.03
Infringement	Green River	Green Ribbon	3.3	.13
Base case	**Coca-Cola**	**Chero-Cola**	**3.6**	**.17**
Infringement	Listerine	Listogen	3.7	.15
No infringement	Sozodone	Kalodont	5.1	.20
Infringement	Gold Dust	Gold Drop	5.2	.12
No infringement	Grape-Nuts	Grain-Hearts	7.0	.13
Infringement	Club	Chancellor Club	7.8	.11
No infringement	Mother's	Grand-Ma's	8.6	.09
No infringement	Holeproof	Knotair	9.5	.08

Source: Rogers, E. S. (1919). An account of some psychological experiments on the subject of trademark infringement. *Michigan Law Review, 18*(2), 94.

umn is the imitation. The fourth column gives the index of likelihood of confusion, and the last column gives the likelihood of error. The objective was to quantify the likelihood of confusion between the marks, with benchmark cases. There was some correlation between the judgment by the court and the results of the psychological research, although it was not conclusive.

More extensive research by Paynter (1920) examined prior cases and their outcomes. The trademarks were tested using standard psychological methods related to vision, such as reaction times to the perception of words, letters, and numbers. For example, it takes longer for an individual to distinguish look-alike names such as hand and band. In a series of recognition experiments, subjects were given brand names, either present or absent, and asked if they were present.

It was found that some imitations the courts had declared not to infringe actually deceived more individuals than other imitations the courts had found to be infringements. Thus it was suggested that decisions were inexact and inconsistent, restraining some good trademarks and allowing some infringing ones to exist. Paynter (1920) determined there was likely a continuum from little or no confusion to absolute confusion using an experiment with several formats: an uninformed treatment, in which imitators were present, but subjects were not informed about imitators; an informed treatment, in which subjects were told about the presence of imitators; and a control treatment, in which no imitations were presented.

Finally, a relative position experiment also was carried out, in which the relative ranking of the similarity of the marks was measured. The results showed a clear continuum of confusion, and it was concluded that although confusion is a subjective fact, it also is a quantitative one. For consumer confusion to be investigated correctly, it needs to be measured on a continuum. A dichotomous measure of present or absent will not suffice. A subset of Paynter's (1920) results is listed in Table 6.4.

In summary, this early research found that when individuals are unaware of the presence of imitations, they confuse, on the average, 44% of the imitations with originals; that when individuals are aware of the imitations, they confuse, on the average, 23%; and that the lower the degree of deceptive similarity of two trademarks, the less the confusion and the greater ability to recognize the change. Despite this early work and the call for a valid and reliable measuring instrument, none exists today. Courts prefer to treat each case individually.

TABLE 6.4
Scale of Visual Recognition Confusion of Trademarks

		Confusion	
Originals	*Imitations*	*Order*	*% Confused*
Welcome	Welcome A. Smith	1	5
Golden Charm	Charm	2	10
Yusea	U-C-A	3	20
Royal Irish Linen	Royal Vellum	4	30
Beats-All	Knoxall	5	35
Shipmate	Messmate	6	40
Six Little	Six Big	7	45
Carbolineum	Creo-Carbolin	8	50
Mormaja	Mojava	9	55
Grenadine	Grenade	10	60
Muresco	Murafresco	11	65
Cottolene	Cottoleo	12	70
Dyspepticure	Dyspepticide	13	75
Siphon	Siphon System	14	80
Nubia	Nubias	15	85

Source: Paynter, R. H. (1920). A psychological study of trademark infringement. *Archives of Psychology, 42,* 45.

Later Marketing-Based Research

Standards for judicial marketing research, supplied by Morgan (1990), are adapted to trademark issues in Table 6.5.

Many different methods have been developed for determining consumer confusion in the marketplace, and some methods may be more suitable for different research questions. A review and critique of various methodologies listed in this section were carried out by Mitchell and Kearney (2002). They examined many of the studies in terms of the market research and the legal advantages and disadvantages. The findings showed that there is no perfect methodology for determining the confusion levels of customers. Each method has some advantages and disadvantages, but no agreement in effectiveness can be found.

Itamar Simonson, Professor of Marketing at Stanford, has written a body of literature on testing for trademark infringement. He examined different ways to test for perception of genericness (Simonson, 1994a) and also the effect of different methods used to measure confusion (Simonson, 1993, 1994b). Using different questionnaire wording, sequencing, and format found in previous cases, he found a great deal of variation in reports of confusion. A summary of these differences is presented in Table 6.6.

Action Plus Words Is the Key

One of the reasons cited for the difficulty in obtaining actual evidence of confusion is that most consumers do not complain about purchasing an imitator product they did not intend to purchase. This is because the imitator product usually is so much lower in price. Another reason for not returning the imitator product is that consumers are reluctant to admit that they made a mistake or were deceived in their purchase. Therefore, controlled research studies are needed to measure the extent to which the choice was attributable to imitation.

The type of data collected depends on the issue. Consumer research data usually fare best when they describe particular behaviors rather than just perceptions. This is especially so if monetary damages are sought. When a company wants to be compensated for lost sales or potential loss of sales, there must be some direct evidence that the loss of these sales was because of the imitator product.

Obtaining data on choices or selections with imitators is ideal, but does not always provide complete information on the case. Even when consumers are observed selecting the imitator over the original, it is important to know why that choice occurred. If a consumer believes two brands to be similar in appearance, it does not necessarily mean that he or she was motivated to purchase one brand instead of the other because of its appearance.

TABLE 6.5
Guidelines for Conducting Research for Brand Imitation

1. Sample selection

   a. Relevant respondents for the sample are those who might purchase, use, or have an opinion about the object of investigation.

   b. Convenience and nonprobability sampling must be relevant respondents.

   c. Sample size should be powerful enough to detect 20% to 30% confusion levels.

2. Design of questionnaire

   a. Questions that appear to predispose respondents must be avoided.

   b. Question wording must be direct, clear, and unambiguous.

   c. Research questions must relate directly to the legal question being litigated.

   d. Objective questions must include properly states, complete sets of response scales.

   e. Objective questions should be simple and elicit answers to one question at a time.

   f. Questionnaires should be pretested to the relevant respondents to ensure the above conditions are met.

3. Administration of questionnaire

   Research designs may be devised in the context of normal marketplace conditions or normal test market conditions subject to the legal research questions being investigated.

4. Interviewers' qualifications and techniques

   a. Interviewers should not know the name of the organization sponsoring the research.

   b. Interviewers should not know the purpose of the research project.

   c. Interviewers must not be associated in any way with the litigants in the lawsuit.

5. Data analysis and presentation

   a. All data should be reported.

   b. Data should be presented by simple frequencies before statistical analysis.

6. Administration of overall project

   a. The research administrator must be a recognized expert, based on peer review, in marketing research.

   b. The research administrator must continuously and closely supervise all steps in the research project.

   c. The research administrator must have minimum contact with and direction from attorneys.

Adapted from F. Morgan (1990). Judicial standards for survey research: An update and guidelines. *Journal of Marketing, 54,* 63.

TABLE 6.6
A Comparison of Likelihood of Confusion Estimates Derived From Different Techniques

Senior Brand	Junior (Infringing) Brand	Exxon* Format (a) (%)	Eveready Format With Other Products Question (b) (%)	Eveready Format With Confidence Question (b) (%)	Squirt Format (c) (%)	Simulated Choice (d) (%)	Simulated Choice as % of Senior Brand Awareness (e) (%)	Simulated Choice With Senior & Junior Brands Side-by-Side (d) (%)
Holiday Inn	Holiday Out (campgrounds)	73% (43)%	20	24	12	6	8	3
Oreo	Reo (cookies)	80 (61)	48	37	12	21	22	3
RCA	RC-Cam (camcorder)	42 (15)	23	33	32	20	24	4
Old Spice	New Spice (deodorant)	73 (64)	28	23	31	33	37	17
Rubbermaid	Plasticmaid (food container)	52 (22)	47	38	24	23	26	5
Dannon	Danfree (light yogurt)	66 (34)	70	55	60	19	22	5
Exxon	Texon (motor oil)	40 (31)	17	15	14			
Hewlett Packard	Packard (PC)	47 (36)	44	53	49	61	65	13
Oral B	Oral Z (tooth paste)	55 (33)	22	16	37	14	23	6
Chicken of the Sea	Tuna of the Sea (tuna)	47 (31)	28	16	37	52	65	18
Panasonic	Wanasonic (VCR)	83 (53)	53	24	7	7	7	3
Rolex	Ronex (watch)	71 (61)	26	16	3	10	10	1
Total		61 (40)	36	29	26	24	28	6

Source: Simonson, I. (1993). The effect of survey method on likelihood of confusion estimates: Conceptual analyses and empirical test. *The Trademark Reporter, 83,* 392.

*The confusion rates in the Table were based on the question "What is the first *company* that comes to mind" … and the numbers in parentheses were derived from answers to the question "What is the first *thing* that comes to mind."

For example, in a study that found customers who bought the brand with a name similar to the original, the judge ruled that confusion was not necessarily demonstrated (*Squirt Co. v. Seven-Up Co.*, 1980). To demonstrate confusion, the judge wanted evidence that explicitly identified why that brand was bought (Crespi, 1987). Therefore, an investigation of motives may be critical.

A valid and useful motivation survey could be based more on investigation to determine whether the trademark generates specifics attitudes and beliefs about the products' attributes. Measures are taken to determine whether these specific attitudes and beliefs cause the consumer to select the product. In *Zippo Mfg. Co. v. Rogers Imports, Inc.* (1963), the final measurement of these attitudes and beliefs was the choice of the product. At the end of the research interview, the respondents were offered their choice of a Zippo lighter or an imitator brand. The original was preferred twice as often as the imitator, and the court noted this as proof of the motivational aspect of the expectations formed by the original brand (Leiser & Schwartz, 1983).

Flash Card Technique Using the Computer

Pre-testing for Infringement. Researchers may carry out some very simple pretests to generate data that might indicate whether more sophisticated controlled studies are worth pursuing. The flash technique is one way to pretest infringement of logo or trademark confusion of products. A series of images is prepared so that each screen displays a trademark, and possibly the term describing the good to which it is applied, such as Ivory soap.

The number of different trademarks may range from 10 to 15. Among the series of screens is one bearing the trademark thought to be infringed upon. These images are shown to a convenience sample, usually a college class or church group. Each person is given several seconds to view each screen. Somewhat later, perhaps after 1 hour, the same group is shown a series of similar images in which there are several repeats (five to eight) from the original series, but in which the original trademark is substituted by the alleged infringing trademark. The respondents are asked at the end of the second series to write down all the trademarks they can recall as having been shown in both the first and second series.

If a critical percentage of the sample indicates that the infringer's logo was shown to them in the first series, then there is some evidence that the two marks are subject to confusion. A further form of testing for confusion of source might then be warranted, because this form of testing is artificial and far removed from the marketplace.

Using Photographs

Sometimes it is difficult to show respondents the object of investigation the way they naturally see it in the environment. Logos or trade dress involving outdoor signs or buildings may cause particular problems. In *Exxon Corporation v. Texas Motor Exchange of Houston, Inc.* (1980), the question was infringement of the logo. It was thought that consumers would believe Texxon was associated with Exxon. Exxon argued that the double x identified its company alone. To test the difference between Texxon and Texon, subjects were shown a photograph of the Texxon sign and asked questions similar to the following:

1. Does anything come to mind when you look at this sign? (if yes) What is it? (record verbatim)
2. What was there about the sign that made you say that? (probe fully)
3. (If no company name is mentioned) What is the first company that comes to mind when you look at this sign? (record name exactly as respondent states it)
4. What was there about the sign that made you mention (the company)? (clarify and probe fully) (Boal 1973, p. 414)

The beauty of these questions lies in the fact that they do not lead the respondent to give any one answer. Perhaps the most informative question is the last one. It allows the respondent to articulate what led to any possible confusion or what caused the confusion if it existed. These questions do not directly ask the respondent about association, sponsorship, or connection. The respondent makes the connection in his or her own mind.

Tachistoscope Research

A basic method of determining threshold levels of perception is with a tachistoscope (T-scope). This device is similar to a slide projector, but is capable of extremely rapid exposures rates. The subject views the screen, watches for the stimulus, and then reports what he or she has just seen. The rate of exposure is varied until there is detection of the stimulus. In cognitive psychology the T-scope is used to determine the level at which a stimulus may be consciously identified.

In marketing research, T-scopes are used to assess a product's shelf visibility and distinctiveness (Valerio, 1992), or confusion of brands for the same product. It has been used to test outdoor poster recognition and comprehension by exposing viewers to only fractional seconds of each poster. T-scope studies investigating the criteria of limited attention are important to manufacturers, because courts have previously rejected some studies on the basis that respondents had too much time to reflect on their decision. The notion of the hurried consumer scanning the shelves (see chapter 2) is very difficult to reproduce in a natural setting. The best way to guarantee limited attention is through the use of a tachistoscope.

Case Study: Oil of Olay.   In determining product confusion, the T-scope has been used in cases such as that involving Oil of Olay (see Smith, Snyder, Swire, Donegan, and Ross [1983] for a complete description of this case). This beauty product has found itself the target of many private label knockoffs, with names such as "Oil of Beauty" and "Oil of Life." To test for consumer confusion, a number of competitive packages and a knockoff were included on a display shelf. Oil of Olay lotion was not on the shelf, but one of the infringing packages was. Subjects then were shown pictures of the store shelves at timed intervals starting at 1/12 of a second. Respondents were asked, "What brands did you see?" Depending on the particular package being tested, a substantial number of respondents misidentified the stimulus product as Oil of Olay.

This test was used in a preliminary way because it helped identify the major package infringers. Such laboratory tests may not be final proof for likelihood of confusion, but they provide data to the expert witness for the basis of opinion. Because this is a basic industry technique used to assess identification, it also is an appropriate tool for assessing misidentification.

Previous criticisms of this technique concern its precision in determining the percentage of customer confusion in the marketplace. Because each person's threshold level for identification may be slightly different, it is difficult to say what exposure time is the correct one for accurate identification of the objects in question. The data were thought best used for demonstration or anecdotal evidence because the data will attract the court's attention and provide a good basis for expert testimony.

Determining Exposure Rates.   Studies by Kapferer and Thoenig (1991), and Kapferer (1995a) sought to develop standards for exposure times used in T-scope tests for courtroom evidence. In the Kapferer and Thoenig (1991) study, consumers were exposed by tachistoscope to the copycat brand either in isolation or paired with the original at exposures of 1/125, 1/60, 1/15, 1/4, 1/2, and 1 second. Consumers viewed four different products and were exposed to each of the original and copycat brands in isolation six times. After each exposure, they were asked three questions: (a) What did you see? (b) What do you think you saw? and (c) What does it represent? The results of the study showed that some brands were confused with their copycat brands up to 42% of the time. The following index of confusion was proposed:

$$I = \frac{\%\,identifying\ brand\ as\ a\ copy}{\%\,identifying\ brand\ as\ original}$$

In some cases, the index of confusion showed little variation over the different exposure times, indicating that a very long detailed look at the copycat brand was necessary for the consumer to be sure it was not the original.

Another study by Kapferer (1995a) was similar, but the research concerned only reactions to brands in isolation. The study found that for most imitators, the highest rate of confusion (perceiving the national brand when the copy is shown) does not take place at the highest speed, but after some exposure time, either 1/15 or 1/4 of a second. Furthermore, the variance in the rates of confusion for different products and consumers is wide, ranging from 0% to 42%. Also, the rates of confusion do not decrease rapidly with time. At one full second of exposure, 22% to 24% of consumers confused certain brands with their imitators.

Blurring Images

A second approach to measuring confusion was then developed by Kapferer (1995b), which relies on the recognition of pictures in which focusing is controlled, varying from a blur to absolute sharpness. The theory behind this methodology is that vision proceeds from the general to details, from approximation to exactitude, and from macro to micro. A review back to the model of Triesman and Schmidt (1982) in chapter 3 may be helpful in explaining the reasoning behind this blurring method. What the consumer does is more or less decode the colors, shapes, and designs until they can be identified.

Using computer technology, the images of each product are blurred into an unclear picture. Over 15 screens, the picture focuses. At any time in these 15 screens, the consumer can offer an identification of the image. A brand recognized on the first slide can be thought of as very strong in visual appearance. The longer it takes to recognize a brand, the weaker the mark. The amount of blur can act as a baseline for measuring overall identity. The imitator brands then can be subjected to the same method. The percentage of consumers identifying the imitator as the original then can be thought to provide an index of the imitation. Throughout this process, when a subject identifies a brand, he or she is asked what cues were used for identification. The most frequently reported cue for identification is color, followed by shape.

Consumer Reaction Tests

A consumer reaction test is not a survey of public opinion. Rather, it involves the direct exposure of an object to consumers, followed by measures of their reaction to or thoughts about what they have just seen. The purpose is not to measure their reactions to the image in their memory, but to measure the direct impression of the object as they see it. The brand impression may be measured in isolation or in the context of other brands.

This type of testing is very important for cases involving alleged infringement of package design, association, or sponsorship. For example, advertising investigated in a passing-off inquiry may be presented to consumers under artificial conditions. Consumers are exposed to the advertisement in isolation rather than in the context of regular television viewing in their homes. After viewing the advertisement in a test theater or a shopping mall format, consumers are asked questions about what they have just seen.

This format likely would cause respondents to attend to the advertisement very closely, thus heightening their awareness of the advertisement's content. Consumers should therefore comprehend the message better than they would if viewing it under natural conditions. This type of testing is conservative in that fewer people may be confused because of the greater attention. It is likely that more evidence of confusion would be found with inattentive but natural viewing. Therefore, controlled attentive viewing is a strong rather than a weak test for confusion because it underestimates the number confused under natural viewing conditions.

The Federal Trade Commission has identified this type of consumer reaction test as the preferred type of extrinsic evidence for determining conveyance in advertising research because it is more direct than other types of research, such as calling people after the advertisement has aired (Preston, 1989a, 1989b). This does not mean that "day-after-recall" tests are totally invalid, but only that failure to show any conveyance of confusion does not conclusively mean that none occurred.

Case Study: Robin Hood.   Another type of reaction test questionnaires and labels is used to determine association or confusion of source. In *International Milling Company v. Robin Hood Popcorn Co.* (1956), the issue was that Robin Hood flour was thought well known to the public. Another company produced and sold Robin Hood popcorn. The flourmill undertook to prove that consumers thought the two products came from the same source. To test this premise, 512 households were shown wrappers or tags from six different products with the name of the producer removed from the label or package.

Respondents were shown the wrappers or labels one at a time and asked, "What is the name of the company that makes ?" They were then shown the labels again, one at a time, and asked, "Have you ever bought ?" The final, but critical, question was "If you can think of any other products put out by each of these companies, please name them." The labels were shown again one at a time to the respondent. If a significant number of consumers mentioned flour in response to the last question, that was a good indication of confusion concerning the source of the product (Pattishall, 1959). The main parts of the questionnaire are presented in Exhibit 6.1.

The questionnaire design shown in Exhibit 6.1 illustrates some important points. First, the questionnaire should be short, but not so short that the key issue is obvious. Second, it should not "trigger" any particular response to the key question. Third, it should be designed to answer a specific question about confusion. Fourth, the questionnaire should hold the interest of the respondent and hence ensure that the answers obtained are given seriously. Fifth, it should be written in a nontechnical manner with words easily understood by those at a high school level. Finally, the results should be presented as a simple tabulation of the percentage confused.

Of the preceding points, the one most likely to cause the most courtroom arguments is the accusation of leading questions. The perception of a question as triggering a particular response is likely to be a subjective matter. It is best to be as conservative as possible, perhaps designing a questionnaire that is just as likely to be used by the opposing company.

Q. 1.   What is the name of the company that makes (show pictures)
        CARNATION?   _____
        IVORY?   _____
        ROBIN HOOD?   _____
        LOG CABIN?   _____
        MONARCH?   _____

Q.2.   Have you ever bought

	Yes	No	Don't Remember
CARNATION?	___	___	___
IVORY?	___	___	___
ROBIN HOOD?	___	___	___
LOG CABIN?	___	___	___
MONARCH?	___	___	___

Q.3.   If you can think of any other product put out by each of these
        companies, please name them.
        CARNATION   _____
        IVORY   _____
        ROBIN HOOD _____
        LOG CABIN   _____
        MONARCH   _____

EXHIBIT 6.1 Consumer Reaction Test for Origin of Manufacturer Adapted from Pattishall (1959), pp. 160–161.

Shopping for the Product

The marketing research house, Angus Reid, consulted on a trademark infringement case involving the Au Coton retail establishment, which situates many of its stores in retail malls. To test for confusion, researchers stopped shoppers in the mall, showed them an ad for Au Coton, and asked directions to the store. The number of times the researcher was directed to the alleged infringing retail store with a similar name was used as the indication of consumer confusion. The court thought this was an excellent indication of actual confusion and ruled for Au Coton because a significant number of shoppers were directed to the wrong store.

In-Store Coupon Test.   To test for the level of confusion between two brands in a retail environment, cooperation might be obtained from one or more retail establishments to carry out an in-store field experiment. There may be several versions of the shelf placement: (a) the competitor may be directly to the left of the target; (b) the competitor may be separated by other brands; (c) the competitor may be directly to the right of the target; and (d) the competitor may be above or below the target. The reason for the different placings is to counterbalance any positioning bias. It is widely accepted that the position of a product on store shelves can influence sales. For example, brand A will sell better than brand B if A is at eye level and B is at ankle level. Aisle-end displays and the number of facings also affect sales. More subtle positional biases (such as right-handed people choosing the brand on the right because of ease of reach) are less obvious, but the possibility can be guarded against by rotation of positions. Each of the different positions then can be used to determine whether different results are obtained on the basis of positioning and to eliminate the possible criticism of positional bias.

In shopping for the product, the consumer is intercepted outside the store and given coupons for different products, valid for that day only. The coupons usually are at a one-third discount, such as one dollar off a three-dollar purchase.[1] The respondents are shown pictures of the brands the coupons represent. The consumer is always given two or three products to shop for so as not to direct his or her attention to the focal product. The shopper is then allowed to enter the store, and the brands purchased are recorded at the checkout counter.

This type of research works well when the brand name under study is not widely known by the consumer, but the look of the brand is very distinctive. For example in *Hartford House Ltd. v. Hallmark Cards Incorporated*

---

[1]The discount is well above the "just noticeable difference" (JND), so the consumer is motivated to purchase (Weber's Law, chapter 3).

(1986), in which the overall look or Gestalt of the card was well known, but perhaps not the brand name, this might have been a very good test to determine the level of confusion among consumers.

Case Study: St. Ives Shampoo.   Consumer shopping was used in the St. Ives shampoo and conditioner case, in which consumers recognized the trade dress but not the brand name (*Ives Laboratories, Inc. v. Darby Drug Co., Inc.*, 1982). The products were sold in containers through which the color of the ingredients could be seen. The shampoo and conditioner bottles were banded together by plastic wrap to form a twin pack, and a promotional tag was placed on top of one of the bottles. The bottle had the trademark "Swiss Formula" printed vertically on the left side of the principal display panel. Imitators in the market adopted the same twin pack concept using a plastic wrap. They were called "Salon Formula" or "European Formula."

In this shopping format test, up to 40% of the shoppers bought the competitors' goods after they had been shown the St. Ives picture before entering the store. This is persuasive evidence for confusion because the test demonstrates actual consumer confusion. It should be noted that this is a strongly conservative test in that it involves a typical consumer setting. Consumer shopping tests are best done for inexpensive, nondurable consumer products.

Shopping for the Product in a Virtual Environment

With the use of three-dimensional modeling and Java-based animation, shoppers can browse store shelves for products, pick up brands, examine them, read labels, select products for purchase, or just give opinions on-line (see www.visioncritical.com). Questionnaires are integrated with the visual screen to collect consumer responses, which then are tallied as data are collected. This technology can easily do the manipulation of the shelf placements or substitute different products on the shelves. The success of this virtual technology in the courts does not yet have a track record.

Motivations to Purchase

Sometimes consumers intend to buy a certain brand A, but once in the retail environment, they encounter a brand B so similar that they purchase it. The purchase could be a mistake, or the purchase could be made because brand B is cheaper and looks just like brand A. The consumer may just disregard the confusion because if brand B meets the consumer's expectations and is sufficiently lower in price (partly due to lower costs by being an imitator), the consumer may switch to the mistaken brand. Here, the consumer is transferring his or her beliefs and attitudes from the original product to the brand imitator because of the similarity or generalization of the two brands. The question in such circumstances is not whether consumers can discriminate between the two products on the basis of some secondary cue, but rather, whether the positive attitudes that have been linked to the first brand are generalized[2] to the second brand in a way that leads to buying behavior (Miaoulis & D'Amato, 1978).

Case Study: Tic Tacs.   An example of measuring this transfer of beliefs and attitudes from brand A to the alleged infringer, brand B, is demonstrated in the investigation of Tic Tac mints versus Dynamints and Mightymints. This case is given in detail in Miaoulis and D'Amato (1978). The premise of the investigation was that consumers have a distinct conception of Tic Tac's taste and product benefits, and that this image is triggered immediately by the visual impact of the product, the package, and the display.

Consumer surveys were conducted in two cities where the infringing brands were not yet sold, but where the original brand was well established. Tic Tac's were replaced by the imitator brands in drug, variety, and grocery outlets in Detroit and New Jersey. Consumers were intercepted after purchasing the test brand, but before they had an opportunity to open the package and taste the product. The basic question asked in this research was "Do people, through the visual impact of the product (the plastic box with the visual configuration of the pellets within), anticipate obtaining the same end benefits and the same experiences that they would with Tic Tac?" Because consumers had not previously experienced or heard of Dynamints or Mightymints, product expectations could be taken to stem from the visual aspects of the product.

The following specific questions asked of the respondents:

1. What do you expect this product to be like?
2. What made you believe it would be like this?
3. Do you believe this product would be like any other product on the market?
4. Which one or ones is it like?
5. Do you believe the same company makes these two products?
6. Why do you feel this way?

At no point during the questionnaire was Tic Tac mentioned by name unless the brand was introduced by the respondent. When the responses to

---

[2]Here stimulus generalization from chapter 2 applies.

the questions were tabulated, the purchasers overwhelmingly referred to the Tic Tac brand. In an out-of-court settlement, the packaging for Dynamints was changed to decrease the visual impact of the scrambled product configuration, and Mightymints withdrew from the market.

The preceding study is slightly different from the previously presented "in-store shopping" scenario because consumers are not instructed to buy the product before entering the store. The obvious problems in gathering data of this type are numerous. First, just obtaining an adequate sized sample that naturally purchases the product could take a very long time. It is rare that a substantial quantity of a product is sold in a given time frame in a self-serve environment. If the goods are not sold in a self-serve environment, the practical difficulties in conducting the study under controlled conditions are immense. It also may be a problem to obtain the cooperation of storeowners and managers because they will benefit little, if any, from the study. The benefits of this method also are its weaknesses. It represents a real purchase situation, yet there is no control over the frequency of people participating.

Signal Detection Theory

Signal detection theory was originally developed to measure a weak signal in a noisy environment. An individual must decide whether some condition is present or absent. Most of the time, the alternatives are obvious and the evidence is clear. However, sometimes the alternatives may be distinct, but the evidence is ambiguous. For example, is the original brand present or absent? The alternatives are distinct, but the other brands may look so similar that the evidence is ambiguous. Therefore, signal detection theory is useful for quantifying the identification of certain target brands among the other competing brands, or for measuring the amount of brand confusion for brands within the same product category.

In a signal detection experiment, the subject experiences two types of trials. In the one type, only the competing brands or background environment is present. In the other type of trial, the target brand or signal is added to the overall brand environment. In both types of trials, the observer is asked to detect the presence of the original brand. Detection of a signal is known as a "hit." Astute observers of distinctive brands have high hit rates, whereas poor observers or the presentation of confusingly similar brands yield low hit rates. Unfortunately, the hit rate is not a true summary of the situation or a good way to indicate the distinctiveness of the brand. The problem lies in the overall look of the available brands or the context of the choice.

To resolve the background problem, it is important not to report the presence of a target brand (signal) when one is not there, a type of error known as a "false alarm." If the brand is correctly identified 85% of the time when it is there, that may be a good hit rate. However, if the brand is identified 60% of the time it is not actually there, then the rate of false alarms indicates a lot of confusion about the presence of the target brand. The brand is likely to be indistinctive and easily confused with another. Researching the problem of confusion may take into account both hits and false alarms to get a complete picture of possible brand imitation.

Methodology.   The procedure for signal detection of brand imitation is adapted from Donovan (1987). Respondents are shown pairs of slides projected on a screen. The first slide contains a matrix of brands, whereas the second slide features just one brand. Thus, two types of slides are prepared: the matrix slides comprising the majority of the brands and the target slides consisting of only one brand. The number of target slides might represent the major competitors and the object of investigation. If, for example, four brands are chosen as the target brands, the original and imitator brands at issue are tested along with two other competitors. The two other competitors should be distinct to indicate the extent of brand differentiation. Testing more than the target brand also helps to camouflage the purpose of the research for the participating consumers.

The possible results for a target brand, as represented in Fig. 6.1, are based on the possible combinations of correct responses (yes or no) and the person's actual answer (yes or no). The hits represent the proportion of times the target brand was correctly detected when it had been present in the preceding matrix slide. This measure gives an indication of how well the brand stands out among its competitors.

The misses represent the proportion of times that respondents thought the brand was not in the matrix when it actually was. The proportion of misses may be taken to indicate the overall similarity within the product

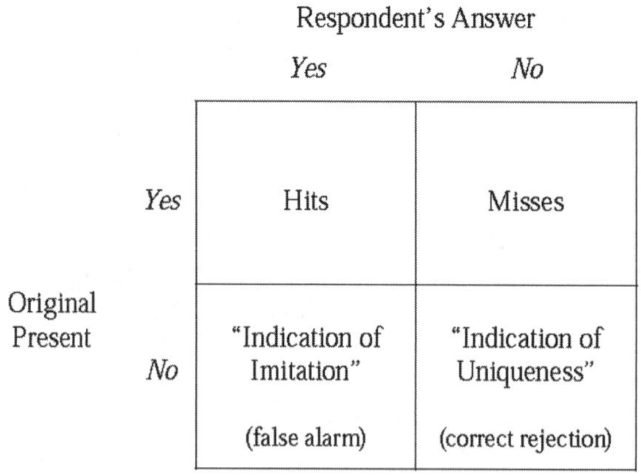

FIG. 6.1. Signal detection matrix for the original brand.

category, or how poorly the target brand stands out from other brands. The false alarms represent the proportion of times that respondents thought the target brand was in the preceding matrix when it actually was not. This measure provides an indication for the degree of confusion about each brand or how easily it is mistaken for another brand.

The correct rejections represent the proportion of times that respondents correctly determined that the target brand was not in the preceding matrix. This gives a good indication for uniqueness of the target brand. The issue here is to compare the detectability of the alleged imitating brand with the original brand. If the original brand stands out and is not confused with the competitors, the results in Fig. 6.2 might occur.

In the following case, depicted in Fig. 6.3, the original brand is easily identified, but also confused with competitors. By establishing this base rate for the original brand, all other results can be compared with it.

FIG. 6.2. Signal detection matrix of distinctive brands.

		Respondent's Answer		
		Yes	No	Total
Original Brand	Present	75 – 90%	10 – 25%	100%
	Absent	10 – 25%	75 – 90%	100%

FIG. 6.3. Signal detection matrix of nondistinctive brands.

		Respondent's Answer		
		Yes	No	Total
Original Brand	Present	75 – 90%	10 – 25%	100%
	Absent	50%	50%	100%

To measure the imitation level of the imitator brand, the matrix would contain the original brand, and the target slide would contain the imitator brand. This would yield a slightly different matrix, as shown in Fig. 6.4.

The pattern of responses under false alarms and hits might indicate the relationship of the imitator to other brands in the marketplace or the extent to which the infringing brand is similar to or different from the original brand. The original brand is not used in the matrix because the issue is not how well the imitator is detected, but how similar the imitator is to the original brand.

Questions for Sponsorship

Sometimes testing for association of two objects is not enough. Instead, the question is whether product A is approved and endorsed by company or product B. For example in *Ideal Toy Corp. v. Kenner Products Division of General Mills Fun Group, Inc.* (1977), a finding of general association that the toys in question looked like characters from the movie Star Wars or reminded the respondents of the movie was not enough for the courts. They ruled that this association did not mean a purchaser thinks the toys are derived from the movie or sponsored by the movie (Boal, 1973).

Getting people to describe sponsorship, endorsements, or approval freely is extremely difficult. Therefore, it usually is best to ask respondents these questions directly. The National Football League has been successful in presenting evidence showing that they did not sponsor or endorse state

Respondent's Answer for
Detection of Original

		Yes	*No*
	Present	"Indication of Imitation" (confusion)	"Indication of Uniqueness" (correct rejection)
Imitator Brand			
	Absent	False Alarm	Hits

FIG. 6.4. Signal detection matrix for imitator brand.

lottery tickets (*National Football League v. Governor of the State of Delaware*, 1977), or clothing (*National Football League Properties, Inc. v. Wichita Falls Sportswear, Inc.*, 1982). In the first case, the respondents were asked whether they agreed that the lottery was conducted with the authorization of the teams. In the second case, the respondents were asked directly if the company producing the clothing had to obtain authorization or sponsorship to make the clothing. Then they were asked from whom the authorization was obtained.

In situations of sponsorship or association, it is best to divide the question into smaller parts that address the specific issues. For example instead of asking "Do you think these two products are made by the same or different producers?" it would be better to ask "Do you think these two products are made by the same producers?" and then "Do you think these two products are made by different producers?"

By asking the question in two parts, one is able to get both positive and negative responses. One question acts as a balance or reliability check on the other. The two questions should also be counterbalanced by sometimes asking the positive question first and sometimes asking the negative question first. By counterbalancing the questions, both positive and negative ideas are equally introduced, and therefore any perceived conditioning of the respondent should be reduced to random error.

Case Study: Paul Hogan. Examples of these two points are found in an Australian case, *Hogan and Another v. Koala Dundee Pty. Ltd. And Others* (1988). Both sides presented research to determine whether consumers thought certain clothing sold by the Koala Dundee shop were associated or licensed by Paul Hogan. The Hogan study, performed by a marketing research firm, showed potential customers three items sold in the respondent's shop: a shopping bag, a T-shirt, and a hat. The consumers were asked five questions with respect to each item:

1. What does this mean to you?
2. Do you associate this with any person or thing?
3. Which person or thing came to mind?
4. Do you think that the person or thing that came to mind has any involvement with the (bag) (T-shirt) (hat)?
5. What do you think that involvement is?

In contrast, the Koala Dundee study was carried out by the shop's employees and did not involve any specific offending merchandise. The shop's customers were given a questionnaire and asked to tick "yes" or "no" to the following questions:
When you saw our shop and our goods on display,

1. Did you wonder whether our goods are sold under an agreement with or by license of Paul Hogan or those who made the film "Crocodile Dundee"?
2. Did you wonder whether our goods are sold with the sponsorship or approval of Paul Hogan or those who made the film "Crocodile Dundee"?

The Koala Dundee questionnaire was leading in that it inherently put the idea of sponsorship in the minds of the person reading the question. This is ironic because Koala Dundee should want to avoid this type of answer.

There were a few other flaws in the market research in this case. First, in the Hogan research, although the hat, shopping bag, and T-shirt should have been rotated in the order of presentation to the consumers, they apparently were not. The criticism was that in showing the hat first, the results could be biased in the favor of Hogan. Second, the importance of using professionally trained interviewers who are naive to the reasons for the data collection also is apparent in this case. In the Koala Dundee survey, conducted by members of their store staff, 8% of customers gave an affirmative answer to one interviewer, and 25% of customers gave an affirmative answer to another interviewer. Therefore, substantial bias might be attributable to the person collecting the data.

QUALITATIVE EVIDENCE AS RESEARCH

No matter how well a consumer reaction test is designed or a consumer survey is prepared and documented, the courts might not have the expertise, confidence, or experience to evaluate its worth independently. Although the social science researcher and courts are concerned with establishing the truth, they operate under very different definitions, precepts, and procedures. Social scientists establish the hypothesis question to be answered and then gather data to support or reject the premise. Their work is reviewed by their peers and evaluated on the methods used to collect and analyze data, as well as underlying theories. The published work represents a premise with evidence to be scrutinized.

The legal system starts with a point of contention. The two parties present evidence that offer support only for their own point of view. It is up to the court to decide whose evidence is better. In this process, each side tries to discredit the other's evidence. The process of discrediting can be irrelevant to uncovering the truth, but each side is paid to win, not to be objective.

Furthermore, the courts treat every case as individual and specific. The ways the courts apply research findings and the criteria they use for accepting the data differ significantly from the "generalizable" world of the social scientist. Judges, who are the final decision makers, often do not have the expertise to evaluate sample sizes and procedures adequately. Testimony that specifies surrounding facts and circumstances is highly valued evidence in aiding the decision. This also is why consumer research can be enhanced with anecdotal and direct testimony instead of being relied upon as the primary basis for reaching a verdict (Crespi, 1987).

The decisions of cases are sometimes based on the impression or credibility of the opposing experts in direct testimony and under cross-examination rather than scientific testing. Because impressions are so relevant and important, it is supportive to bring the numbers to life. Individual witnesses' uncontradicted evidence as to what they thought they said or bought can make a vivid impression in the courtroom (*A & M Pet Products, Inc. v. Pieces, Inc. and Royal K-9*, 1989). The ascertaining and parading of consumers as witnesses in the courtroom is a costly and tedious task. Furthermore, both sides can easily produce individual witnesses to support their point of view. However, getting individual respondents who participated in the consumer test to testify undermines the confidentiality of the respondent. It could grossly decrease the response rate if subjects knew there was a possibility they would be served with a subpoena to testify in court.

Alternative methods of bringing the data to life involve the use of videotapes. Because judges and juries have little or no experience with consumer research, videotaping the procedure followed in consumer reaction tests is most informative. Focus groups might be beneficial in cases involving secondary meaning, advertising, defamation, or dilution of trademarks. Videotaping reactions from a dozen people giving free-flowing ideas and emotions lends a side to the evidence that drab numbers on a page can never do.

The importance of qualitative methods to support and enhance quantitative data is exemplified in *Grotian, Helfferich, Schultz Steinweg Nach v. Steinway & Sons* (1975). In this case, the quantitative data showed 8½% of consumers were confused as to the origin of the pianos, one of the lowest percentages in trademark infringement cases. However, detailed tape-recorded interviews with purchasers of Steinweg pianos were accepted to show the tendency of these consumers to believe Steinweg pianos to be the German-made Steinway ones.

EVIDENCE FROM SECONDARY SOURCES

Misdirected mail, telephone calls, or other real mistakes are useful anecdotal evidence to back up statistical data. These types of occurrences show actual confusion about the source of the goods. It is a mistake to rely solely on this kind of evidence to establish consumer confusion because there is no control over gathering the data. Hence, the courts might think these data are a result of carelessness rather than the imitative nature of the competing product or service under scrutiny.

Nonetheless, companies should keep track of wrong numbers by telephone logs, noting the time and nature of the call (*IMS Ltd. v. International Medical Systems Inc.*, 1986; *Wells Fargo & Co. v. Wells Fargo Construction Co.*, 1985). Notation of mail addressed correctly but intended for the other company also may be invaluable in the courtroom (*Harlequin Enterprises Ltd. v. Gulf & Western Corp.*, 1981; *Purofied Down Products Corp. v. Puro Down International of New Jersey Corp.*, 1982).

Advertising that depicts the wrong product is another form of secondary data (*Parkdale Custom Built Furniture Proprietary Limited v. Puxu Proprietary Limited*, 1981–1982; *Smith v. Sturm, Ruger & Co., Inc.*, 1985). In these cases, retailers ran advertisements that showed one brand, but clearly labeled it as the competitor's brand. In some of these, cases the retailer might have requested reimbursement for running an advertisement from the competitor rather than the manufacturer who was mislabeled (*Jockey International, Inc., v. Burkhard*, 1975). Retailers also may send coupons for redemption to the wrong manufacturer (*Glamorene Products Corp. v. Boyle-Midway, Inc.*, 1975; *Helene Curtis Industries, Inc. v. Church & Dwight Co., Inc.*, 1977). Advertising that mistakenly promotes one item as another may be very important for the courtroom.

FLAWS JUDGED TO DISCREDIT RESEARCH

It may be best for the researcher to imagine him- or herself working for the opposing party while designing the research. It is always best to be as conservative as possible in one's research approach for the courtroom. The results from consumer research studies seeming to be liberal in their approach or deemed subject to flaws of bias often are heavily discounted by the courts even though the studies were carried out by experts. For example, in *Amstar Corp. v. Domino's Pizza Inc.* (1980), the court attacked the marketing research of both parties, finding that the samples in each study failed to include a fair sampling of purchasers most likely to partake of the other party's product. Of the 10 cities in which Amstar's study was conducted, 8 had no Domino's Pizza outlets, and the outlets in the remaining 2 cities had been open for less than 3 months. The trial court discounted Domino's research because it was conducted on the premises of Domino's Pizza outlets and therefore thought not to examine a proper sample.

It also is advisable not to use informal surveys that include respondents not naive to the issues. Although this last point may seem odd, it is not unheard of for law firms to do this. The problem is that most people in the firm likely will have heard about the issues and will be eager to give their opinions. Because the area of brand confusion usually surrounds consumers, and because everyone is a consumer, it is likely that people will be eager to give their opinions.

Getting Approval Before the Research: The Online Experience

Avoiding flaws in research and guaranteeing that the courts will find consumer research valid and reliable for courtroom evidence is reason to get one's research methodology pre-approved by the court. The difficulty in finding an accepted methodology is demonstrated in the online case of *Simon Property Group, L.P. (SPG) v. mySimon, Inc.* (see Sarel & Marmorstein, 2002). The SPG operated retail shopping malls, and mySimon operated a comparative shopping service on the Web. The SPG sued mySimon Inc., alleging that the Web address www.mysimon.com and the "Simon" character infringed on SPG's federal trademarks. The SPG presented three consumer surveys (Home Page Survey, Print Survey, and Television Advertising Survey), as tests for confusion to the court for pre-approval. The SPG wanted to make sure their research would not only be admissible to the court, but also be granted substantial weight.

In the Home Page Survey, the consumer was shown a card depicting the mySimon home page. While looking at the page, the consumer was asked about the services of interest offered on that site. After recording the answers and removing the page, the interviewer handed the consumer a card depicting the SPG home page and asked the same question. After recording the answers and removing the second card, the interviewer asked, "Do you believe that the two Web pages just shown to you are put out by (a) two unrelated sources, companies, or organizations; (b) the same source, company, or organization; (c) related but different sources, companies, or organizations; (d) or don't you know?"

If the consumer answered a, b, or c, the interviewer then asked, "Why did you say that?" What else?

The court found three major design flaws with this methodology. First, it did not reflect the market condition. Second, the controls were inappropriate. Finally, there were demand effects.

Market Conditions. The court said that because consumers were not asked to view actual search engine results containing hyperlinks to real sites, the research had little value. The proposed methodology was judged "nothing more than a meaningless memory or word association exercise that bears no relationship to the marketplace" because the two home pages were presented together. The methodology was thought to exaggerate greatly any confusion that might be detected.

Adequate Controls.   The court argued that many Simons existed online, and that there were no controls to establish the research around only the two marks in question. Given the fact that consumers are likely to encounter other 'Simon' sites during a search, such other names should be included in the research. The court said proper controls should show that consumers have no trouble distinguishing most Simon sites from one another, and then SPG would have to show confusion between its site and mySimon.

Demand Effects.   The court decided that there were demand effects in answers a, b, and c to the questions about association or affiliation. It said there were two positive answers, but only one negative answer. The court did not like the c option, which was "related but different," because it determined this option to be biased by inferring a relationship.

In the two other proposed methodologies, Print Survey and Television Advertising Survey, consumers were asked to view print or video ads for five online shopping services, one of which was mySimon. After viewing the ads, the consumers were presented with cards that displayed www.simon.com or www.mysimon.com. The consumers were asked whether they would use the address to access the Web site mySimon. The court said demand effects were obvious because none of the other ads had a connection with the name "Simon." The methodology tested only memory and common sense.

The conclusion is that research conducted to measure likelihood of confusion on the Internet needs to ensure that it is they are capturing real-world market conditions. The court observed that in searching for information on the Internet, consumers are used to finding many sites with similar-sounding names. It is necessary to demonstrate that the site accused of infringement is causing more confusion than the ordinary noise created by the search process.

SUMMARY

The laws dealing with trademark infringement vary from country to country. The points to be considered in testing for likelihood of confusion are numerous, and all may not apply to any one case. The main overall point to consider is "Does the alleged imitating trademark cause the consumer to think about the original brand and derive inferences from its presence?" In other words, is there confusion in the broadest sense of the word?

Designing research to determine consumer confusion usually is a difficult task because of time constraints, confidentiality, and the need for extremely carefully worded questions. Measuring actual confusion by consumer choice behavior is preferred to measuring opinions. In addition to choice behavior, it also is useful to determine specific motivations behind the behavior to get an understanding of what led to the confusion.

An important step in doing research on brand confusion is to determine the number of people needed for the study. This is an extremely difficult concept to demonstrate and explain in the courtroom, because not all involved will understand the techniques of statistical sampling. A novice of statistics will not know there is an inverse relationship between sample size and critical effect. And to determine that sample size, the critical effect needs to be determined or estimated in advance.

Just as critical as the number of people sampled is the type of people sampled. Although courts have ruled that there is no need for samples to be representative of national probability samples or to include only users of the product, or only those exposed to media running the advertisement (Preston, 1990), it is preferable to be as close to these points as possible. Research for consumer reactions is different from research for public opinion polls. Unfortunately, due to the overwhelming abundance of political party research in the form of polling, polling is sometimes considered by those not knowledgeable in marketing research to be the norm or the correct way to gather information. When data are collected in one location, those who do not understand the generalizability of consumer research gathered using less than random samples of the entire population might devalue it. Small test markets in localized geographic areas are the norm in market research. Test marketing provides marketing managers with data good enough for making decisions. Random probability samples are not practical, perhaps impossible, and certainly not necessary.

With respect to the other two points on the type of sample, it may be extremely desirable, if not necessary, to have respondents who are users or aware of the product category. It is important that respondents have the knowledge to respond accurately to the questions of the investigation. Much consumer research in court cases is judged to be flawed on the basis of inappropriate samples.

There are various techniques for evaluating brand imitation. The particular technique chosen should correspond to the specific problem at hand. The research does not necessarily have to take place in a natural purchase environment. Tests of perception often involve laboratory settings set up to provide the controls for measuring the degree of imitation with reliable precision. Field experiments in the way of prompted or natural shopping provide very conservative tests of confusion with respect to consumer purchase behavior.

Despite the need for some quantification of the confusion level, courts often are swayed by some very qualitative experiences on the part of consumers. Videotapes of focus groups or detailed recorded in-depth interviews of customers often brings life to very unexciting statistical information. Everyone can understand and relate to experiences told by others. Other useful anecdotal information presented to the court that provides understandable concrete evidence of confusion is misdirected mail, phone calls, or both. Advertising that shows one brand but labels it as another is also an example of confusion through a secondary source.

The general objective in testing for brand imitation is to determine how similarly the consumer perceives the two objects in question. Gathering data for the courtroom must be a careful process. Because judges and lawyers usually are not trained in the nuances of statistics, it is up to the researchers to convey their information in a clear and simple manner. This may be a difficult task.

Recently courts have taken to approving consumer research methodology before it is carried out. The research methodology is submitted to the judge before the data are collected. The judge decides whether the questions, the sample, and the procedure are indeed unbiased. This pre-approval before data collection is the ideal and should lead to a more efficient decision-making process as to the acceptability of the resulting data.

REFERENCES

A & M Pet Products, Inc. v. Pieces, Inc. and Royal K-9. Case No. CV 89-4923 (Southwest United States District Court, Central District of Los Angeles 1989).

Amstar Corp. v. Domino's Pizza, Inc., 615 F.2d 252, 205 USPQ 969 (CA 5 1980), rehearing denied 617 F.2d (CA 5, 1980), Cert denied 449 US 899, 208 USPQ 464 (CA 5 1980).

Boal, R. B. (1973). Techniques for ascertaining likelihood of confusion and the meaning of advertising communications. *The Trademark Reporter, 73,* 405–435.

Chumura Kraemer, H., & Thiemann, S. (1987). *How many subjects? Statistical power analysis in research.* Newbury Park, CA: Sage.

Crespi, I. (1987). Surveys as legal evidence. *Public Opinion Quarterly, 51,* 84–91.

Donovan, R. (1987). *Brand detectability research.* Perth, Australia: Donovan Research.

Exxon Corporation v. Texas Motor Exchange of Houston, Inc., 628 F2d 500 (5th Cir. 1980).

Federal Glass Co. v. Corning Glass Works, 162 USPQ 279, 282-83 (TTAB 1969).

Gastwirth, J. (2003, March). Issues arising in using samples as evidence in trademark cases. *Journal of Econometrics, 113*(1), 69–82.

Glamorene Products Corp. v. Boyle-Midway, Inc., 188 USPQ 145 158-59 (SDNY 1975).

Grotrian, Helfferich, Schultz Steinweg Nach v. Steinway and Sons, 523 F2d 1331, 186 USPQ 436 (CA2 NY 1975).

Harlequin Enterprises Ltd. v. Gulf & Western Corp., 644 F2d 946,949 210 USPQ 1 (CA 2 1981).

Hartford House Ltd. v. Hallmark Cards Incorporated, CA (Colo), 846 F2d 1268 - Fed Cts. 815,862; Trade Reg 43, 334, 576, 626, (1986).

Helene Curtis Industries, Inc. v. Church & Dwight Co., Inc., 560 F2d 1325,1331, 195 USPQ 218 (CA 7 1977).

Hogan and Another v. Koala Dundee Pty. Ltd. and Others, 83 A.L.R. 187, (Federal Court of Australia, Pincus, J. 1988).

Humble Oil and Refining Co. v. American Oil Co., 405 F 2d 803, 160 USPQ 289 (CA8 Mo 1969), cert den 395 US 905, 23 L Ed 2d 218, 89 S Ct 1745, 161 USPQ 832.

Ideal Toy Corp. v. Kenner Products Division of General Mills Fun Group, Inc., 433 F Supp 291, 308, 197 USPQ 738, 752 (SDNY 1977).

IMS Ltd. v. International Medical Systems, Inc., USPQ 2d 1268, 1274-75 (EDNY 1986).

International Milling Company v. Robin Hood Popcorn Co., 110 USPQ 368, 46 TMR 1306,1308, (1956).

Ives Laboratories, Inc. v. Darby Drug Co., Inc., 601 F2d 631, 634, 202 USPQ 548 (CA 2 1979), on remand 488 F Supp 394, 206 USPQ 238 (EDNY 1980), revd 638 F2d 538, 209 USPQ 449 (CA 2 1981), revd 72 TMR 104, 214 USPQ1 (US 1982).

Jacoby, J. (1985). Survey and field experimental evidence. In S. M. Kassin & L. S. Wrightsman (Eds.), *The psychology of evidence and trial procedure* (pp. 175–200). Beverly Hills, CA: Sage.

Jenkins Bros v. Newman Hender & Co. Ltd., 123 USPQ 50, 329 (TTAB 1959).

Jockey International, Inc. v. Burkard, 185 USPQ 201 (1975, SD Cal).

Kapferer, J. N. (1995a). Brand confusion: Empirical study of a legal concept. *Psychology and Marketing, 12*(6), 551–568.

Kapferer, J. N. (1995b, May). Stealing brand equity: Measuring perceptual confusion between national brands and copycat' own-label products. *Marketing and Research Today, 23*(2), 96–103.

Kapferer, J. N., & Thoenig, J. C. (1991). *Les consommateurs face a la copie: Prodimarques.* Paris, France: Association Pour La Promotion a la Diffusion des Marques.

Leiser, A. W., & Schwartz, C. R. (1983). Techniques for ascertaining whether a term is generic. *The Trademark Reporter, 73*, 376–390.

Liefeld, J. P. (2003, July–August). How surveys overestimate the likelihood of consumer confusion. *The Trademark Reporter, 93*(4), 939–963.

Mead Data Central Inc. v. Toyota Motor Sales, U.S.A., Inc., 702 F. Supp 1031 9 USPQ2d 1442 (SDNY) revd 875 F2d 1026, 10 USPQ2d 1961 (CA2 1989), (S.D.N.Y. 1988).

Miaoulis, G., & D'Amato, N. (1978, April). Consumer confusion: Trademark infringement. *Journal of Marketing, 42*, 48–55.

Mitchell, V. W., & Kearney, I. (2002). A critique of legal measures of brand confusion. *Journal of Product and Brand Management, 11*(6), 357–379.

Morgan, F. (1990, January). Judicial standards for survey research: An update and guidelines. *Journal of Marketing, 54*, 59–70.

National Football League v. Governor of the State of Delaware, 435 F Supp 1372, 1379, 195 USPQ 803, 807 (D. Del 1977).

National Football League Properties, Inc. v. Wichita Falls Sportswear, Inc., 532 F Supp 651, 215 USPQ 175 (W.D. Wash 1982).

National Hockey League v. Pepsi-Cola Canada Ltd. No. C902104 (Supreme Court of British Columbia, June 2 1992).

Parkdale Custom Built Furniture Proprietary Limited v. Puxu Proprietary Ltd. (High Court of Australia 1981–1982).

Pattishall, B. W. (1959). Reaction test evidence in trade identity cases. *The Trademark Reporter, 49,* 145–174.

Paynter, R. H.(1920, January). A psychological study of trademark infringement. *Archives of Psychology, 42,* 1–72.

Preston, I. L. (1989a). The Federal Trade Commission's identification of implications as constituting deceptive advertising. *Cincinnati Law Review, 57,* 1243–1309.

Preston, I. L. (1989b). False or deceptive advertising under the Lanham Act: Analysis of factual findings and types of evidence. *The Trademark Reporter, 79,* 508–553.

Preston, I. L. (1990). The definition of deceptiveness in advertising and other commercial speech. *Catholic University Law Review, 39*(4), 1035–1079.

Price Pfister, Inc. v. Mundo Corp. (Superior Court of the State of California 1989).

Purofied Down Products Corp. v. Puro Down International of New Jersey Corp., 530 F Supp 134, 135 fn 2, 218 USPQ 720, 721 (EDNY 1982).

Reiner, J. P. (1983). The universe and the sample: How good is good enough? *The Trademark Reporter, 73,* 366–375.

RJR Foods, Inc. v. White Rock Corp. 201 USPQ 578 (1978, SD NY), Affd 603 F2d 1058, 203 USPQ 401 (CA2 NY).

Rogers, E. S. (1919, December). An account of some psychological experiments on the subject of trademark infringement. *Michigan Law Review, 18*(2), 75–103.

Sarel, D., & Marmorstein, H. (2002). Designing confusion surveys for cyberspace and trademark litigation: The admissibility vs. weight debate. *Intellectual Property and Technology Journal, 14*(9), 12–17.

Simon Property Group L.P., v. mySimon, Inc., 104 F Supp. 2d 1033 (SD Ind. 2000).

Simonson, I. (1993). The effect of survey method on likelihood of confusion estimates: Conceptual analysis and empirical test. *The Trademark Reporter, 83,* 364–393.

Simonson, I. (1994a). An empirical investigation of the meaning and measurement of "genericness." *The Trademark Reporter, 84,* 199–223.

Simonson, I. (1994b). Trademark infringement from the buyer perspective: Conceptual analysis and measurement implications. *Journal of Public Policy and Marketing, 13*(2), 181–199.

Smith, J. G., Snyder, W. S., Swire, J. B., Donegan, T. J., Jr., & Ross, I. (1983, October/November). Legal standards for consumer survey research. *Journal of Advertising Research, 23*(5), 19–35.

Smith v Sturm, Ruger & Co., Inc., 39 Wash. App. 740 695 F2d 600 (1985).

Sorensen, R. C., (1983). Survey research execution in trademark litigation: Does practice make perfection. *The Trademark Reporter, 73,* 349–365.

Squirt Co. v. Seven-Up Co., 207 USPQ 12 (ED Mo), aff'd 628 F2d 1086, 207 USPQ 897 (CA 8 1980), (1979).

Treisman, A., & Schmidt, H. (1982). Illusory conjunctions in the perception of objects. *Cognitive Psychology, 14,* 107–141.

Valerio, P. (1992). Case histories in the use of T-scopes in design research. Unpublished manuscript, Landor and Associates, San Francisco, CA.

Weight Watchers International v. The Stouffer Corporation, No. 88 Civ 7062 (MBM) (United States D 1990).

Weiss, P. (1990, January–February). The use of survey evidence in trademark litigation: Science, art, or confidence game. *The Trademark Reporter, 80,* 71–86.

Wells Fargo & Co. v. Wells Fargo Construction Co., 619 F Supp 710, 712-3 229 USPQ 938 (D. Ariz 1985).

Zippo Manufacturing v. Rogers Imports, Inc. (1963, SDNY) 216 F. supp. 670, 137 USPQ 413.

The Special Case of Cyberspace[1]

Commensurate with the increase in popularity of online purchasing, there has been a steady increase in counterfeit merchandise. According to Evans (2001), 25% of all branded goods sold on the Internet are counterfeit, causing companies to suffer $25 to $30 billion in lost revenues. The huge industry of online distribution of counterfeit pharmaceuticals is not only a threat to commerce, but also a threat to the safety of consumers. Evans suggested that the Internet facilitates this process because of its low barriers to entry and its capacity to give "criminals the ability to look professional and legitimate."

Counterfeiting is just one illegal activity occurring online and having a negative impact on companies and their customers. Online trademark infringement currently is quite common as "infringers" now have adopted the Internet to sell "replica" branded goods, imitators, and counterfeits that infringe on the trade dress and the trademark of well-known brand names, and to facilitate the process of confusing and misleading the consumer about the source of the goods or services they are seeking.

The different techniques used to create confusion in online search include cybersquatting (registration of a known trademark and selling it to the trademark owner), typosquatting (registration of a domain name consisting of a common typographic error for a trademark), framing (linking a site shown inside the layout of another Web site), and deep linking (connecting to specific content while bypassing a home page).

---

[1]Much of this chapter is based on Laurie Allen's Masters of Business Administration project completed at Simon Fraser University, Canada, 2003.

ONLINE LEGISLATION

Separate legislation is necessary for trademarks and domain names because there are some very basic differences between the two, despite the fact that the consumer may use them as one. Table 7.1 lists differences as itemized by Stephen Selby, the Director of Intellectual Property Government of Hong Kong.

Trademark owners could appeal to the courts under traditional trademark legislation with any trademark infringement cases, whether they involved the Internet or not. However, the Anti-Cybersquatting Consumer Protection Act (ACPA) was adopted in the United States in 1999 to deal specifically with online cases. The ACPA "provides relief to the trademark owner in those cases where a domain name has been registered in bad faith

TABLE 7.1
Main Differences Between Registering Trademarks and Domain Names

	Domain Names	*Trademarks*
Similarity	A domain name does not clash with a previous name as long as it is not identical. The concept is very simple and a computer can do the check without human intervention.	A trademark would clash with a previously registered mark if it were similar enough to mislead the consumer about the source of the goods or services. This concept is sophisticated and supported by much complex case law. Special training and human judgment are necessary to apply it.
Descriptive	A domain name can describe the property of the goods or services it is registered for (e.g., "freshbread.com" for a bakery).	A trademark must not simply be a property normally associated with the goods or services for which it is registered. "Fresh Bread" is not an allowable trademark for bakery products (although it would be fine for clothing).
Unrelated goods or services	A domain name does not get registered against a specific class of goods and services	Trademarks are registered for classes of goods and services. An application that clashes with a registered mark in one class may be allowed into another class if it does not mislead.

Adapted from Selby (2001). Cybersquatting. Available: http://www.info.gov.hk/ipd/eng/information/studyaids/cybersquatting.htm

with intent to profit, traffic in, or use a domain name that (a) is identical or confusingly similar to a mark that was distinctive when the domain name was registered, (b) is identical or confusingly similar to or dilutive of a mark that was famous when the domain name was registered, or (c) infringes marks and names protected by statute such as the Olympic Symbol or Red Cross" (Kitts & Caditz, 2002).

The complexity of determining whether the preceding points support a lawsuit for court or not is found in *Chatam International Inc. v. Bodum, Inc.* (2001). In this case, the suit was dismissed because of a summary judgment (or no trialable issue of fact). The dispute involved competing claims for the use of the Internet domain name "Chambord" and the registration and use of chambord.com. Whereas Chatam International sells various products such as preserves, liqueur, and chocolate under the name Chambord, Bodum sells a specific coffeemaker called Chambord (Exhibit 7.1).

In a previous suit in the 1980s involving these companies, the court ruled that Bodum could call its Chambord coffeemaker, but not any coffee it sells, because Chatam was in the business of edible goods and beverages. The court observed that the two companies had coexisted peacefully until the second domain name suit in 2000. Hence, there was little chance of confusion on the Net if there was none in person at the grocery store. There was therefore no need to reassign the domain name. Since early 2004, the

EXHIBIT 7.1   Bodum Webpage: While the name Chambord is registered to a company selling preserves, liqueur and chocolate, only Bodum can use the name to direct customers on the web.

domain name does not appear on the Web. Instead, the consumer who types in chambord.com is sent directly to the Bodum page when the name is entered.

ALTERNATIVE RESOLUTION AVENUES

Administrative avenues were established to address the issue of online trademark infringement after the seriousness of online trademark infringement was identified in a 1998 study by MARQUES, the European association of trademark-owning companies, in response to a request for comments posted by the World Intellectual Property Organization (WIPO). The study found that 85% of organizations had experienced infringement on their intellectual property, with 78% suffering domain name infringement, 40% suffering copyright infringement, and 29% percent claiming defamation (Wood, 1999). The consumer issue also was raised loud and clear: The public must have confidence that they can connect to the Internet with the party they are seeking. The clear message was that domain names needed to be allocated with much greater care.

The fact that the Internet has no borders creates a great legal challenge. Consider the following example, which occurred in 1999. Desktop Technologies Inc. of Boyerton, Pennsylvania, was the registered trademark holder in the United States of the name Colorworks, but the domain name colorworks.com was owned by Colorworks Reproduction and Design of Vancouver, Canada. A suit was brought forward by Desktop for trademark infringement. The argument was that there had to be more than simple registering of a mark as a domain name and posting of a Web site. There had to be proof of cross-border commerce. Hence, Colorworks Reproduction was allowed the name because no business of the firm crossed over to Desktop Technologies. However, Colorworks, small company it was, ceased operations before the judge's decisions (Akin, 1999).

The Internet Corporation for Assigned Names and Numbers (ICANN) implemented the resulting Uniform Domain Name Dispute Resolution Policy (UDRP), in 1999.[2] The UDRP was developed for the resolution of "disputes between a domain-name registrant and a third part over the abusive registration and use of an Internet domain name" (Kitts & Caditz, 2002). The UDRP has jurisdiction for the generic top-level domains such as

---

[2]Canada has its own policy under the Canadian Internet Registration Authority (CIRA). Its policy, the CIRA Domain Name Dispute Resolution Policy (CDRP) is meant to "provide a forum in which cases of bad faith registration of domain names registered in the dot-ca country code top-level domain name registry operated by CIRA can be dealt with relatively inexpensively and quickly" (CIRA, http://www.cira.ca/en/cat_dpr_policy.html). The CDRP closely follows that of the UDRP.

.com, .net, .org, .info, .biz, and .name, as well as country code top-level domains such as .jp for Japan, .uk for United Kingdom, and .br for Brazil.

A domain name complaint to the UDRP must meet the following criteria: (a) the domain name registered must be identical or confusingly similar to a trademark or service mark in which the complainant has rights; (b) a domain name registrant has no rights or legitimate interest with respect to the domain name in question; and (c) the domain name has been registered and is being used in bad faith. The UDRP procedure is not binding on federal courts, but it is a more efficient and cost-effective way to resolve domain name disputes. The UDRP is considerably less formal than the courts, in which the decision makers are experts in areas such as international trademark law, domain name issues, electronic commerce, and dispute resolution. The UDRP provides a mechanism for resolving a domain name dispute regardless of geographic borders. However, the only remedy available under the UDRP is cancellation or transfer of the domain name at issue. The cost to file a complaint is said to be less than $1,000, and takes less than 2 months to resolve.

One example of the type of problem appropriate for the UDRP is *Northern Light Technology v. Northern Lights Club, Jeffrey K. Burgar* (2001). Northern Light Technology, an American company, registered its Web site domain and operated a search engine under the name. Jeffrey K. Burgar, a resident of Canada, registered thousands of domain names based on the names of popular people and organizations, including northernlights.com. Burger stated that he was the President of Northern Lights Club, an unincorporated association with a listed address in Las Vegas, Nevada. The mission of the Club was to bring together devotees of the northern lights or aurora borealis, but the club had no actual members. Burger then licensed the name to FlairMail, a vanity e-mail service owned indirectly by his spouse. Negotiations for the Northern Light Technology to buy the domain name from Burger failed after 2 months. Ultimately, the court ruled that Burger's modus operandi of registering domain names containing the famous trademarks of others in hopes of selling them for profit was an act in bad faith.

A more targeted and typical dispute across foreign borders is found in *Quokka Sports Inc. v. Cup Int'l Ltd, Cup Int'l Internet Ventures* (1999). Quokka, an American Company, operated a Web site at americascup.org. Cup Int'l was a New Zealand company that registered the domain name americascup.com. The U.S. court found that personal jurisdiction could be asserted over the New Zealanders under California's long-arm statute and concluded that www.americascup.com was likely to cause consumer confusion. The Web site appeared to be masquerading as an official Web site associated with the America's Cup event. Several e-mails documenting possible advertising agreements from U.S. companies in U.S. dollars further provided the court with further evidence for their decision.

THE WEB AS A COMPLAINT MEDIUM

Americans are among the most vocal consumers in the world when it comes to satisfaction and consumer rights. Remember, it was John F. Kennedy who signed the Consumer Bill of Rights in 1963, and then Ralph Nader who led the attack on corporate America. Now, the World Wide Web has given consumers all over the world a medium for voicing their dissatisfaction with little cost and great convenience. Many disgruntled consumers who become frustrated when they fail to get satisfaction from a firm are motivated to go to the Net so that someone, somewhere, will pay attention to their complaints. In a case about topsoil, for example, a homeowner was dissatisfied with the work a local landscape company did on her yard. Unable to get satisfaction, she registered the name of the nursery online (lucasnursery.com) to voice her complaints. Of course, she was sued by the landscape company, but Public Citizen, the watchdog of the market founded by Ralph Nader, defended her actions. She won the case, but was left with a $20,000 legal bill because the costs of the litigation had to be covered personally.

Public Citizen also defended a customer who wanted a sunroof in his car. The dealership installed it aftermarket, hence, voiding part of the car warranty. The disgruntled consumer registered crownpontiacnissan.com and was sued for trademark infringement. Public Citizen argued that "using a trademark in a domain name is the same as using it in a book title, which is protected under the free speech clause of the constitution, because it is a way of calling attention to the content of the work in question" (Waldmeir, 2004, p. 7). This argument prevailed, and the car buyer was awarded his legal fees ($766) and another $6,000 for anguish and deprivation of free speech.

Currently, sophisticated companies, such as Cyveillance (www.Cyveillance.com), search the net and alert companies to content that relates to their firm, trademarks, and trade dress. They claim there are more than 40 million registered domains and more than 20 million live Web sites to monitor. Clearly, they serve big business well by identifying and alerting companies to sites that may defame them. For example, the name peta.org was registered for a Web site called People Eating Tasty Animals. The real PETA (People for the Ethical Treatment of Animals) was outraged and through the courts managed to claim and own the site peta.org. Sites such as Netscapesucks.com or ballysucks.com are constantly put up by disgruntled people and can be found easily by Cyveillance for the real company (Murray, 2004).

ONLINE TRADEMARK INFRINGEMENT TECHNIQUES

The legislation and regulating bodies discussed earlier have been implemented in an attempt to protect trademark owners from the different

From: "6.95domains@registrationgroup.com"
          <6.95domains@registrationgroup.com>
To: bus-faculty@sfu.ca
Date: Fri, 2 Jul 2004 07:17:47 -0400 (EDT)
Subject: **SPAM** Domain Names only $6.95/year

www.registrationsgroup.com

300 Park Avenue Center New York NY 10022

EXHIBIT 7.2   Spam Selling Web Addresses.

methods used by online trademark "infringers." One must look at the different types of infringements as "fluid" because of the constantly changing nature of Web sites and their content. The Web has come a long way from the early days, when astute college students saw the commercial benefits of registering many brand names in the hopes of selling them back to their rightful owners for a quick profit. The original investment of $70 for a 2-year right to use the domain name on the Web led to the registration of thousands of names by people who had no logical claim to them. Currently, domain names are priced according to the length of registration (1 to 10 years), and then can be sold again in aftermarkets in online auctions such as Afternic.com.

Many current problems with online infringement of intellectual property come when the consumers do not know the domain name of the company they are searching for. When users do not know the name, they either guess the name or use a search engine. When they guess, they may use the name of the brand or company followed by .com. When they use a search engine, their request goes through an index of Web sites relating to the entered key word. Each search engine may use a different algorithm to arrange the sites that relate to the keyed-in search name. The hierarchy in which discovered sites appear depends on a variety of factors, including getting paid by the search engine company.

Cybersquatting

The most well-known infringement technique is cybersquatting, which occurs when a company or person registers a domain name consisting of a known trademark and then attempts to sell it to the trademark owner. This problem arose because the governing body that first ran the Internet refused responsibility to check for trademark violations, but sold and assigned names on a "first come, first served" basis. This lack of accountability resulted in mass registration by entreprenuring young people, some of whom registered a dozen or more corporate names such as hertz.com. This mass registration was no doubt helped by articles such as the one in *Wired* magazine entitled "Billions Registered: Right Now There Are No Rules to Keep You From Owning A Bitchin' Corporate Name as Your Own Internet Address" (Dean, 1997). More recently, Spam is sent that invites one to register for only $6.95 per site (Exhibit 7.2). One can see how easy it is be become an owner of a Web address.

Registrars usually do not investigate whether a requested domain name matches a trademark held by someone else, because registering a domain name does not provide intellectual property rights (Butera, 2000). This type of infringement affects the company or trademark owner directly and the consumer indirectly, because in most cybersquatting cases, no Web site actually is designed for the domain name in question. For example, Miami college student Rafael Fortuny expressed, "I thought it was a cool thing. Then you get sued, and it's not so cool anymore." He had registered the Internet domain names that closely resembled the addresses of companies, such as PaineWebber and Citigroup, and routed that online traffic to an adult Web site.

Typosquatting

Typosquatting is an offshoot of cybersquatting, in which the "infringer" first determines the Web sites with the most traffic, then registers domain names that "consist of the likeliest typographical errors" (Kopp & Suter, 2000, p. 123). These errors range in variety, including misspellings (e.g., silliconvalley.com), alternative domain names (e.g., yaleuniversity.edu), or omitted punctuation (e.g., wwwbarnesnoble.com).

Various studies have estimated that 10% to 20% of all hand-entered uniform resource locators (URLs) are mistyped, adding up to 20 million wrongly reached addresses per day (Boutin, 2005). This type of infringement can be difficult to prove because the omission of punctuation may not be considered a cause for confusion.

The *Toronto-Dominion Bank v. Boris Karpachev* (2002) case is a good example of typosquatting. Mr. Karpachev became a customer of TD Waterhouse and its online brokerage service in June 1999. In November 1999, a dispute arose between Karpachev and TD Waterhouse over an alleged change order and short sale, which resulted in a loss of about $35,000 to Karpachev and the closing of his account. In March 2002, Toronto-Dominion Bank complained that Boris Karpachev deliberately registered 16 domain names confusingly similar to its proprietary TD Waterhouse mark (www.tdwaterhouse.com), such as tdwoterhouse.com, and dtwaterhouse.com. On the Internet sites associated with these domain names, Karpachev wrote disparaging comments about TD Waterhouse, such as alleged accusations of its involvement in white-collar crime, and asked other visitors to the site to write the courts about TD Waterhouse.

The Toronto-Dominion Bank was concerned that its customers would be confused as to the source of the information found on Karpachev's similar Web sites. Karpachev did not dispute Toronto-Dominion Bank's right to the TD Waterhouse domain name, nor did he dispute that he registered and used domain names noticeably similar to the TD Waterhouse mark. Karpachev, in fact, admitted that it was his intent to divert consumers from www.tdwaterhouse.com by creating confusion as to the source of the site. Consequently, Karpachev was ordered to forfeit the 16 domain names identified, and not to register any further domain names for the purpose of creating confusion with the TD Waterhouse trademark (*Toronto-Dominion Bank v. Boris Karpachev*, 2002).

Other similar disputes have occurred with mixed results. In particular, a dispute arose in January 1999 between Buy.com and a number of its competitors. The online retailer, Buy.com, had registered domain names that closely resembled its competitors' names, such as www.10percentoffamazon.com, www.10percentoffreel.com, and www.10percentoffegg.com. With these domain names, Buy.com created Web sites designed to lure business away from the competitor (Wood, 1999). Whereas the sites resembling Reel.com and Egg.com are no longer active, www.10percentoffamazon.com still works and links directly to Buy.com's book department site (www.buy.com).

Linguistic Issues

Another factor that could cause confusion involves any alphabetic, acronymic, phonetic, and linguistic issues. It could easily be the case that the "pronunciation of a brand name may be different from its spelling or abbreviation as a domain name" (Kopp & Suter, 2000, p.124). This is particularly a problem when the company has customers or information seekers who are not familiar with the language in which the brand name is stated. A consumer who is not familiar with the spelling of a brand name may search for the brand based on the way it sounds, and may arrive at a Web site selling similar products. The consumer may go ahead and purchase without knowing that the product is not the brand he or she intended to purchase.

Search-Related Issues

Search-related infringement issues often involve metatags and keywords. Metatags are "software codes used by Web search engines to find and return records …. The practice of using metatags is intended to ensure that a site is among the first listed in a user's search" (Kopp & Suter, 2000, p. 120). Metatag trademark infringement is known as 'invisible infringement' because metatags are not visible, but are the code behind the Web site. If individuals use trademarked words they do not own in their Web site's metatags, resulting in the diversion of traffic to their Web site rather than the trademark owner's Web site, then this can be considered trademark infringement.

Key words have become targets for potential trademark infringement cases because search engines have taken up the business strategy of actively directing users to Web sites that purchase key words and, therefore, placement on the results page (Lastowka, 2002). The difficulty is that search engines are seen as unbiased. However, by their promotion of Web sites that have purchased a particular word, users are being herded toward a particular site. Trademark infringement becomes a possibility when the key words for sale are trademarked words.

The first case of metatag "invisible" trademark infringement was *Playboy vs. Calvin Designer Labels* (1997). In this case, the court ruled that the word "playboy" could not be used as a metatag to lure customers to a rival sex site. Conversely, trademark rights also were limited in a Playboy case involving the 1981 Playmate of the year, Terri Wells. Ms. Wells promotes her own Web site, which carries pictures of her in various activities wearing next to nothing, with the metatags "playboy" and "playmate." *Playboy* sued for trademark infringement and lost. Ms. Wells was judged as using the *Playboy* trademark fairly for her descriptive purposes. Otherwise, she would have to describe herself as "the nude model selected by Mr. Hefner's magazine as its number one prototypical woman for the year 1981." *Playboy* had more or less given its "brand" to Ms. Wells when it crowned her.

Perhaps one of the best cases, which outlines the complex issues with metatags, is *Brookfield Communications Inc. v. West Coast Entertainment Corporation* (1995). Brookfield is a computer company, which designed a program called "moviebuff" to search for movies through a database. West Coast Entertainment, a movie rental store, registered the same domain name for its Web site. The issue was whether federal trademark and unfair competition laws prohibit a video rental store chain from using an entertainment industry information provider's trademark in the domain name of its Web site and in its Web sites metatags.

The court stated: "Registration of a domain name for a Web site does not trump long-established principles of trademark law. When a firm uses a competitor's trademark in the domain name of its Web site, users are likely to be confused as to the source or sponsorship. Similarly, using a competitor's trademark in the metatags of said Web site is likely to cause *initial interest confusion.*" These forms of confusion are exactly what the trademark laws are designed to prevent, and the decision went to Brookfield although West Coast claimed to have spent 15 million dollars in advertising.

Linking and Framing Issues

Because the Internet itself is a web or network of computers all over the world, it is possible to access files stored in other computers. Linking is a simple matter of connecting the content of two different files or parts of files on computers located in different places. A single Web page may contain dozens of links to different computers and files, and it, in turn, may be linked to hundreds or thousands of other different Web sites. The issue for confusion is that the consumer may not know to which source of the goods they are linked. A very good discussion of linking is found at www.bitlaw.com/internet/linkinking.html (Bolin, 2000).

There are new technologies to prevent users from linking without consent. These technologies include registration and passwords for gaining access to a site and dynamic web pages whose URLs change at set periods. The effectiveness of these measures remains to be proven.

Framing occurs when "a linked site is displayed inside another's Web site so that the content of the linked site is literally framed on the linking site" (Kopp & Suter, 2000, p. 125). Framing may cause confusion about the source of the content because to users, it appears that they never leave the original Web site. Deep Linking occurs when "a link bypasses a home page and connects instead to specific content within a Web site"(Kopp & Suter, 2000, p.125). Again, confusion about the source of the information may occur because the user is not shown who the owner of the content is, and the owner has no control over how the content is displayed.

THE DISCLAIMER

Disclaimers appear to be used in an effort to solve confusion problems, without much thought to their effectiveness pertaining to the magnitude of the disclaimer and placement issues. In *Interstellar Starship Services v. Epix Incorporated* (2001) (a local Portland theater group vs a technical firm), the court ruled against claims for trademark dilution and cybersquatting of epix.com by Starship. The court found that Starship Services' past use of the epix.com in conjunction with the promotion of technical services and digital image processing did infringe on the EPIX trademark and prohibited Starship from using their Web site for those purposes. The court ruled that any time Starship used epix.com as a logo on their Web site, it needed to provide an annotation explaining that epix.com was not affiliated with EPIX on each page displaying the epix.com logo. Adding a disclaimer seems to be the usual method of selling imitation goods on the Internet, especially imitations of luxury brands. A typical example of the disclaimer found on these Web sites follows:

> All products sold within this website are replicas, imitations or reproductions. They can be used for entertainment or educational and novelty purposes only. The replica items, including but not limited to watches, sunglasses, pens, belts, umbrellas, sports and handbags, wallets, hats, suitcases, t-shirts, and etc. are NOT being represented as the originals. Although the details look similar to the originals, they do not have any relation with the brands mentioned in this website whatsoever, and this does not mean to damage in any way the brands mentioned. The replica items from this site bear no relationship to the name brand(s) they may bear and are not from nor can authorized dealers service them. We strongly recommend that if you want an original one, buy it from an official dealer. We do not sell originals. The customer accepts not to sell or show them as legitimate ones, and is completely responsible to the law for their actions after buying them. If you enter or shop from this site you declare to have read in detail all the terms and conditions above, and understand and agree with every item mentioned above. By entering this site, you are agreeing not to prosecute anyone affiliated with this site, or anyone who shops here. If you work for any of the companies mentioned above, you give up the right to prosecute anyone affiliated with this website, view this website, and you also give up the right to shop here. Shopping here means you comply and agree to these terms. If you work for Louis Vuitton, Chanel, Fendi, Coach, Prada, Hermès or any of the names mentioned above, you may not enter or shop from this site. By viewing this site, you give up all rights to prosecute anyone affiliated with this site. If you are viewing this site, any page on it, you agree to these terms (http://www.luxeinthecity.com/).[3]

These disclaimers seemingly try to intimidate anyone wishing to complain about the Web site or to protect his or her intellectual property. They also add a very official line about "violating code 431.322.12 of the Internet Privacy Act signed by Bill Clinton in 1995" and go on to state that "you cannot threaten our ISP(s) affiliated with this page which includes family, friends, or individuals who run this Web site." The effectiveness or legality of these statements is unclear. In *Rolex Watch U.S.A., Inc. And Prl Usa Holdings, Inc. v. Todd Jones* (2000), the Internet site was selling the same product with the same name of Rolex watches and polo shirts, but stated openly that the goods were "replicas." The court ruled that there was bad faith in Jones' marketing tactics, and that his products were likely diluting the famous marks.

---

[3]Accessed October 28, 2003, Web site domain name expired September 10, 2005.

REMEDIES

Company Directed

As discussed in an earlier section on the legal aspects of online trademark infringement, a trademark owner who feels that its mark is being infringed upon can choose to place a complaint with the UDRP or CDRP, or issue a lawsuit under the ACPA or the more traditional trademark infringement legislation. The remedies under the UDRP and CDRP are limited to the cancellation or transfer of the domain name at issue. Under legislation, the remedies are much broader. Specifically, under the ACPA, remedies include cancellation or transfer of the domain name, as well as compensatory or statutory damages of $1,000 to $100,000 per domain name, plus attorneys' fees, costs, and injunctive relief (Kitts & Caditz, 2002).

Companies have begun implementing their own methods to protect against online trademark infringement. These techniques include placing a unique identification marker on products to verify authenticity and increasing Internet monitoring, including the use of various new products that track chat rooms, message boards, UseNet groups, and e-commerce sites to report pricing structures and erosion, channel manipulation, product integrity, and customer satisfaction. Companies now initiate investigation of potential infringement leads and then hand them off to their attorneys (Evans, 2001). Finally, it is important for trademark owners with online capabilities to create a domain name management system to control renewals and the necessary domain name maintenance (Wood, 1999).

Consumer Directed

Few studies have looked at how companies can protect or minimize confusion for the consumer. Whereas companies focus on minimizing trademark infringement through court cases, administrative processes, or both, there has been little focus on what can be done on the demand side. Currently, the consumer is left to manage the existence of confusion on his own. Mitchell and Papavassiliou (1999) identified the use of generic confusion-reducing strategies used by consumers when they are aware of their confusion. These strategies include doing nothing, postponing or abandoning the purchase, clarifying the buying goals, seeking additional information, narrowing down the set of alternatives, and sharing or delegating the purchase.

Most of these confusion-reducing strategies are not encouraging for the marketer. Thus, any solutions that would clarify the confusion so that the consumer need not invoke these reduction strategies would be beneficial. A review of the past research on consumer confusion has identified a few constructs that have had as having an impact in the traditional in-store setting.

Degree of Care

First, degree of care appears to be a moderating factor for the courts in assessing likelihood of confusion. Degree of care denotes "the extent to which consumers consider product information when making purchases, such that they will be more or less likely to distinguish trademarks and other source-related information" (Howard, Kerin, & Gengler, 2000, p. 250). It is particularly important in online trademark infringement cases because the Internet has a significant impact on consumer information search behavior. The Internet is being used for searches "when a consumer's objective is specific product or service information in anticipation of a purchase as well as when the objective is to obtain general information about a brand or product or service category" (Peterson & Merino, 2003, p.104).

Given this understanding, consumers "are likely to spend less time searching for specific product or service information in prepurchase information searches" (Peterson & Merino, 2003, p. 110) because they assume all necessary knowledge has been accumulated during the general information search stage. The problem with this behavior is that the consumer's detailed knowledge of various trademarks in the product category they are evaluating may be lower than if they performed their regular specific product information search. This reduced level of information potentially could affect their degree of care, thus increasing their likelihood of confusion.

Product Involvement

Directly related to degree of care and level of information search is the construct of involvement. Involvement plays a pivotal role in explaining the amount of information search and information processing consumers exhibit when considering brands. In a high-involvement situation, consumers generally increase their level of information search, and are thus better able to detect even small differences in stimuli. In low-involvement purchase decisions, consumers are less motivated to perform an information search, making it more difficult for them to differentiate between subtle differences in products. Or, it could be that they are not interested in expending the mental effort needed.

For example, in *Mars Musical Adventures, Inc., a Wisconsin Corporation v. Mars Inc., a Florida Corporation* (2001), the first company (MMA) sold vintage music equipment, instruments, and recording services. In 1998, the company registered mars-music.com, and used it as its principal Web address. The second Mars is a nationwide chain of superstores that offer musical instruments (new and vintage), supplies, and recording services. In 1996, Mars acquired and registered the Internet domain name marsmusic.com. In March 1999, Mars demanded that MMA "cease and desist" from using the domain name mars-music.com. In response, MMA sued, but offered to sell its Web address to MARS for $650,000.

Although there were many legal issues in this case, the court found that for the type of products Mars Inc. sold and the level of involvement consumers had with these products, customers would expend more time and effort in their decision. There could be no confusion by consumers other than diversion by the Web site address. The offer to sell the address for $650,000 was in bad faith because Mars Inc. had bought the same name without the hyphen for $3,000. The court ruled against the mom and pop small store and for the large retail chain.

Product Experience

Another potential modifier of confusion, also linked closely with degree of care and product involvement, is product experience. With product experience, a consumer's level of knowledge concerning a given product will expand so that he or she should be able to identify more subtle distinctions between competing brands. Product experience can include actual purchase of the product or exposure through a friend or family member, as well as familiarity with a product's advertising and promotion. When goods are bought online because they are otherwise unavailable to the consumer, there is no direct consumer experience on which to draw on. For example, if a man has never taken Viagra before, he may not be familiar with its distinctive shape or its real manufacturer. It may be very easy for the man to believe that whatever he gets in the mail is indeed the Viagra that he thinks is the real product.

In countries, such as China, where the language is totally different from that of the original manufacturer and the goods may be unavailable, it is very difficult to know how the real good should appear. Many people may not be aware that they are purchasing imitation goods. In a study of imitation goods and the Chinese, Lai and Zaichkowsky (1999) found that the people from mainland China were the least likely to identify real brands. The most accurate identifiers were the people from Hong Kong and Taiwan. Almost 90% of the mainland Chinese respondents reported buying imitation goods when they wanted the "real" brand. Moreover, they reported that they felt cheated by the experience.

ONLINE VERSUS IN-STORE SHOPPING

Internet usage for purchasing products and services has steadily increased over the past few years. Sources, such as Jupiter Research, have suggested that consumer online purchases will reach $199 billion by 2005 (Wolfinbarger & Gilly, 2001). Why the flood to online shopping? What makes it different from traditional in-store shopping? Li and Gery (2000) outlined the major differences between online and in-store shopping:

1. Alternatives for consideration (wider choice)
2. Shopper's ability to screen and select alternatives (selecting best option)
3. Availability of information for making purchase decisions (informed decision)
4. Ordering and servicing of merchandise (convenience)
5. Shopping experience (functional).

Online consumers have access to a greater number of products (alternatives) than in a store, and all are available at a click of a mouse. This accessibility should help consumers find the best product for them. However, more alternatives can mean increased information search costs, and thus a decreasing marginal return for each additional search conducted. Too much choice has been documented to overwhelm consumers and create stress. In-store shopping can minimize information overload because sales associates may disseminate important information and focus on the critical characteristics of the merchandise that may not be accurately conveyed on the Internet (e.g., color, smell, style).

The Internet enables users to order products from anywhere, at any time, suggesting lower transaction costs. However, customers will not have the usual immediate gratification gained from a purchase, because they will need to wait a day, usually longer, for their purchase to be delivered. After-sales service may also be troublesome for online shoppers, depending on the retailer's return policy. Without the interaction with people, be it family, friends, or sales associates, online shopping becomes more functional than social or entertaining.

It is reported that two-thirds to four-fifths of online shoppers engage in narrowly defined searches for specific products, over a 15-minute or less time frame. In fact, many do not view shopping online as "shopping," but think of it as "buying," and consider themselves much more impulsive in an offline setting (Wolfinbarger & Gilly, 2001). Shoppers feel much more committed to offline purchases, a sentiment that is confirmed with the feeling of regret if they come home empty-handed after shopping offline. Online purchasing lacks this pressure because it is viewed as "always there." Although this may appear to be negative, online shoppers actually enjoy this lack of commitment, suggesting that it increases their efficiency and minimizes the effort needed to make a purchase.

Online and offline environments provide different shopping experiences even if the same products are available. However, the two shopping experiences can complement each other well, and it is for this reason that many shoppers use both. For example, consumers may take advantage of the convenience of online shopping to purchase, but visit a store before a purchase for a personal inspection of the product. The reverse also occurs, in which the consumer uses the Internet as a source of information, but then purchases the product in-store. The consumer still identifies brands in two ways: by the company providing the good, and by the trademark and trade dress, regardless of the purchase medium.

A STUDY OF CONSUMER BEHAVIOR ON THE NET

Academic studies have targeted the impact of trademark infringement on the consumer only in the traditional store setting. Besides discussing the different techniques used by "infringers" online, no research has been done to investigate the specific ways consumers deal with these sites. What specifically about a Web experience will make the consumer confused? For those who are not confused, what do they do differently? Is there something companies can do that will prevent consumer confusion so that the courts do not have to get involved? These are some of the questions addressed through exploration of online search behavior and encounters with infringing sites.

Different Ways of Searching the Net

When a consumer decides to search the Net for some product or service, they may start by guessing the domain name. For example, if you are looking to book a flight on Delta Airlines, you might start with typing in the name delta.com. However that search leads you to a Web site for Delta Financial Corporation. The Web address for Delta Airlines is deltaairlines.com. Therefore, sometimes the Web address you think is the obvious one is not the one you want.

If you do not know the Web address, the next method is to use a search engine such as Google or Yahoo. If you type in Delta Airlines as the key words, not only will you connect to get the real Delta Airlines site, but you also might be directed to a variety of travel agencies, for example, Expedia.com, or Travelocity.com. You also may be directed to BoycottDelta.com, which is of course a Web site that the company prefers that you do not see. These different sites emerge because when a search word is entered, the search engine processes it through an index of Web sites to generate a list related to the entered word. Search engines look for these key words in places such as domain names, actual text on the Web page, and metatags. The more often a term appears in the metatags and in the text of a Web page, the more likely it is that the Web site will be counted as a "hit," and the results of the search are determined by the number of hits entered for the key word.

Sometimes the search does not provide the Web page that the consumer really wants. The consumer ends up looking through these sites, which offer alternate choices. Because a particular domain name is like a street or mailing address, it is important for every legitimate company to have its obvious and intuitive name as its domain name and Web address, so that the search produces its name without the help of a search engine. This is especially important because there is no exhaustive central listing of Internet domain names for companies similar to the Yellow Pages (*Obh, Inc. and Columbia Insurance Company v. Spotlight Magazine and Claude Tortora*, 2000).

In-Depth Interviews With Online Shoppers

To investigate online consumer confusion, an exploratory, qualitative study with a series of 11 in-depth interviews was undertaken with consumers who regularly purchased online. The participants ranged in age from 21 to 36 years. All the participants used the Internet on a daily basis, primarily for correspondence, research related to their studies, and purchase-related activities.

The initial questionnaire was composed of nine broad topic questions:

1. What types of products have you purchased online?
2. If you were going to purchase <insert a product they listed above> online, how would you go about doing so?
3. Can you show me some of the Web sites you use to purchase products online? Take me through a typical purchase.
4. Why do you use these Web sites?
5. What information provided on these Internet sites is most useful to you?
6. What information do you not like?
7. a. Have you come across a Web site where you are not sure of the connection between the good and the provider of the information?
   b. Can you show me an example?
   c. What made you unsure?
   d. What were your feelings/emotions? How did you react? What did you do?
   e. Have you come across this situation in an offline setting?

8. Scenario: You need to buy textbooks for your classes. Your friend says to try online as you can get them cheaper than at the campus bookstore. What do you do?

   a. Your friend refers you to the domain: *www.10percentoffamazon.com*. What are your initial thoughts/expectations of this site?

b. Please visit *www.10percentoffamazon.com*. What are your impressions now? How are they the same/different from your initial feeling? How do you feel about that?

c. How does this site compare with its competitors?

- Chapters
- Barnes & Noble
- Amazon
- Compare your feelings of *10percentoffamazon.com* with *whitehouse.com*? Are they different? Why?

9. Have you purchased a product online that you have not purchased in a regular retail environment?

Insights into the direction the interviews might go highlighted areas such as the influence of word-of-mouth on the consumer's choice of Web sites used, as well as the use of branding by the consumer to determine a company's legitimacy. The interviews were performed both with participants who acknowledged having experienced confusion online and with those who had not knowingly experienced confusion before entering the interview. There were several cases with the latter group in which the participant described experiencing confusion without labeling it as such.

Once the interviews were completed, they were transcribed verbatim from the tape-recordings of the interviews. Categorization began during the open process of coding the transcripts. Here, concepts were identified both deductively from the literature and inductively using in-vivo codes (in which the researcher used the exact term given by the participant) (Strauss & Corbin, 1990). Once a close reading of all the interviews was completed, the conceptualization process evolved into abstraction, in which the concepts were grouped into higher level constructs. At this point, a second reading of the transcripts occurred because some concepts were recoded and new ones presented themselves on the basis of the newly defined constructs. Some axial coding was performed to analyze the relationship between categories and their subcategories. Throughout the process, comparison opportunities were identified. For example, the participants' responses to online and offline confusion discussions were grouped into separate categories for consideration.

A Model of Online Confusion

The suggested theoretical model for online consumer confusion that emerged from the data is found in Fig. 7.1. The findings focus on the Process of Online Search, which has organized into seven major constructs. The Outcomes From Search are not discussed at length.

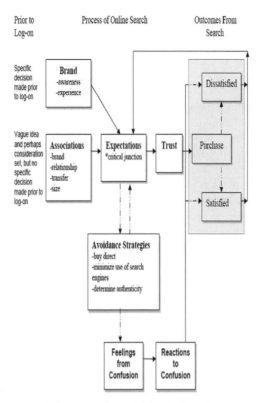

FIG. 7.1.   Suggested Theoretical Model for Online Consumer Confusion.

The Seven Constructs of Online Confusion

Brand

The brand construct is divided into two categories: brand awareness and brand experience. For the purpose of this study, *brand awareness* was defined as "knowledge of the brand." Participants' comments such as "I was familiar with the name, I'd heard it" (Kyle, male, 25) or "a company already in my head" (Jane, female, 21) are examples of utterances coded under awareness. *Brand experience* was defined as "experience with the brand either directly through purchase or vicariously." Examples of comments coded in this section included "I've shopped there before" (Jane, female, 21); "Also, too, I've heard of the name in my past experience somewhere else" (Dana, female, 23); and "I've used it back at, when I was working" (Robert, male, 23).

Many of the participants suggested that shopping online occurs for a preplanned situation. In such instances, consumers already know what they want. They have a list of providers in their mind, and they go directly to the Web sites of these companies to find the product they want. In consideration of this behavior, the model begins with identification of the brand for those online shoppers who already have made a specific decision before logging-on. For this to occur, the consumer must be aware and perhaps have some prior experience with the brand.

Associations

An association is a feeling or thought that connects two items. Participants seem to use associations to get an understanding of something unknown or unfamiliar to them. They use something known to help explain the unknown in an attempt to limit the uncertainty in an unfamiliar purchase situation. Consumers who have not made a specific decision regarding their online purchase before using the Internet enter the model at this juncture. They, however, do not take the time to determine whether the association they have made is correct or not, which can open them up to confusion. If the association is incorrect, the consumer will have formed expectations (the critical junction in the model) based on incorrect associations.

Associations have been divided into four types: brand, relationship, transfer, and size. A brand association occurs when the association relates to a brand. A participant might say, "I associated that if this is Casio, then it must have some sort of guarantee behind it" (Robert, male, 23) or "If, for example, Buy.com looks similar to Amazon, then I guess it gives me more comfort" (Ben, male, 21). In both examples, the participant uses his understanding or an idea about a familiar brand to connect it with an unknown, potentially unrelated item.

A relationship association occurs when there is a perceived formal relationship between two items. Examples of this category from the study include "I see this as not Amazon; I would wonder if they have a deal with Amazon"(Michelle, female, 36) or "or something like maybe a promotion affiliated with Amazon that they are having or it would connect back to the Amazon Web site, like the Amazon home page" (Dana, female, 23).

A transfer association occurs when the properties of a familiar item are transferred to the unfamiliar item. Examples include the following:

> Yahoo sponsored it and Yahoo is a credible name, so even though the company I'd never heard of before, it was associated with a credible company, so I thought that I'd be safe again to buy from them so I did. (Ben, male, 21)

> I thought that because these guys were popping up on a site that I visited regularly and I thought was pretty reputable, so I guess that made me think okay these guys should be legitimate as well. (Ben, male, 21)

The final classification is size association. Here, the consumer makes an association based on the size of the company. For example,

If you're a big company, and you have all these resources and if you can't prevent this [trademark infringement], then God knows what else you are not able to do. Maybe you are not able to actually give me good products or good quality service at the end. (Robert, male, 23)

No matter on which route consumers enter the model, they use the information gathered to form expectations for the good, the Web site, and the company behind the Web site.

Expectations

Expectations are classified as the consumer's preconceived notions before purchase. These expectations are developed from the brand, from any associations made, and from external factors, such as experience using the Internet or the product category. Examples of expectations include such statements as "It would depend on what I was trying to get out of my purchase" (Jane, female, 21) and "I expected it to still say 10percentoffamazon.com" (Dan, male, 22).

The expectations construct is a critical juncture in the model because it is from this point that the consumer has the potential to be confused. It will be recalled that confusion occurs when there is a disconnect between the consumer's expectations and reality. The importance of expectations is addressed well in this statement from a participant:

If I go into a store like Wal-Mart to buy clothes, I don't care if I'm being mislead, 'cause I'm not going to buy that brand name anymore. I'm just going to get some clothes. So whatever they give me for whatever price. Then if, and if I'm going into a store like Old Navy or American Eagle and I'm going in, that's what they offer. (Jane, female, 21)

Jane had different expectations from her Wal-Mart shopping experience than from a shopping experience at Old Navy or American Eagle. She expects more from the brand name stores because she is going there specifically for their product.

Expectations represent a crossroads of sorts in the model. If the expectations formed are equal or very similar to reality, then the consumer will develop trust and purchase from the Web site when needed. But if the expectations formed do not equal reality, confusion may occur. It is important to note that when a consumer's expectations and reality are clearly different, then confusion does not occur:

I just tried to type what I was thinking, but it went to something totally different, so I think *Gap.ca* is something different. But it is not really confusion because once it goes there you automatically know it's not, I think it's some sort of travel agency, so it becomes apparent pretty soon. (Dana, female, 23)

Trust

Trust has been defined as "the ability to believe or have confidence in the Web site, organization, or situation in which the consumer finds him- or herself" (Liu & Leach, 2001). It became clear that this was a very important construct for the online consumer because trust was mentioned in all interviews. Participants expressed the fact that trust is much more important for online shopping than for offline shopping: "There's a certain amount of trust on a Web site; you can see pictures, but it's not the same as being able to handle something; it's not the same as being able to know what's in your hand"(Kyle, male, 25), and "on the net you're basing your trust on a picture and someone else's word" (Ed, male, 21). One participant summarized it well when he said, "Actually, it's all about trust" (Kyle, male, 25).

However, trust is fragile. It can be formed easily: "I immediately trust because of a brand name or the Web site address," (Jane, female, 21), which is what "infringers" play off of. However, it can be easily broken, as one participant put it, due to "the fear of being scammed" (Ben, male, 21). Participants, although they may not have been personally involved in an online transaction that went poorly nor know someone involved in one, fear that it might happen to them. Consumers therefore tend to guard against such problems, as the following participants explain:

> I don't trust a lot of the Web sites because a lot of them, there's certain suppliers and they set up lots of portals at different Web sites, but there's no actual company behind it. (Ed, male, 21)

> I don't really have a trust for the other Web sites because I'm pretty confident that they will eventually deliver what I want, but I don't know how fast they're going to deliver. (Ed, male, 21)

Trust between a consumer and supplier can be broken in two ways: when the supplier does not perform as expected, and when the supplier does not hold honest motivations or attitudes toward the consumer. Confusion occurs during the time when the consumer interacts with the supplier in a way that is not what was expected, or receives a good that was not as expected. They are unsure about what happened, why it is not as expected. The reaction to not receiving what was expected can be broken trust and the formation of distrust, unless what is received exceeds expectations, in which case trust can be developed further. With trust being so fragile, consumers avoid seeking out new alternatives when they already have a supplier in which they trust: "I figured, since I already have the ebgames, I've tried it and it works and the prices seem to be the same, there's little motivation for me to try ign.com" (Dan, male, 22).

Avoidance Strategies

The participants identified a number of ways in which they tried to avoid confusion, and these have been categorized as avoidance strategies in the model. Although these strategies are enacted at all times throughout the purchase process, they are relied on most heavily during the short on-line search stage before the purchase is made. As discussed earlier, due to "the fear of being scammed" (Ben, male, 21), consumers automatically use precautions to minimize risk. These avoidance strategies can help consumers to identify potentially high-risk transactions, and thus provide them with an avenue for readjusting their expectations if necessary. The primary strategies identified in this study include buy direct, minimize the use of search engines, and determine authenticity.

Buy Direct. Consumers buy direct when they purchase from the manufacturer instead of a dealer or distributor. This was a fairly common occurrence as it was mentioned in more than half of the interviews. Participants described this phenomenon as follows:

> I'll take the brand names that actually make the product that I'm looking for and go to their site directly. (Ben, male, 21)

> If I was looking for something, if I know I want a shirt, maybe I will type in something like, I don't know, whatever company it is that I'm looking for and just go to their Web site. (Ben, male, 21)

> I go to the product Web site, you can buy from their own store right, I buy direct. (Dan, male, 22)

Participants buy direct to avoid the excess information provided to them by search engines.

Minimize the Use of Search Engines. The participants in this study preferred to minimize their use of search engines because it was deemed that search engines often are the cause of "being scammed." As one participant described, "Those type of situations I usually get into when I pop into a search engine. So that's why I really have problems with shopping by search engines" (Ben, male, 21). It appears that search engines are useful for gathering information, but during the purchasing process, consumers prefer to avoid using them. Several of the participants discussed their preference for using search engines within a site to navigate the site over other methods, although there was not a consensus on this matter.

When forced to use search engines, the participants tended to use the domain name as cues to determine the legitimacy of the site:

> Certain domain names, like certain porno Web sites will disguise themselves as legitimate websites to try to drive traffic and then drive sponsors, and often, so you can't really trust what it says here; you can often tell that something's wrong with the address, and you can then stay away. (Kyle, male, 25)

Often the participants used a combination of the information search engines provided them in an attempt to filter unwanted sites.

Determine Authenticity. The participants in the study appeared to have four primary methods for determining authenticity: referrals, availability of contact information, use of trademarks, and level of professionalism. The participants mentioned referrals most often. In fact, referrals were mentioned in seven of the eight interviews. Referrals were through word-of-mouth, most commonly by friends, but also through Web site features, such as feedback forums in which postings were placed by those involved in a transaction.

Availability of contact information was used to determine whether there actually was a company behind the Web site. The importance of knowing "that there's a physical location" (Kyle, male, 25) was identified. The fact that "sometimes contact information is so hard to find on some sites" (Dana, female, 23) gave credibility to those that openly displayed contact information. It gives the company credibility because "that kind of tells me that they're not afraid to have people call them, but they kind of want people to be able to contact them, and they make it really easy to find" (Dana, female, 23).

Trademarks, such as logos, are commonly used for identification. But as one participant discussed, it is important for the consumer to ensure that the correct format of the trademark is used: "Well, and then their name, as long as it's in the right lettering, as part of the brand" (Jane, female, 21).

Level of professionalism was a criterion used by the participants to determine authenticity. The participants discussed professionalism usually in the context of what poor professionalism meant to them:

> Just the user interface, a poor interface, I kind of infer that the store itself, the professionalism, might also be kind of poor, so I tend not to buy from them as well, because if they can't get their Web site nicely organized and functional, why would we trust them with getting a computer, my computer, up and running. (Dan, male, 22)

> I wasn't quite sure if it was really legit or not because they seemed to sell a lot; it wasn't really well-structured, the site; it seemed that the package they put up it didn't seem very professional so of course I didn't buy from there; it just didn't seem like it could be a store. (Dan, male, 22)

> Bad color coordination and, how should I say, bad fonts, no links, no pictures, nothing up there, then I would go like, yeah, I'm not using this; no one has put any effort in. (Robert, male, 23)

However, the participants also were careful to note that the level of professionalism, although an important criterion, could not be used on its own to determine authenticity sufficiently. As one participant noted, "I mean it's professional, but I mean it's easy to create a professional Web site I guess" (Dana, fFemale, 23). Thus, professionalism is used in conjunction with the other methods of authenticity identification. This can be said to be true for all the criteria discussed. As one participant described determining authenticity: "It's kind of an instinct" (Ben, male, 21) that incorporates everything about a Web site.

Feelings From Confusion

Participants were asked for their emotions during a time that caused them confusion. They described their feelings in the following terms:

Disappointment

I usually like to be informed, well informed when I make a decision, and in this case I just felt like I did not know what I was buying. If I knew beforehand it's a refurbished cam, maybe I would of changed my decision, maybe not, but either way, I would like to know beforehand. So that, in that respect, yeah I was kind of disappointed. (Michelle, female, 36)

Frustration

… Take away from my experience with the company that I was trying to find. Like, starting off the search frustrated. (Jane, female, 21)

Taken advantage of

I felt, one that I paid the money, but also kind of taken advantage of, yeah pretty much taken advantage of. (Dana, female, 23)

Lack of Control

They are leading me somewhere and I have no control over that …. I am giving information to them over the Internet that I have no control over what happens to it, and I don't even know what's going to end up coming to me on the other end. (Jane, female, 21)

These feelings were exhibited toward the company that did the misleading as well as toward the company that the participant was searching to find. In most cases, the participants exhibited negative feelings and general dissatisfaction from confusion. However, this was not always the case. One participant described a transaction in which she experienced confusion, but the result, nevertheless was a good experience because she described it as a "good surprise" (Michelle, female, 36). She was left with a higher opinion of the company than when she first purchased. In this case, the participant's expectations were not equivalent to reality, but they were exceeded, and thus resulted in satisfaction from the purchase. Consequently, it cannot be suggested that confusion always results in dissatisfaction. The satisfaction level depends on the expectations initially formed, as with any purchase situation.

The feeling of lack of control was very Internet specific, as the participant stated: "There is way more control in just going into a mall, then being online" (Jane, female, 21). The uncertainty of the Internet leads to this feeling of lack of control on a regular basis, which could suggest the reason behind the mistrust of the Internet. However, this lack of control becomes extremely apparent to the consumer during confusion. Because it is possible for consumers not to realize that they were confused until after receiving a purchased good, it is possible for consumers to go through the entire transaction process feeling in control, and to feel a lack of control only after the fact.

Although it would appear that the feeling of lack of control can never completely disappear due to the nature of the Internet, consumers use repeat purchases as a way to feel more in control. The increased feeling of control is based on the fact that they had a good experience previously, and expect that repeating the process will result in a similar outcome. The assumption of it working again gives the consumer more confidence and a feeling of control. As compared with feelings from confusion offline, the feelings expressed seemed to be stronger. The participants described offline situations as "I was slightly disappointed" (Michelle, female, 36) and "I was kind of disappointed but okay with it. It wasn't a big deal" (Michelle, female, 36).

Reactions to Confusion

The participants then were asked how they reacted to being misled or deceived. The reactions were triggered by the affective response ("feelings") as discussed earlier. One participant described her reaction as follows:

> You're disoriented for a second, at first, I'll end up going to either a company that has the same name or similar characteristics, so I end up going to their Web site and then, and it has nothing to do with it but, maybe it should have something to do with it, so you kind of get caught up in the site for a couple of minutes or seconds trying to figure out if there is either a link to where you really want to be going or if this is like a parent company or something like that, so, and then having to start the search all over again and avoiding that site that you were at before. (Jane, female, 21)

Others commented:

> I wouldn't want to buy something from this because of where I thought I was going. I wouldn't trust it at all. (Jane, female, 21)

> I am probably going to hit the back button, go to Google, and look for it there. (Dan, male, 22)

> From that experience I wouldn't even purchase from a small company now, or something that's used. (Dana, female, 23)

One clear reaction that separated itself from other reactions was that of blame. Half of the participants mentioned that they blamed themselves for what happened:

> I would first assume that I did something wrong and the computer just took me somewhere and redo it again. (Robert, male, 23)

> And part of it is my mistake too; I guess I could have clarified it in some way or been a little more vigilant. (Dana, female, 23)

> And a little bit silly that I had maybe not done enough research on my own to make sure, or even thought about that this could happen. (Dana, female, 23)

Also, their experiences transferred to future purchases and to other companies:

> You become skeptical, okay; why are these guys selling it for 10 dollars when they are supposed to be 50 dollars. So if a deal that comes along it's suppose to be too good to be true, compared to say other things then I guess you become skeptical, and then maybe that transfers to the other stuff. (Ben, male, 21)

> I know that after that happened, I stopped shopping online through smaller sites; now if I shop online, it's only through trusted sites that I know I can trust pretty much because they're bigger brands, or bigger names that can't really get away with it, not tricking people but like its obvious what you're buying. (Dana, female, 23)

The latter participant will not purchase from small companies after her confusion experience because she has associated the confusion with the size of the company. She assumes that bigger companies are not able to "get away with it," so she is more comfortable purchasing from them. She has created associations (size, in this case) that will have an impact on her future expectations of purchasing online. Her experience has transferred forward to any future online purchases she will make, and driven her back to her safe, "trusted brands." This is classified as a "strong" reaction because it will affect future behavior in terms of online purchasing. The strength of the reaction seems dependent on whether the purchase has actually taken place. If consumers realize the confusion before purchase, the strength of the reaction tends to be less. They will leave the site and then go on with their search, trying to avoid the same site again. If they should come across it again, they will just leave. The reaction is not to the same degree, because their purchase behavior is not dramatically changed.

One participant described how his reaction was dependent on what was lost: "You're not going to start a fuss about it because its only six bucks; you just want to watch the movie, so a lot of times people get away with that" (Ed, male, 21). Similarly, one participant put a limit on the price of the items she would be willing to buy online. Items costing more than $200 were purchased only offline.

Interestingly, no one stopped purchasing online completely. One participant mentioned that friends had recommended that she stop purchasing online:

> I've had some people say, "Okay, you didn't do the research so what can you expect you know, I mean you should've read more about it and you should've I don't know, things like that, so or just refrain from buying," which I usually, unfortunately, don't do. (Michelle, female, 36)

She says it with regret, yet confusion appears not to be a motivating factor for halting online purchasing. It appears that participants have just accepted it as a risk of transacting online, and may alter their behavior after experiencing it.

Discussion of the Model

To offer a perspective on the findings of this study, it is important to reconsider the differences between online and offline shopping to set the stage for online consumer confusion. The participants in the study reflected previous research findings, which showed that consumers shopped online for preplanned purchases. It was clear that preplanned meant having the brand name identified, or at least a very small consideration set, before going online. Also mentioned was the Internet's lack of social appeal, suggesting that online shopping never will completely eliminate offline shopping for many consumers.

Although the Internet provides the consumer with access to vast amounts of product information and thus the ability to evaluate multiple alternatives before identifying the perfect choice, it appears that the consumer is not interested in this "benefit." Consumers' preference to "stick with what works" highlights the importance of generating trust because there is more to purchasing online than just finding what the customer is looking for. There has to be a level of trust or they will not purchase. This could explain why participants experienced stronger feelings when they were confused online versus offline. The strong trust they had developed was broken. Furthermore, the feeling of receiving a gift when ordering online enhances the disappointment for the consumer when something goes wrong with the transaction.

The findings also confirm Peterson and Merino's (2003) suggestion that consumers will spend less time searching for specific product information. The reduction in search occurs because the consumer already has a specific brand in mind at the purchase stage and does not want or need more information. Consumers actually will use specific techniques that will limit their access to additional alternatives, thereby reducing the chance of information overload and the possibility of confusion. However, this limited search could result in the choice of a good that is not the best option for the consumer because he or she is not aware of the superior alternative. Also, it suggests that there is a new criterion for the consumer in an online purchasing decision that does not exist offline, that is, the confidence the consumer has that the transaction will transpire as anticipated. This transaction uncertainty relates to the consumer's feeling of lack of control in the online environment, and the consumer's preference for purchasing in situations wherein he or she feels more control. By providing fewer options, and by making these options alternatives that have been experienced by the consumer or referred to him or her by someone, the consumer's confidence that the next transaction will be successful is heightened.

With regard to the factors potentially moderating consumer confusion (degree of care, product involvement, and product experience), it was difficult to determine specifically their implications, because this was a qualitative study. What became evident was that brand experience did have a significant impact, because it is from this that consumers form their expectations.

RECOMMENDATIONS TO PREVENT
ONLINE CONSUMER CONFUSION

One key objective of this study was to suggest ways for companies to protect consumers from online confusion. It became clear from the study that companies need to be concerned regarding consumers' expectations and trust. The following recommendations have taken this uncertainty into consideration.

Professionalism

Professionalism appears to be the easiest recommendation to implement. Although the participants recognized that professional-looking Web sites are easy to create, they were automatically distracted if the site was not functional and appealing. Professionalism involves integrating aesthetic appeals such as color, graphics, and fonts within a functional user interface. Competitors function as industry benchmarks because consumers feel some degree of comfort when Web sites within a product category are similar in layout and functionality. The concepts of color, picture placement, typeface and organization-linking act to protect the look and feel of the Web site.

Contact Information

Contact information such as physical location, telephone, and email needs to be included and made easily accessible for the user. Giving consumers this information involves placing multiple links within the text to the *Contact Us* section of the Web site, as well as including *Contact Us* as a major heading on the home page. The inclusion of a company history section (usually called *About Us*) also is recommended because the consumer will use this information to develop trust with the company. It is important to include information in this section that will suggest to the consumer that the company has expertise in its chosen field. J. Crew does an excellent job with both of these criteria on its Web site www.jcrew.com. J. Crew ensures that its *Contact Us* is easy to find by including it in the footer that appears on every page. Contact information also is included in the *About Us* section of J. Crew's Web site.

Word of Mouth

Word-of-mouth plays as significant a role in generating business online as it does in the traditional marketing arena. Consequently, it is important to be conscious of the online location of any information regarding the company. Companies should do regular searches of the Internet to ensure that their trademark is not being infringed upon. If consumers can purchase the product online, the Web site needs to be considered as important a channel as any retail store. Customers should be able to receive the same level of service online as they do offline to ensure that the consumer has a positive experience interacting with the brand at all times, and to make them more likely to refer the Web site to someone looking to purchase in that product category.

Brand Awareness

Brand awareness needs to be created both offline and online. By advertising in traditional media, the consumer is given access to information about the company in more than one arena. This offline information will generate the feeling that they have had a longer experience with the company, and develop the trust that is crucial for a purchase to take place online. Chapters Bookstore is a good example of this because it include its Web site address in traditional media, such as the signs included on their buildings and the bags used for packaging purchased items.

Also, one should ensure that the brand image is consistent throughout the organization. This means paying attention to the little details, such as ensuring that the font, color, and the like are the same every time the brand is presented. This continuity will present a clear meaning for the brand, and give the consumer a way to identify the true brand if alternatives are available.

Buying Direct

Buying direct appears to be the approach preferred by consumers for on-line shopping, and should be facilitated. Dealers and distributors should consider linking directly to manufacturers for product information and even for purchase. Arrangements can be made so that sales generated from a dealer's Web site are tracked so that remuneration can occur. This action will restrict accessibility of products online, and should be communicated to the consumer as such: "Our products are available only at ourcompany.com". With this knowledge, consumers will know that if they come across a product at a site other than that of the manufacturer, it will be an imitation, and therefore no confusion will arise. This linking will decrease the incentive for "infringers" because it will reduce the likelihood that they will have any benefit.

Manufacturers also should consider having a Web store for their products so that consumers can purchase directly from them, even if they do not have a retail store. Manufactures also may consider developing separate Web sites for each of their subbrands for which a connection between the subbrand and the parent brand is not obvious. A subbranding strategy also may be considered in which the name of the parent brand remains on all products to be sold online.

Expectations are difficult to anticipate because each consumer will have a different level of brand awareness or experience, or make a different set of associations. Companies may find it useful to have planning sessions when introducing a new brand to anticipate the types of expectations a consumer might form. Are there competitors already operating with similar positioning? If so, will it be obvious to the consumer that you are different? By considering these suggestions, expectations can be managed, and trust developed, so that when products are offered for sale online, confusion by consumers is minimized.

REFERENCES

Akin, D. (1999, March 25). B.C. Firm wins domain name case. *Financial Post*, C16.

Bolin, B. (2000). Linking and liability. [On-line]. Available: www.bitlaw.com/internet/linking.html Accessed October 27, 2003.

Boutin, P. (2005, March 5). There's a thriving economy in typos. *Financial Post,* FW9.

Brookfield Communications, Inc., v. West Coast Entertainment Corporation, No. 98-56918, 174 F.3d 1036; U.S. App. Lexis 7779; 50 U.S.P.Q.2d (United States Court of Appeals for the Ninth Circuit 1999).

Butera, C. M. (2000). Domain name piracy and trademark infringement. *Marketing Management, 9*(3), 58–61.

Buy.com Inc. [online] Available: www.buy.com Accessed April 30, 2003.

Canadian Internet Registration Authority (CIRA). (2001). CIRA domain name dispute resolution policy. [On-line]. Available: http://www.cira.ca/en/cat_dpr_policy.html Accessed April 16, 2003.

Chatam International, Inc. v. Bodum, Inc. Civil Action No. 00-1793, 157 F. Supp. 2d 549; U.S. Dist. Lexis 11514 (United States District Court for the Eastern District of Pennsylvania 2001).

Dean, J. R. (1997). The sheriff is coming to Cyberville: Trademark and copyright law and the Internet. *BYU Journal of Public Law, 11*(1), 75–103.

Evans, L. (2001). Brand fraud grows online. *Sporting Goods Business, 34*(13), 38.

Howard, D. J., Kerin, R. A., & Gengler, C. (2000). The effects of brand name similarity on brand source confusion: Implications for trademark infringement. *Journal of Public Policy & Marketing, 19*(2), 250–264.

Interstellar Starship Services, v. Epix Incorporated, Civil No. 97-107-Jo, 125 F. Supp. 2d 1269; U.S. Dist. Lexis 100 (United States District Court for the District of Oregon 2001).

Kitts, K. T., & Caditz, C. L. (2002, September). Domain-name registrations and on-line trademark infringement. *Washington State Bar News.* [On-line]. Available: http://www.wsba.org/barnews/2002/09/kitts-caditz.htm Accessed March 6, 2003.

Kopp, S. W., & Suter, T. A. (2000). Trademark strategies online: Implications for intellectual property protection. *Journal of Public Policy and Marketing, 19*(1), 119–131.

Lai, K., & Zaichkowsky, J. L. (1999). Brand imitation: Do the Chinese have different views. *Asia Pacific Journal of Management, 16*(2), 179–192.

Lastowka, F. G. (2002). Search engines under siege: Do paid placement listings infringe trademarks? *Intellectual Property and Technology Law Journal, 14*(7), 1–7.

Li, Z. G., & Gery, N. (2000). E-tailing—For all products? *Business Horizons, 43*(6), 49–54.

Liu, A. H., & Leach, M. P. (2001). Developing loyal customers with a value-adding sales force: Examining customer satisfaction and the perceived credibility of consultative salespeople. *Journal of Personal Selling and Sales Management, 21*(2), 147–156.

Mars Musical Adventures, Inc., a Wisconsin Corporation, v. Mars, Inc., a Florida Corporation, Civil File No. 99-669 (MJD/JGL), 159 f. Supp. 2d 1146; U.S. Dist. Lexis 18565 (United States District Court for the District of Minnesota 2001).

Mitchell, V. W., & Papavassiliou, V. (1999). Marketing causes and implications of consumer confusion. *Journal of Product and Brand Management, 8*(4), 319–339.

Murray, B. H. (2004). *Defending the brand: Aggressive strategies for protecting your brand in the online arena.* New York: American Management Association.

Northern Light Technology, Inc., v. Northern Lights Club, Jeffrey K. Burgar, and 641271 Alberta Ltd., D/B/A Northern Lights Club, No. 00-1641, 236 F.3d 57; U.S. App. Lexis 161; 57 U.S.P.Q.2d (Bna) 1277 (United States Court Of Appeals For The First Circuit 2001).

Obh, Inc. and Columbia Insurance Company, v. Spotlight Magazine, Inc. and Claude Tortora, 99-Cv-746a, 86 F. Supp. 2d 176; U.S. Dist. Lexis 4462; 54, U.S.P.Q.2d (Bna) 1383 (United States District Court for the Western District of New York 2000).

Peterson, R. A., & Merino, M. C. (2003). Consumer information search behavior and the Internet. *Psychology & Marketing, 20*(2), 99–121.

Playboy Enterprises, Inc. v. Calvin Designer Label, Calvin Fuller, and Calvin Merit, No. C-97-3204 CAL. U.S.D.C, N.D. California, Sept. 8, 1997.

Quokka Sports, Inc., v. Cup Int'l Ltd., Cup Int'l Internet Ventures, Arron John Brett, Justin Nicholas, and Does 1-50, No. C-99-5076-Dlj, 99 F. Supp. 2d 1105; U.S. Dist. Lexis 21000 (United States District Court for the Northern District of California 1999).

Rolex Watch U.S.A., Inc., and Prl Usa Holdings, Inc., v. Rufus Todd Jones A/K/A Todd Jones, Deals By Todd; Deal By Todd; Replica4u; and Shirts Are Us, 99 Civ. 2359 (Dlc), U.S. Dist. Lexis 15082 (United States District Court for the Southern District of New York 2000).

Selby, S. (2001). Cybersquatting. [On-line]. Available: http://www.info.gov.hk/ipd/eng/information/studyaids/cybersquatting.htm Last updated April 24, 2004. Accessed May 10, 2004.

Strauss, A. & Corbin, J. (1990). *Basic qualitative research: Techniques and procedures for developing grounded theory,* 2nd ed. Thousand Oaks, CA: Sage.

Toronto-Dominion Bank v. Boris Karpachev 188 F. Supp. 2d 110 U.S. Dist. of Massachusetts 3647 (2002).

Waldmeir, P. (2004, March 29). Our inalienable right to whinge on the Web. *Financial Times,* p. 7.

Wolfinbarger, M., & Gilly, M. C. (2001). Shopping online for freedom, control, and fun. *California Management Review, 43*(2), 34–55.

Wood, N. (1999). Protecting intellectual property on the Internet: Experience and strategies of trademark owners in a time of chance. *International Review of Law, Computers and Technology, 13*(1), 21–28.

8

Trademark Infringement in China[1]

Asia, especially China, is of special interest for her inability to protect intellectual property. Both China and Taiwan were placed on the E.U. and U.S. sanction list throughout the 1990s for the lack or insufficiency of trademark enforcement (Sun, 1998). The U.S. Patent and Trademark Office reports that 66% of the counterfeit goods seized at American borders now come from mainland China, up from 16% five years ago (Roth, 2005). As one example, the toy industry is estimated at $12 billion a year. China makes 70% of the world's toys and accounts for 49% of all toy counterfeit seizures in the United States by Customs Service (Fowler, 2003).

New technology seems to have made the issue even worse. Before new models and designs of products can even hit the store shelves, counterfeiters can beat the originals to market and sell them as if they were the originals. Using rapid-prototype machines, copiers can take three-dimension digital scans of objects shown at trade fairs in Hong Kong and then reproduce a prototype across the border in Shenzhen factories within hours. For example, the Chery QQ Minicar of China is virtually a twin of the Chevrolet Spark developed by the General Motors (GM) in South Korea. The Chinese manufacturer was accused of stealing mathematical formulas and design information from GM before production, and many parts from the two cars are interchangeable (Hutzler, 2005).

High-quality manufacturing equipment, along with high-quality raw materials (often imported) and high quality consultants allow the Chinese to produce high-quality end goods. These goods are worthy of being marketed under unique Chinese names, but most Chinese manufacturers choose to steal the name brand of someone else at this time. Trademark in-

---

[1]Most of this chapter was prepared by Felix Tang, PhD student at the Chinese University of Hong Kong.

fringement is so pervasive in China that 95% of CD and DVD sales and 90% of computer software are either knockoffs or counterfeit. Wang Jingchain, China's top intellectual property officer has said that the central government is making progress against counterfeiters by clamping down on use pirated software in central government offices! (Kirkpatrick, 2005). As much as 90% of certain daily use products, such as shampoo and clothing, are either knockoffs or counterfeits (York, 2003). On the average, 20% of all consumer products sold in China are counterfeit (Goodspeed, 2005).

The pervasiveness of imitation products in China may be surprising to many consumers living in the North America, Europe, and other developed countries. Most people in developed countries may think that knockoffs and counterfeits are meaningful only if the genuine article is well known. They also may believe knockoffs and counterfeits are reserved for luxury brands of accessory items, such as watches, designer purses, and scarves. Nevertheless, the phenomenon is much more widespread in China. Intellectual property practitioners have found counterfeit and knockoff analog chips, auto parts, airplane parts, apparel, cosmetics, fertilizers, sunglasses, condoms, snooker tables, videotapes, distilled water, car vacuums, canned soup, computer software, fragrances, children's toys, prescription drugs, animal medicines, health and beauty aids, and food products (Bamossy & Scammon, 1985; Feedstuffs, 1992; Fortune, 1991; Grossman & Shapiro, 1988a; Harvey & Ronkainen, 1985; McDonald & Roberts, 1994; Ott, 1992; Yu & Lu, 2004).

Besides economic harm, substandard imitations of food products and drugs pose health risks and safety hazards to everyone in the society (*China Daily*, 2004). For example, 13 children died and 200 more were taken ill after being fed fake formula (Goodspeed, 2005). Cultural influences may not be salient in the Western context, but do have significant influences on the purchase of imitation products in Asia. An understanding of consumer behavior in the Chinese context not only helps international marketers to market their products into China, a 1.2-billion consumer market, but also may enlighten researchers about various motivational factors that drive the consumption of fraudulent products.

There seems to be a lack of investigation on the demand side. Many researchers have investigated the phenomenon of knockoffs and counterfeits from the supply perspective and have looked at the production and distribution of knockoffs in the context of the legal structure and law enforcement in the People's Republic of China (PRC) or China, (Chen, 2001; Chow, 2000; Lu, 1998; Mertha, 2001; Schlesinger, 1995; Shen, 2000; Spierer, 1999; Sun, 2001; Yatsko, 2000), the Republic of China (ROC), or Taiwan, (Formasa Transnational Attorneys at Law, 2003; Shen, 2000; Sun, 1998), and Hong Kong Special Administrative Region (Hong Kong SAR) (Cheung, 1999, 2001; Selby, 2000a, 2000b). However, little is written about the phenomenon from the demand or consumer behavior perspective. What is written tends to focus on the problem of counterfeits. Relatively few studies have investigated the broad problem of brand imitation in general.

Perhaps the story of La Chemise Lacoste, the French producer of leisure- and sportswear, epitomizes the complexities of trademark infringement in China. Lacoste's direct competitor in Asia is a brand called Crocodile, which appears to use a mirror image of the Lacoste crocodile logo. Crocodile was registered in Singapore in 1951. LaCoste was registered in France in 1933. The Crocodile brand preempted the Lacoste brand in China by being first to the market. In November 2000, Crocodile was registered as a trademark in China with the National Copyright Bureau. La Chemise Lacoste had applied for registration of the crocodile with the state trademark office of China in 1995 (registered in 1999). Crocodile then sued La Chemise Lacoste in 2004 for trademark infringement in China and won its case, asking for $1.00 in damages (*Mr. Tan Hian Tsin and the Crocodile International PTE Ltd. v. La Chemise Lacoste*, 2004).

The Chinese court ruled that the Crocodile logo is original and different from the Lacoste crocodile in terms of the combined words, as well as the shape and expressions of the reptiles. Crocodile has since opened 100 stores in China. It is said that a gentleman's agreement was reached between the two companies, with Crocodile consenting to change its look. However, in July 2005 an appeals court in Shanghai threw out the 2004 ruling which favored Crocodile (*Marketing News*, August 15, 2005, p. 4).

A brief summary of the current legal status in trademark protection in the three regions of China (mainland China, Hong Kong SAR, and Taiwan) is provided in this chapter. Previous literature on confusion, utility, social influence, cultural influence, ethical perception, risk perception, and local interest is presented to explain why Chinese consumers purchase imitation products, including knockoffs and counterfeits.

TRADEMARK LAW AND LEGAL ENFORCEMENT

Mainland China

The current Chinese trademark system can be traced back to the 1950s, right after the establishment of the PRC. The objectives of setting up the trademark system were to guarantee the quality of products bearing marks and to protect the consumer's interest. The development of the trademark system was interrupted during the Cultural Revolution from 1966 to 1976. The first modern Trademark Law was enacted in 1982. The Implementing Regulations for the Trademark Law, which provides rules for the application, examination, registration and protection of trademarks, also was enacted in 1982 (China Law, 2003).

China has made several important revisions and updates in her trademark law. China acceded to the Paris Convention for the Protection of Industrial Property in 1985, the Berne Convention in 1992, the Madrid Agreement Concerning the International Registration of Marks of the World Intellectual Property Organization (WIPO) in 1989, and the World Trade Organization's 1995 Agreement on Trade-Related Aspects of Intellectual Property Rights (TRIPS) Agreement (Schlesinger, 1995). To comply with these international treaties and the China–United States' Memorandum of Understanding (MOU) in 1992 and 1994, PRC developed more stringent intellectual property protection policies and made many major amendments to its Trademark Law throughout the 1980s and 1990s to ensure the proper protection of foreign intellectual property rights in China (Spierer, 1999).

Many supplemental laws also were enacted to supplement the existing legislation, for example, the Measures on the Registration and Administration of Collective Marks and Certification Marks (the "Collective and Certification Marks Measures"). In 2004, China stiffened punishment for copyright and trademark violations. Sellers can be prosecuted if caught with goods values at $6,000. If more than one brand is being sold or made, the threshold is $3,600. Offenders can be jailed for 3 to 7 years if the goods are worth five times the limit (*Vancouver Sun*, 2005).

Currently, the Trademark Law, along with other intellectual property protection laws, is covered by the General Principles of the Civil Law of the People's Republic of China. Under the current Trademark Law, trademark registration is voluntary. Article 37 explicitly states the exclusive right to use a registered trademark. However, only those who have registered their trademarks on approved goods may enjoy the exclusive right to use such trademarks (Lu, 1998). This is different from the law of many Western countries, such as the United Kingdom and the United States, which recognize the acquisition of trademark rights without registration. Once approved, a trademark is registered for 10 years, and renewal is allowed. Where any trademark approved and registered is not used for three consecutive years, the approval may be withdrawn. The use of a trademark includes its use in advertisements and exhibitions (China Law, 2003).

The Chinese Trademark Law also protects the registrants from further similar marks. The registration of a trademark or the granting of an exclusive right to use the registered trademark excludes the use of the same or similar marks for products closely related to the listed products under registration, if such use is likely to cause confusion to the public. If an application for the registration of the same or similar trademark is not refused or has been approved, the owner of the registered trademark may file an opposition to the registration and contest the decision.

Judicial protection is afforded in two ways: civil and criminal. Criminal responsibility includes fines and/or a fixed term of imprisonment levied against the person found guilty of infringement. On most occasions, intellectual property rights are treated as civil rather than criminal cases. For a business, civil remedies are the remedies necessary for damage control. According to the Trademark Law, the trademark registrant may ask the court to issue judgment to stop infringement, to award damages, or to award an apology when an unauthorized party has used an identical or similar trademark without the consent of the trademark registrant. These remedies may be granted jointly or separately.

The people's courts try cases in strict accordance with substantive and procedural law, following the principles of "no suit no trial" and "the one who claims has the burden of proof." These courts follow an open trial system, a challenge system, a trial supervision system, and a system of the second instance as the final instance (Lu, 1998).

China recently became a member of the World Trade Organization (WTO). This breakthrough implies that the Chinese government would need to phase in the provisions in the TRIPS Agreement beyond the minimum national standards of Intellectual Property Rights (IPR) laws/protection, enforcement standards, and a binding dispute settlement process (China Law, 2003). To show its cooperation with Western practices, Chinese TV showed authorities using wood chippers to destroy 42 million counterfeit DVDs and CDS (York, 2003).

Hong Kong SAR

Hong Kong became a special administrative region of China in 1997, and it is known as the Hong Kong Special Administrative Region (Hong Kong SAR) since 1997. Intellectual property has been protected in Hong Kong for a very long time. The Trade Mark Registry started operating in 1874, and copyright has been protected since 1912. Hong Kong follows the English Common Law system, and its intellectual property system before 1997 reflected the British intellectual property protection regime. Under sections 139 and 140 of the Basic Law of Hong Kong SAR, Hong Kong SAR retained its autonomy in intellectual property protection, legislation, and litigation. This link to the British system allows Hong Kong to maintain a body of law that can respond to and benefit from developments in common law within the UK as well as other common law jurisdictions. For example, the Hong Kong courts can assess important precedents from other common law countries. Meanwhile, Hong Kong SAR develops its localized system of intellectual property law to reflect Hong Kong's special needs and its status as a part of China.

Under Hong Kong SAR's trademark law, a trademark indicates the origin of products or services. A trademark proprietor has the exclusive right to use it to identify its goods or services, and the period of registered protection can be renewed indefinitely. Because Hong Kong follows the English common law system, in the case of infringement, the remedies available are similar to those of other commonwealth countries. In general, civil remedies include injunction, damages, and public apology. Criminal responsibility includes fines and/or a fixed term of imprisonment levied against the person found guilty of infringement.

In 2000, the Hong Kong SAR Legislative Assembly passed a new trademark law to modernize the intellectual property protection law, and the new law came into force in 2002. The new intellectual property laws have incorporated wording directly from international treaties to ensure that the local laws fully comply with the international standards, such as the WTO's TRIPS standards. The new law simplified licensing and assignment and allowed for multiclass filing. Furthermore, the new law also attempts to deal with issues arising from the Internet and to allow e-commerce in filing. The new law also broadened the range of trademarks to encompass three-dimensional marks, sounds, and scents that can be represented graphically (Cheung, 2001).

Taiwan

Taiwan, or the Republic of China (ROC), is generally considered a region of China under the one-China policy. However, the legal structure of Taiwan is independent and different from that of mainland China. Taiwan began developing its legal system in 1911. The National Bureau of Standard was authorized to administer patent affairs in 1950 and trademark affairs in 1954 (Taiwan Intellectual Property Office, 2003). The booming development of Taiwan's industrial and commercial activities at the international level in the 1980s caused the number of new trademark applications to expand rapidly. Meanwhile, numerous Taiwanese businesses were involved in infringement disputes, and the alarm of insufficient intellectual property protection was raised. This catalyzed the modernization of the country's intellectual property protection laws, and the Taiwanese government made many amendments to the intellectual property rights protection laws and regulations, including the Trademark Law, throughout the 1980s and 1990s. Besides, an Anti-Counterfeiting Committee also was formed under the Ministry of Economic Affairs to strengthen enforcement of counterfeit investigation and interdiction tasks so as to improve the national image (Taiwan Intellectual Property Office, 2003). The main purpose of the Trademark Law, according to Article 1 is to protect the right to the exclusive use of a trademark and the interests of consumers in order to promote the normal development of industrial and commercial enterprises.

Taiwan's Trademark Law affords a 10-year protection term for all marks, commencing from the date of filing, and permits indefinite renewal, as long as the renewal application is filed within 1 year before expiration, and "use" of the mark is established within 3 years immediately before the filing for renewal. Legal redress and remedies are similar to those provided in China and Hong Kong SAR.

Similarities and Differences Among Trademark Laws in China, Hong Kong SAR, and Taiwan

Trademark Protection

All registered trademarks are protected to the same extent in China, Hong Kong SAR, and Taiwan. In Hong Kong, trademarks enjoy double protection from the Trade Mark Ordinance by registration and the common law through usage. Thus, unregistered trademarks also are protected. In China and Taiwan, only registered trademarks are protected under the Trademark Law. Unregistered trademarks are not protected.

Trademark Classification

Trademarks registered in China and Hong Kong SAR are classified according the international classification scheme into 34 categories. Taiwan has its own classification system. Product trademarks registered in Taiwan are classified into 95 categories, and service marks are classified into 12 categories.

Trademark Registration

In Hong Kong, a registrant must either use the trademark during the application or show an intention to use the trademark. Trademark law in China and Taiwan do not have this requirement. Registration in Hong Kong SAR and Taiwan are completely voluntary. Registration in mainland China is mostly voluntary, except for certain health and public welfare–related products such as drugs or tobacco products. If the registration is disapproved, the applicants can appeal. In Hong Kong and Taiwan, the ultimate decision for the registration of a trademark is made in court. In China, the Business and Industry Administration Bureau makes the final decision.

Length of Protection and Cancellation of Trademarks

In Hong Kong, the length of protection is 7 years since the date of application, and 14 years for renewal. In China and Taiwan, the length of protection is 10 years since the date of approval, and 10 years for renewal. Trademark registration can be canceled if the trademark has not been used for the past 2 years in Taiwan, 3 years in China, or 5 years in Hong Kong SAR (Table 8.1).

TABLE 8.1
A Comparison of Trademark Laws in China

Issue	*China*	*Hong Kong SAR*	*Taiwan*
Registered trademark	Protected under the trademark law	Protected under the Trademark Ordinance and Common Law	Protected under the trademark law
Unregistered trademark	Not protected	Protected under common law through usage	Not protected
Classification	Follows the international classification scheme, classify trademarks and service marks in 34 categories	Follows the international classification scheme, classify trademarks and service marks in 34 categories	Own classification system, classify trademarks into 95 categories and service marks into 12 categories
Registration	Mostly voluntary[a]	Completely voluntary	Completely voluntary
Usage requirement during registration	No requirement	The mark must be currently in use or there is an "intention-to-use"	No requirement
Length of protection	10 Years since the date of approval, 10 years for renewal	7 Years since the date of application, 14 years for renewal	10 Years since the date of approval, 10 years for renewal
Trademark cancellation	Possible, if the mark was not used for 3 years	Possible, if the mark was not used for 5 years	Possible, if the mark was not used for 2 years
Registration appeal	Final decision is made by the Business and Industry Administration Bureau	Final decision is made in court	Final decision is made in court

[a]Trademarks for health and public welfare–related products, such as drugs and tobacco products, must be registered.

The Problem of Enforcing Trademark Laws in China

The previous section on trademark law in mainland China, Hong Kong SAR, and Taiwan demonstrates that the laws on intellectual protection are on a par with the international standards, such as WIPO's Madrid Agreement and WTO's TRIPS Agreement. However, mainland China, Hong Kong SAR, and Taiwan continue to face different levels of trademark infringement activity.

Mainland China has faced several major impediments to effecting legal enforcement, such as inability to police the vast countryside (Sun, 2001), a mazelike legal structure (Mertha, 2001), corruption (Bian, 1996), lax enforcement (Chow, 2000), and vague legal language (Spierer, 1999). Hong Kong SAR and Taiwan also have suffered a lesser extent of the legal enforcement problem and have faced difficulty in controlling trademark infringement activities at the grass roots level.

The one event that may change China as the center of imitation and counterfeit production is the 2008 Olympics in Beijing. The original prediction of a $16 billion Olympic windfall to the country is at risk of being eroded from within by local counterfeit merchandise (York, 2003). Chinese authorities are likely to crack down hard on local counterfeiters to protect their interests. This crackdown could benefit all legitimate brands, not just the Olympic merchandise.

SEVEN FACTORS INFLUENCING THE PURCHASE OF IMITATIONS IN CHINA

From a Legal to a Consumer Behavioral Perspective

A less than perfect legal enforcement system may lead to the supply of knockoffs and counterfeits. However, the supply of goods is neither a necessary nor a sufficient condition for the demand of goods. If knockoffs or counterfeits cannot fulfill any wants or needs of consumers, no matter how large the supply is, no consumer will purchase or consume these imitation products. On the other hand, if the imitations can satisfy some needs that the genuine ones cannot otherwise, even if there is a short of supply, there still will be demand for it. Thus, it is important to understand the demand side of these products (e.g., purchase and consumption activities). Most of the previous researchers investigating the issue in the Chinese context, for one reason or another, tended to focus on the legal aspect in China, Taiwan, and Hong Kong. However, the phenomenon from the demand or consumer behavioral perspective in the Chinese context has been seriously overlooked.

On the basis of insight drawn from the extant literature, personal interviews, and direct experiences, seven factors are postulated to affect the demand and consumption of imitation products: confusion, utility, social influence, cultural influence, ethical perception, risk perception, and local interest. Together, these seven factors provide a multiperspective and overarching framework for understanding the consumer behavior related to the purchasing and consumption of imitation products.

Confusion

Generally speaking, most of the literature on consumer brand confusion assumes that consumers are fundamentally good in nature, or seeking to buy the original branded goods. According to this view, consumers purchase imitation products only when they are confused about the identity of the products. Several factors such as product familiarity, product experience, involvement attention, and presence or absence of the original brand are found to play a moderating role in the relationship between product similarity and consumer brand confusion (Foxman, Muehling, & Berger, 1990; Kapferer, 1995).

In most rural parts of China, the coverage of mass communication (e.g., advertising) and personal communication (e.g., word-of-mouth) usually outreach the coverage of the distribution system of the products being imitated. Thus, many of the original brands are not available in most parts of China, and imitators are frequently misjudged as the genuine products. This phenomenon is consistent with Kapferer's (1995) findings that the risk of confusion increases with brand similarity and is greater when the original brand is not present. If the consumer never used a particular brand before and learned about it only via commercial advertising or from a casual conversation, then found an imitation brand appearing similar to what he or she had learned about, without a direct comparison with the original brand, the consumer is likely to believe that the imitating product is the original brand.

Even if the original brand were present, many Chinese consumers still would have difficulty identifying an original due to the problem of illiteracy. The problem of consumer confusion is highly relevant in China (and arguably, other developing countries), where the illiteracy rate is high. According to the Human Development Report 2003, the adult illiteracy rate in mainland China was 14.2% in 2003. Chinese government officials agree that the problem is even more pervasive in rural areas.

As suggested in chapter 2, illiterate people rely on simple heuristics and cues to guide their consumption decisions. Thus, the high penetration rate of imitation products in rural areas of China can be partially attributed to the consumer's inability to differentiate the imitators from the originals.

This illiteracy–consumer confusion linkage also is likely to play a significant role in the consumption of imitation products in other developing countries. Chow (2000) found that the rise in education level in Taiwan led to a decrease in Taiwan's counterfeiting industry in the 1990s. This study showed that education level and knowledge in general could have a moderating effect on consumer confusion.

Copycats use various methods, such as rhyming, spelling similarity, or use of the same font and logo style of the original brand, to create an illusion that the product is being made by the original producer. For example, Procter & Gamble's brand name tissue paper "Tempo" has been imitated extensively in southern China. "Tampo," "Tango," and "Tembo" are some uncreative brand names of imitating brands aiming to deceive unaware consumers into believing that they are the original Tempo brand. Some others meticulously copy all aspects of the packaging except the brand name of "Tempo" to confuse consumers into believing that they are associated or produced by the same manufacturer. Yatsko (2000) described some copycat furniture retailers who even dare to display the logo of the original brand or the original company's catalogs and models in their showrooms in an attempt to confuse and mislead potential consumers into thinking that the copycat retailers are carrying the original products. Some salespeople even dare to lie to their customers that they are buying the designs from the trademark owner.

Chinese consumers not only need to distinguish the "me-too" look-alike brands from the originals, but they also need to guard themselves from counterfeit products. For example, Tempo tissue paper has been a favorite target of counterfeiters for a long time. Although the confusion created by counterfeits is similar to that of the look-alike brands, counterfeiting creates at least one more source of confusion because counterfeiters in China have recently begun to manufacture counterfeits of parallel imports. Counterfeits are passed off as products manufactured by the brand owner or by authorized manufacturers abroad that have then been imported into China (Chow, 2000). For example, counterfeiters manufacture a product from another location outside mainland China, such as Taiwan, and package the product differently from the genuine product in mainland China. This is done because Chinese consumers generally believe that imported goods are of higher quality than locally made products. In short, even highly involved consumers still may be confused about the origin of almost all products with the various kinds of creative deceptive techniques.

Utility

Although some unwary consumers may be deceived to believe falsely the originality of counterfeits and knockoffs, in some other cases, especially with prestige and luxury goods, some sophisticated consumers are not victims of deception, but choose to buy an imitation, knowing at the time of purchase that the product is a fake. Nia and Zaichkowksy (2000) pointed out that consumers can distinguish counterfeits from the authentic items by inspecting the quality of the goods or by evaluating the place of sales. Most counterfeits and knockoffs are of poor quality or sold outside the legitimate distribution channel. Grossman and Shapiro (1988b) called these purchasing activities nondeceptive counterfeiting.

The willful purchase of an imitation can be seen as a carefully evaluated transaction in which the consumer balances the perceived benefits derived from a transaction against the cost of it. In economic terms, consumers are willing to purchase knockoffs and counterfeits because the utility they derive from the imitators is greater than that from the original goods. That is, a consumer will buy an imitation knowingly if the unit of happiness that arises from the purchase of an imitation is higher than the unit of happiness they receive from the genuine product. According to this perspective, consumers will buy a knockoff if they perceive the knockoff to be of comparable quality with the original good (same benefits) at a lower price (lower monetary cost).[2] However, consumers might not buy the same knockoff if they think their friends would know the product is a fake, which would make them lose face (high social cost). Of course, whether a consumer's friends actually can distinguish the imitation from the original is irrelevant in the decision to purchase because it is the *perception* of whether a consumer's friends can differentiate the product that affects the decision making. Acquisition utility and place utility are two example sources of utility highly relevant in the purchase of a brand imitation.

Acquisition Utility

Similar to the economic concept of consumer welfare, acquisition utility "is a measure of the value of the good obtained relative to its price" (Thaler, 1999). That is, consumers receive acquisition utility from a purchase if the price they paid is less than what the product is worth to them: the larger the discrepancy, the higher the utility the consumer experiences.

Imitation products are priced at a fraction of the genuine products, and hence are much more affordable for the general public in mainland China. When the price of the original product is present for comparison, the difference in price creates a great incentive for the consumer to switch from the original brand to the imitator brand, if the perceived quality is the same or if the quality is not important at all. In Schoenfeld's (2003) case study on the infamous Taiwan-made Callaway golf club knockoffs, the salesperson

---

[2]See chapter 1 for a more detailed discussion of this concept.

showed the customer the genuine brand first, then introduced the much lower-priced knockoff brand to stimulate and encourage price comparison.

Acquisition utility is especially relevant in China because imported goods often are relatively more expensive than local goods. In mainland China, compounded by high tariffs and agency fees, the genuine products are prohibitively expensive for the average Chinese consumer (Bian, 1996; Lewis, 2001). It is estimated that more than 200 million mainland Chinese live on less than US$1.00 a day. The acquisition utility provided by the knockoffs is simply too overwhelming when consumers are given the opportunity to substitute the imitator brand for the original brand. Even many of the more affluent Hong Kong Chinese cannot resist the temptation to purchase a very "similar" product at a much lower price. Chow's (2000) study confirmed that less affluent and less educated mainland Chinese are willing to purchase counterfeit shoes, apparel, and daily use products. He explained that this creates a niche market for imported knockoffs and counterfeits, which are perceived to be of higher class with the same quality and price as the local brands.

This phenomenon is not unique to Chinese culture. For example, Cordell and Wongtada (1991) found that students, when faced with a paper-and-pencil choice of a counterfeit versus a legitimate good, selected the counterfeit without regard for legality or public welfare. Bloch, Bush, and Campbell (1993) found that consumers selected the counterfeit when the counterfeit had a distinct price advantage over the genuine product. Tom, Garibaldi, Zeng, and Pilcher (1998) found that it was the superior price and not the brand, quality, or function of pirated CDs that attracted consumers to buying fake CDs. Similarly, Collins-Dodd and Zaichkowsky's (1999) study suggests that North American customers are willing to buy lower priced imitators because of the greater value if the product is of the same quality as the brand it imitates. Three aspects of acquisition utility (brand imagery, customization, and localization) are described in the following sections. Whereas the brand imagery aspect is well documented in the literature, the importance of product customization and localization has been overlooked.

Brand Imagery.   Advertising is becoming increasingly effective in generating awareness of brands in modern China, and as a result, more Chinese are now brand conscious (Bian, 1996). The appearances of well-known brands or products are broadcasted over the media. Because Chinese consumers' consumption patterns symbolize their social class position, similar to their North American counterparts, the Chinese want to associate themselves with their current social class position or the class above them.

The display of wealth and the desire to impress others is not new to the Chinese, and many Chinese consumers purchase luxury goods primarily to satisfy an appetite for symbolic meanings. Status conscious consumers often purchase branded products, which convey an image of affluence, wealth, and social class. In this sense, products are obtained as means to an end. However, most Chinese cannot afford the expensive originals, so to satisfy their desire to impress others, many turn to counterfeit products as cheap substitutes for the originals. Knockoff luxury goods similar in appearance to the genuine goods they wish to imitate gain extra product utility for the image associated with the original brand. Image attributes reflect how consumers feel about themselves, and subsequent use of the product associates them with a desired group, role, or self-image.

Schoenfeld (2003) suggested that most of customers visiting "knockoff" stores are locals who are well aware that they are buying knockoffs or counterfeit goods. They simply want the brand name at a lower price. One of the knockoff gurus in Taiwan interviewed by Schoenfeld (2003) suggested that whereas some counterfeiters do not care about product quality, some do, and they test their products for quality to make sure the quality is there.

Kapferer (2004) reported that the head of Louis Vuitton was shown counterfeits of its handbags by the Chinese manufacturer, in the hope that Louis Vuitton would buy the Chinese company. The company felt that their counterfeit product had quality good enough to pass for the original. Thus, because product quality is only one of the many sources of product utility, high quality knockoffs can be a superior alternative to branded goods, and consumers may prefer knockoffs to the genuine products. Therefore, by offering the same value at a lower price, these imitations provide higher acquisition utility than the original products.

Localization. Localization is another good example of how knockoffs provide great product utility to the consumer. Whereas genuine goods usually have a great aesthetic appearance and design, knockoffs sometimes add extra value to the consumer. For example, the Japanese brand "Pioneer" is a leading electronics equipment manufacturer in Japan, and some of its phones were imported into China targeting the upscale market. The importing company did not localize these phones because Japanese goods are perceived to be of higher class and quality than local brands. Therefore, the built-in voice system of the phone spoke Japanese, and the characters on the buttons of the phone and the user menu all were written in Japanese.

Shortly afterward, several imitation brands (one even called "Pioner") appeared on the market. These telephones were very similar to the Pioneer telephones, with identical designs and features. Moreover, these phones were well localized, bearing the same design with Chinese characters imprinted on the cover case rather than the original layout with Japanese characters and accompanied by a photo-intensive, user-friendly Chinese user manual rather than the bible-like, Japanese user manual. Although these imitations were not much cheaper than the original goods produced by Pioneer, such localization features satisfied the needs of the Chinese market very well, and the imitated phones were very popular in China during the late 1990s. The brand existed for a few years, but has now disappeared from the marketplace.

Most counterfeiters generate this extra product utility by localizing and adapting the original product to meet the needs of the local market. These practices are more relevant in China because, contrary to the general belief that China is a unified market with more than 1.2 billion consumers, China is a diversified marketplace with hundreds of different dialects and countless complicated local customs, rules, and preferences.

Customization.   Besides adapting the products to meet the needs of the local market, some imitating brands also personalize the products to offer additional product utility to the consumers. Custom tailoring is a good example of how knockoffs provide great product utility to consumers and can be superior alternatives to branded goods.

When customers visit a knockoff custom tailor store, they are invited to suggest the design of the clothing they want. Of course, most consumers do not have a particular design or cutting in mind that they want the tailor to make. Rather, most of them rely on the professional advice of the tailors. Most of the stores have stacks of the latest fashion and design magazine available for the customer to browse for "suitable" styles. Not surprisingly, most of the latest designs featured in these magazines are the patented designs of well-known international brands. Some places even organize the design according to the designers and paste pictures on the wall to facilitate easy selection. After the customers make their selection, the tailor takes their measurements and delivers the clothing of their choice within a few days.

Besides direct copying of the designer clothing appearance, these custom tailors are willing to personalize the product according to the customer's specification. Extra pockets can be added, and unwanted laces and accessories can be removed. Types and colors of fabrics also can be changed. If the original design has only a shirt, the tailor can even make a matching skirt upon request, and the sky is the limit. It is easy to imagine why someone would like an imitation more than the original.

A personal interview with one of these "tailors," actually a salesperson, in Hong Kong reveals a well-developed network of the "custom tailoring" industry, in which brand name apparel, usually clothing, shoes, handbags, or anything that a tailor can make, are reproduced. Everything is the same except the label. The informant disclosed that most of the production happens in China, and that the factory is just a telephone call away. The craftsmanship and quality are not greatly different from those offered by the genuine authorized dealer, and the price is on a par with that of the local brands, but much lower than the price of the original brand being imitated.

Another example of how customization offers greater product utility is the manufacturing of knockoff furniture. As Yatsko (2000) pointed out, imitators copy the design of a famous designer and make furniture to the customers' specifications. Length, width, and color are just some of the specifications that the imitators can change to fit the needs of the customers. A furniture store in Guongdong offers major brand names and the latest design in office furniture. After a customer has placed an order for a piece, the salesperson asks whether there is any customization the customer would like to have. If there is, the salesperson suggests another brand guaranteed to be identical to the original brand and usually at a slightly lower price. The author speculates that some customers would accept the salesperson's "kind" offer and, knowingly or unknowingly, purchase some knockoff furniture.

Place Utility

Consumers experience place utility when they have convenient access to a product or service. To provide place utility, marketers need to have the product available where the customer wants it. Whereas it is relatively easy to advertise a brand in China, Taiwan, and Hong Kong through multinational marketing campaigns to create demand for well-known brands (Bush, Bloch, & Dawson, 1989), it is relatively more challenging to offer the right amount of the product at the right place at the right time. This job is even more difficult in China because of its vast geographic area and complex distribution channels.

Most trademarked foreign goods are premium goods with limited or exclusive distribution channels. The physical accessibility of foreign imports is limited primarily to major urban centers and the coastal provinces. Most suburbs in the interior and rural areas rely on the local distribution centers, such as Hanzhen Street in Wuhan City for the Hubei Province, Wuai Market in Shenyang for the Liaoning Province, and the China Small Commodities City in Yiwu City in the Zhejiang Province, where most knockoffs and counterfeits are widely available. The buyers and sellers in these local distribution centers may not have the knowledge to distinguish the knockoffs and counterfeits from the genuine products. Even if they possess the knowledge, the genuine products are simply not available, and the buyers can only choose between different qualities of imitation products.

Chow (2000) provided a thorough description of one of these local distribution centers, the China Small Commodities City in Yiwu City. With more than 30,000 wholesale stalls and 3,500 full-sized wholesale stores, Yiwu City is renowned for the amount of its trading. According to Chow (2000), approximately 200,000 visitors visit the city daily, and 2,000 tons of goods are purchased every day. What is most special about Yiwu City is that at least 90% of the daily use consumer products found there are counterfeits, knockoffs, or other intellectual property–infringing products. Two open transport areas, each of the size of a football field, are filled with imitation products. On one side, trucks unload imitation products that newly arrive from the factories. On the other side, trucks are loading recently bought goods for delivery.

Imitation products then are distributed further down the chains from these wholesale markets to all parts of China: some into the rural villages and some into the metropolitan areas. Without a formal complaint lodged from the original trademark holders, the police and custom investigators are unwilling to prosecute small vendors. Thus, it is a common scene for hawkers to carry bags or trolleys of knockoffs and counterfeits and sell them on the streets. Some shops and convenience stores carry the entire line of knockoffs, knowingly or unknowingly, mixing them with up other genuine products. Such distribution networks offer excellent geographic coverage and penetration for the imitation products unmatched by the authentic brands.

In the United States, when some toys are in high demand, it is not uncommon to see parents camping out by the stores to get the presents their children want for Christmas. When there is a short supply, desperate parents surf the Internet toy stores and auction Web sites to look for the toys, and they are willing to buy knockoffs knowingly to please their children (D'Innocezio, 2002). The situation in China is in some sense similar to this U.S. scenario. Some well-known brands are simply never available in certain parts of the country. The power of mass media and word-of-mouth communication helps to accumulate demand for these unavailable products, creating opportunities for some shrewd but unethical businesses to prey off the famous brands. It also is possible that the Chinese who brought the knockoffs have never heard of the genuine brand name of the trademark registrant. Because of to the poor communication infrastructure in the interior and Western parts of China, most Chinese living in these rural areas are isolated from the rest of the world, and their knowledge of brand names is severely limited. Because there is no mental association between the original brand and the imitated product, there is no consumer brand confusion. Customers buy the product simply because the imitation is available in the right place at the right price at the right time.

In summary, the preceding examples of imitation products may provide utility above and beyond that of the original branded goods. These imitators have extended beyond the traditional "me-too" imitation strategies, offering extra functional benefits to the consumers.

Social Influence

During the contemplation of a purchase decision, most consumers look beyond the immediate benefit they would receive in the purchase and consider the social ideals and standards imposed by others (Bearden, Netemeyer, & Teel, 1989). Social influence is a "process whereby attitudes and behavior are influenced by the real or implied presence of other people" (Vaughan & Hogg, 2002, p. 177). The proliferation of designer handbags among high school teenage girls is an example of this driving social force. The leaders of the style parade want the real Louis Vuitton bags, whereas those who cannot possibly afford the $600 to $2,000 price tags are driven to find the counterfeits. As one girl stated, "If one girl gets one, they all have to have get one. Its kind of sad because it shows that people have no originality and can't think for themselves" (Harris, 2004).

The Chinese have a strong cultural motivation toward "face saving" and group conformity. They are likely to follow stricter ethical standards in public (Hofstede, 1980). However, when a consumer is alone, the restraints imposed by intimate circles are relaxed, and the consumer is more likely to disregard the reaction of others and act in accordance with his or her impulses. Chan, Wong, and Leung (1998) found that the Chinese considered unethical consumption behavior carried out in private, such as recording a CD, to be more ethical than questionable social acts in public, such as drinking a can of soda in a supermarket. Such relaxation of ethical standards also was found in the West, where Gellerman (1986) reported that people were more likely to engage in misconduct when they thought the act would not be found out and publicized.

A darker aspect of social influence is the tolerance and acceptance of corrupt acts within peer groups. For instance, Conger (1980) suggested that when a person has friends who exhibit deviant behavior, then he or she is more likely to exhibit deviant behavior. Research on compliance, obedience, and conformity suggests that social influence can lead people to both follow rules and break rules. Peer pressure to conform reportedly is a factor leading to inappropriate consuming behavior (Bearden, Rose, & Teel, 1994; Powers & Anglin, 1996).

Using high school and college student consumers, Bearden et al. (1994) found correlational evidence that consumers are likely to conform to illicit consumption behaviors when family and friends also display such behaviors. Powers and Anglin (1996) found empirical evidence that deviant consumer behavior of couples reciprocally reinforced the consumption of each other. They also found that the female is more likely to conform to the spouse's behavior than the male. Although the preceding studies are not linked directly to the consumption of imitation products, per se, the influence of others on consumption behavior is nonetheless clearly demonstrated. Thus, it is reasonable to conjecture that consumers who otherwise would not purchase imitation and counterfeit products might be influenced by others to do so.

Cultural Influence

Besides the expected utility derived from the product and the social influence from family and friends, culture also plays an influential role in the widespread disregard of intellectual property rights in China. Western philosophy values the importance of creativity, and students are taught to respect the works of others and to avoid copying and plagiarism. The mainstream view on copying and imitation is distinguishingly clear: Copying is theft of intellectual property. Such a view is based on the premise that intellectual property rights create an incentive for the creation and investment of creative ideas and products. However, traditional Chinese culture may not share the same philosophy, as exemplified in the Chinese proverb "He that shares is to be rewarded; he that does not, condemned" (Swinyard, Rinne, & Kau, 1990, p. 656).

As Lai and Zaichkowsky (1999) correctly pointed out, copying enjoys a long tradition in China, and the Chinese regard it as important to "copy" the good aspects of all things. The traditionally accepted practice of copying or imitating the "good aspects" of everything has a profound impact in the Chinese culture. In school, Chinese students learn by reproducing the works of the teachers at school, and they have been taught for centuries to copy their teachers as accurately as possible before attempting to create. At home, parents encourage their children to "copy" the good behavior of their brothers and sisters. Furthermore, in traditional Chinese art, copying a masterpiece was historically considered an art form in its own right. In Asian calligraphy, for example, a hallmark of mastery is demonstrated when the student's work becomes indistinguishable from the teacher's. In publishing, when books are translated into different languages, the name of the translator stands on equal footing with the original author's name on the title page to acknowledge the effort of the translator in helping to share the knowledge.

The value of copying or imitating also can be seen in entertainment. Lewis (2001) attributed the widespread success of karaoke to the traditional Chinese value of imitation or copying. Imitators are praised for their ability to mimic all aspects of the original singers. Thus, most Chinese are brought up in an environment in which copying and imitating are acceptable and encouraged.

This philosophy is demonstrated in the following example. A major equipment manufacturer from Canada tells a story of an international trade show held in China. Major industrial machinery from companies who hoped to sell their wares in China was displayed in a huge convention center. One evening, a reception and dinner was held for the delegates of the trade show, and the wares on display were left under the watchful eye of Chinese security guards hired by the exposition. When the Canadian delegates returned the next morning to their display booth, they found that all the paint around the nuts and bolts of the equipment was damaged. During the night, the complete machine was taken apart, apparently measured and perhaps photographed, and then reassembled by morning. The only evidence was that all the paint surrounding the joints and bolts was broken and damaged.

Ang, Cheng, Lim, and Tambyah (2001) believe that the Singaporeans' perception that buying counterfeits is not unethical may stem from the Asian philosophy of sharing, which teaches that one's expertise should be shared to maximize the benefit to the society as a whole. Thus, it is selfish and antisocial for the individual to insist on special compensation for the contribution (Mittelstaedt & Mittelstaedt, 1997). Consumers may feel reluctant to buy from selfish businesses that do not share their expertise with the rest of the society. Recent empirical studies also have found a significant relationship between a country's level of individualism and the extent to which intellectual property rights are protected (Husted, 2000; Ronkainen & Guerrerro-Cusumano, 2001).

Although senior government officials and judges understand the importance of intellectual property protection for the long-term growth and advancement of the nation, most people at the grass roots level do not share the same philosophy as the central government. For instance, in mainland China, local officials do not hold intellectual property law in the same light as their counterparts in Western countries (Schoenfeld, 2003). Some Chinese bureaucrats still hold the attitude that it is reasonable for others to copy successful products or their strategies (Yatsko, 2000). Their rationalization is simple: Success breeds competition. If something sells, why will others not try to sell something similar? Thus, enforcement of intellectual property is sometime less than diligent.

Consumers in Hong Kong are a well-educated group exposed to Western influence for international status in finance, tourism, trading, and shipping. Some would expect the Hong Kong Chinese to respect intellectual property rights and to behave ethically on a par with their Western counterparts for their similar income, wealth and education level. Despite such education and Western influence, counterfeits and knockoffs still can be easily obtained in certain parts of the metropolis, such as the Lady's Market on the Kowloon side, and many Hong Kong Chinese have admitted that they consume counterfeits and knockoffs on a regular basis.

Although the Hong Kong Chinese generally appreciate that there is "something wrong" with using pirated or counterfeit goods (Selby, 2000a), they have a poor grasp of why piracy and counterfeiting are wrong, and why protection of copyright, trademarks, designs, and patents represent a social and economic benefit (Selby, 2000b). Consumers in Hong Kong underestimate the amount of resources invested in the creation of intangible property. The business community in Hong Kong generally has a good understanding of the principles of trademark protection. However, they still have limited comprehension of the system of protection for designs and patents.

The consumption of imitation products by the Hong Kong Chinese can be attributed to their Chinese roots. This further supports the notion that cultural influences play an influential role in the predisposition of the Chinese to accept knockoffs and counterfeits even when they have the money to purchase the genuine products and the education to comprehend the importance of intellectual property rights. Similar situations are reported in Singapore, where a large proportion of the Singaporean population is Chinese or descents of Chinese (Ang et al., 2001). The problem of counterfeiting and product imitation is a long-standing problem in Singapore despite its well-educated population and tight legal enforcement.

In short, because of this culture value of copying, most Chinese consumers do not share the philosophy regarding the importance of intellectual property rights. They are more receptive to brand imitation products, and they do not see a problem in buying knockoffs and counterfeits. It seems that they rather have difficulty buying the idea of paying a high premium for an item when a similar item with better features, perhaps at a lower price, can be easily obtained.

Ethical Perceptions

If the consumer is unaware that the product under inspection is an imitation, as in the case of confusion or a total lack of ability to judge, there is no ethical concern on the part of the consumer. However, the purchase of imitation products becomes an ethical decision if the consumer knows that the product under evaluation is a knockoff or a counterfeit. Muncy and Vitell (1992) developed a consumer ethics scale to investigate consumers' ethical judgment. Specifically, consumers in different cultures use similar rules to assess the ethicality of a given situation. If consumers think a behavior is unethical, they are less likely to engage in, or at least overtly display, such behavior in public.

Consumer ethics is "the moral principles and standards that guide behavior of individuals or groups as they obtain, use, and dispose of goods and services" (Rallapalli, Vitell, Wiebe, & Barnes, 1994; Vitell & Muncy,

1992). These authors have suggested that consumer ethical judgments are affected by three major factors: (a) whether the buyer (i.e., the consumer) or seller (i.e., the original manufacturer) is at fault or not, (b) whether the activity is perceived as illegal or not, and (c) whether there is a direct harm to the seller or not. On the basis of the literature and personal observation, the author argues that there exists a fourth factor: whether the activity benefits the society as a whole. The acceptance and prevalence of the consumption of imitation products in China can be explained by using these four factors.

First, those who purchase counterfeits and knockoffs blame the original manufacturers for making the originals unavailable (because of limited distribution channels) or unaffordable (because of a premium pricing strategy).[3] Such a rationale is consistent with Yau's (1988) finding that the Chinese tend to be situation oriented and pragmatic. For example, a decision about whether it is right or wrong to buy a counterfeit product might depend on the availability and price of the genuine article. If a genuine product is not available in the local market, or if it is priced too high, consumers may feel that it is acceptable to buy counterfeit products. On the other hand, if a genuine product is available in the local market at a reasonable price, they may feel it is wrong to commit such an offense. Many Chinese, especially Chinese with low incomes, think high-profile businesses are guilty for asking unacceptably high prices for their products, and hence the Chinese hold an unfavorable attitude toward these businesses (Wee, Tan & Cheok, 1995).

Other consumers blame the counterfeit or knockoff manufacturers for producing the items in the first place. If there were not a supply of imitation products, they would have no choice but to buy the originals. However, because the imitations are available, they think there is nothing wrong in buying them (Cordell, Wongtada, & Kieschnick, 1996). These consumers do not see themselves as confederates of the counterfeiters, but rather as bargain hunters and penny-wise shoppers. Thus, many Chinese excuse themselves from any accusation by deflecting the blame to both the original manufacturers and the imitation manufacturers.

Second, there seem to be some misunderstandings regarding intellectual property. Most Chinese believe the purchase and consumption of imitation products, including counterfeits, are totally legal. Some consumers hold a double standard in that they think selling counterfeits and knockoffs is illegal but buying them is legal. These misperceptions are widely held. Most Chinese consumers have learned by observation that

---

[3]It is interesting to note that the same reasoning was used in Germany to allow counterfeit and imitation products of Hermès to be manufactured and then sold on the street. The proliferation of the Jelly Handbag was allowed because a sufficient supply of the real article could not be made widely available.

product imitation is part of their lives. Sellers are sometimes caught and put on trial, but it is almost unheard of that buyers are ever prosecuted. These incidents have been conducive to the public misunderstanding of their legal responsibility.

Third, many Chinese believe that imitation products do not cause great harm to the original trademark holders. Some consumers may reason that the value of their transaction is unlikely to affect the business well-being, whereas others argue that they are not going to purchase the originals anyway because the prices the original manufacturers charge are too high. Empirical evidence supports this rationale. For example, although consumers thought that pirated CDS were not fair to the original manufacturers and singers, they did not think it was unethical to buy them. This is because most people have learned from the media that both the entertainment industry and the entertainers still earn high incomes despite the widespread pirating of CDS (Ang et al., 2001).

Arguments pointing out the harm of imitation products, such as people confusing the imitation products with the originals and the brand image and equity of the original brand being affected by the lower quality of the imitation, falls on deaf ears. This is because most of these arguments require a high level of intellectual capability to be comprehended. Even if consumers understood the arguments, these arguments may not be easily remembered when the consumers make their purchase decision. What is more salient to the consumer is that the companies targeted by imitators make lucrative profits year after year. Therefore, most Chinese view the loss of sales to product imitation as a small price to pay for mass popularity and have difficultly accepting the idea that product imitation hurts the original company in any serious way.

Fourth, many Chinese consumers may see product imitation as beneficial to the society by allowing consumers who cannot afford the authentic goods an alternative choice. This view is documented in Cordell et al.'s (1996) study, in which consumers thought that by making a product widely available to the public, counterfeiters benefit the society. This notion is consistent with the aforementioned Chinese philosophy of sharing. Ang et al. (2001) also found a significant difference between buyers and nonbuyers in terms of their belief about the social impact of imitation products. They found that buyers of counterfeit products believe piracy benefits the society, whereas nonbuyers believe otherwise.

Risk Perceptions

The perception of risk also is an important potential factor relating to the purchase and consumption of imitation brands. Economists have traditionally investigated the concept of risk perception. Marketing and psychology researchers have studied risk in the context of ethical consumption. For example, on the basis of the reasoning that fear of criminal penalty deters aberrant behavior, Albers-Miller (1999) used perceived criminal risk as a predictor of the purchase of illicit goods. Similarly, users of imitation goods risk disapproval of others. Harvey and Walls (2003), modeled the full price of a counterfeit good as its monetary price minus the risk of detection times the value of the penalty.

Risks can arise both during the purchase of the products (i.e., purchasing risks) and during the consumption of the products (i.e., consumption risks). For purchasing risks, legal enforcement is the most directly related factor. In general, because of lax legal enforcement, both the buyer's and seller's risk for being caught by intellectual property enforcing agents is minimal. Occasionally, there is news that knockoff manufacturers or sellers are caught and found guilty, but most consumers believe that buying or possessing knockoffs or counterfeits for domestic consumption is not illegal. Besides, Sun (2001) also pointed out that large foreign companies or trade associations are not likely to sue an individual for buying knockoffs or counterfeits as their public relations may suffer because they will be perceived as the Goliath going after small domestic consumers. This makes consumers feel less risk in their purchases and encourages future purchase of imitation goods.

The most directly related factor in the category of consumption risks should be product quality. Although the quality of some imitation products is on a par with the originals, for many it is not. When consumers end up with an inferior, faulty product, they lose their investment in the imitation product. For some product categories, such as pharmaceutical products, product quality is very important, and the risk of consuming a substandard knockoff drug can be life threatening. However, for other product categories, such as clothing, shoes, and watches, consumption risk is much lower because the product quality of the imitator is either not important or perceived to be similar to that of the genuine product.

Social risk is another kind of consumption risk associated with reference groups. As discussed in chapter 3, if the reference group to which a person belongs or aspires to belong does not approve the consumption of imitation products, consumers run the risk of being ostracized for using such products. As discussed in the social influence section, the influence of the real or implied presence of others affects people's attitude and consumption behavior.

An interesting observation worth noting is consumption pattern adjustment in anticipation of potential consumption risk. Because the product imitation phenomenon is so pervasive in China, when consumers know or suspect their products to be counterfeits or knockoffs, they adjust their usage pattern to lower their consumption risk. Chow (2000) found during interviews with the Chinese Consumer Group in Shanghai that some consumers may use an inferior knockoff soap to wash their hands only, but not other parts of their body. Similarly, these consumers may use a counterfeit detergent to wash their work clothes, but not their bed sheets. Through this behavior, consumers lower the risk associated with a potential substandard imitation product.

Another example of consumption pattern change is the use of an imitation as a decoy for the genuine product. Some consumers buy an original and also an identical imitation. A personal interview with one of these consumers, a Hong Kong Chinese, showed that she frequently needs to travel to Shenzhen and Dongguan in the Guangdong Province for work-related matters. Because Shenzhen is thought to be a problematic area, she worries about being the target of thieves and robbers, and therefore saves her authentic Louis Vuitton handbag for special occasions, using the imitation bag for day-to-day purposes. She does not mind telling her friends that the handbag she brings to work every day is a fake, but she reminds her friends and coworkers that she does own an authentic Louis Vuitton handbag. She brings the real Louis Vuitton handbag to her Christmas party and allows her coworkers to inspect the handbag closely to verify its authenticity. Such strategic arrangements are aimed at improving the expected life span of the authentic good by shifting the daily wear-and-tear and the potential risk of theft to the imitation.

In summary, consumers also consider the risks associated with the purchase and consumption of imitation products. If the perceived risk related to the imitation product is high, consumers are likely to forego buying the product and discontinue using it. The same applies to authentic brands, if the consumption is risky. Consumers of these brands also adjust their consumption behavior accordingly to mitigate the risk.

Local Interests

Another unique factor influencing the behavior of Chinese consumers is the fact that many counterfeits or knockoffs are produced locally. The imitation product–manufacturing industry hires many skilled and unskilled laborers in the local areas. Because these manufacturers are integrated into the local community, the locals view them as legitimate businesses representing the local interest. The situation of Yiwu City, mentioned in a previous section, is a good example of local interest. Many of the imitation products in Yiwu are not produced there. However, the distribution of these products supports the entire logistic industry, such as transportation companies and warehousing companies. The hospitality and retail industries also benefit indirectly from the massive traffic in the area. Thus, brand imitation is viewed as a legitimate source of employment and economic development.

Because most famous, well-known brands are imported goods, these genuine branded goods are generally perceived to be of foreign interest. Sun (2001) suggested that most Chinese believe intellectual property laws protect the foreign interest and are skeptical whether intellectual property protection is beneficial to Chinese society in the long run. Those who share this view are willing to purchase knockoffs and counterfeits to "support" their fellow citizens rather than the foreigners. As Schoenfeld (2003) also pointed out, businesses that help foreign companies to maintain their trademarks in Taiwan are scorned by many Taiwanese. These companies are seen as evil businesses that rob the locals and give their wealth to the foreigners. This further encourages the locals to purchase the locally made knockoffs.

SOLUTIONS

The previous paragraphs suggest that the consumption of imitation products in Asia is a complex and multifaceted problem caused by a host of different factors. Most legal experts, such as Harvey and Walls (2003), have suggested that more stringent enforcement of intellectual protection legislation on both the buyers and the sellers is needed. They have suggested further that a high penalty for violating the law would be the most direct and appropriate policy response to dampen down the demand for imitation products.

Legal enactment and enforcement can surely deter unethical and illegal behaviors. However, it is not the penicillin for the problem. From the marketing and consumer behavioral perspective, consumers purchase these imitation products because either they were misled into believing that these imitations are the originals or these imitations can better satisfy the needs of the consumers, and consumers chose to buy them knowing that these brands were not authentic. The seven factors discussed in the previous section provided a multiperspective and overarching framework to help governments and businesses solve the trademark infringement predicament in China, Taiwan, and Hong Kong from the demand side.

Reduce Confusion

Teaching consumers simple methods for identifying the imitations and the genuine brands might reduce the purchases of imitation brands attributable to consumer confusion. For example, educational advertisement can be used to teach consumers how to spot a counterfeit or knockoff. The use of high-tech labels, which are difficult to duplicate, allows easy differentiation on the part of consumers and discourages imitation of the brand by low-tech manufacturers. Wee et al. (1995) suggested that publishing of a list of legitimate distributors and retailers can reduce confusion because consumers will know exactly where the genuine products are sold.

Consumers with higher education, such as Hong Kong Chinese and Taiwanese Chinese, are less likely to be confused by imitation products than the mainland Chinese (Lai & Zaichkowsky, 1999). Thus, the government should continue its effort to reduce the illiteracy problem.

Increase Utility

To improve acquisition utility of nonluxury products, multinationals might reconsider their pricing strategy. Although price provides a signal of a product's quality and most Chinese consumers expect nonlocal brands to be more expensive, consumers may nonetheless consider the prices charged for the originals to be too high, despite their excellent production quality. Marketers should keep in mind that a higher profit margin may invite more imitators. Setting an affordable and reasonable price is strongly recommended to reduce the risk of the product being imitated. Place utility can be improved by increasing the number of distribution channels.

The lessons from custom tailoring and phone localization suggest that marketers should customize and localize their products to meet the needs of the local markets. Doing so can increase the product utility of the genuine products, with the result that more people will prefer to purchase them. Marketers also can emphasize the concept of authenticity and the value of owning an authentic item. Once consumers buy into the concept of authenticity, no imitation products will ever satisfy them, and they will always strive for the originals.

Use Social Influence Strategically

The Chinese have a strong cultural motivation toward "face saving" and group conformity. Consumers avoid consumption of imitation products in public if their friends disapprove of such behavior. Similarly, consumers also avoid buying and using questionable goods in private if people close to them are going to find out and condemn such consumption. Education of youngsters in school about intellectual property rights is a good beginning because the students can have a social influence on their friends outside the classroom and family members at home. The government can organize a special intellectual property–training program to educate people, such as salespersons, teachers, entertainers, and actors on the importance of intellectual property rights. The program would aim to train these people into "intellectual rights ambassadors" so they can influence friends, family members, and others, inspiring them to be more sensitive to product imitation and use only the genuine products.

Similarly, businesses also can integrate intellectual property rights education into their loyalty and/or referral program, in which "brand ambassadors" are trained to differentiate the imitations from the originals and encouraged into spread the message and knowledge to their friends and family members. Such a network of social influence should encourage the public to attend to the problem and deter them from buying and consuming the imitations for the sake of "face saving" and social conformity.

Harmonize the Impact of Culture

The situation in Hong Kong sends a clear signal to marketers that a high education is not the equivalent of a high respect for intellectual property rights. Government needs to start educating children at an early age about the importance of intellectual property rights, and to instill a sense of integrity and righteousness among the students when the influence of culture is not profound. The philosophy of sharing should be encouraged and passed on to the new generation because it is a core part of Chinese culture. Even more important, the children must be taught to make ethical judgments as to what can and cannot be shared, copied, and imitated. By showing similarities to other commonly accepted unethical behavior such as shoplifting and stealing, students can be helped to comprehend that intellectual property rights violation is a crime. Although the effect of education cannot be seen for a long time, intellectual property education, not general education, is the only feasible and long-term way to influence some fundamental values of a culture.

Inform the Consumer About Unethical Behavior

When consumers evaluate whether a consumption decision is ethical or not, they will judge it along four dimensions. Research on information processing suggests that ease and fluency of retrieval affect whether and how the information retrieved will be used. By making certain facts more salient and accessible, consumers may be more likely to recall these facts and thus be more likely to take these claims into consideration when making their ethical judgments. For example, by consistently educating the population that the counterfeiting industry does not pay any tax on its profits, and that it free rides on a lot of social resources, consumers may be more likely to hold a negative attitude toward counterfeiting and recall this fact when they see a counterfeit product. Although the price of a counterfeit may be very attractive, many consumers cannot excuse themselves of their conscience because any claim that counterfeiting benefits society is discounted or rejected by their knowledge that these deceitful business do not pay any tax.

One caveat is that the message must not be easily counterargued. Empty threats such as "do not buy counterfeits and knockoffs or you will be prosecuted" must be avoided because most people have learned by observation or experience that the chance of getting caught when buying imitation products is extremely infinitesimal. Unless the government is serious, it must avoid threatening the public with penalties or other empty threats. Keeping the message simple, easy, and vivid, such as, "counterfeiters do not pay tax," should make its recall easy.

Increase the Salience of Risks

Customers will be discouraged from buying imitation products if they perceive such purchases to be a risky venture. That is, the higher the risk involved with the purchase, the less likely it is that a consumer will make the purchase. Both ethics and risk are perceptions that lie in the eye of the beholder. If the public can be taught to recall various risk factors associated with the purchase of imitation products, consumers are likely to buy from the original manufacturers to reduce their perceived risk. Again, for this strategy to work, the risk factors must be direct and prominent. Indirect and difficult-to-remember arguments (e.g., piracy reduces the creativity of music and software producers and leads to the closedown of entertainment businesses, lowering the quality of life of all consumers [Ang et al., 2001]) are too distant from the consumer and not salient. Social risk such as social rejection and "losing face" for wearing knockoff apparels and physical risk such as loss of life attributable to substandard food or medicine are dreadful yet plausible consequences of consuming imitation products. When these kinds of risky consequences flash by the minds of consumers during their product evaluation process, they are more likely to reconsider their choices in favor of original brands.

Make Friends, Not Foes

If the original manufacturers are perceived as socially responsible to the local community, this would give the consumers one more reason to purchase the genuine brands and one less reason to purchase the knockoffs or counterfeits. This perception can be achieved by foreign direct investment for manufacture of the product locally, partly, or wholly. Media space can be purchased to feature locals hired by the company making improvement in their quality of life. Many traditional Chinese ideas and doctrines encourage the notion of "helping each other around the neighborhood." Thus, supporting the product of the company indirectly will help fellow citizens to improve their quality of their life. With this human side of the company, consumers may sense an obligation to purchase original branded goods.

If direct foreign investment is not possible, for marketing or managerial reasons, to maintain a prestige brand image, or there is not enough skilled labor available, marketers can sponsor or participate in suitable local events to foster a local responsible image. Maintaining a positive image of corporate citizenship is effective in dampening down the rationalization of local interests, which encourage the growth of knockoffs and counterfeits. People are more willing to support a company that cares for the locals than a company that cares only about its profit.

SUMMARY

The infringement of intellectual property and copycat manufacturing are embedded in China. The introduction and updating of intellectual property protection legislation alone cannot solve this problem. In fact, the intellectual property protection laws enacted in mainland China, Hong Kong SAR, and Taiwan are on a par with the international standards, for example, WIPO's Madrid Agreement and WTO's TRIPS Agreement. However, the legal enforcement of these intellectual property protection laws in China is found to be less than diligent. Legal experts have called for more stringent legislation and stricter enforcement to control the current brand imitation situation in China.

From the marketing perspective, legal issues are not the major driving force for the widespread consumption of imitation products. The demand and consumption of imitation products purportedly are affected by seven factors: confusion, utility, social influence, cultural influence, ethical perception, risk perception, and local interest. Together, these seven factors provide managers and researchers a multi perspective and broad-reaching framework for understanding consumer behavior related to the purchasing and consumption of imitation products.

Consumer brand confusion occurs when consumers cannot differentiate the original products from the imitating ones. This factor is especially relevant in developing countries, such as mainland China, in which the original products are not available and much of the population is illiterate. Even when consumers can distinguish the imitations from genuine articles, some still may choose to purchase the imitations if they believe that the imitations can provide some unique benefits to them that the original brands cannot.

Consumers also are likely to be influenced by their peers and family members. For example, a consumer with friends who buy counterfeits is more likely to behave similarly to his or her friends. Cultural influence is another important factor that has an impact on imitation product consumption. Traditional Chinese philosophy stresses the importance of sharing, and most Chinese are bought up in an environment in which copying the good aspects of others is acceptable. Thus, the prevalence accepting and supporting product imitations can be partially attributed to this aspect of the Chinese culture.

In addition, consumer ethical evaluations also play a role in the decision to purchase an imitation product or not. Many Chinese consumers believe that the original manufacturers are at fault for making the original products unavailable or unaffordable. Others believe that it is legal to purchase counterfeits and knockoffs, and they think such a purchase would not affect the original manufacturer's profits. On the basis of these beliefs, many Chinese consumers think that the purchase of imitation products is not unethical.

Besides, consumers also think that the risk associated with imitation purchases is low. Purchasing risk is low because most consumers believe it is legal to buy counterfeits and knockoffs.

The last of the seven factors is local interest. Some Chinese consumers think that imitation products produced locally represent the local interest, and the authentic goods imported from abroad represent foreign interests. Thus, some consumers further justify their purchase decision by thinking that by buying locally made imitation products, they are helping their fellow Chinese citizens.

On the basis of insights from this seven-factor framework, while intellectual property enforcing agents crack down on the brand imitation problem from the supply side, policymakers and marketing managers can help by resolving the same problem from the demand side. Educating the consumers with product-specific information can lower consumer mistakes that result from confusing the imitation products with the authentic ones. By customizing and localizing their products, marketers can increase the utility of their products and encourage the consumer to buy the originals. Social influence can be used in different ways to encourage ethical consumption behavior.

The influence of deep-rooted cultural values can be harmonized by specifically educating children and students about the importance of intellectual property protection when these young consumers are still receptive to new ideas and values. Other methods for lowering the consumption of brand imitation problem from the demand side include educating consumers to understand that the purchase of imitation products is unethical and increases the salience of risks (health, social, and economic) associated with the consumption of imitation products, and forming ties with local community to cultivate a good corporate citizenship brand image among the consumers.

China is a profitable market with great potential. Despite the challenges marketers are currently facing, the rewards to be reaped after overcoming these obstacles are enormous.

REFERENCES

Albers-Miller, N. D. (1999). Consumer misbehavior: Why people buy illicit goods. *Journal of Consumer Marketing, 16*(3), 273–87.

Ang, S. H., Cheng, P. S., Lim, E. A. C., & Tambyah, S. K. (2001). Spot the difference: Consumer responses towards counterfeits. *Journal of Consumer Marketing, 18*(3), 219–235.

Bamossy, G., & Scammon, D. L. (1985). Product counterfeiting: Consumers and manufacturers beware. In E. C. Hirschman & M. B. Holbrook (Eds.), *Advances in Consumer Research, 12* (pp. 334–339). Provo, UT: Association for Consumer Research.

Bearden, W. O., Netemeyer, R. G., & Teel, J. E. (1989, March). Measurement of consumer susceptibility to interpersonal influence. *Journal of Consumer Research, 15,* 473–481.

Bearden, W. O., Rose, R. L., & Teel, J. E. (1994). Correlates of conformity in the consumption of illicit drugs and alcohol. *Journal of Business Research, 30*(1), 25–31.

Bian, Z. (1996). Intellectual property protection in China. *Economic Reform Today, Property Rights and Democracy, Number 1.* [On-line]. Available: http://www.cipe.org/publications/fs/ert/e19/zizhen.htm Accessed May 24, 2003.

Bloch, P. H., Bush, R. F., & Campbell, L. (1993). Consumer "accomplices" in product counterfeiting: A demand-side investigation. *Journal of Consumer Marketing, 10*(4), 27–36.

Bush, R. F., Bloch, P. H., & Dawson, S. (1989, January–February). Remedies for product counterfeiting. *Business Horizons, 32,* 59–65.

Chan, A., Wong, S., & Leung, P. (1998). Ethical beliefs of Chinese consumers in Hong Kong. *Journal of Business Ethics, 17*(11), 1163–1170.

Chen, K.(2001, March 22). The rule of law in Asia: A measure of political and economic change in the 21st century. *Harvard Asia Quarterly.* [On-line]. Available: http://www.people.fas.harvard.edu/~asiactr/haq/200102/0102a001mi3.htm Accessed May 20, 2003.

Cheung, P. K. F. (Ed.). (1999). *The jig-saw of intellectual property protection on information technology: Proceedings of the conference on the International Symposium on Intellectual Property and Information Technology 1999.* Hong Kong: Hong Kong SAR Government.

Cheung, P. K. F. (2001). *How E-intellectual property management impacts on E-commerce.* [On-line]. Available: http://www.info.gov.hk/ipd/eng/information/studyaids/eIP_ecommerce.htm Last Updated Jan 01, 2001 Accessed Mar 1, 2003.

China Law. (2003). *China intellectual property law, rights, protection: Trademark Law.* [On-line]. Available: http://www.china-laws-online.com/china-tradmarks-patents-law/trademark-law/index.htm Accessed Mar 8, 2003.

China renews attack on pirating. (2005, May 18) *Vancouver Sun,* D6.

Chow, D. C. K. (2000). Counterfeiting in the People's Republic of China. *Washington University Law Quarterly, 78*(1), 1–39.

Collins-Dodd, C., & Zaichkowsky, J. L. (1999). National brand responses to brand imitation: Retailers versus other manufacturers? *The Journal of Product and Brand Management, 8*(2), 96–105.

Conger, R. (1980). Juvenile delinquency: Behavior restraint or behavior facilitation. In T. Hirschi & M. Gottfredson (Eds), *Understanding crime: Current theory and research* (pp. 131–142). Beverly Hills, CA: Sage.

Cordell, V. V., & Wongtada, N. (1991). Consumer responses to counterfeit products. In T. L. Childers, T. Leigh, S. Skinner, J. G. Lynch, S. E. Heckler, H. Gatignon, et al. (Eds.), *Marketing theory and applications* (p. 247).

Cordell, V. V., Wongtada, N., & Kieschnick Jr., R. L. (1996). Counterfeit purchase intentions: Role of lawfulness attitudes and product traits as determinants. *Journal of Business Research, 35*(1), 41–54.

D'Innocenzio, A.(2002, December 11). Too few top toys. *The Washington Times*.

Formasa Transnational Attorneys at Law. [On-line]. Available: http://www.taiwanlaw.com/en/c.php?cat=51 Accessed May 1, 2003.

Fowler, G. (2003, January 31). Copycats take the joy out of making toys. *Wall Street Journal Europe*, A6.

Foxman, E. R., Muehling, D. D., & Berger, P. W. (1990). An investigation of factors contributing to consumer brand confusion. *Journal of Consumer Affairs, 24*(1), 170–189.

Gellerman, S. W. (1986, July-August). Why "good" managers make bad ethical choices. *Harvard Business Review, 64*, 85–90.

Goodspeed, P. (2005, April 6). No product piracy too paltry. *National Post*, p. 1.

Grossman, G. M. & Shapiro, C. (1988a, February). Foreign counterfeiting of status goods. *The Quarterly Journal of Economics, 103*, 79–100.

Grossman, G. M., & Shapiro, C. (1988b, March). Counterfeit-product trade. *The American Economic Review, 78*, 59–78.

Harris, M. (2004, April 6). Designer bags the latest for teenage fashion slaves. *Vancouver Sun*, p. F5.

Harvey, M. G., & Ronkainen, I. A. (1985, Fall). International counterfeiters: Marketing success without the cost and risk. *Columbia Journal of World Business, 20*, 37–45.

Harvey, P. J., & Walls, W. D. (2003). The revealed demand for pirate goods: Probit analysis of experimental data. *International Journal of Management, 20*(2), 194–201.

Hofstede, G. (1980). *Cultural consequences: International differences in work-related values*. Beverly Hills, CA: Sage.

How Copycats Steal Billions. (1991, April 22). *Fortune*, pp. 157–164.

Husted, B. W. (2000). The nature of national culture on software piracy. *Journal of Business Ethics, 26*, 197–211.

Hutzler, C. (2005, January 14–15). China auto firm uses GM design, U.S. official says. *Wall Street Journal Europe*, A1.

Kapferer, J. N. (1995, May). Stealing brand equity: Measuring perceptual confusion between national brands and "copycat" own-label products. *Marketing and Research Today*, pp. 96–103.

Kapferer, J. N. (2004). *The new strategic brand management*. London and New York: Kogan-Page.

Kirkpatrick, D. (2005, June 27). China won't protect IP until it gets its own IT. *Fortune*, p. 50.

Lacoste-ly legal battle falls short. (2005, August 15). *Marketing News*, p. 4.

Lai, K., & Zaichkowsky, J. L. (1999). Brand imitation: Do the Chinese have different views. *Asia Pacific Journal of Management, 16*(2), 179–192.

Lewis, O. (2001, March 22). China: Protecting the knowledge-based economy and intellectual property rights. *Harvard Asia Quarterly*. [On-line]. Available:

http://www.people.fas.harvard.edu/~asiactr/haq/200102/0102a001cp5.htm
Accessed May 20, 2003.

Lu, G. (1998, Summer). Advances in the protection of intellectual property rights in China. *Harvard China Review*, p. 1. [On-line]. Available: http://www.harvardchina. org/magazine/article/intell-property1.html. Accessed March 1, 2003.

McDonald, G., & Roberts, C. (1994). Product piracy: The problem that will not go away. *Journal of Product and Brand Management, 3*(4), 55–65.

Merck names more with drug counterfeiting. (1992, May 4). *Feedstuffs*, p. 4.

Mertha, A. C. (2001). *Pirates, politics, and trade policy: Structuring the negotiations and enforcing the outcomes of the Sino–U.S. intellectual property dialogue, 1991–1999.* Ph.D. Dissertation, University of Michigan, Ann Arbor, Michigan.

Milk powders kill babies in Anhui Province. (2004, April 20). *China Daily.*

Mittelstaedt, J. D., & Mittelstaedt, R. A. (1997). The protection of intellectual property: Issues of origination and ownership. *Journal of Public Policy & Marketing, 16*(1), 14–25.

Mr. Tan Hian Tsin and the Crocodile International PTE Ltd. v. La Chemise Lacoste, People's Republic of China Shanghai No. 2 (Intermediate People's Court, March 25, 2004).

Muncy, J. A., & Vitell, S. J. (1992). Consumer ethics: An investigation of the ethical beliefs of the final consumer. *Journal of Business Research, 24,* 297–311.

Nia, A., & Zaichkowsky, J. L. (2000). Do counterfeits devalue the ownership of luxury brands? *Journal of Product and Brand Management, 9*(7), 485–497.

Ott, J. (1992, May).U.S. expects many indictments against bogus parts makers. *Aviation Week and Space Technology, 136,* 18.

Powers, K. I., & Anglin, D. M. (1996). Couples' reciprocal patterns in narcotics addiction: A recommendation on treatment strategies. *Psychology and Marketing, 13*(8), 769–783.

Rallapalli, K. C., Vitell, S. J., Wiebe, F. A., & Barnes, J. H. (1994). Consumer ethical beliefs and personality traits: An exploratory analysis. *Journal of Business Ethics, 13,* 487–495.

Ronkainen, I., & Guerrero-Cusumano, J. (2001, Spring). Correlates of intellectual property violation. *Multinational Business Review, 9,* 59–65.

Roth, D. (2005, January 10). China tries to kick the piracy habit. *Fortune,* pp. 56, 58.

Schlesinger, M. N. (1995). A sleeping giant awakens: The development of intellectual property law in China. *Journal of Chinese Law, 9,* 93–138.

Schoenfeld, B. (2003). *Duped.* [On-line]. Available: http://www.golfjournal.org/ features/98/sept/duped.html Accessed March 8, 2003.

Selby, S. (Ed.). (2000a). *One country, three systems: The Hong Kong Special Administrative Region.* Proceedings of the conference on the Symposium 2000: Hong Kong, an intellectual property gateway. Hong Kong: Hong Kong SAR Government.

Selby, S. (Ed.). (2000b). *Intellectual property public education.* Proceedings of the conference on The Mainland–HKSAR Intellectual Property Symposium 2000. Hong Kong: Hong Kong SAR Government.

Shen, Y. (2000). Conception and receptions of legality: Understanding the complexity of law reform in modern China. In K. G. Turner, J. V. Feinerman, & R. K. Guy (Eds.), *The limits of the rule of law in China* (pp. 20–44). Seattle, WA: University of Washington Press.

Spierer, J. C. (1999, Summer). Intellectual property in China: Prospectus for new market entrants. *Harvard Asia Quarterly*, (3). Available: http://www.fas.harvard.edu/~asiactr/haq/199903/9903a010.htm Accessed Mar 1, 2003.

Sun, A. Y. (1998). From pirate king to jungle king: Transformation of Taiwan's intellectual property protection. *Fordham Intellectual Property, Media and Entertainment Law Journal, 9*(1), 67, 73–76.

Sun, A. Y. (2001). *Reforming the protection of intellectual property: The case of China and Taiwan in light of WTO accession*. Maryland Series in Contemporary Asian Studies, No. 4-2001(165). University of Maryland School of Law. [On-line]. Available: http://apli.org/ftp/IPR Reform in China and Taiwan.pdf.. Accessed May 4, 2003.

Swinyard, W. R., Rinne, H., & Kau, A. K. (1990). The morality of software piracy: A cross-cultural analysis. *Journal of Business Ethics, 9*, 655–664.

Taiwan Intellectual Property Office. (2003). A brief introduction to Intellectual Property Office Ministry of Economic Affairs. [On-line]. Available: http://www.moeaipo.gov.tw/eng/information/system-e.html Accessed May 1, 2003.

Thaler, R. H. (1999). Mental accounting matters. *Journal of Behavioral Decision Making, 12*(3), 183–206.

Tom, G., Garibaldi, B., Zeng, Y., & Pilcher, J. (1998). Consumer demand for counterfeit goods. *Psychology and Marketing, 15*(5), 405–421.

Vaughan, G. M., & Hogg, M. A. (2002). *Introduction to Social Psychology*. Frenchs Forest: Pearson Education Australia.

Vitell, S. J., & Muncy, J. (1992). Consumer ethics: An empirical investigation of factors influencing ethical judgments of the final consumer. *Journal of Business Ethics, 11*, 585–597.

Wee, C. H., Tan, S. J., & Cheok, K. H. (1995). Non-price determinants of intent to purchase counterfeit goods. *International Marketing Review, 12*(6), 19–46.

Yatsko, P. (2000, October 2). Rip-offs: Knocking out the knockoffs. *Fortune*, 213–218.

Yau, O. H. M. (1988). Chinese cultural values: Their dimensions and marketing implications. *European Journal of Marketing, 22*(5), 44–56.

York, G. (2003, August 16). Counterfeiters racing for gold. *The Globe and Mail*, A13.

Yu, S., & Lu, J. (2004, January 2). Fake analog chips spreading in China, damaging consumer products. *DigiTimes.com*. [On-line]. Available: www.digitimes.com Accessed May 16, 2004.

CHAPTER 9

Where to From Here?

The registration of new trademarks shows no sign of slowing down. In 2003, 227,000 trademark applications were processed in United States alone, and the European Union registered nearly another 60,000. Each new product development brings a host of new ideas and names to the marketplace. Protecting one's brand identity may not be an easy task, especially when goods need to be registered separately in different countries. A trademark or trade dress, which might be easily registered in one country, might be rejected in another. For example, Wrigley's Doublemint chewing gum, on the shelves for decades in North America, was not allowed to register its name in Europe because the name was thought be descriptive (Tait, 2004).

Therefore, preventing and stopping brand imitators and counterfeiters may become ever more bothersome. A decade ago, the results of a survey among European companies manufacturing branded goods showed that more than 80% of the respondents had seen some of their products imitated at least once within the preceding 5 years, yet only half of them had taken legal action against the imitators. Manufacturers cited cumbersome procedures, high costs, and uncertainty of outcomes as the main reasons for not defending their rights (Lego Group, 1993). Globalization and the increased use of China as a manufacturing base has further exacerbated this situation to a point that imitation and fake goods enter all aspects of legitimate supply chains, big and small.

Some of this might change with the Madrid Protocol, a treaty that facilitates the protection of trademark rights throughout most of the world with the World Intellectual Property Organization and China's link to the World Trade Organization. The Madrid Protocol allows one filing in English, through the U.S. Patent and Trademark Office, and companies can be registered in many countries simultaneously (Lans Retsky, 2003). However, The European Union, Canada, and most of South America are not part of the Madrid Protocol, and applications to these countries must be made directly and separately to each country.

In addition to the increase in the number of trademarks, there is the problem of a growing cavalier attitude by consumers and local regulators toward brand imitators and counterfeit goods. Canal Street in New York, known for its stalls of counterfeit goods, is even written up in tourist guides as a great place to shop. However, Canal Street is only the tip of the iceberg of a worldwide distribution system that relies heavily on the Internet and a network of middlemen.

Consumers buy imitation goods because they can afford them, and then pass them off as higher priced originals. By and large, consumers see knockoffs as fun and feel no shame in buying, owning, and wearing them. Local areas tolerate these goods and their sellers because they feel they have more serious crime to deal with, and they do not perceive the possible link between organized crime and knockoff goods.

But it is a fact that imitation and counterfeit goods rob governments of tax dollars, usually rely on exploited labor, and can fund a broad range of criminal activities. Recently, two Chinese gangs met with an undercover U.S. Immigration and Customs Enforcement agent and paid him $1 million to clear containers through customs without inspection (McCarthy, 2004). The seriousness of this consumer-based crime business to fund organized crime can be vastly underestimated.

CAN CHINA CHANGE?

It is estimated that two-thirds of counterfeit goods seized in the United States originated in China. This is likely attributable to the increased move of manufacturing to China and the ease with which design and manufacturing information can be stolen from the original owner. The car manufacturing business is just now learning how difficult it is to protect their designs from local companies (Hutzlar, 2005). Although arrests and fines for counterfeiting in China are rare, highly visible cases are publicized.

Recently, three men were sentenced to prison terms up to 1 year for making copies of Microsoft software. The manufacturers were fined $11,000 and had their profits from sales seized. Seizure of profits from sales is key. When a Guang Dong businessman was fined $97,000 and given a suspended sentence for producing 15 different brands of automotive windshields, the comment was that the fine was in no way commensurate with his sales (Balfour, 2005).

There is some indication of pressure within China for more vigilance against thieves of intellectual property as legitimate local Chinese manufacturers find themselves subject to imitators and fakes. For example,

Beijing Scholar Digital Technology made available online published works on piracy (e.g., "Knowing the Enemy and Yourself: Winning the Intellectual Property War," written by a Chinese expert on copyright abuse, Zheng Chensi). Professor Chensi sued the Beijing company for offering pirated digital versions of his book and won $8,000 in damages (Dickie, 2005). When companies within China see their own profits evaporate, aggressive legal action takes place.

Perhaps the greatest change and pressure from within the country will come from Beijing and the 2008 Olympics. A number of counterfeiters and unauthorized merchants have already flooded the market and robbed the authorities of millions of dollars in profits from the Olympic connection. Inspections for unauthorized Olympic products are now a daily routine regarded with the utmost importance.

TO LITIGATE OR NOT?

The decision to proceed with legal action might depend on the size of the original brand's firm, the size of the imitator brand's firm, and the estimated value of the intellectual property. When the original is a large corporation, it might be more likely to take legal action against any imitating firms immediately. These large corporations are likely to have in-house legal counsel. When the original is a small firm, it may be less likely to take legal action in the beginning. A small firm might be more likely to seek cooperation by the offending imitator company out of the courtroom. If no solution is resolved out of court, then the small firm might proceed with legal action.

One of the problems for small firms is that they may be countersued for their rightful ownership of the intellectual property. And if they lose, they may be liable for the court costs of both parties. Insurance may be purchased for this possibility, but it is expensive.

When the imitator is a direct competitor as well as a retail distributor of the original brand, the legal journey is less clear. Some manufacturers are very reluctant to go after retail store imitator brands for fear of losing shelf space in the retailer's store, or even worse, being dropped from the retail chain's distribution system. However, most manufacturers who do litigate against store brands are not intimidated by this threat (Collins-Dodd & Zaichkowsky, 1999).

If manufacturers are afraid of retailer imitators, ignoring them may not be the best strategy. Monetary evidence to date favors the prosecution of imitators. Lost sales and dilution of brand image cannot be beneficial to the original brand. Clearly, more research is needed to document the costs and benefits to the original brand under conditions of legal action, as opposed to no legal action.

Estimating the Value of Intellectual Property.

The value of one's trademark, trade dress, or brand name can be estimated through projection and accounting practices (Davidson, 2004). The issue is to capture sustainable future cash flow generated from one's intellectual property by looking at revenue, costs, and carryover.

On the revenue side one has premium pricing due to trademark (trade dress, brand name), incremental volume due to trademark, and estimation of revenue without permission pricing and volume due to trademark. The cost factors are economies of scale, such as high volumes triggering discounts on the purchase of raw materials; reduced costs through efficiencies in product promotion and administration; and enhanced return on the assets used in the business. The carryover benefit, in the example of advertising, could be the lack of depreciation in advertising costs.

These factors are used to estimate the additional revenue and profits to the firm through the ownership of its intellectual property. This is a complex and imprecise way to estimate because it is difficult to know the future. We see how firms such as Google are constantly under- and overestimated in value, and how opinions on worth vary over time.

WINNERS AND LOSERS

An attempt was made to measure the value of trademarks through stock market data of corporations involved in trademark litigation (Bhagat & Umesh, 1992). The premise of the study was that lawsuits are filed to protect trademarks, and that this is a positive signal to the market that the firm is serious about fighting brand imitation in the marketplace. The lawsuit is seen as a signal blaming another company for any erosion of sales or market share.

Bhagat and Umesh (1992) postulated that a corporation would decide to file a lawsuit to protect its trademark or brand name if the expected value of the settlement exceeded the expected legal and nonlegal costs. The benefits to the corporation might be monetary damages paid by the defendant, court-ordered injunctive relief, a settlement that might require the defendant to stop infringing on the plaintiff's trademark or brand name, and possible prevention of future imitators. These benefits might be reflected in the price of the corporation's stock. In contrast, the imitator is seen as having few long-term benefits and many costs in defending the lawsuit.

Therefore, the researchers hypothesized that the shareholder wealth of the original brand should increase and the shareholder wealth of the imitating brand should decrease with the filing of a trademark lawsuit. Using data available between 1975 and 1990, the study concluded that trademarks have value. The mere filing of a lawsuit led to a drop in the stock value of the alleged infringing firm. When the verdict went against the imitator, the loss was considerable, but a favorable verdict did not lead to a gain in returns. The researchers deduced that lawsuits produced a net negative effect on the alleged infringer. However, the stock losses by the imitator brand were not matched by stock gains for the original brand.

This study was restricted to firms with public holdings and did not address the more common occurrence of brand imitations by small private companies. Small firms may not be able to absorb legal fees, and any legal action may lead to bankruptcy for them. Therefore, small firms may be highly motivated to settle out of court and immediately stop the imitation process. However, when a small firm is the original and a larger firm the infringer, the legal action is a much riskier process because of the legal costs involved.

Currently, luxury houses such as that of Louis Vuitton report spending more than $16 million a year on legal fees and investigations. General Motors employs seven full-time people to look for infringement activities around the globe, whereas Pfizer employs five people in Asia alone (Balfour, 2005). These costs are minuscule compared with the billions of dollars of profit at stake.

RELIEF IN INFRINGEMENT CASES

Relief can be in the form of either injunctive relief against future infringement or damages (including lost profits) from past infringement. Recovery of damages seems to have been difficult in the past, but court cases in the United States show a different trend (Exhibit 9.1). Under the copyright law in effect since 1996 (and amended in 1999 to increase awards), a winning plaintiff may recover its actual damages as well as any additional profits of the infringer, or statutory damages per work of not less than $750 and not more than $30,000. Moreover, if the infringement is committed wilfully, the court may increase the award of statutory damages to a sum of not more than $150,000.

In *Viacom International Inc. v Fanzine International Inc.* (2001), the issue involved unauthorized use of cartoon characters. The courts ruled that the intellectual property owner was entitled to enhanced damages because the infringer had been sued at least two other times for copyright infringement within the span of 1 year. It was judged that five works had been infringed upon, and $100,000 was awarded for each one, for a total $500,000 damage award to the original company.

Courts also may choose a commonsense approach to awarding damages. In the Big O tire case, Goodyear was required to pay Big O 25% of the

EXHIBIT 9-1
Examples of Awards in Trademark Infringement Cases

Case	Amount ($)	Comment
A.C. Legg Packaging Co. v. Olde Plantation Spice Co. Inc. (1999)	223,143.30 (+ costs)	Damages times profits, by judge.
Arachnid Inc. v. Medalist Marketing (1991)	100,000	Awarded by jury—based on imitator's profits
Broan Mfg. Co. Inc. v. Associated Distributions Inc. (1991)	523,000	Awarded by jury—imitator judged lower quality and possible harm to purchaser
Celebrity Service International Inc. v. Celebrity World Inc. (1988)	248,745	Based on 3 times lost revenue from subscriptions
Fax Express Inc. v. Halt (1988)	687,500	Based on 3 times lost revenue, plus $200,000 loss of goodwill and reputation
Limelight Prods. Inc. v. Limelite Studios, Inc. (1992)	2,500,000	Jury awarded for damages
Sands, Taylor & Wood v. Quaker Oats Co. (1990)	24,730,000	Court inferred that 10% of the brand's success resulted from infringement period. 10% of profits equals damages.
Sturm, Ruger & Co. Inc. v. Arcadia Machine Tool Inc. (1988)	2,804,924	Based on lost profits
Viacom International Inc. v. Fanzine International, Inc. (2001)	500,000 + 124,033.33	Statutory damages plus profits
Walt Disney Co. v. Powell (1988)	15,000	Based on defendant's sales, no records kept
Zazu Designs v. L'Oreal S.A. (1988)	1,000,000	Based on lost profits, advertising costs, and punitive damages

advertising budget spent promoting the major tire company's Big Foot Line. This amount was nearly $5 million. In a Utah case, Godfathers Pizza opened several company-owned outlets under the Godfathers name in full knowledge that a Godfathers Restaurant existed in Salt Lake City. The restaurant sued for name infringement. The judge ruled that Godfathers Pizza could continue to use the name if it paid Godfathers Restaurant 25% of Godfathers Pizza's total advertising expenditures in the Utah market each year. This amounted to $50,000, which could be used by the restaurant for advertising to clarify in people's minds the difference between the two companies or pocketed by the restaurant. The restaurant was now assured of a profit (Hunt, 1990).

There may be an advantage in trial by a jury rather than by a judge in that juries seem to award damages to the original creator more often. In *Tavern Pizza Restaurant v. S. & L. Food Services Inc.*, the dispute was over recipes for pizza. A jury was used to decide the case rather than a judge. The jurors never tasted either pizza, but after comparing written recipes, they unanimously sided with Tavern Pizza restaurant and awarded $465,000 in damages (Woo, 1992). In another food case, the jury awarded $100,000 in damages to Chocolates à la Carte after declaring Presidential Confection to be guilty of copying the seashell shapes of their competitors (Felsenthal, 1992).

The seriousness of the courts in addressing trademark infringement is also evident in *Merriam-Webster v. Random House* (*Publishers Weekly*, 1991). The dictionaries of both companies had red covers with the name "Webster's" in similar white typeface on the cover and spine. Merriam-Webster has been using the same cover since 1973. Random House, which originally called its dictionary *The Random House Dictionary* changed its name and began using a red cover in 1991. The jury awarded Merriam-Webster $1.7 million in compensatory damages and $500,000 in punitive damages. The judge then ordered the compensatory award to be more than doubled to $3.5 million and personally redesigned the infringing book jacket himself, specifying requirements for type size, color, and word arrangement for a new Random House jacket.

Sometimes the relief in the form of damage is merely symbolic. In *Walt Disney Co. v. Triple Five Corp.*, Disney wanted to stop the firm from using the name "Fantasyland" for its amusement area and hotel in West Edmonton Mall, Canada, and sought $1 in damages (Coulter, 1992). After the Canadian courts ordered the mall to stop using the name Fantasyland, the case was unsuccessfully appealed.

It appears generally that brand imitation is an expensive risk to the imitating company. Although initial profits from imitating successful brands might appear to be worthwhile, the resulting legal fees and judgments could likely determine the closure of the imitating company. The clear winner, in any case, is the legal firm hired to represent those involved.

KEEPING BRAND IMITATION IN PERSPECTIVE

It is so easy to be different in the marketplace that it actually may be unethical to be similar. Innovative companies that invest in their image should be able to keep their image to themselves. They do not have to share it. The purpose of this book is to make people aware of the various issues, not to serve as a guide on creating imitators. Yet there is danger of creating more imitation, not less, by providing information. As my colleague Dennis Rook commented, "There is obviously an audience for the book among those interested in protecting their intellectual property innovation. There is, also, probably, an audience among manufacturers who pursue imitative strategies. *Both* are interested in the question: How far can you go before legal infringement occurs? This duality is the source of considerable controversy, yet it seems central to the (sometimes competing) issues of property protection, fair competition, and consumer protection."

These are extremely important thoughts that have not totally escaped me while writing this book. I have had several conversations with brand managers about dealing with imitators. In some cases, when the imitator is another relatively large company with a product not too significantly different in quality, that imitator evolves into a competitor. The evolution takes place, with the imitator changing some of the offending strategy and developing its own unique advertising and positioning. Some of the "new" approaches by the imitator may even be "copied" by the original. Hence, in some rare cases, the original and imitator learn from each other.

Perhaps this is what has happened with Lego and Mega-Bloks Inc. For years, Lego has been accusing Mega Bloks of trademark infringement, since they expanded their original product, jumbo bricks for infants, into Lego-sized blocks. In 2004, Lego launched a new line of over-sized bricks aimed at the toddler market segment that was originally developed by Mega Bloks. Like Mega Bloks toys, the new Lego line, known as Quatro, is made of a softer plastic and is lower priced than the traditional Lego playsets (Pereira, 2004).

Both companies are constantly in court around the globe. In 2004, Lego reported a loss of $70 million dollars, whereas Mega-Bloks reported net earnings of $29 million dollars (Austen, 2005). Clearly, something is amiss in the state of Denmark.

Some companies view brand imitation strictly as a legal problem in the beginning. It is not until the imitator continues on the market for some time that the brand imitation becomes a marketing problem for the original. This may be because the originating firm believes that if the imitator is inferior, it will disappear because the consumer will not buy it. That is, the consumer will determine the importance of the imitator to the market by sales and market share. If the brand is inferior, consumers will not buy it, and the imitator will have a short shelf life. However, if the imitator brand comes close to matching the quality of the original and gains significant market share, then there is a problem with imitation. Attention is then paid to the original brand's declining market share and sales.

There are several problems with this strategy from the consumer's perspective. If the product is inferior, the consumer loses, and the image of the product category as a whole also may be diminished. This is always the case with counterfeit products. It is vital to prosecute the infringers with poor quality products and those producers who deceive the public. Poor quality helps no one. The company may lose not only in the economics of lost sales, but also in the destruction of brand equity.

The dilemma in direct brand imitation, when product quality is as good or hypothetically perceived as better, is that the whole language of branding is at risk. This is good for neither consumers or corporations. The marketplace cannot have one set of judicial standards for good imitators and another set of standards for poor imitators. All imitators need to be treated equally, irrespective of quality offered to the consumer.

THE CONCLUSION

"What's real is always worth it."

The solution to the influx of counterfeit and imitation brands and products is in the ability of manufacturers to get customers to believe the beginning quote. The line is from a novel called *White Oleander* by Janet Fitch (1999). The story is about a young girl named Astrid and her journey through a series of foster homes. The book details her efforts to find a place for herself in impossible circumstances. She is an unpaid maid, housekeeper, and babysitter most of the time, but finds escape at the home of a neighbor.

The neighbor takes Astrid with her on a shopping trip to Rodeo Drive and buys Astrid a fine blue cashmere sweater. She shows Astrid how the details in the making of the sweater define its quality through shoulders knit together with a separate yoke rather than a seam. Astrid learns what is real as they move from shop to shop. The analogy is that "stores like churches in worship of real." Astrid learns above all that "to own the real (is) to be real." Marketers need to teach consumers what is real, and how that ownership reflects one's self-worth and value system.

REFERENCES

A.C. Legg Packaging Co. v. Olde Plantation Spice Co. Inc., 61 F. Supp. 2d 426 (U.S. Dist. Lexis 12453 1999).

Arachnid Inc. v. Medalist Marketing Corp., 18 USPQ 2d 1941 (WD Wash 1991).

Austen, I. (2005, February 3). Lego plays hardball with rights to bricks. *International Herald Tribune*, p. 11.

Balfour, F. (2005, February 7). Fakes. *Business Week*, 54–64.

Bhagat, S., & Umesh, U. N. (1992). *The market value of trademarks measured via trademark litigation*. Cambridge, MA: Marketing Science Institute, pp. 92–131.

Broan Mfg. Co. Inc. v. Associated Distributors Inc., 923 F2d 1232, 17 USPQ 2d 1617 (CA 6 1991).

Collins-Dodd, C., & Zaichkowsky, J. L. (1999). National brand responses to brand imitation: Retailers versus other manufacturers. *Journal of Product and Brand Management, 8*(2), 96–105.

Coulter, D. (1992, August 12). WEM wins reprieve in fantasyland battle. *The Edmonton Journal*, B1.

Davidson, A. S. (2004, September). When TTBs get valued. *CA Magazine*, pp. 36–38.

Dickie, M. (2005, January 15/16). Digital pirates published books on how to protect copyright. *Financial Times Europe*, A2.

Fax Express Inc. v. Halt, 708 F. Supp 649, 8 USPQ 2d 1618 (ED Pa 1988).

Felsenthal, E. (1992, July 16). Ice sculptors view this outcome as a means to a lasting legacy. *The Wall Street Journal*, B1.

Fitch, J. (1999). *White oleander*. Boston: Little, Brown and Company, p. 143.

Fletcher, A. L. (1991). Trademark infringement and unfair competition in courts of general jurisdiction. *Trademark Reporter, 81*, 718–791.

Hunt, H. K. (1990). Second-order effects of the FTC initiatives. In P. E. Murphy & W. L. Wilkie (Eds.), *Marketing and advertising* (pp. 88–93). Notre Dame: University of Notre Dame.

Hutzlar, C. (2005, January 15/16). China auto firm uses GM design, U.S. official says. *Wall Street Journal Europe*, A1.

Lans Retsky, M. (2003, September 29). Review international filing process for marks. *Marketing News*, p. 8.

Lego Group. (1993). *Fair play*. Denmark: Billund.

Limelight Prods., Inc. v. Limelite Studios, Inc., No. 89-965- CIV-Aronvitz (U.S. District Ct., S.D. Fla. 1992).

McCarthy, S. (2004, August 30). Crackdown on New York's Canal Street. *Globe and Mail*, B1.

Merriam-Webster wins doubled award in Random House suit. (1991, November 22). *Publishers Weekly*, p. 13.

Pereira, J. (2004, February 4). Lego has blocks ready to build up market share. *Wall Street Journal Europe*, A.7.

Sands, Taylor & Wood v. Quaker Oats Co., 18 USPQ 2d 1457 (ND ILL 1990).

Sturm, Ruger & Co., Inc. v. Arcadia Machine & Tool Inc., 10 USPQ 2d 1522 (CD Calif 1988).

Tait, N. (2004, April 30). Protection demand picks up. *Financial Times*, p. 26.

Viacom International Inc., v. Fanzine International, Inc., 98 Civ 7448 (RCC) 2001 U.S. Dist. Lexis 11925; Copy. L. Rep (CCH) P.28,297.

Walt Disney Co. v. Powell, 698 F Supp 10, 9 USPQ 2d 1234 (DC 1988).

Woo, J. (1992, September 30). He proved he knew his onions and pepperoni, and sausage, etc. *The Wall Street Journal*, B1.

Zazu Designs v. L'Oreal S.A., 9 USPQ 2d 1972 (ND ILL 1988).

Glossary

Actual confusion: Whether or not there have been any reported instances of individuals who actually have been confused as to the source of the defendant's products because of the similarity between the parties' trademarks.

Affidavit: A written statement of facts confirmed by the oath of the party making it before a notary or officer having authority to administer oaths.

Appeal: A request made after a trial asking another court to decide whether the trial was conducted properly. One who appeals is called the appellant.

Attention: The direction and duration of one's mental activities.

Balance theory: A theoretical perspective on social interaction suggesting that people organize their perceptions of people and objects into units and strive for some consistency in the positive and negative feelings among them.

Brand equity: The value held in the consumer's mind toward a particular brand usually based on the marketing efforts of the brand.

Brand identity: The physical features used to distinguish the brand on the marketplace: brand name, logo, symbols, package shape, graphics, colors, and/or product descriptions and benefits.

Brand imitation: Another word for passing-off. Brand imitation is based on similarities, and what is perceived to be similar by one party may not be perceived as such by others. It may result in damage to the original brand.

Brand name: A commodity, service, or process having a trade name; a name given to a product or service.

Brief: A written statement submitted by the lawyer for each side in a case that explains to the judges why they should decide the case or a particular part of a case in favor of that lawyer's client.

Classical conditioning: Description of one type of associative learning in which there is no contingency between response and reinforcer.

Competing brands: Similar products that have the same target market, which result in the competition for customers.

Complaint: A written statement by the plaintiff stating the wrongs allegedly committed by the defendant.

Concrete reasoning: The basing of decisions and behaviors on the literal or concrete meaning of single pieces of information (e.g., price, size) without regard for the product attributes represented by the isolated bits of information.

Confusion: Similarity between the parties' trademarks that result in customers being confused about the sources of the products.

Consumer deception: Situation in which two marks elicit the same psychological impression, or look so much alike, or sound so much alike that unscrupulous dealers are led to believe they can sell the imitation good for that of the original without fear of detection, or if detected, with an excuse believed sufficient to excuse the action.

Consumer mistake: Consumer purchase of one product/brand when the other is intended.

Counterclaim: A claim that a defendant makes against a plaintiff.

Counterfeit good: A "direct" copy that may or may not deceive the consumer concerning its origin.

Credence good: A good for which the consumer cannot readily objectively judge the value or quality through experience of consumption (e.g., vitamins).

Critical effect: The level, magnitude, or size of the finding that determines whether an action is present or absent (e.g., the number of deficiencies allowed on the assembly line before a problem in the method of production is determined).

Cybersquatting: Situation in which a company or person registers a domain name consisting of a known trademark, and attempts to sell it to the rightful trademark owner.

Damages: Money paid by defendants to successful plaintiffs in civil cases to compensate plaintiffs for their injuries.

Deep link: Linking is a simple matter of connecting the content of two different files or parts of files on computers located in different places. Deep linking involves burying the connection into pages of the Web and perhaps jumping over information that indicates the true source of the good.

Defendant: In a civil suit, the person complained against.

Descriptive brand name: How well the trademark describes the products or vice versa.

Design: The general arrangement or layout of a product.

Dilution: Injury to an original trademark when that trademark is used or in conjunction with noncompeting goods or unrelated categories.

Disclaimer: A statement affixed to the good that alerts the consumer about the use, content, or affiliation of the good.

Discovery: Lawyers' examination, before trial, of facts and documents in possession of the opponents to help the lawyers prepare for trial.

Feature integration theory: Features are perceived before objects, and in parallel across the field of vision. Objects are identified only later with focused attention.

Figurative logo: A logo that incorporates a pictographic representation of the brand name into its design.

Functional design: How the design of the product performs the function of relating the uniqueness of the product.

Generic: Not having a trademark or brand name, a product or substance sold under or identified by a generic name, common or descriptive and not entitled to trademark protection.

Gestalt: A configuration or pattern of elements so unified as a whole that it cannot be described merely as a sum of its parts.

Heuristics: Attributes used to make decisions in a usual and repeated manner.

Illusory conjunctions: Individual features of objects registered separately, and in the absence of focused attention, wrongly combined.

Imitators: Goods or services that attempt to copy elements of another's brand name, trademark, or trade dress.

Imperfect recollection: Errors that occur in what people say they saw as opposed to what they actually saw when objects are reconstructed from memory.

Implied association: The act of associating or the state of being associated that is not specifically and explicitly made known.

Industrial design: The ornamental or aesthetic aspect of an article. The design may consist of three-dimensional features, such as the shape or surface of an article, or of two-dimensional features, such as patterns, lines, or color.

Infringement: Intentional integration of the name, shape, symbol, color, or look associated with a successful brand to another brand.

Initial interest confusion: Capture of the consumer's attention although no actual sale is completed as a result.

Involvement: A person's perceived relevance of the object based on inherent needs, values, and interests. It is a motivational construct.

Knockoffs: An unauthorized copy or imitation.

Lawsuit: A legal action started by a plaintiff against a defendant based on a complaint that the defendant failed to perform a legal duty, resulting in harm to the plaintiff.

Limited users: Users restricted within certain limits.

Logo: The design element associated with a brand name.

Meta tags: Software codes used by Web search engines to determine the nature of the Web pages' content. The metatag determines the priority with which the site is listed after the search.

Opinion: A judge's written explanation of a decision of the court or of a majority of judges. A dissenting opinion disagrees with the majority opinion because of the reasoning and/or the principles of law on which the decision is based. A concurring opinion agrees with the decision of the court, but offers further comment.

Parody: A composition that imitates a trademark or trade dress in a humorous or satirical way.

Passing-off: Situation in which a trade or service mark is not registerable, but still may be entitled to certain protection (i.e., a passing-off action). Passing-off is available where there is a prospect of confusion of identity through the unauthorized use of similar marks or get-up, or likely damage to the goodwill and reputation of a business. Unregistered marks and passing-off can apply to virtually any name, mark, logo, or get-up that distinguishes a company, business, product, or service.

Perception: Interpretations of stimuli made in light of one's previous experience.

Pictographic thinking: The attachment of literal and concrete meaning to pictorial elements, such as color, font, package illustrations and even words, instead of the abstract and metaphorical meaning often intended.

Piracy: The unauthorized use or reproduction of copyrighted or patented material.

Plaintiff: The person who files the complaint in a civil lawsuit.

Precedent: A court decision in an earlier case with facts and law similar to a dispute currently before a court. Precedent ordinarily will govern the decision of a later similar case unless a party can show that it was wrongly decided, or that it differed in some significant way.

Qualitative research: Research generated outside the framework of a quantitative approach. Collected data is not subjected to formulaic analysis for the purpose of generating projections. It provides more detail on behavior, attitudes, and motivation relative to quantitative research.

Quantitative research: Market research that provides numeric measurement and reliable statistical predictability of the results to the total target population. The data usually are gathered using more structured research instruments. The results usually are based on larger sample sizes that are representative of the population. The analysis of the results is more objective relative to qualitative research.

Reference groups: An actual or imaginary individual or group conceived as having significant relevance on an individual's aspirations or behaviors.

Related products: Products associated with each other in terms of their usage, function, or target market. Related products could be shampoo, hairdryers, and styling gel.

Secondary meaning: A developed association in the public's mind between the mark, name, or trade dress of a product and a specific manufacturer originating it that renders the mark, name, or trade dress protectable under trademark law.

Signal detection theory: A theory that provides a precise language and graphic notation for analyzing decision making in the presence of uncertainty. Signal detection theory holds that the detection of a stimulus depends on both the intensity of the stimulus and the physical and psychological state of the individual.

Stimulus generalization: The transfer of a learned response to one stimulus to a similar stimulus.

Symbols: Something that represents something else by association, resemblance, or convention, especially a material object used to represent something invisible.

Trade dress: Visual features of a product or its packaging (or even the façade of a building, such as a restaurant). These features can include the three-dimensional shape, graphic design, color, or even smell of a product and/or its packaging. To be legally protected, trade dress must be nonfunctional to be legally protected. Otherwise, it is the subject of patent law.

Trademark: A name, symbol, or other device identifying a product officially registered and legally restricted to the use of the owner or manufacturer. Law protects a mark used by a manufacturer or merchant to identify the origin or ownership of goods and to distinguish them from others.

Transcript: A written, word-for-word record of what was said, either in a proceeding, such as a trial, or during some other conversation, as in a transcript of a hearing or oral disposition.

Typosquatting: An offshoot of cybersquatting in which the infringer registers domain names that consist of likely typographical errors, misspellings, missed punctuation, and/or alternative domain names. The goal is not always to sell the name back to the original. Sometimes the goal is to divert people to other sites.

Unrelated products: Products are not associated with each other in terms of their usage, function, or even target market.

Weber's Law: The concept that a just-noticeable difference in a stimulus is proportional to the magnitude of the original stimulus.

Witness: A person called upon by either side in a lawsuit to give testimony before the court or jury.

World Intellectual Property Organization (WIPO): Headquartered in Geneva, Switzerland, WIPO is one of the 16 specialized agencies of the United Nations' system of organizations. It administers 23 international treaties dealing with different aspects of intellectual property protection.

Appendix 1

As the economy has moved to a global marketplace, the World Intellectual Property Organization (WIPO, www.wipo.int), based in Geneva, hopes to harmonize the different trademark laws of the different countries of the world. The WIPO developed the Madrid Protocol, which allows a central registry of a trademark and protection throughout many foreign countries. The overall success of the system is still being tested, and the European Union and Canada are not members. The WIPO may be more successful in its efforts toward the dispute resolution of the World Wide Web rather than in face-to-face commerce due to the borderless nature of the Web.[1]

Around the world, trademark laws are similar, but vary from country to country. Laws and decisions about trademark rights also are subject to change over time, and the interpretation of the laws varies within country and from case to case. The specific laws of any country are retested often. Therefore, the law is fluid, and the information in this appendix may have changed since it was written.

Some general background with respect to the definitions used in the language of the law, the various considerations and interpretations, and the spirit of the law is outlined in this appendix. Because the specifics of each country's laws are subject to change and interpretation over time, laws should be interpreted and dealt with by lawyers not lay people. The following excerpts from the laws of various countries are intended to provide the reader with some reference points, not legal advice. They are not complete and are heavily edited for ease of reading. The reader is cau-

---

[1] See Brody, M. J., Morin, L. O. & Skelton, T. L. (2000). The new world of the World Wide Web: Internet liability issues. *Defense Council Journal, 64,* 47–60.

tioned from using this appendix in any formal manner for the court. It is intended to show the similarities, differences, and complexities of the law.

TRADEMARKS AND THE UNITED STATES

Trademark laws in the United States are outlined under what is commonly known as the Lanham Act (1988). There are two judicial systems in the United States. One system consists of 90 plus district courts established under the authority of the state and territorial governments. The other is the Supreme Court and federal court system created by Congress. The state courts have the power to decide most local business cases. The jurisdiction of the federal courts encompasses the many cases that involve commerce among the states. When a state court decides a case involving federal law, it in a sense acts as a federal court, and its decisions on federal law may be reviewed by the U.S. Supreme Court.

A business or person involved in a suit in a U.S. Court may proceed through three levels of decisions. Usually, the case is be tried by one of the 94 district courts (California, Texas, New York, and Oklahoma have four districts each). If a party is dissatisfied with the decision, it may have the decision reviewed in one of the 12 courts of appeals. If the party still is dissatisfied, it may move its case to the Supreme Court of the United States. However, the Supreme Court hears only cases judged to be of national importance, and these cases are few in number.

The federal courts are meant to give uniformity to the judicial system and can correct errors made in the state court system. Between the routes from complaint to judgment are discovery, motions related to discovery, pretrial, and courtroom trial. All these phases can take months to years to complete.

Definition of a Trademark

A trademark is any mark, word, letter, number, design, picture or combination thereof in any form of arrangement which

(a) is adopted and used by a person to denominate goods which he or she markets and is affixed to the goods, and

(b) is not a common or generic name for the goods or a picture of them, or a geographic, personal, or corporate or other association name, or a designation descriptive of the goods or of their quality, ingredients, properties, and functions (Trademark Act [TA] s.2, 715).

A tradename is any designation which

(a) is adopted and used by a person to denominate goods which he or she markets or services which he or she renders or a business which he or she conducts, or has to be so used by others, and
(b) through its association with such goods, services, or business has acquired a special significance as the name thereof (TA s. 716).

Infringement. One infringes another's trademark or tradename, if

(a) without a privilege to do so, he or she uses in his or her business, in the manner of a trademark or tradename, a designation which is identical with or confusingly similar to the other's trademark, though he or she does not use the designation for the purpose of deception, and
(b) the other's interest in his tradename is protected with reference to

   i) the goods, services or business in connection with which the actor uses his or her designation, and
   ii) the markets in which the actor uses the designation;

(c) the other's trademark is not a clear likeness of a third person's prior and subsisting trademark or tradename in substantially the same market for the same or clearly related goods (TA s. 717).

Passing-Off. The false designations of origin and false descriptions are forbidden as follows:

(a) Any person who, on or in connection with any goods or services or any container for goods, uses in commerce any word, term, name, symbol, device, or any combination thereof, or any false designation of origin, false or misleading description of fact, or false or misleading representation of fact, which

   i) is likely to cause confusion, or to cause mistake, or to deceive as to the affiliation, connection, or association of such person with another person, or as to the origin, sponsorship, or approval of his or her goods, services, or commercial activities by another person, or
   ii) in commercial advertising or promotion, misrepresents the nature, characteristics, qualities, or geographic origin of his or her or another person's goods, services, or commercial activities, shall be liable in a civil action by any person who believes that he or she is or is likely to be damaged by such act.

Testing for Likelihood of Confusion

The determination of trademark infringement sometimes depends on determining whether the public has been confused by the alleged infringer. The courts consider the following various points in testing for likelihood of confusion:

(a) the similarity or dissimilarity of the trademarks in their entireties as appearance, sound, connotation, and commercial impression;

(b) the similarity or dissimilarity and nature of the goods or services as described in an application;

(c) the similarity or dissimilarity of established, likely-to-continue trade channels;

(d) the conditions under which and buyers to whom sales are made (i.e., impulse vs careful, sophisticated shopping);

(e) the fame of the prior mark (sales, advertising, length of use);

(f) the number and nature of similar marks in use on similar goods;

(g) the nature and extent of any actual confusion;

(h) the length of time during and conditions under which there has been concurrent use without evidence of actual confusion;

(i) the variety of goods on which a mark is or is not used (house mark, family mark, product mark);

(j) the market must interface between applicant and the owner of a prior mark:

i) a mere consent to register to use,

ii) agreement provisions designed to preclude confusion (i.e., limitations on continued use of the marks by each party),

iii) assignment of mark, application, registration, and goodwill of the related business,

iv) laches and estoppel attributable to the owner of the prior mark and indicative of lack of confusion;

(k) the extent to which the applicant has a right to exclude others from use of its mark on its good;

(l) the extent of potential confusion;

(m) any other established fact prohibitive of the effect of use (TA s. 2 [d] p. 159).

It is worthwhile to mention that among the different legal jurisdictions in the United States, there is very little agreement among the courts on what factors to consider in testing for likelihood of confusion (Fletcher, 1989). Some circuits apply equal weight to many factors; some apply equal weight to only a few factors; and some focus only on one or two factors. Each circuit also may consider different factors as the most important.

TRADEMARKS IN CANADA

Any term, symbol, design, or combination of these that identifies a business or a product are called trademarks in Canada, and they are protected under the federal Trademarks Act (1985). A trademark must be registered in order to be protected under the statute. Exclusive rights and protection are granted for use throughout Canada and in other countries party to the International Trademark Agreement. This protection is granted for 15 years and is renewable.

Definition of a Trademark

In chapter T-13, section 2 of the Trademarks Act, a trademark is defined as a mark used for the purpose of distinguishing or so as to distinguish goods or services of a defined standard with respect to

(a)   the character or quality of the goods or services;
(b)   the working conditions under which the goods have been produced or the services performed;
(c)   the class of persons by whom the goods have been produced or the services performed; or
(d)   the area within which the goods have been produced or the services performed from goods or services that are not of that defined standard.

Confusion.   When the distinguishing aspect is not met, it is said the goods or services are confused. The word "confusing," when applied as an adjective to a trademark or tradename, means a trademark or tradename, the use of which causes confusion with another trademark or tradename in the same area. This confusion would be likely to lead to the inference that the goods and services associated with

(a)   those trademarks
(b)   the trademark and those associated with the business carried on under the tradename
(c)   the business carried on under the tradename and those associated with the trademark are manufactured, sold, leased, hired, or performed by the same person, whether or not the wares or services are of the same general class (c. T-13, s. 6).

Consideration of What Is Confusing.   In determining whether trademarks or tradenames are confusing, the court regards the following:

(a)   the inherent distinctiveness of the trademarks or tradenames and the extent to which they have become known;
(b)   the length of time the trademarks or tradenames have been in use;
(c)   the nature of the wares, services, or business;
(d)   the nature of the trade; and
(e)   the degree of resemblance between the trademarks or tradenames in appearance or sound or in the ideas suggested by them (c. T-13, s. 6[5]).

Unfair Competition and Prohibited Marks.   No person shall

(a)   make false or misleading statements tending to discredit the business, wares, or services of a competitor;
(b)   direct public attention to his or her wares, services, or business in such a way as to cause or likely cause confusion in Canada, at the time he or she commenced so to direct attention to them, between his or her wares, services, or business and the wares, services, or business of another;
(c)   pass off other wares or services as and for those ordered or requested;
(d)   make use, in association with wares or services, of any description that is false in material respect and likely to mislead the public as to

   i)   the character, quality, quantity, or composition,
   ii) the geographical origin, or
   iii) the mode of the manufacture, production, or performance of the wares or services (c. T-13, s. 7).

Infringement.   The right of the owner of a registered trademark to its exclusive use shall be deemed to be infringed by a person not entitled to its use under this Act who sells, distributes, or advertises wares or services in association with a confusing trademark or tradename, but no registration of a trademark prevents a person from making

(a)   any bona fide use of his personal name as a tradename; or
(b)   any bona fide use, other than as a trademark,

   i)   of the geographical name of the place of business, or
   ii) of any accurate description of the character or quality of his wares or services, in such a manner as is not likely to have

the effect of depreciating the value of the goodwill attaching to the trademark (c. T-13, s. 20).

Concurrent Use of Confusing Marks. Where, in any proceedings respecting a registered trademark the registration of which is entitled to protection, it is made to appear to the Federal Court that one of the parties to the proceedings, other than the registered owner of the trademark, had in good faith used a confusing trademark or tradename in Canada before the date of filing of the application for that registration, and the court considers that is not contrary to public interest that the continued use of the confusing trademark or tradename should be permitted in a defined territorial area concurrently with the use of the registered trademark, the Court may order that the other party may continue to use the confusing trademark or tradename within that area with an adequate specified distinction from the registered trademark (c. T-13, s. 21[1]).

Depreciation of Goodwill

No person shall use a trademark registered by another person in a manner that is likely to have the effect of depreciating the value of the goodwill attaching thereto. In any action to the above, the court may decline to order the recovery of damages or profits and may permit the defendant to continue to sell wares marked with the trademark that were in his or her possession or under his or her control at the time the notice was given to him or her that the owner of the registered trademark complained of the use of the trademark (c. T-13, s. 22).

TRADEMARKS AND THE EUROPEAN UNION

In contrast to the use-based system in the United States, the European Economic Community (EEC) Trademark system is registration based. It is the first registration that determines ownership of the trademark (Elsmore, 1999).

Definition of a Community Trademark

A community trademark may consist of any signs capable of being represented graphically, particularly words, including personal names, designs, letters, numerals, the shape of goods or of their packaging, provided that such signs are capable of distinguishing the goods or services of one undertaking from those of other undertakings (Trademarks, Dir. 89/104, A. 2).

The Council and the Commission consider that the word "shape" also is intended to cover the three-dimensional form of goods and that where goods are packaged, the expression "shape of goods" includes the shape of the packaging. Adoption of this law will make it easier for a trademark to qualify for registration, allowing companies to register three-dimensional shapes such as Johnny Walker whiskey bottles that form part of the brand. Therefore, a distinctively-shaped bottle will become just as registrable as a brand name.

This definition of a trademark also does not rule out the possibility

- of registering as a Community trademark a combination of colors or a single color;
- of registering in the future, as Community trademarks, sounds (i.e., distinctive audibles), provided that they are capable of distinguishing the goods or services of one undertaking from those of other undertakings. Additionally, the European Court of Justice has ruled that word combinations with a syntactically or structurally unusual inversion of words can be registered (Bodoni, 2004).

Ineligible Trademarks.   The following shall be refused registration as a trademark:

(a)   signs which do not conform to the requirements outlined in defining EEC trademarks;

(b)   trademarks which are devoid of any distinctive character;

(c)   trademarks which consist exclusively of signs or indications which may serve, in trade, to designate the kind, quality, quantity, intended purpose, value, geographical origin, or the time of production of the goods or rendering of the service, or other characteristics of the goods or service;

(d)   trademarks which consist exclusively of signs or indications which have become customary to designate the goods or service in the current language or bona fide and established practices of the trade;

(e)   signs which consist exclusively of

i) the shape which results from the nature of the goods themselves, or

ii) the shape of goods which is necessary to obtain a technical result, or

iii) the shape which gives substantial value to the goods;

(f)   trademarks which are contrary to public policy or to accepted principles of morality;

(g) trademarks which are of such a nature as to deceive the public, for instance as to the nature, quality, or geographical origin of the goods or service;

(h) trademarks which have not been authorized by the competent authorities;

(i) trademarks which include badges, emblems, or escutcheons (Dir. 89/104. A.3).

Unfair Competition.   The Council and the Commission consider that the reference to the law of Member States relating in particular to civil liability and unfair competition is to be construed as including passing-off. Passing-off is a term used in common-law countries such as the United Kingdom. It occurs when one person presents goods or services in a way which is likely to injure the business or goodwill of another person, for example by causing the public to believe that they are goods or services associated with that other person. In order to succeed in an action for passing-off, a plaintiff must show that the way his or her goods or services are presented by the defendant is likely to be injured by that confusion. It is not however necessary to show that the defendant intended to mislead or confuse the public.

Licensing.   There are five points put forth by the commission with respect to licensing:

1. A community trademark may be licensed for some or all of the goods or services for which it is registered and for the whole or part of the community. A license may be exclusive or nonexclusive.

2. The proprietor of a Community trademark may invoke the rights conferred by that trademark against a licensee who contravenes any provision in the licensing contract with regard to duration, the form covered by the registration in which the trademark may be used, the scope of the goods or services for which the license is granted, the territory in which the trademark may be affixed, or the quality of the goods manufactured or of the services provided by the licensee.

3. Without prejudice to the provisions of the licensing contract, the licensee may bring proceedings for infringement of a Community trademark only if its proprietor consents thereto. However, the holder of an exclusive license may bring such proceedings if the proprietor of the trademark, after having been given notice to do so, does not bring infringement proceedings.

4. A licensee shall, for the purpose of obtaining compensation for damage suffered, be entitled to intervene in an infringement action brought by the proprietor of the Community trademark.

5. On request of one of the parties the grant or transfer of a license in respect of a Community trademark shall be entered in the Register and published (EC Regulation, 4595/91, A. 22[21]).

REFERENCES

Bodoni, S. (2004, March). ECJ develops descriptive trademark definition. *Managing Intellectual Property, 137,* 5.

Elsmore, M. (1999, August). European Trademark Law: The provisions of the Community Trademark: Part 1. *The Licensing Journal,* pp. 16–23.

Fletcher, A. L. (1989). Trademark infringement and unfair competition in courts of general jurisdiction. *Trademark Reporter, 79,* 794–882.

Lanham Act. (1988). 15 U:S:C: 1051-1127.

Trademarks Act. R.S.C. (1985). c T-13, s. 1., Canada.

Understanding the federal courts. Administrative Office of the United States. Washington, D. C. Accessed October 31, 2005 from http://www.uscourts.gov/4FC99.pdf

Appendix 2

LEGAL CASES SORTED BY TYPE OF PRODUCT CATEGORY AND ISSUE BEING DEALT WITH

1		Same Name, Same Product	Point of Contention	Outcome	Type of Evidence	Issue	Country	Comments
1	1	Westfair Foods Ltd. v. Jim Pattison Industries Ltd. (1990) 45 B.C.L.R. (2d) 253 (C.A.)	Logo "permanent discount"	Dismissed	Surveys	Secondary meaning, Unrealistic	Canada	No secondary meaning
1	2	ErwenWarnink B.V. v. J. Townend & Sons (Hull) Ltd. (1979) A.C. 731 (H.L.)	Name "avocaat"	Held	Opinions	Confusion	England	
1	3	Ewing v. Buttercup Margarine Co. Ltd. (1917) 2 Ch. 1 (C.A.)	Name "buttercup"	Held	Opinions	Confusion	Scotland	History
1	4	Rodgers (Joseph) & Sons Ltd. v. W. N. Rodgers & Co. (1924) 41 R.P.C. 277 (Ch. D.)	Name "Rodgers"	Held	Opinions	Confusion	England	History
1	5	Montgomery v. Thompson (1891) A.C. 217 (H.L.)	Name "Stone Ale"	Held	Opinions	Confusion	England	Ch. 4, history
1	6	Spalding (AG) & Bros. v. A.W. Gamage Ltd. (1915), 32 R.P.C. 273 (H.L.)	Name "orb footballs"	Held	Opinions	Confusion	England	Ch.4. history
1	7	Reddaway (Frank) & Co. Ltd. v. George Banham & Co. Ltd. (1896) A.C. 199 (H.L.)	Name "Camel hair belting"	Held	Opinions: jury	Secondary meaning, unrealistic	England	History
1	8	Orkin Exterminating Co. Inc. v. Pestco Co. of Canada Ltd. (1985), 50 O.R. (2d) 726 (C.A.)	Name "Orkin" and logo		Customer testimony	Confusion	Canada	

1		Same Name, Same Product	Point of Contention	Outcome	Type of Evidence	Issue	Country	Comments
1	9	Regal Toy Ltd. v. Goodtime Toys Inc. (1974), 19 C.P.R. (2d) 98 (F.C.T.D)	Name "Star Dolls" and tag line	Held	Opinions	Confusion	Canada	
1	10	Customglass Boats Ltd. v. Salthouse Brothers Ltd. (1976) R.P.C. 589 (N.Z.S.C., Mahon, J.)	Name "Cavalier" boats	Held	Surveys	Confusion	New Zealand	
1	11	Carefree Trading Inc. v. Life Corp.83 F. Supp. 2d 1111, 1117*; 2000 U.S. Dist.	Name "Life v. Life masks"	Held	Opinions	Confusion	Arizona	
1	12	Colston Investment Company & Colston Commercial Properties Inc. v. Home Supply Company No. 1999-CA-000491-MR, 74 S.W. 3rd 759; 2001 Ky	Name "Executive Inn"	Add disclaimer	Opinions	Confusion	Kentucky	
1	13	Carnival Corp. v. Seascape Casino Cruises Inc.74 F. Supp. 2d 1261; 1999 U.S.; Dist. Lexis 17546;52 U.S.P.Q.2D(BNA) 1920;13 Fla. L. Weekly Fed. D. 237	Tag line "fun ship"	Refused	Surveys	Confusion	Florida	Ch. 4, dilution argument
1	14	Igloo Products Corp. v. Brantex Inc. 202 F.3d 814; 2000 U.S. App. LEXIS 1839; 53 U.S.PQ.2D(BNA) 1753	Name "kool pak, Cool Pak"	Held	Jury	Confusion	Texas	
1	15	HPF LLC v. Nu Skin Enterprises Inc. (1999) U.S. Dist. LEXIS 15200	Name Cholestin v. Cholestene	Held	Opinions	Confusion	Pennsylvania	

1	Same Name, Same Product	Point of Contention	Outcome	Type of Evidence	Issue	Country	Comments
16	Jerusalem Restaurant Ltd. v. Jerusalem Food Processing & Packaging Company Ltd. et al. (1985), 6 C.P.R. (3d) 493 (Ont. H. Ct.)	Jerusalem Restaurant	Held	Opinions	Confusion	Canada	
17	Rolex Watch U.S.A. Inc. & PRL U.S.A. Holdings Inc. v. Rufus Todd Jones	Rolex watches and Polo shirts	Held	Opinions	Confusion	New York	Selling on www Disclaimer
18	Alaska Incorporated v. Alaska Ice Cream Company 1995 U.S. Dist. Lexis 2165; 34 U.S.P.Q.2D (BNA) 1145	Name "Alaska"	Held	Opinions	Confusion	Pennsylvania	
19	Alphagraphics Inc. v. Andy Shapiro, Vicky Shapiro and Printshop & Copy center of MT. Prospect Inc 1995 U.S Dist. Lexis 19371	Transfer of telephone numbers	Denied	Opinions	Unrealistic	Illinois	
20	AT&T Corp. v. Vision One Security System 1995. U.S Dist. Lexis 11279; 37 U.S.P.Q.2D (BNA) 1114	Name "AT&T"	Held	Opinions	Confusion	California	
21	August Storck K.G and Storck USA L.P. v Nabisco Inc 59 F.3d 616; 1995 U.S. App. Lexis 14352; 35 U.S.P.Q.2D (BNA)	Trademark and trade dress, Werther's Original	Reversed	Opinion	Confusion	United States	

1		Same Name, Same Product	Point of Contention	Outcome	Type of Evidence	Issue	Country	Comments
1	22	Bambu Sales Inc v. Ozak Trading Incorporated and Doron Gratch,58 F.3d 849; 1995 U.S. App. LEXIS 15859; 35 U.S.P.Q.2D (BNA) 1425; 32 Fed. R. Serv. 3d 761	Name "Bambu" cigarette rolling paper to be sold only offshore	Held	Opinion	Confusion	New York	Appeal court upheld the entire $9,375,000 verdict
1	23	Chauvin International Ltd v. David M. Goldwitz 927 F. Supp. 40; 1996 U.S. Dist. Lexis 7829	The name "BUM"	Held	Opinion	Confusion	Connecticut	
1	24	Deva Singh Sham Singh v. Patel & Sons Inc 851 F. Supp. 318; 318; 1994 U.S Dist. Lexis 5768; 31 U.S.P.Q.2D (BNA) 1933	Trademark for basmati rice	Denied	Opinion	Confusion	Illinois	
1	25	Forschner Group Inc, v. New trends, VROLIXS J. -C. 1994 U.S. Dist. LEXIS 18516	Trademark "Swiss Army"	Held	Opinion	Confusion	United States	Ch. 4
1	26	Forschner Group Inc, v. Phoenix Universal, LTD 1994 U.S. Dist. LEXIS 14434	Trademark "Swiss Army"	Held	Opinion	Confusion	Phoenix	Ch. 4
1	27	Marion Kusek, v. The Family Circle, Inc 894 F. Supp. 522; U.S. Dist. LEXIS 16540	Trademark "Speed Cooking"	Held	Opinion	Unrealistic	United states	
1	28	Microsoft Corporation, v. CMOS Technologies 872 F. Supp. 1329; 1994 U.S. Dist. LEXIS 15402; Copy. L Rep. (cch) p27,388	Infringement of computer software programs on Microsoft	Held	Opinion	Confusion	United States	

1		Same Name, Same Product	Outcome	Type of Evidence	Issue	Country	Comments
1	29	Petrolon Management Inc, v. Howe Laboratories 1994 U.S. Dist LEXIS 4281	Denied	Opinion	Confusion	Wilmington, Delaware	
1	30	Sea-Roy Corporation v. Parts R Parts Inc, Multiquip Inc and Rammax 907 F. Supp. 921; 1995 U.S. Dist. LEXIS 12014; 36 U.S.P.Q.2D (BNA) 1188	Denied	Opinion	Confusion	North Carolina	
1	31	Texaco Inc. v. Edward Leavitt 1994 U.S. Dist. LEXIS 4924	Held	Opinion	Confusion	Massachusetts	
1	32	The Gazette Newspaper. v. The New Paper inc 934 F. Supp. 688; 1996 U.S. Dist. LEXIS 12053; 40 U.S.P.Q.2D (BNA) 1900; 25 Media L. Rep. 1428	Held	Opinion	Confusion	Maryland	
1	33	Totalplan Corp of America.v. Lure Camera Limited and	Dismissed	Opinion	Confusion	New York	Pocket camera, 7 day bench trial
1	34	Totalplan Corp of America v. Northwest Pipe & Supply Co. 1996 U.S. Dist. LEXIS 13612; 40 U.S.P.Q.2D (BNA) 1851.	Dismissed	Opinion	Confusion	New York	No infringement found
1	35	Vogel v. Sandri Inc 898 F. Suoo. 254; 1995 U.S. Dist. LEXIS 17913;27 U.C.C.R. Serv. 2d (Callaghan) 1167	Reversed	Opinion	Contract Agreement	Vermont	

2	Same Name, Related Product	Point of Contention	Outcome	Type of Evidence	Issue	Country	Comments
2	36	The Clock Ltd. v. Clock House Hotel Ltd. (1936), 53 R.P.C 269 (C.A.)	Name "clock house"	Held	Customer testimony	Confusion	England	Ch. 4, history
2	37	Mountain Shadows Resort Ltd. v. Pemsall Enterprises Ltd. (1973), 9 C.P.R. (2d) 172 (B.C.S.C.)	Name "Mountain Shadow"	Held	Opinions	Confusion	Canada	Ch.4
2	38	Abundant Earth Pty. Ltd. v. R & C Products Pty. Ltd. (1985) 59 A.L.R. 211 (Fed Ct. Of Aust, Full Ct)	Name "pure and simple"	Held	Opinions	Confusion	Australia	Disclaimer
2	39	Cartier Incorporated v. Cartier Optical Ltd. (1988), 17 F.T.R. 106 5F.C.T.D. Dube,J)	Name "Cartier"	Held	Surveys	Confusion	Canada	
2	40	Oshawa Holdings Ltd. v. Fjord Pacific Marine Industries Ltd. (1981), 55 C.P.R. (2d) 39 (F.C.A.)	Name "Dutch Boy"	Refused	Opinions	Confusion	Canada	
2	41	Canadian Jewellers Association v. McElroy (1988), 21 C.P.R. (3d) 102 (B.C.S.C.)	Name "Jewellry World"	Held		Confusion	Canada	
2	42	Culinar Inc. v. Gestion Charaine Inc. Et al. (1987), 16 F.T.R. 205	Name "Grillettes"	Held		Confusion	Canada	
2	43	Jeld-Wen Inc. v. Dalco Industries Inc. (1999) U.S. App. Lexis 29548	Name "elite"	Dismissed	Opinions	Confusion	Missouri	High involvement product

2		Same Name, Related Product	Point of Contention	Outcome	Type of Evidence	Issue	Country	Comments
2	44	The Gideons International Inc. v. Gideon 300 Ministries Inc. (1999) U.S. Lexis 6239	Name "Gideon"	Dismissed	Opinions	Confusion	Pennsylvania	Ch. 4
2	45	St. Croix of Park Falls Ltd. v. Maurice Sporting Good Inc. & Southbend Sporting Good Inc.(2000) U.S. Dist. LEXIS 11112; 55 U.S.P.Q. 2D (BNA) 1749	Name "elite"	Denied	Opinions	Confusion	Illinois	Fishing rods, fishing reels
2	46	AC Legg Packaging Company Inc. v. Olde Plantation Spice Co. Inc.61 F. Supp. 2d 426; 1999 U.S. Dist. Lexis 12453	Old Plantation v. Olde Plantation Spice	Held	Opinions	Confusion	Maryland	Spices, damages of $223,143.30
2	47	GB Electrical Inc. v. Thomas & Betts Corporation 1995 U.S. Dist. LEXIS 20116; 37 U.S.P.Q.2D (BNA) 1177	Name "CYCLONE"	Denied	Opinions	Confusion	Wisconsin	
2	48	Illinois High School Assn. v. GTE Advantage 99 F.3d 244; 1996 U.S. App. LEXIS 28258;40 U.S.P.Q.2D (BNA) 1633	Trademark through use of "March Madness"	Held	Opinions	Confusion	Illinois	Appeal, novel issue
2	49	Sears Roebuck & Co. v. Sears Reality 1996 U.S. Dist. LEXIS 10651	Name "SEARS"	Denied	Opinions	Confusion	New York	Ch. 4

		Same Name, Different Product	Point of Contention	Outcome	Type of Evidence	Issue	Country	Comments
3	50	Visa International Service Association v. Visa Motel Corp. (1985), 1 C.P.R. (3d) 109 (Proudfoot, J. aff'd by C.A.)	"Visa" with same color scheme	Held	Opinions	Confusion	Canada	Credit cards vs modular structures, Damages plus costs
3	51	Lego System A/S v. Lego M. Lemelstrich (1983) F.S.R. 155 (Ch.D)	Lego	Held		Confusion	Canada	Toys vs irrigation equipment, Ch. 4
3	52	Glen-Warren Productions Ltd. v. Gertex Hosiery Ltd. (1990), 29 C.P.R. (3d) 7 (F.C.T.D.)	Name "Miss Canada"	Held		Confusion	Canada	Beauty pageants, hoisery
3	53	Falconbridge Nickel Mines Ltd. v. Falconbridge Land Development Co. (1974) 5 W.W.R. 385 (B.C.S.C.)	Falconbridge	Held		Confusion	Canada	Mine vs land development
3	54	Sun Life Assurance Company of Canada v. Sunlife Juice Ltd. (1988) , 65 O;R; (2d) 496 (ONT. H. Ct)	SunLife	Held	Survey	Confusion	Canada	Insurance vs juice
3	55	Jaguar Cars Ltd., and Jaguar Cars, a division of Ford Motor Co., v. Manufactures des Montres Jaguar, S.A., Festina, U.S.A. 196 F.R.D. 306; 2000 U.S. Dist. LEXIS 13027	Name "Jaguar"	Divided		Confusion	Michigan	Cars/ watches, Ch. 4

	Same Name, Different Product	Point of Contention	Outcome	Type of Evidence	Issue	Country	Comments
3	56	M2 Software Inc. v. Viacom International Inc.119 F. Supp. 2d 1061; 2000 U.S. Dist. Lexis 11753	M2	Dismissed		Confusion	California	Television/ software, Ch. 4
3	57	Origins Natural Resources Inc. v. Ben Kotler & LDI, L.L.C. 2001 U.S. Dist. LEXIS 5906	Origins	Denied		Confusion	New York	Cosmetics/ clothing
3	58	Bonus Foods Ltd. v. Essex Packers Ltd. (1946), 29 F.P.R. 1 (Exch Ct.)	Bonus meats	Held	Opinions	Confusion	Canada	Human food and dog food
3	59	A & H Sportswear Inc. & Mainstream Swimsuit Inc. v. Victoria's Secret Stores Inc. & Victoria's Secret Catalogue Inc. 166 F. 3d 191; U.S. App LEXIS 718; 49 U.S.P.Q.2D (BNA) 1493	Miracle Bra v. Miracle Suit	Denied	Opinions	Confusion	Pennsylvania	Bras and swimsuits
3	60	Revlon Consumer Products Corporation v. Jenniferleather Roadway inc 858 F. Supp. 1268; 1994 U.S. Dist. LEXIS 10944; 32 U.S.P.Q.2D (BNA) 1659	Name "Revlon"	Held	Opinions	Unsuitable association which may affect Revlon's reputation and sales	New York	Enjoin defendant from using the statement "only Revlon has more colors" for advertising
4		**Same Name**						
4	61	Havana Club Holding, S.A. v. Galleon S.A, Bacardi-Martini USA Inc 1997 U.S. Dist. LEXIS 2643	Name "Havana Club"	Held	Opinion	Confusion	New York	

		Same Name	Point of Contention	Outcome	Type of Evidence	Issue	Country	Comments
4	62	Internmatic Incorporated v. Dennis Toeppen 947 F. Supp. 1277; 1996 U.S. Dist. LEXIS 14878;40 U.S.P.Q.2D (BNA) 1412	Internet domain name "intermatic.com"	Plaintiff: partly granted, Defendant: Denied	Opinion	Confusion	Illinois	
4	63	Sterling Drug Incorporated v. Bayer AG, Bayer USA Incorporated 14 F.D3 733; 1994 U.S. App. LEXIS 373;29 U.S.P.Q.2D (BNA) 1321	Name "Bayer"	Partly affirmed	Opinion: chief judge	Confusion	New York	
5		Similar Name, Same Product						
5	64	Alberto-Culver Co. v. Trevive Inc.199 F. Supp.2d 1004; 2002 U.S. Dist. LEXIS 9725	Trevive v. Tres Hair products	Held	Opinions	Confusion	California	Hair products
5	65	CSC Brands LP v. Herdez Corp.191 F. Supp. 2d 1145; 2001 U.S. Dist. LEXIS 23025	V8 v. Verduras 8	Held	Survey	Confusion	California	15% Confusion
5	66	Slazenger & Sons v. Feltham & Co. (1889), 6 R.P.C. 531 (Ch.D.)	Demon v. Demotic	Held	Opinions	Confusion	England	Tennis racquets
5	67	Professional Publishing Associates Ltd. v. Toronto Parent Magazine Inc. (1986), C.P.R. (3d) 207 (F.C.T.D)	Todays Parent v. Toronto Parent	Denied	Annecdotal	Confusion	Canada	Magazines

5		Similar Name, Same Product	Point of Contention	Outcome	Type of Evidence	Issue	Country	Comments
5	68	Canadian Schenley Distilleries Ltd. v. Canada's Manitoba Distillery Ltd. (1975), 25 C.P.R. (2d) 1 (F.C.T.D)	Tovarich v. Tsarevitch	Held	Survey	Confusion	Canada	Vodka
5	69	Sea-Roy Corp. & Ameramax Contractors Equipment & Supplies Inc. v. PRP Inc.No. 98-1028, No. 98-1546, 1999 U.S. App. LEXIS 3383.	Industrial equipment	Held	Opinions	Confusion	United States	Gestalt, trench rollers, color
5	70	Door Sys. v. Pro-Line Door SYS 83 F. 3d 169; 1996 U.S. App. LEXIS 10411;38 U.S.P.Q.2D (BNA)	Name "Door Systems"	Denied	Judge opinion	Confusion	Illinois	Garage doors, generic
5	71	Eventide Inc. v. Dod Electronics Corp 1995 U.S. Dist. LEXIS 5404	Term "Intelligent harmonizer"	Held	Opinions	Confusion	New York	Audio processor, vocalist
5	72	Malaytex USA Inc. v. Colonial Surgical Supply Inc 1997 U.S. Dist. LEXIS 5304	Term "CHANBERRY" vs "BLUEBERRY"	Held	Opinions	Confusion	California	Gloves
5	73	Mckay v. Mad Murphy's Inc 899 F. Supp. 872; 1995 U.S. Dist. LEXIS 13476	Name "Mad Muphy" or "Mady Murphy's"	Reversed	Opinions	Confusion	Connecticut	Cafe, restaurant and bars
5	74	Milmar Shoe Co. v. Shonac Corp 75 F. 3d 1153; 1996 U.S. App. LEXIS 1508; 37 U.S.P.Q.2D (BNA) 1633	Name "Shoe Warehouse"	Held	Opinions	Confusion	Wisconsin	Injunction

		Similar Name, Same Product	Point of Contention	Outcome	Type of Evidence	Issue	Country	Comments
5	75	Monotype Corp. v. URW Unternehmensberatung Karow Rubow Weber 1995 U.S. Dist. LEXIS 13267	Typeface designs in similar name and same format	Docketed	Opinions	Confusion	Illinois	Digitized Typographic products format
5	76	Sara Lee Corp. v. Kayser-Roth Corp 81 F.3d 455; 1996 U.S. App. LEXIS 8266; 38 U.S.P.Q.2D (BNA) 1449	"L'eggs" vs Leg looks	Held	Opinions	Confusion	North Carolina	Pantyhose, hosiery products
5	77	The Board of Trustees of the University of Arkansas v. Professional Therapy 873 F. Supp.1280; 1995 U.S. Dist. LEXIS 867; 34 U.S.P.Q.2D (BNA) 1241	Unauthorized use of the "RAZORBACK" name and design logo	Held	Memorandum Opinion	Confusion	Arkansas	
5	78	Thomas & C131Betts Corporation v. Panduit Corporation 940 F. Supp. 1337; 1996 U.S. Dist. LEXIS 16033	Trademark "BARB-TY"	Held	Opinions	Confusion	Illinois	Patent issues
5	79	Ultrapure SYS v. Ham-Let Group 921 F.Supp. 659; 1995 U.S. Dist. LEXIS 21258	Trademark infringement for the mark "GAZLINE"	Denied	Industry Buyers	Confusion	California	Fittings
6		Similar Name; Related Product						
6	80	Icarumba Inc. v. Inter-Industry Conference on Auto Collision Repair 2000 U.S. Dist. LEXIS 19291; U.S.P.Q.2D (BNA) 1151	ICAR v. ICARUMBA	Denied	Opinion	Confusion	Washington DC	Training to auto repair, online auto services

6		Similar Name, Related Product	Point of Contention	Outcome	Type of Evidence	Issue	Country	Comments
6	81	E. &J. Gallo Winery v. Pasatiempos Gallo, s.a and Don Clemente Inc 905 F. Supp. 1403; 1994 U.S. Dist. LEXIS 20889	Infringement of plaintiff's trademark	Filed	Opinion	Confusion	California	
6	82	Fisions Horticulture Inc. v. Vigoro Indus 30 F.3d 466; 1994 U.S. App. LEXIS 18227;31 U.S.P.Q.2D (BNA) 1592	The brand "Fairway" vs "Fairway Green"		Opinion of the court		United States	
6	83	Jim Beam Brands Co Inc. v. Beamish & Crawford Ltd 852 F. Supp. 196; 1994 U.S. Dist. LEXIS 5759; 31 U.S.P.Q.2D (BNA) 1518	Trademark infringement and false advertising on the brand "BEAMISH"	Held	Judge opinion	Confusion	New York	
6	84	The Upjohn Co. v. American Home Products 1996 U.S. Dist. LEXIS 8049	Infringement of "PROVERA" trademark by "PREMPO"	Held	Opinion	Confusion	Michigan	Drugs
7		Similar Name, Different Product						
7	85	Brunckhorst Co. v. G.Heileman Brewing Co, Inc 875 F. Supp. 966; 1994 U.S. Dist. LEXIS 19742;35 U.S.P.Q.2D (BNA) 1102	Trademark infringement and false designation of origin on the name "Boar's Head"	Held	Opinion	Confusion	New York	Beer
7	86	Hormel Foods Corp. v. Jim Henderson Productions 73 F. 3d 497; 1996 U.S. App. LEXIS 338;37 U.S.P.Q.2D (BNA) 1516	Luncheon meat (SPAM) vs film (Spa'am)	Denied	Circuit judge opinion	Infringe-ment and dilution of trademark	New York	Limited merchandise sold

287

		Similar Name, Different Product	Point of Contention	Outcome	Type of Evidence	Issue	Country	Comments
7	87	Hormel Foods Corp. v. Jim Henderson Productions 1995 U.S. Dist. LEIS 13886;36 U.S.P.Q.2D (BNA) 1812; 1995-2 Trade Cas.(CCH) P71, 154	Luncheon meat (SPAM) vs film (Spa'am)	Denied	Opinion	Infringement and dilution of trademark	New York	Name of a muppet
7	88	Sunmark Inc. v. Ocean Spray Cranberries Inc 1994 U.S Dist. LEXIS 15186	"SweeTARTS" vs "sweet-tart"	Denied	Opinion	Confusion	Illinois	
8		*Similar Name*						
8	89	Baron Phillippe De Rothschild S.A. v. Paramountdistillers, Inc 1995 U.S. LEXIS 20116;37 U.S.P.Q.2D (BNA) 1177	Infringment of the trademark "CYCLONE"	Denied	Opinion	Confusion	Wisconsin	Conduit benders
8	90	O-M Bread Inc. v. United States Olympic Comm 65 F.D3 933; 1995 U.S. App. LEXIS 25188; 36 U.S.P.Q.2D (BNA) 1041	The name "OLYMPIC KIDS" for bakery product	Affirmed	Opinion	Infringement of trademark	United States	
9		*Partial Name, Same Product*						
9	91	Nabisco Inc. & Nabisco Brands Co. v. Warner-Lambert Co. 220 F.3d 43; 2000 U.S. App. Lexis 12244; 55 U.S.P.Q. 2D (BNA)	Ice Breakers v. Dentyne Ice	Denied	Opinions	Confusion	New York	Chewing gum/colors

10	Unauthorized Selling of Procedure Gestalt, Same Product	Point of Contention	Outcome	Type of Evidence	Issue	Country	Comments
10	Children's Television Workshop Inc. v. Woolworth's (N.S.W.) Ltd. (1981) 1 N.S.W.L.R. 273 (Equity Div.) Helsham, C.J.	Sesame street toys	Held	Opinions	Confusion	Australia	Useless disclaimer
10	Processed Plastic Company v. Warner Communications Inc. (1982), 675 F. 2d 852 (U.S.C.A., 7th Cir.)	Dukes of Hazard toys	Held	Survey	Confusion	United States	
10	Mirage Studios v. Counter-Feat Clothing Company Limited (1991) F.S.R. 145 (Ch. D;, Browne-Wilkinson, V.C.)	Ninja turtles	Held	Opinions	Confusion	United Kingdom	Destroying reputation through bad quality
11	*Unauthorized Use of Name, Likeness or Image*						
11	Pacific Dunlop Ltd. v. Hogan (1989), 87 A.L.R. 14 (Fed. Ct. Of Aust., Full Ct.)	Advertising Crocodile Dundee figure	Held	Opinions	Confusion	Australia	Ch. 6
11	Pacific Dunlop Ltd. v. Hogan (1988) 83 A.L.R. 403 (Fed. Ct. of Aust., Gummow, J)	Advertising Crocodile Dundee figure	Held	Opinions	Confusion	Australia	Ch. 6
11	Paramount Pictures Corp. v. Howley (1991), 5 O.R. (3d) 573 (Ont. H.Ct;)	Unauthorized sale of merchadise	Held	Opinions	Confusion	Canada	Damages totaling $18,000 over 3 stores

11		Unauthorized Use of Name, Likeness or Image	Point of Contention	Outcome	Type of Evidence	Issue	Country	Comments
11	98	Brockum Company v. Blaylock (1990), 729 F. Supp. 438 (U.S.D.C., E.D. Penn.)	Unauthorized sale of merchandise	Held	Opinions	Confusion	United States	Disclaimer noted as useless
11	99	Hutchence v. South Sea Bubble Ltd. (1986), 64 A.L.R. 330 (Aust. Fed. Ct.)	Unauthorized sale of merchandise	Held	Opinions	Confusion	Australia	Disclaimer noted as useless
11	100	National Football League v. Governor of the State of Delaware (1977), 435 F. Supp. 1372 (U.S. Dist. Ct, D. Delaware)	Unauthorized use of name/implied association/lottery		Opinions	Confusion	Delaware	Disclaimer ordered by judge
11	101	Hogan v. Koala Dundee Pty. Ltd. (1988), 83 A.L.R. 187 (Fed Ct. Of Aust., Pincus, J.)	Unauthorized sale of merchandise	Held	Opinions	Confusion	Australia	Ch. 6
11	102	Lyngstad v. Anabas (1977) F.S.R. 62 (Ch. D., Oliver, J.)	Unauthorized sale of merchandise	Held	Opinions	Confusion	Australia	ABBA buttons
11	103	WCVB-TV v. Boston Athletic Association (1991), 926 F. 2d 42 (U.S. C.A. 1st Cir.)	TV station aired the Boston marathon	Denied	Opinions	Confusion	United States	Boston marathon wanted to be paid for TV coverage
11	104	Boston Athletic Association v. Sullivan (1989), 867 F. 2d 22 (U.S.C.A., 1st Cir.)	Unauthorized sale of merchandise	Held	Anecdotal	Confusion	United States	Ch. 4
11	105	Boston Professional Hockey Association Inc. v. Dallas Cap & Emblem Mfg. Inc.510 F. 2d 1004 (U.S.C.A., 5th Cir.) 1975	Unauthorized sale of merchandise	Reversed	Opinions	Confusion	United States	NHL wear

11		Unauthorized Use of Name, Likeness or Image	Point of Contention	Outcome	Type of Evidence	Issue	Country	Comments
11	106	National Football League Properties Inc. v. Wichita Falls Sportswear Inc. (1982)	Unauthorized sale of merchandise	Held	Opinions	Confusion	United States	NFL wear
11	107	Henderson v. Radio Corporation Pty. Ltd. (1969) R.P.C. 218 (N.S.W.)	Unauthorized use of picture	Held	Opinions	Implied endorsement	Australia	Picture on record album
11	108	University of Georgia Athletic Association v. Laite (1985), 756 F. 2d 1535 (U.S.C.A., 11th Cir.),	Unauthorized use of emblem on beer cans	Held	Opinions	Confusion	United States	Disclaimer deemed inefficient
11	109	Viacom International Inc. v. Fanzine International Inc., 98 Civ. 7448 (RCC) 2001 U.S. Dist. LEXIS 11925; Copy. L. Rep. (CCH) P28,297	Unauthorized use of cartoon characters	Damages	Opinions	Confusion	New York	$50,000 plus $124,033 plus attorney's fees
11	110	National Football League & National Football League Properties v. Coors Brewing Co. & National Footbal League Players Inc. 99-7921 1999 U.S. App. LEXIS 32547	Unauthorized use of name	Held	Opinions	Confusion	United States	"Official beer of the NFL players"
11	111	Gianni Sport Ltd. v. Metallica 00 Civ. 0937 (MBM) 2000 U.S. Dist. LEXIS 17339	Unauthorized use of name	Held	Opinions	Confusion	New York	Rock group Metallica
11	112	Ford Motor Co., Jaguar Cars Ltd., & Aston Martin Lagonda Ltd. v. Lloyd Design Corp.00-2046, 2001 U.S. App. LEXIS 23668; 22 Fed. Appx. 464	Unauthorized use of name "Jaguar"	Vacate	Opinions	Confusion	United States	Floor mats for autos, disclaimers

11	Unauthorized Use of Name, Likeness or Image	Point of Contention	Outcome	Type of Evidence	Issue	Country	Comments
11	113	ETW Corp., v. Jireh Publishing, Inc., 99 F. Supp. 2d 829; 2000 U.S. Dist. LEXIS 4816	Unauthorized use of Tiger Woods image	Denied	Opinions	Art defended by first amendment	Ohio	Ch. 4 paintings
12		Advertising; Unauthorized Use of Name, Likeness, Image, Media						
12	114	Astrud Oliveira v. Frito-Lay Inc., Pepsico Inc., BBDO Worldwide Inc. & Omnicom Group Inc.251 F.3d 56; 2001 U.S. App. LEXIS 10486; 58 U.S.P.Q.2D (BNA° 1767; 29 Media L. Rep. 2101	Original singer said Girl from Ipanima was "her" signature song	Affirmed / vacated	Opinions	Dilution	United States	Singer not paid for her work, she was not entitled
12	115	Associated Newspapers PLC v. Insert Media Ltd. et al. (1990) 2 All E.R. 803 (Ch.D.) (aff'd C.A. The Times March 11, 1991)	Inserting unauthorized ads in plaintiffs publications	Held	Opinions	Confusion	England	Disclaimers thought to be ineffective
12	116	EMI Catalogue Partnership & EMI Robbins Catalogue Inc. v. Hill, Holliday, Conors, Cosmopulos Inc. & Spalding Sports Worldwide,2000 U.S. App. LEXIS 30761	Sing sing sing, swing swing swing	Reversed	Opinions		United States	Defendant could not afford royalties, then found new song

13	13	Implied Association Defamation, Parody	Point of Contention	Outcome	Type of Evidence	Issue	Country	Comments
13	117	IPC Magazines v. Black and White Music Corp. (1983) F.S.R. 348 (Ch.D.)	Judge Dredd	Denied	Opinions	Defamation		Record
13	118	New York Stock Exchange Inc. v. New York, New York Hotel and Casino LLC,69 F. Supp. 2d 479; 1999 U.S. Dist. LEXIS 15208; 52 U.S.P.Q.2D (BNA) 1884	New York Stock Exchange v. New York Slot Exchange	Denied	Survey	Defamation	New York	Casino, Las Vegas
13	119	Tommy Hilfiger Licensing Inc. v. Nature Labs, LLC 99 Civ. 10713 (MBM) 2002 U.S. Dist. Lexis 14841	Dog perfumes	Denied	Opinions	Defamation	New York	Tommy Hilfiger v. Timmy Holedigger
13	120	Dallas Cowboys Cheerleaders Inc. v. Pussycat Cinema Ltd. (1979), 604 F. 2d 200 (U.S.C.A., 2nd Cir.)	Pornographic movies	Held	Opinions	Defamation	United States	Dallas Cowboys cheerleader uniforms
13	121	Charles Atlas, Ltd. v. DC Comics Inc., 99 Civ. 4389 (NRB) 112 F. Supp. 2d 330; 2000 U.S. Dist. LEXIS 12337; 56 U.S.P.Q.2D (BNA) 1176	Charles Atlas	Denied	Opinions	Confusion	New York	Comic books, first amendment, involvement
13	122	Ford Motor Co. v. Ultra Coachbuilders Inc. 2000 U.S. Dist. LEXIS 20173; 57 U.S.P.Q. 2D (BNA) 1356	Stretch limos	Granted/ denied	Opinions	Dilution	California	User not buyer

14		Implied Association Defamation/Parody, Web Sites	Point of Contention	Outcome	Type of Evidence	Issue	Country	Comments
14	123	OBH Inc. & Columbia Insurance Co. v. Spotlight Magazine Inc. & Claude Tortora, 99-CV-746A 86 F. Supp. 2d 176; 2000 U.S. Dist. LEXIS 4462; 54 U.S.P.Q. 2D (BNA) 1383	Buffalonews, parody news	Held	Opinions	Confusion	United States	Disclaimer ineffective
14	124	Toronto Dominion Bank v. Boris Karpachev, 188 F. Supp. 2d 110; 2002 U.S. Dist. LEXIS 3647	Defamation campaign by disgruntled trader	Held	Opinions	Confusion	United States	Extortion seeking to divert business
15		Web Sites, Same or Similar Name						
15	125	Quokka Sports, Inc. v. Cup Int'l Ltd., Cup Int'l Internet Ventures, Aaron John Brett, Justin Nicholas, and Does 1-50, No. C-99-5076-DLJ, 99 F. Supp. 2d 1105; 1999 U.S. Dist. Lexis 21000	Americas cup	Held	Opinions	Confusion	California	Domain name
15	126	Northern Light Technology Inc. v. Northern Lights Club, Jeffrey K. Bungar and 641271 Alberta Ltd.No. 00-1641, 236 F.3d 57; 2001 U.S. App. LEXIS 161; 57 U.S.P.Q. 2D (BNA) 1277	Northern lights	Held	Opinions	Confusion	United States	First amendment

15		Web sites, Same or Similar Name	Point of Contention	Outcome	Type of Evidence	Issue	Country	Comments
15	127	Mars Musical Adventure Inc. v. Mars Inc.159 F. Supp. 2d 1146; 2001 U.S. Dist. Lexis 18565	Mars-music	Held	Opinions	Confusion	Minnesota	Level of involvement
15	128	Chatam International Inc. v. Bodum Inc. 157 F. Supp.2d 549; 2001 U.S. Dist. LEXIS 11514	Chambord	Dismissed	Opinions	Confusion	Pennsylvania	Noncompeting products
15	129	Interstellar Starship Services v. Epix Inc., 125 F. Supp. 2d 1269; 2001 U.S. Dist. LEXIS 100	Epix.com	Denied	Opinions	Confusion	Oregon	Some similar services, some not
15	130	Darrell J, Bird v. Marshall Parsons, Stephen Vincent, George deCarlo, et al. 289 F.3d 865, 2002 U.S. App. LEXIS 9543; 2002 FED App. 0177P (6th Cir.); U.S.PQ.2D (BNA) 1905; Copy. L. Rep. (CCH) P28,434	Financia, efinancia	Affirmed	Opinions	Confusion	United States	Failed at claiming dilution
16		Gestalt						
16	131	Black&Decker (US), Inc, Black&Decker, Inc. v. Catalina Lighting, Inc 953 F. Supp. 134; 1997 U.S. Dist. LEXIS 2073	Direct infringement of product	Held	Opinion	Copyright violation	Virginia	
16	132	Decor Grates, Inc. v. Frank C. Fararo 1997 U.S. Dist LEXIS 3328	Misappropriated trade dress	Held	Opinion	Confusion	Illinois	
16	133	Hanig & Company, Inc. v. Fisher & Company, Inc 1994 U.S. Dist. LEXIS 20422	Copied plaintiff's design for a desktop calculator	Docketed	Opinion	Confusion	Illinois	

16		Gestalt	Point of Contention	Outcome	Type of Evidence	Issue	Country	Comments
16	134	Kransco Manufacturing, Inc. v. Hayes Special Corp 1996 U.S. App. LEXIS 2459; 37 U.S.P.Q.2D (BNA) 1722	Infringement for registered trademark and patent for a gamefootbag	Divided between trademark and patent	Opinion	Confusion	United States	Hackysack
16	135	Nelson/Weather-Rite, Inc. v. Leatherman Tool Group 1995 U.S. Dist. LEXIS 16575; 40 U.S.P.Q.2D (BNA) 1239	Trademark infringement, "Leatherman Pocket Survival Tool" vs "American Camper Camper's Tool"	Denied	Opinion		Illinois	Similar pocket tools
16	136	P.T.C Brands, Inc. v. Conwood Company L.P 887 F. Supp. 963; 1995 U.S. Dist. LEXIS 11937	Trademark infringement on packaging	Held	Opinion	Confusion	Kentucky	Similar packaging for both companies
16	137	Pebble Beach Company, Resorts of Pinehurst, Inc. v. Tour 19 I, LTD 942 F. Supp. 1513; 1996 U.S. Dist. LEXIS 13186	Replication of golf hole designs, service marks in advertisements etc.	Held	Opinion		Texas	
16	138	Winning Ways, Inc. v. Holloway Sportware, Inc 913 F. Supp. 1464; 1996 U.S. Dist. LEXIS 1831	Duplication of Winning Ways' Clipper and Victory jackets	Reversed	Opinion	Confusion	Kansas	

17		Logo	Point of Contention	Outcome	Type of Evidence	Issue	Country	Comments
17	139	Alaska Incorporated v. Alaska Ice Cream Company 1995 U.S. Dist. Lexis 2165; 34 U.S.P.Q.2D (BNA) 1145	Name Alaska	Held	Opinions	Confusion	Pennsylvania	
17	140	Deva Singh Sham Singh v. V. Patel & Sons Inc 851 F. Supp. 318; 318; 1994 U.S Dist. Lexis 5768; 31 U.S.P.Q.2D (BNA) 1933	Trademark for the basmati rice	Denied	Opinion	Confusion	Illinois	
17	141	Levy C100 v. Kosher Overseers Association of America, Inc 1994 U.S. Dist. LEXIS 9262	"Circle-K" vs "Uncircled, half moon-K"	Held	Opinion	Confusion	New York	
17	142	Marion Kusek v. The Family Circle, Inc 894 F. Supp. 542; 1995 U.S. Dist. LEXIS 16540	Infringement by Family Circle on the trademark "Speed Cooking"	Held	Opinion	Confusion	Massachusetts	
17	143	The Board of Trustees of the University of Arkansas v. Professional Therapy 873 F. Supp.1280; 1995 U.S. Dist. LEXIS 867; 34 U.S.P.Q.2D (BNA) 1241	Unauthorized use of the "RAZORBACK" name and design logo	Held	Memorandum opinion	Confusion	Arkansas	
18		*Shape*						
18	144	Reckitt & Coleman Products Ltd. v. Borden Inc. (1990) 1 All E.R. 873 (H.L.)	Jif Lemon Juice in a plastic lemon	Held	Opinions	Confusion	England	
18	145	Aerogroup International, Inc. v. Marlboro Footworks, LTD 1997 U.S. Dist. LEXIS 1417	Trademark for "Waffle" shoe sole design	Reversed	Opinions		New York	

18	Shape	Point of Contention	Outcome	Type of Evidence	Issue	Country	Comments
18	146 GNB Battery Technologies, Inc. v. Exide Corporation 886 F. Supp. 420; 1995 U.S. Dist. LEXIS 6879	Infringement of battery	Held	Opinions	Damage	Delaware	Not established trade dress is protected
18	147 Thomas & Betts Corp. v. Panduit Corp 65F.3d 654; 1995 U.S. App. LEXIS 26011;36 U.S.P.Q.2D (BNA) 1065	Infringement of trade dress on cable ties	Reversed	Circuit judge opinion	Confusion	United States	
18	148 Thomas & Betts Corp. v. Panduit Corp 935 f. Supp. 1399; 1996 U.S. Dist. LEXIS 11952	The name "BARB-TY"	Held	Opinion	Confusion	Illinois	
18	149 Versa Products Co. Inc. v. Bifold Co 50f. 3D 189; 1995 U.S. App. LEXIS 2838;33 U.S.P.Q.2D (BNA) 1801	Trade dress for B-316 directional control valve	Denied	Court opinion	Confusion	United States	
18	150 Versa Products Co. Inc. v. Bifold Company LTD1994 U.S.Dist. LEXIS 19053	Trade dress infringement for valves	Held	Opinion	Confusion	New Jersey	

ABBA, name of singing group (Rock band); NFL, National Football League; NHL, National Hockey League.

Author Index

Subject Index